CBSE

CHAPTERWISE QUESTION BANK

2024-2011

Geography

Class 12

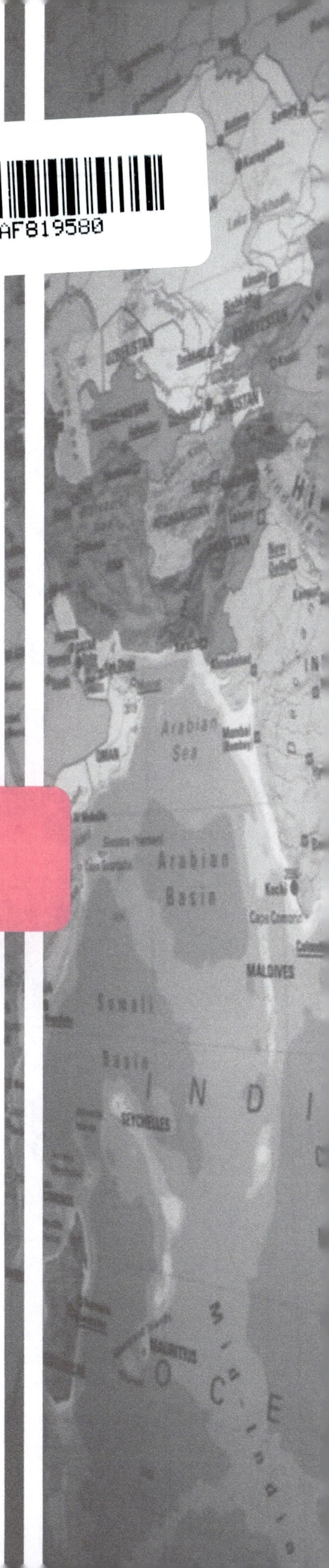

CBSE

CHAPTERWISE QUESTION BANK

2024-2011

Geography

Class 12

Author

Susmita Dhar

arihant

SUCCESS AND NOTHING LESS

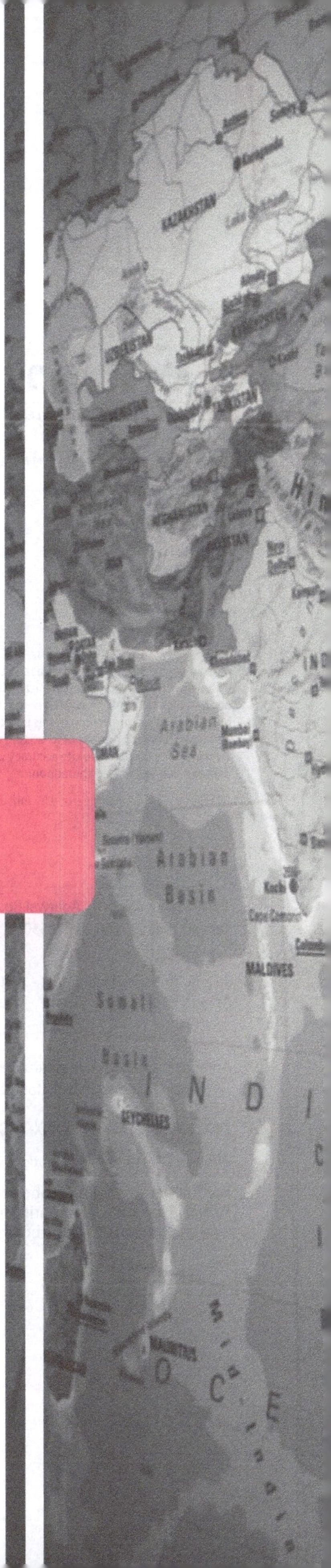

arihant
SUCCESS AND NOTHING LESS

ARIHANT PRAKASHAN
(School Division Series)

卐 ADMINISTRATIVE & PRODUCTION OFFICES

Regd. Office
'Ramchhaya' 4577/15, Agarwal Road, Darya Ganj, New Delhi -110002
Tele: 011- 47630600, 43518550

Head Office
Kalindi, TP Nagar, Meerut (UP) - 250002, Tel: 0121-7156203, 7156204

卐 SALES & SUPPORT OFFICES

Agra, Ahmedabad, Bengaluru, Bareilly, Chennai, Delhi, Guwahati, Hyderabad, Jaipur, Jhansi, Kolkata, Lucknow, Nagpur & Pune.

卐 **PO No :** TXT-XX-XXXXXXX-X-XX

Published By Arihant Publications (India) Ltd.

For further information about the books published by Arihant, log on to www.arihantbooks.com or e-mail at info@arihantbooks.com

卐 **PRICE** ₹275.00

Follow us on

Achieving 99+
Marks in Board Exams

Achieving 99+ marks in board exams is definitely an ambitious goal, but with the right approach and these 7 tips from toppers, you can definitely increase your chances of success!

Here are the 7 Topper Tips to ace your board exams:

1. Master the art of consistency

Consistency builds understanding and confidence, both crucial for excelling in exams.

2. Build a winning study strategy

Create a personalised timetable that prioritises subjects based on your strengths and weaknesses.

3. Befriend the syllabus

Focus on high-weightage topics and prioritise mastering core concepts before moving on to advanced ones.

4. Embrace active learning

Explain concepts to yourself or in study groups to solidify understanding.

5. Conquer the past

Solve Past years' papers and Sample Papers under timed conditions to practice time management and understand paper pattern.

6. Seek help, when needed!

Don't hesitate to clarify doubts with teachers, tutors, or study groups. Asking questions strengthens your understanding and prevents confusion.

7. Prioritise well-being

Eat nutritious meals, get enough sleep, have regular exercise and practice stress management techniques like meditation, to stay calm and focused during exams.

These tips are just a starting point, and you can personalise them to fit your learning style and preferences.

Description of

Newly Added Features

01

Human Geography: Nature and Scope

TREND ANALYSIS 3 YEARS

TOPIC 01 Nature of Human Geography

Average No. of Questions Across all Sets

Types of Questions	2023	2020	2019
1 Mark	-	-	-
3 Marks	5	1	1
5 Marks	-	-	-

Trend Analysis

At the start of each chapter, Trend Analysis is given to indicate the types of Questions asked from different topics of the chapter. This feature helps students to know the importance of different topics of the given chapter from exam point of view and helps them to prepare accordingly.

1. Examine the geographical factors that influence distribution of population in the world. ***(CBSE 2023)***

Other Similar Questions

Or "There are various geographical factors that influence distribution of population in the world." Explain.

Or What are the factors that influence distribution of population in the world?

Other Similar Questions

Other Similar Questions are given with selected questions that can be asked in different formats but their answers remain same. This feature help students to identify and answer the question correctly.

11. What is the subject matter of the study of human geography? Explain any three facts. ***(Delhi 2015)***

Ans. The subject matter of the study of human geography are as follows

To Understand the Inter-relationship There is a close relationship between the physical/natural environment and the human world, so human geography studies and establishes that relation.

Study the Spatial Distribution Human geography also studies the spatial distribution of human phenomena.

Subject matter of the study of Human Geography

- To Understand the Inter-relationship
- Study the Spatial Distribution

Heading Boxes

Heading Boxes are given in those questions whose answers are divided into different headings. This feature will help students to remember the answer through headings only.

5. Describe any three characteristics of the first stage of 'Demographic Transition Theory'. ***(Delhi 2014)***

Ans. Characteristics of first stage of Demographic Transition Theory are as follows

Additional Info

Other characteristics of the first stage of Demographic Transition Theory are

- Life expectancy is low in this stage. People are mostly illiterate and have low levels of technology.

Additional Info

Additional Info is given in selected questions with the purpose to give extra information about the concept asked in the question.

1. "Human beings were able to develop technology after they developed better understanding of natural laws." Evaluate the statement in the context of naturalisation of humans. ***(CBSE 2023)***

HINT *Dear students, this question simply ask you to describe the importance of knowledge and understanding of natural laws while developing a technology.*

Hint

Hint provides a clue to the students about what the question is asking to write in the answer. This feature help students to write the answer correctly in sync with the question.

Mastering

CBSE Board Exams

Tips and Strategies From Top Scorers!

Raksha Gopal
Class 12 Topper

Hansika Shukla
Class 12 Topper

Karishma Arora
Class 12 Topper

Students put their heart, soul, and sweat into their board exam preparation. In a bid to score the best they can, aspirants often look to previous toppers to draw inspiration from them.

Here we have covered some tips & strategies shared by few former toppers - Raksha Gopal, Hansika Shukla, and Karishma Arora. So, what makes them special? Did they study for 24 hours a day? Did they burn the midnight oil days before the exam? Or even lock themselves up inside a room to avoid distractions? No, they did none of these things.

How to handle the exam pressure?

Raksha: The best way to handle pressure is to not overthink. Treat the board exams as a stepping stone in your life and do not let them define your entire life. It is helpful to keep a calm mind and if you can meditate for some time, nothing like it.

Hansika: One should have a healthy conversation with parents in this situation and reach out for help. Studying excessively won't help and it will blur your mind.

Karishma: It is important to keep aside some time for relaxation. Pursuing your hobby even while preparing for the exams act as a stress reliever.

Top time management skills while writing the exams

Raksha: Try to answer the questions according to the marks allocated to them. Do not spend too much time on one question neglecting other questions. And always keep some buffer time to review your answers.

Hansika: Time management is important, especially for language papers, as one cannot predict how long a paper will be. For instance, students can always divide the papers into different sections such as section A, section B, and so on. They must aim to finish a section within a certain time limit

Karishma: While writing the exam, keep in mind that the length of your answers should be according to the weightage of marks allotted for it.

How to approach the exams - attempt the easy and known answers first and then try to solve the difficult ones or take on each question chronologically?

Raksha: Try to attempt the questions chronologically as it is easier for the examiner to check.

Hansika: It depends on the student. Solving the questions chronologically may help. However, a preferred method would be tackling the easy answers first before moving to the difficult ones.

Karishma: Usually, I try to answer the questions in chronological order.

Is it true 'Neat and clean answer sheets have more chances of getting good marks than untidy ones'.

Raksha: Yes, of course! An examiner should be able to read your answers easily. Good handwriting or not, you should present your answers in a neat manner.

Hansika: Whether neat and clean papers would get more marks depends on the examiner. In most cases, having neat and clear handwriting does help.

Karishma: When the examiner checks an answer sheet and it has good handwriting and neat and clean work, he or she will assume that the student is well-prepared. Often there is a chance that the examiner might even miss your careless mistakes.

Should student should review the paper again after completing it, to check if any mistakes have been committed

Raksha: You should keep the last 5-10 minutes to review your answers again and check for any mistakes. But once you are out of the exam hall, no point going through the paper again to check for mistakes.

Hansika: I firmly believe that one should review the paper thoroughly after the exam. This way, any errors committed during the exam can be rectified.

Karishma: Revising the answers before submitting your sheet is important to check for any last-minute mistakes.

Some miscellaneous exam writing tips for Students.

Raksha: Always underline the important points of your answer. It helps in scoring. And try to mark your answers neatly.

Hansika: Students should remain calm and tackle one question at a time. In case they come across a question which they find difficult, they should try to write what would be the most relevant and appropriate answer.

Karishma: Make sure that you know the distribution of marks for all the topics in that subject. This way you can plan the length of your answers accordingly.

Most Important Topics

from each Chapter

On the basis of analysis of last 4 Years' Board Examination Papers, we have identified Important Topics from each chapter.

Part I : Fundamentals of Human Geography

Chapter Name	Important Topics	Weightage in Last 4 Years' Boards			
		2024	2023	2020	2019
Human Geography: Nature and Scope	Nature of Human Geography	3M	15M	3M	3M
The World Population	Patterns of Population Distribution	5M	13M	1M	6M
	Population Growth/Change	-	2M	1M	-
Human Development	Human Development	3M	20M	7M	9M
Primary Activities	Hunting and Gathering, Pastoralism	-	14M	-	2M
	Agriculture & Mining	1M	8M	2M	5M
Secondary Activities	Manufacturing	5M	21M	-	20M
Tertiary and Quaternary Activities	Tertiary Activities and Quaternary Activities	3M	18M	1M	12M
	Quinary Activities	-	4M	-	-
Transport and Communication	Transport	3M	29M	-	10M
	Communication	-	-	-	-
International Trade	History of International Trade	-	-	-	-
	WTO & Gateways to International Trade	3M	-	-	-

Part II : India : People and Economy

Chapter Name	Important Topics	2024	2023	2020	2019
Population : Distribution, Density, Growth and Composition	Population : Distribution, Density Growth and Composition	-	10M	-	3M
Human Settlement	Rural Settlement	3M	-	3M	3M
	Urban Settlement	5M	5M	-	-
	Urbanisation	3M	-	-	9M
Land Resources and Agriculture	Types of Farming	1M	3M	-	-
	Agricultural Development in India	-	5M	-	-
Water Resources	Water Resources	-	3M	-	10M
	Water Conservation and Management	3M	11M	-	-
Minerals and Energy Resources	Types of Mineral Resources	2M	16M	3M	3M
	Types of Energy Resources	-	11M	-	15M
Planning & Sustainable Development in Indian Context	Planning and Sustainable Development	3M	5M	-	10M
Transport and Communication	Means of Transport	-	10M	5M	15M
	Communication Networks	12M	-	3M	3M
International Trade	Changing Patterns of India's Export and Import	3M	5M	-	3M
	Major Ports of India	-	5M	-	-
Geographical Perspective on Selected Issues and Problems	Environmental Pollution	5M	-	-	10M
	Land Degradation/Slums	-	5M	-	5M

Contents

CBSE Chapterwise Solved Papers
2024-2011

PART I Fundamentals of Human Geography

PART II India : People and Economy

Latest Syllabus

Geography Class XII

Fundamentals of Human Geography

Chapter No	Chapter Name	No. of Periods	Marks Allocated
	Unit - I		
1	Human Geography	7	3
	Unit - II		
2	The World Population Density Distribution and Growth	9	8
3	Human Development	7	
	Unit - III		
4	Primary Activities	12	19
5	Secondary Activities	10	
6	Tertiary and Quaternary Activities	10	
7	Transport, Communication and Trade	15	
8	International Trade	10	
Map Work (Based on identification of features on World Political Map)		**10**	**5**
	Total	**90**	**35**

India : People and Economy

Chapter No	Chapter Name	No. of Periods	Marks Allocated
	Unit - I		
1	Population Distribution Density Growth and Composition	10	5
	Unit - II		
2	Human Settlements	8	3
	Unit - III		
3	Land Resources and Agriculture	9	10
4	Water Resources	9	
5	Mineral and Energy Resources	9	
6	Planning and Sustainable Development in Indian Context	7	
	Unit - IV		
7	Transport and Communication	11	7
8	International Trade	9	
	Unit - V		
9	Geographical Perspective on selected issues and problems	8	5
Map Work (Based on Marking and labelling on a Political Map of India)		**10**	**5**
	Total	**90**	**35**

Map items for identification only on outline political map of the world
Fundamentals of Human Geography

Chapter No	Chapter Name	No. of Periods
1	Human Geography	Nil
2	The World Population Density Distribution and Growth	Nil
3	Human Development	Nil
4	Primary Activites	• Areas of subsistence gathering (Fig 4.2) • Major areas of nomadic herding of the world (4.4) • Major areas of commercial livestock rearing (4.6) • Major areas of extensive commercial grain faming (4.12) • Major areas of mixed farming of the World (4.14)
5	Secondary Activities	Nil
6	Tertiary and Quaternary Activities	Nil
7	Transport, Communication and Trade	• Terminal Stations of Transcontinental Railways– Trans-Siberian, Trans Canadian, Trans-Australian Railways **Major Sea Ports** • **Europe:** North Cape, London, Hamburg • **North America:** Vancouver, San Francisco, New Orleans • **South America:** Rio De Janeiro, Colon, Valparaiso • **Africa:** Suez and Cape Town • **Asia:** Yokohama, Shanghai, Hong Kong, Aden, Karachi, Kolkata • **Australia:** Perth, Sydney, Melbourne **Major Airports:** • **Asia:** Tokyo, Beijing, Mumbai, Jeddah, Aden • **Africa:** Johannesburg and Nairobi • **Europe:** Moscow, London, Paris, Berlin and Rome • **North America:** Chicago, New Orleans, Mexico City • **South America:** Buenos Aires, Santiago • **Australia:** Darwin and Wellington **Inland Waterways** Suez Canal, Panama Canal, Rhine Waterways and St Lawrence Seaways
8	International Trade	Nil

Map items for locating and labelling on political outline map of India
India : People and Economy

Chapter No	Chapter Name	No. of Periods
1	Population Distribution Density Growth and Composition	State with highest population density and state with lowest population density (2011)
2	Human Settlement	Nil
3	Land Resources and Agriculture	Leading producing states of the following crops: (a) Rice (b) Wheat (c) Cotton (d) Jute (e) Sugarcane (f) Tea and (g) Coffee
4	Water Resources	Nil
5	Mineral And Energy Resources	**Mines:** • **Iron-ore mines:** Mayurbhanj, Bailadila, Ratnagiri, Bellary • **Manganese mines:** Balaghat, Shimoga • **Copper mines:** Hazaribagh, Singhbhum, Khetari • **Bauxite mines:** Katni, Bilaspur and Koraput • **Coal mines:** Jharia, Bokaro, Raniganj, Neyveli • **Oil Refineries:** Mathura, Jamnager, Barauni
6	Planning and Sustainable Development in Indian Context	Nil
7	Transport and Communication	Nil
8	International Trade	Mark and label the major sea ports and airports on an outline map of India. • **Major Sea Ports:** Kandla, Mumbai, Marmagao, Kochi, Mangalore, Tuticorin, Chennai, Visakhapatnam, Paradip, Haldia • **International Air ports:** Ahmedabad, Mumbai, Bengaluru, Chennai, Kolkata, Guwahati, Delhi, Amritsar, Thiruvananthapuram and Hyderabad.
9	Geographical Perspective on Selected Issues and Problems	Nil

Human Geography: Nature and Scope

TREND ANALYSIS 3 YEARS

TOPIC 01 Nature of Human Geography

Average No. of Questions Across all Sets

Types of Questions	2023	2020	2019
1 Mark	–	–	–
3 Marks	5	1	1
5 Marks	–	–	–

Geography is a science that is concerned with the study of Earth and its lands, features, inhabitants and phenomena. It is an integrative, empirical and practical subject that studies each and every event or phenomena which varies over space and time. Therefore, geography can be broadly classified into two branches i.e, **physical geography** and **human geography.**

Physical geography is concerned about the physical features of the Earth such as mountains, plains, atmosphere, soils, etc. On the other hand, human geography is the study of mankind over the surface of the Earth and spatial distributions of the human phenomena.

Nature of Human Geography

- Human Geography studies the inter-relationship between the physical environment and socio- cultural environment created by human beings through mutual interaction with each other.
- The elements like villages, cities, road-rail networks, etc and all other elements of material culture have been created by human beings using the resources provided by the physical environment. Thus, In the saying of **Ellen Semple** ''Human Geography is a study of changing relationship between unresting man and unstable Earth''.

Naturalisation of Humans and Humanisation of Nature

- Humans interact with their physical environment with the help of technology. This indicates the level of cultural development.
- The interaction of primitive societies with the physical environment is termed as **environmental determinism** which is naturalisation of humans.
- With the development of technology, humans began to modify nature and created cultural landscape. This is called **possiblism** or humanisation of nature.
- A middle path of **neo-determinism** was introduced by **Griffith Taylor** which means that neither is there a situation of absolute necessity (environmental determinism) nor is there a condition of absolute freedom (possibilism).

Field and Sub-fields of Human Geography

- Human Geography is inter-disciplinary in nature and develops vast linkages with other sister disciplines in social sciences.
- The fields and sub-fields of human geography explains every aspect of all elements of human life on the surface of the Earth.

Human Geography and Sister Disciplines of Social Sciences

Fields of Human Geography	Sub-Fields	Interface with Sister Disciplines of Social Sciences
Social Geography	—	Social Sciences-Sociology
	Behavioural Geography	Psychology
	Geography of Social Well-being	Welfare Economics
	Geography of Leisure	Sociology
	Cultural Geography	Anthropology
	Gender Geography	Sociology, Anthropology, Women's Studies
	Historical Geography	History
	Medical Geography	Epidemiology
Urban Geography	—	Urban Studies and Planning
Political Geography	—	Political Science
	Electoral Geography	Psephology
	Military Geography	Military Science
Population Geography	—	Demography
Settlement Geography	—	Urban/Rural Planning
Economic Geography	—	Economics
	Geography of Resources	Resource Economics
	Geography of Agriculture	Agricultural Sciences
	Geography of Industries	Industrial Economics
	Geography of Marketing	Business Studies, Economics, Commerce
	Geography of Tourism	Tourism and Travel Management
	Geography of International Trade	International Trade

PYQs Previous Years' Questions

1 Mark Questions

Multiple Choice Questions

1. Who among the following has introduced the concept of neo-determinism? *(CBSE SQP Term I 2021)*
   (a) Ratzel (b) Griffith Taylor
   (c) Ellen C Semple (d) Paul Vidal de La Blache

Ans. (b) Griffith Taylor

2. Which one of the following concepts is related to naturalisation of humans? *(CBSE SQP Term I 2021)*
   (a) Environmental Determinism
   (b) Possiblism
   (c) Humanism
   (d) Neo Determinism

Ans. (a) Environmental Determinism

3. Arrange the following approaches in a sequential order according to their development. *(CBSE SQP Term I 2021)*
   I. Spatial organisation II. Regional approach
   III. Areal differentiation IV. Humanistic approach

   Codes
   (a) I, IV, II, III (b) IV, I, III, II
   (c) II, III, I, IV (d) III, II, IV, I

Ans. (c) II, III, I, IV

4. This age was marked by use of computers and sophisticated statistical tools. Laws of Physics were often applied to map and analyse. Select the correct option. *(CBSE SQP Term I 2021)*
   (a) Regional analysis (b) Quantitative revolution
   (c) Areal differentiation (d) Spatial organisation

Ans. (d) Spatial organisation

5. Match the following. *(CBSE SQP Term I 2021)*

	List I (Period)		List II (Approach)
A.	Early colonial period	1.	Exploration & Description
B.	Late 1950s to the late 1960s	2.	Regional Analysis
C.	Later colonial period	3.	Areal Differentiation
D.	1930s through the inter-war period	4.	Spatial Organisation

Codes

	A	B	C	D		A	B	C	D
(a)	1	4	2	3	(b)	4	1	3	2
(c)	2	3	4	1	(d)	1	2	3	4

Ans. (a)

6. Who among the following defined "Human geography is the study of the changing relationship between the unresting man and the unstable Earth"? *(CBSE SQP Term I 2021)*
   (a) Ratzel (b) Griffith Taylor
   (c) Ellen C Semple (d) Paul Vidal de la Blache

Ans. (c) Ellen C Semple

7. Behavioural school of thought emphasised on which of the following aspects? *(CBSE SQP Term I 2021)*
   (a) Lived experience
   (b) Causes of poverty and social inequality
   (c) Different aspects of social well-being
   (d) Housing, health and education

Ans. (a) Lived experience

8. Arrange the following approaches in ascending order on the basis of time. *(CBSE SQP Term I 2021)*
   I. Post modernism in geography
   II. Exploration and description
   III. Areal differentiation
   IV. Regional analysis

   Codes
   (a) I, II, III, IV (b) IV, III, II, I
   (c) III, I, IV, II (d) II, IV, III, I

Ans. (d) II, IV, III, I

9. Match the following. *(CBSE SQP Term I 2021)*

	List I (Sub-fields of Human Geography)		List II (Sister disciplines)
A.	Behavioural Geography	1.	Anthropology
B.	Geography of Leisure	2.	Business Geography
C.	Geography of Marketing	3.	Sociology
D.	Cultural Geography	4.	Psychology

Codes

	A	B	C	D		A	B	C	D
(a)	4	3	2	1	(b)	1	2	3	4
(c)	2	1	4	3	(d)	3	4	1	2

Ans. (a)

10. "Humans are restricted by the constraints of the natural environment." This idea can be described as
(a) Environmental Determinism (b) Neo-liberalism
(c) Possibilism (d) Spatial Analysis

Ans. (a) Environmental Determinism

11. "Nature provides opportunities and human beings use these opportunities slowly and nature gets humanised." The statement above describes which of the following ideas?
(a) Possibilism
(b) Environmental Determinism
(c) Spatial Analysis
(d) Areal Differentiation

Ans. (a) Possibilism

12. "The approach of spatial organisation emerged in geography during which period"?
(a) Late 1960s to early 1970s
(b) Late 1950s to late 1960s
(c) 1970s
(d) 1990s

Ans. (b) Late 1950s to late 1960s

13. The subject matter of population geography is taken from which field ?
(a) Economics (b) Welfare Economics
(c) Demography (d) Anthropology

Ans. (c) Demography

14. Which of the following is considered as the middle path between determinism and possibilism ?
(a) Neo-liberalism (b) Neo-possibilism
(c) Dualism (d) Neo-determinism

Ans. (d) Neo-determinism

15. Which of the following concepts were given by Griffth Taylor?
(a) Neo-determinism (b) Neo-possibilism
(c) Neo-liberalism (d) Dualism

Ans. (a) Neo-determinism

16. Complete the following table using the given options.

Field of Human Geography	Sub-Field	Interface with sister discipline
Social Geography	Behavioural Geography	A.........
	Geography of Leisure	B.........

(a) A → Sociology, B → Psychology
(b) A → Psychology, B → Sociology
(c) A → Anthropology, B → History
(d) A → History, B → Anthropology

Ans. (b) A → Psychology, B → Sociology

3 Marks Questions

1. "Human beings were able to develop technology after they developed better understanding of natural laws." Evaluate the statement in the context of naturalisation of humans. ***(CBSE 2023)***

Or "The knowledge about nature is extremely important to develop technology." Support this statement by giving three examples. ***(All India 2015)***

Or How is the knowledge of nature important to develop technology? Explain with suitable examples. ***(Delhi 2010)***

HINT *Dear students, this question simply ask you to describe the importance of knowledge and understanding of natural laws while developing a technology.*

Ans. Human beings interact with their physical environment with the help of technology. Technology also indicates the level of cultural development of society. Human beings were able to develop technology only after they developed better understanding of natural laws.

The following examples can be considered to understand the given statement

- It was the understanding of concepts of friction and heat which helped us to discover fire.
- Similarly, understanding of the secrets of DNA and genetics enabled us to conquer many diseases.
- Likewise, understanding and knowledge of the laws of aerodynamics helped us to develop aeroplanes to carry passengers and goods.
- Thus, knowledge and understanding about natural laws are extremely important to develop technology, and the use of this technology results in greater cultural development of society.

Hence, we can say that knowledge about nature is extremely important to develop technology.

2. "The imprints of human activities are created everywhere." Evaluate the statement in context of humanisation of nature. ***(CBSE 2023)***

HINT *Dear students, this question simply ask you to explain the extent and impact of human activities on our nature.*

Ans. Humanisation of nature can be traced from human geography by understanding the following points

- With social and cultural development, humans began to understand their environment and the forces of nature and they developed better and more efficient technology. With better technology, they moved from a state of necessity to a state of freedom and created possibilities with the resources obtained from the environment.
- Humanisation of nature simply means that human have tendencies of grabbing opportunities which are given by the nature so that they are no longer constrained by the limitations imposed by nature.
- The imprints of human activities are created everywhere i.e. health resorts on highlands, huge urban sprawls, fields or orchards and pastures in plains and rolling hills, ports on the coasts, oceanic routes on the oceanic surface and satellites in the space.

3. ''The physical and human phenomena are described in metaphors using symbols from human anatomy.'' Support the statement with example. ***(CBSE 2023)***

Or "The physical and human phenomena in geography are described in metaphors using symbols from the human anatomy." Explain the statement by giving examples. ***(CBSE Compartment 2020)***

Ans. Both physical and humans phenomena are described in metaphors using symbols from the human anatomy. We often talk about the 'face' of the earth, 'eye' of the storm, 'mouth' of the river, 'snout' (nose) of the glacier, 'neck' of the isthmus and 'profile' of the soil. Similarly regions, villages, towns have been described as 'organisms'. German geographers describe the 'state/country' as a 'living organism'. Networks of road, railways and waterways have often been described as "arteries of circulation".

4. ''Nature and humans are inseparable in all geographical studies.'' Examine the statement. ***(CBSE 2023)***

Or ''Nature and humans are inseparable elements''. Justify the statement with suitable examples. ***(Delhi 2017)***

Or ''The nature and human beings are so intricately intertwined that they cannot be separated.'' Justify the statement. ***(Delhi 2016)***

Ans. The nature and human beings cannot be separated as they are inseparable because man became social, economic and technologically advanced. He broadened his nature by creating his own environment through his design and skill to have provision for better food, shelter, access and comfort.

Both nature and humans are described metaphors using symbols from the human anatomy, like we often talk of the face of the Earth, eye of storm, mouth of the river, snout (nose) of the glacier, neck of the isthmus and profile of the soil.

All the above nick names are given by the humans to the natural phenomena. By doing so, human can interact easily with the nature. All these physical features are described as organism and man-made structure like road, railways and waterways have been described as arteries of circulation.

5. Explain systematic or regional approach to the study of Geography. ***(CBSE 2023)***

Ans. **Systematic Approach**

The systematic geography approach was introduced by Alexander Von Humboldt, a German geographer. In systematic approach, a phenomenon is studied world over as a whole and then the identification of typologies or spatial patterns is done.

For example, if one is interested in studying natural vegetation, the study will be done at the world level as a first step. The typologies such as equatorial rainforests or softwood conical forests or monsoon forests, etc will be identified, discussed and delimited.

Regional Approach

Regional geography approach was developed by another German geographer and a contemporary of Humboldt, Karl Ritter.

In the regional approach, the world is divided into regions at different hierarchical levels and then all the geographical phenomena in a particular region are studied. These regions may be natural, political or designated.

For example, if one is interested in studying natural vegetation, the study will be done for different region like equator, monsoon region, Desert region, Tundra region, etc.

6. How is 'Naturalisation of Human' different from 'Humanisation of Nature'? **(CBSE SQP 2022)**

Ans. 'Naturalisation of Humans' and 'Humanisation of Nature' can be studied in terms of relation between man and environment and their interaction.

Technology has enabled human beings to interact with their physical environment. The technologies can be developed after understand the natural laws. This understand help human to go beyond the limitations posed by nature. For example, the understanding of friction and heat helped the humans to discover fire and use it to make their lives easier by cooking food and keeping themselves warm.

Similarly, DNA technology is helping humans to cure many diseases.

7. 'The approaches to the study of human geography have been evolving over a period of time'. How have these schools of thought changed the approaches of study to human geography? **(CBSE SQP 2022)**

Ans. The approaches to the study of human geography have been evolving over a period of time. These schools of thought have changed the approaches of study to human geography in the following ways

- Welfare or humanistic school of thought in human geography was mainly concerned with the different aspects of social well-being of the people. These included aspects such as housing, health and education.
- Radical school of thought employed Marxian theory to explain the basic cause of poverty, deprivation and social inequality. Contemporary social problems were related to the development of capitalism.
- The Behavioural school of thought laid great emphasis on lived experience and also on the perception of space by social categories based on ethnicity, race and religion, etc.

8. Explain how human geography in the early 20th century has become more integrative and inter-disciplinary in its approach. **(CBSE SQP 2020)**

Ans. The subject matter of human geography continues to grow since a long period of time. It has widened its scope considerably. In the early 20th century, several new branches emerged out of it such as population geography, political geography, agricultural geography, etc. Its aim was to study emerging issues and problems like political dimensions and social relevance. In doing so, human geography has not only become more integrative and inter-disciplinary in nature but has also incorporated several new approaches into its field. For example, it gives the necessary spatial and systematic view point to the other social sciences which they otherwise lack. At the same time, human geography draws on other sciences, the analysis and identifies with its sub-fields such as political, economic and social geography.

9. How is possibilism different from environmental determinism? Explain with suitable examples. **(CBSE SQP 2019)**

Ans. The differences between Possibilism and Environmental determinism are

Possibilism	Environmental Determinism
With the passage of time, humans developed better and efficient technology. This gave them many choices and possibilities to use resources offered by the environment. They became free to use natural resources according to their convenience and necessity.	In the earlier stages of human evolution, there was no technology available to man to modify the environment. Thus, human beings adapted to dictates of nature.
Man has created health resorts on highlands, huge urban sprawls, fields, orchards and pastures in the plains, ports on the coasts and satellites in space. This was termed as 'Possibilism' by earlier scholars.	The naturalised human was afraid of nature and worshipped the forces of nature such as fire, floods, rains, etc. This has been termed as 'Environmental Determinism'.

10. 'Technology loosens the shackles of environment on human being'. Justify. **(CBSE SQP 2018)**

Or How does technology loosen the shackles of environment on human beings? Explain with examples. **(All India 2010, CBSE SQP 2018)**

Ans. It is true that technology loosen the shackles of environment on human beings because human beings interact with their physical environment with the help of technology. Here technology indicates the level of cultural development of society.

Earlier stages of their interaction with their natural environment, humans were greatly influenced by the nature, but contemporary human understands the nature and its forces. They use their understanding for new era of soreness i.e. humanisation of nature.

The examples are as follows

(i) In early stages of human history, the concepts of friction and heat helped in discovering fire.

(ii) In modern times, understanding the secrets of DNA and genetics enabled us to conquer many diseases.

11. What is the subject matter of the study of human geography? Explain any three facts. ***(Delhi 2015)***

Ans. The subject matter of the study of human geography are as follows

To Understand the Inter-relationship There is a close relationship between the physical/natural environment and the human world, so human geography studies and establishes that relation.

Study the Spatial Distribution Human geography also studies the spatial distribution of human phenomena.

Social and Economic Variations The subject matter is also concerned about studying the social and economic differences between different parts of the world.

Subject matter of the study of Human Geography

- To Understand the Inter-relationship
- Study the Spatial Distribution
- Social and Economic Variations

12. "There is mutual interaction between the elements of physical geography and human geography." Support the statement with suitable examples. ***(Delhi 2014)***

Ans. Physical geography includes natural environment like landforms, climate, flora and fauna. Human geography includes the inter-relationship between the human beings and the physical environment. Humans through the use of technology create the socio-cultural environment of the cultural landscape.

These creations are the action of mutual interaction between physical and human geography.

For instance, on highlands, health resorts are created, oceanic routes are discovered on the surface of the oceans, houses in villages and cities are made to use the physical environment in a better way. These examples show that there is mutual interaction between these two.

13. Explain the concept of 'possibilism', with three suitable examples. ***(Delhi 2013, All India 2009)***

Ans. The concept of possibilism was propounded by Lucian Febvre who described that there are no necessities, but possibilities everywhere and man is referred to as a master of these possibilities who judges their use. Man can adopt, adjust and modify the forces of his physical environment with his strength. His imprints could be seen everywhere.

For instance, health resort on highlands, huge urban sprawls (spread), fields, orchards and pastures in plains and rolling hills, ports on the coasts, oceanic routes on the oceanic surface and satellites in the space.

14. Define 'human geography' in your own words. Mention any four fields of human geography. ***(All India 2013)***

Ans. Human geography studies the inter-relationship between the physical environment and socio-cultural environment created by human beings through mutual interaction with each other. It attempts to explain the relationship between all elements of human life and space they occur over. The four fields of human geography are as follows

Social Geography It is a field of human geography which is connected with social sciences and sociology. Its sub-fields are behavioural geography, geography of social well being, historical, medical geography, etc.

Urban Geography It is a field of human geography connected with the urban studies and planning.

Political Geography It is a field of human geography connected with the science. Its sub-fields are electoral geography, military geography, etc.

Population Geography It is a field of human geography connected with the demography.

Fields of Human Geography

- Social Geography
- Urban Geography
- Political Geography
- Population Geography

15. Define 'human geography'. Give four examples of elements of material culture created by humans, using the resources provided by nature. ***(All India 2012)***

Ans. Human geography studies the inter-relationship between the physical environment and socio-cultural environment created by human beings through mutual interaction with each other. It attempts to explain the relationship between all elements of human life and space they occur over. Elements of physical environment are landforms, soils, climate, water, natural vegetation, rivers, flora and fauna, etc.

Example of elements of material culture created by humans, after using the resources provided by nature are as follows

(i) Furniture from tree wood.

(ii) Machines using iron ore.

(iii) Houses using stone and soil.

(iv) Clothes from cotton.

16. Explain the concept of 'neo determinism' with suitable examples. *(All India 2011)*

Or What is the new concept of Griffith Taylor in the field of human geography? Describe the concept with examples. *(All India 2008)*

Ans. The concept of neo-determinism was introduced by Griffith Taylor which emphasises the middle path or Madhyam Marg between two ends of environmental determinism and possibilism. It can be understood by the following points

(i) The concept envisages that there is nothing absolute whether it is absolute necessity (i.e. environmental determinism) and absolute freedom (i.e. possibilism).

(ii) A human being can inhibit nature by obeying it, as possibilities can be created within limit.

(iii) Over exploitation of natural resources for the development of economy, causes environmental problems like green house effect, ozone layer depletion, global warming, receding glaciers and degrading lands.

An example of neo-determination i.e. middle path is traffic signals. Red light means stop while green means go and amber light provides a gap between red and green lights 'to get set'. Amber light is middle path just as neo-determinism is in between two ends of environmental determinism and possibilism.

17. Explain the concept of 'determinism' with suitable examples. *(Delhi 2011, 2009)*

Or What is the meaning of environmental determinism? How did naturalisation of humans lead to the development of this concept? *(CBSE Compartment 2009)*

Ans. The concept of determinism explains that human is a passive agent, influenced by the environmental factors that are physical factors like climate, flora, fauna, etc which determine the attitude of decision-making and lifestyle of human beings.

For instance, the Eskimos of Tundra adapted to the extremely cold climate. Their main food is whale, seals and walrus. They use animal oil for cooking, heating and lighting. They live in igloos. Whereas Samang and Sakai of Malaysia and Pygmies of Congo basin live in hot and humid condition. They live on vegetable, hunting and fishing.

Naturalisation of human means when nature is stronger than humans and therefore humans are controlled by nature. This type of interaction was between primitive human society and nature. At the time, forces of nature were stronger and humans struggled to survive in that environment. Humans were passive agents. This gave rise to the term environmental determinism.

18. State the six approaches of human geography. *(Delhi 2008)*

Ans. The six approaches of human geography are as follows

(i) Exploration and description

(ii) Regional analysis

(iii) Areal differentiation

(iv) Spatial organisation

(v) Emergence of humanistic, radical and behavioural schools

(vi) Post-modernisation in geography

19. State six different fields of human geography. *(Delhi 2008)*

Ans. The six different fields of human geography are as follows

(i) Social Geography

(ii) Urban Geography

(iii) Political Geography

(iv) Population Geography

(v) Settlement Geography

(vi) Economic Geography

20. State any six sub-fields of social geography. *(All India 2008)*

Ans. The six sub-fields of social geography are as follows

(i) Behavioural geography

(ii) Geography of social well-being

(iii) Geography of leisure

(iv) Cultural geography

(v) Gender geography

(vi) Historical geography

21. Which are the six sub-fields of economic geography? *(All India 2008)*

Ans. The six sub-fields of economic geography are as follows

(i) Geography of resources

(ii) Geography of agriculture

(iii) Geography of industries

(iv) Geography of marketing

(v) Geography of tourism

(vi) Geography of international trade

5 Marks Questions

1. Describe various schools of thought that have developed in geography.

Ans. The various schools of thought developed in geography are discussed below

- **Welfare or Humanistic School of Thought** This school of thought seeks to put humans at the centre of geography. It is a part of human geography that is concerned with the different aspects of social well-being of the people like housing, health, education, etc. It deals with the concepts like human awareness, human agency, human consciousness and human creativity.
- **Radical School of Thought** The origin of radical school of thought can be traced to the radical geography movement which started in 1960s in the USA. It is only a 25 year old approach in geography, which has a strong Marxist base and holistic view of economics, society and polity. It explains the basic cause of poverty, deprivation and social inequality. According to this theory, capitalism creates the contemporary social problems in societies.
- **Behavioural School of Thought** This came in response to the dissatisfaction with the models and theories developed by the positivists. This school of thought lays great stress on lived experience and also perceives the notion of space by social categories based on ethnicity, race and religion.

Various School of Thought
- Welfare or Humanistic School of Thought
- Radical School of Thought
- Behavioural School of Thought

2. Why deterministic approach faded out with the passage of time? Discuss.

Ans. Despite its success in the early 1900s, environmental determinism's popularity began to decline in the 1920s, as its claims were often found to be wrong. In addition, critics claimed it was racist and perpetuated imperialism.

Carl Sauer's Criticisms

One of the critics of this approach was Carl Sauer, who said (1924) that environmental determinism led to premature generalisations about an area's culture and did not allow for results based on direct observation. Spate also criticised that "environment taken by this approach is a meaningless phrase; without man, environment does not exist."

Other Criticisms

It has also been criticised on the ground that people make their own history, culture and civilisation under definite conditions and circumstances. Men act through a world of rules which our action makes, breaks and renews.

By the 1950s, environmental determinism was almost entirely faded out and replaced in geography by possibilism (to explain cultural development) and lost its prominence as the central theory in geography.

CHAPTER TEST

01 Mark Questions

1 Which one of the following is the most important factor in the interaction between people and environment?
(a) Human brotherhood (b) Technology
(c) Human intelligence (d) People's perception

2 Which of the following pairs is correctly matched?

(Sub-fields of Human Geography)		(Sister disciplines)
(a) Behavioural Geography	–	Psephology
(b) Geography of Leisure	–	Business Geography
(c) Geography of Marketing	–	Sociology
(d) Cultural Geography	–	Anthropology

3 Arrange the following approaches of human geography in ascending order on the basis of time.
I. Post-modernism in geography
II. Exploration and description
III. Areal differentiation
IV. Regional analysis

Codes
(a) I, II, III, IV (b) II, IV, III, I
(c) IV, III, II, I (d) III, I, IV, II

4 **Assertion** (A) The imprints of human activities are created everywhere.

Reason (R) Health resorts on highlands, huge urban sprawls, fields, orchards and pastures in plains and rolling hills, ports on the coasts, oceanic routes on the oceanic surface and satellites in the space are examples of cultural landscape.

Codes
(a) Both A and R are true and R is the correct explanation of A
(b) Both A and R are true, but R is not the correct explanation of A
(c) A is true, but R is false
(d) A is false, but R is true

5 Consider the following about the later colonial period and choose the correct answer.
I. Regional analysis was used to study geography.
II. Elaborate descriptions of all aspects of a region were undertaken.

Codes
(a) Only statement I is correct
(b) Both the statements are true and statement II correctly present the reason for statement I
(c) Only statement II is correct
(d) Both the statements I and II are incorrect

Answers

1. (b) | 2. (d) | 3. (b) | 4. (a) | 5. (b)

03 Marks Questions

6 The scope of human geography holds a vast area. Discuss the scope of human geography in your own words.

7 Describe various schools of thought that have developed in geography.

8 Compare and contrast between determinism and possibilism.

05 Marks Questions

9 The concept of 'neo-determinism' was introduced by Griffith Taylor which emphasises the middle path or 'Madhyam Marg'. Explain the concept in brief.

10 Define human geography. Give four examples of elements of material culture created by humans using the resources provided by nature.

11 State about the subject matter of the study of human geography. Explain any three facts.

02

The World Population

TREND ANALYSIS 3 YEARS

Average No. of Questions Across all Sets

	Types of Questions	2023	2020	2019
TOPIC 01 Patterns of Population Distribution	1 Mark	3	1	1
	3 Marks	–	–	–
	5 Marks	2	–	1
TOPIC 02 Population Growth/Change	1 Mark	2	1	–
	3 Marks	–	–	–
	5 Marks	–	–	–

The people of a country are its real wealth as they put the natural resources into use and also decide various policies, and finally a country is known by its people. It is important to know the number of males, females, birth and death rate to make necessary decisions for social and economic development.

Patterns of Population Distribution

- Population distribution means arrangement or distribution of people over the Earth's surface. Population is not evenly distributed as 90 per cent of the world's population lives in about 10 per cent of its land area.
- The 10 most populous countries of the world contribute about 60 per cent of the world's population. Out of these 10 countries, 6 are located in Asia.

Density of Population

- This means the ratio between the number of people to the size of the land. It is usually measured in persons per sq km density of population/area. Some areas are densely populated like North-Eastern USA, North-Western Europe, South, South-West and East Asia.
- Some areas are sparsely populated like near the polar areas and high rainfall zones near the equator while some areas have medium density like Western China, Southern India, Norway, Sweden, etc.

$$\text{Density of Population} = \frac{\text{Population}}{\text{Area}}$$

Factors Influencing Population Distribution

The population distribution is influenced by three factors i.e., geographical factors, economic factors and social and cultural factors.

Geographical Factors

Environmental or natural factors such as landforms, fertile soil, suitable climate for cultivation and availability of adequate source of fresh water are the geographical factors that affect the population distribution. Some geographical factors are

Landforms Flat plains and gentle slopes are preferred by people, because these are favourable for the production of crops and to build roads and industries.

Climate Area with less seasonal variation attract more people.

Soil Area which have fertile loamy soil have more people living on them as these can support intensive agriculture.

Water People prefer to live in areas where fresh water is easily available. Because, it is the most important factor for life.

Economic Factors

Places having employment opportunities like mineral rich areas, industrial units and urban centres have high concentration of population. Some economic factors are

Industrialisation Industries provide job opportunities and attract large numbers of people.

Minerals Minerals deposits attract industries, mining and industrial activities generate employment.

Urbanisation Good civic amenities and the attraction of city life draw people to the cities.

Social and Cultural Factors

Places having religious importance and cultural significance are also very densely populated areas.

Population Growth/Change

This refers to the change in number of inhabitants of a territory during a specific period of time. When change in population is expressed in percentage, then it is called **Growth Rate of Population**.

When there is an increase in population by taking the difference between births and deaths, then it is called **Natural Growth of Population**. There is also **Positive Growth** of Population which happens when birth rate is more than death rate and **Negative Growth** of Population when birth rate is lower than death rate.

Components of Population Change

There are three components of population change i.e., births, deaths and migration.

Crude Birth Rate (CBR)

Number of births in a year per thousand of population is expressed as Crude Birth Rate (CBR). It is calculated as

$$CBR = \frac{Bi}{P} \times 100$$

Here, Bi= live births during the year; P = Mid- year population of the area

Crude Death Rate (CDR)

Number of deaths in a year per thousand of population is expressed as Crude Death Rate (CDR). It is calculated as

$$CDR = \frac{D}{P} \times 100$$

Here, D= Number of deaths; P = Estimated mid-year population of that year.

Migration

It is movement of people across region on permanent, temporary or seasonal basis. The place they move is called place of origin and the place they move to is called place of destination.

Push and Pull Factors of Migration

The **push factors** make the place of origin seem less attractive for reasons like unemployment, poor living conditions, political turmoil, unpleasant climate, natural disasters, epidemics and socio-economic backwardness.

The **pull factors** make the place of destination seem more attractive than the place of origin for reasons like better job opportunities and living conditions, peace and stability, security of life and property and pleasant climate.

Demographic Transition Theory

This theory studies the changes in the population of a region as it moves from high births and high deaths to low births and low deaths. This happens when a society progresses from rural agrarian and illiterate to urban, industrial and literate.

There are three-staged model of Demographic Transition Theory. They are

First Stage

- This stage is marked by high fertility, high mortality rate because people reproduce more to compensate for the deaths due to epidemics and variable food supply.
- People are poor, illiterate and mostly engaged in agriculture. Life expectancy is low and population growth is slow.

Second Stage

- Level of technology increases and other facilities like medical, health, sanitation improves due to which the death rate reduces.
- But the fertility rate and birth rate remains high due to which there is huge rise in population. Population expands rapidly as there is wide gap between birth and death rate.

Third Stage

- The birth and death rate both reduces and the population moves towards stability.
- People become literate, urbanised and control the size of the family. There is good judicious use of technology also.

Population Control Measures

- Family planning is the spacing and preventing the birth of children. Thomas Malthus theory (1793) states that the number of people would grow faster than the food supply thus leading to famine, diseases and war.
- Therefore, it is essential to control the population. This is undertaken through measures like awareness for family planning, free availability of contraceptives, tax disincentives and active propaganda.

PYQs Previous Years' Questions

1 Mark Questions

Multiple Choice Questions

1. Which among the following is an economic factor responsible for uneven distribution of population in the world? *(CBSE 2023)*

(a) Urbanisation (b) Soils
(c) Climate (d) Political unrest

Ans. (*a*) Urbanisation

2. Which one of the following is a thickly populated region? *(CBSE 2023)*

(a) The Himalayan region
(b) Osaka-Kobe region of Japan
(c) Siberian region of Russia
(d) Central Chile

Ans. (b) Osaka-Kobe region of Japan

3. Which one of the following is the push factor responsible for migration? *(CBSE 2023)*

(a) Better job opportunities
(b) Unpleasant climate
(c) Peace and stability
(d) Security to life and property

Ans. (b) Unpleasant climate

4. Which one of the following is related to push factor of migration? *(CBSE 2023)*

(a) Natural disasters (b) Pleasant climate
(c) Security of life and property (d) Peace and stability

Ans. (a) Natural disasters

5. Which one of the following is a social factor affecting the distribution of population? *(CBSE 2023)*

(a) Minerals (b) Urbanisation
(c) Industrialisation (d) Unrest

Ans. (d) Unrest

6. Which of the following may be interpreted as a spontaneous effort to achieve a better balance between population and resources? *(CBSE SQP 2022)*

(a) Migration (b) Growth Rate
(c) Birth Rate (d) Death Rate

Ans. (a) Migration

7. Which of the following features is related to the second stage of Demographic Transition Theory? *(CBSE 2022)*

(a) Fertility and mortality decline considerably
(b) Decline in mortality but fertility remains high
(c) Fertility and mortality are high
(d) Fertility declines and mortality high

Ans. (b) Decline in mortality but fertility remains high

8. **Assertion** (A) Mediterranean regions have been inhabited from early periods in history.
Reason (R) Plain areas are favourable for the production of crops and to build roads and industries. *(CBSE SQP 2022)*

Codes
(a) Both A and R are true and R is the correct explanation of A
(b) A is true, but R is false
(c) A is false, but R is true
(d) Both A and R are true, but R is not the correct explanation of A

Ans. (d) Both A and R are true, but R is not the correct explanation of A

9. Which one of the following states has the lowest population density? *(CBSE Term I 2021)*
(a) Mizoram (b) Nagaland
(c) Assam (d) Himachal Pradesh

Ans. (a) Mizoram

10. Which one of the following is the most serious problem due to increasing population? *(CBSE Term I 2021)*
(a) Increased epidemics
(b) Decreased resources
(c) Shortage of education institutions
(d) Shortage of opportunities of employment

Ans. (b) Decreased resources

11. Which one of the following is a main component of population change? *(CBSE Term I 2021)*
(a) Density of population
(b) Urbanisation
(c) Industrialisation
(d) Migration

Ans. (d) Migration

12. Which one of the following is a main cause for the excess of females in urban areas of United States of America (USA)? *(CBSE Compartment 2020)*
(a) Males prefer to live in rural areas.
(b) Out-migration of males to other countries.
(c) Low birth rate of male child.
(d) Influx of females from rural to urban areas to avail vast job opportunities.

Ans. (d) Influx of females from rural to urban areas to avail vast job opportunities.

13. Which one of the following refers to actual growth of population? *(CBSE Compartment 2020)*
(a) Change of population in a particular area between two points of time.
(b) Population increases by difference between births and deaths.
(c) Population increases by the difference of births and deaths plus in-migration minus out-migration.
(d) Increase in population by births plus in-migration

Ans. (c) Population increases by the difference of births and deaths plus in-migration minus out-migration.

14. Relate the most important factor responsible for high density of population found in Katanga, Zambia Plateau located in Africa. *(CBSE SQP 2020)*
(a) Availability of copper in abundance
(b) Availability of forests resources
(c) Close social ties
(d) Scenic natural beauty

Ans. (a) Availability of copper in abundance

15. If a country is having large proportion of young population, it would mean *(CBSE SQP 2020)*
(a) high birth rate and the population is youthful.
(b) large working population.
(c) expenditure on healthcare facilities.
(d) heavy pressure on government to arrange basic facilities.

Ans. (a) high birth rate and the population is youthful.

16. Study the given graph carefully and answer the following questions. *(CBSE SQP 2020, CBSE SQP Term I 2021)*

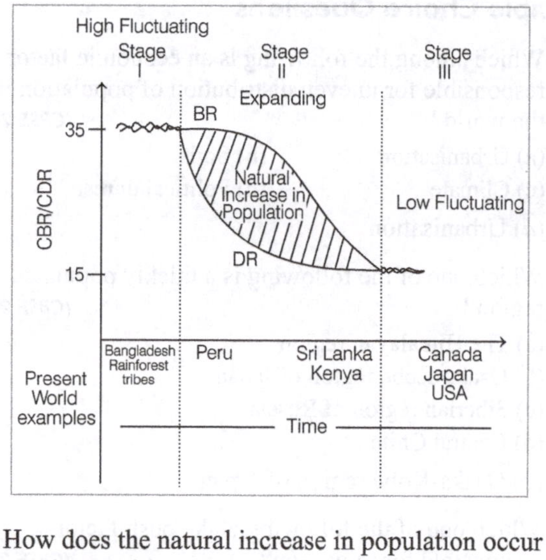

(i) How does the natural increase in population occur as per the graph?
(a) Birth Rate – Death Rate
(b) Death Rate + Birth Rate
(c) Growth Rate – Birth Rate
(d) Birth Rate + Migration

Ans. (a) Birth Rate – Death Rate

(ii) What does the transition from high fluctuating stage to low fluctuating stage indicate?
(a) Shift from Urban Industrial Economy to Rural Agrarian Economy
(b) Shift from Rural Agrarian Economy to Urban Industrial Economy
(c) Low Birth and Death Rate to High Birth and Death Rate
(d) Migration from Urban to Rural areas

Ans. (a) Shift from Urban Industrial Economy to Rural Agrarian Economy

(iii) From the given graph, what condition can you infer about the developing countries?
(a) High Birth Rate and High Death Rate
(b) Low Birth Rate and Low Death Rate
(c) High Birth Rate and Low Death Rate
(d) Low Birth Rate and High Death Rate

Ans. (a) High Birth Rate and High Death Rate

(iv) In which stage of Demographic Transition, population explosion took place
(a) Stage I (b) Stage II
(c) Stage II (d) Post Stage III

Ans. (b) Stage II

17. Which one of the following is not a push factor? ***(CBSE SQP 2019)***
(a) Water shortage
(b) Medical/Educational facilities
(c) Unemployment
(d) Epidemics

Ans. (b) Medical/Educational facilities

18. Which of the following is not a geographical factor which influences the distribution of population ?
(a) Industrialisation (b) Climate
(c) Landforms (d) Availability of water

Ans. (a) Industrialisation

19. CBR stands for
(a) Combined Birth Rate (b) Crude Birth Ratio
(c) Complete Birth Rate (d) Crude Birth Rate

Ans. (d) Crude Birth Rate

20. Which of the following areas are characterised by dense population?
(a) Mountainous regions (b) Plateau regions
(c) River valleys (d) Deserts

Ans. (c) River valleys

21. Which of the following countries is in the first stage of demographic transition ?
(a) Peru (b) Canada
(c) Bangladesh (d) India

Ans. (c) Bangladesh

19. Complete the following table.

Terms	Formulas
Population Density	$\frac{\text{Population}}{\text{Area}}$
Crude Birth Rate	?
Crude Death Rate	$\frac{D}{P} \times 100$

Ans. Crude Birth Rate $= \frac{\text{Bi}}{\text{P}} \times 1000$

Very Short Answer Questions

1. Differentiate between positive and negative growth of population. ***(CBSE SQP 2018)***

Ans. Positive growth of population takes place when the birth rate is more than death rate between the two points of time. Negative growth of population occurs when birth rate falls below the death rate.

2. Differentiate between immigration and emigration. ***(CBSE SQP 2018)***

Ans. The difference between emigration and immigration are as follows

Emigration	Immigration
It means movement of people from a country where they earlier reside. It means to move out.	It means movement of people to a new country where they decide to live and work for future prospects. It means to move in.
A person who emigrates from a country is called as emigrant.	A person who immigrates into a country is called as immigrant.

3. How is density of population of a region calculated? ***(Delhi 2015)***

Ans. Density of population refers to a ratio between the total population and the total land area in a country. It can be calculated as

$$= \frac{\text{Total population of area}}{\text{Total area}}$$

4. Define the term 'population distribution'. ***(Delhi 2015)***

Ans. Population distribution means arrangement of people over the Earth's surface. The population distribution in the world is uneven.

5. Name the most densely populated region of North America. ***(All India 2013)***

Ans. The most densely populated region of North America is North-Eastern part of USA.

6. Give the meaning of 'Crude Birth Rate (CBR)'. ***(Delhi 2013)***

Ans. The Crude Birth Rate (CBR) is expressed as number of live births in a year per thousand of population. It is calculated as

$$CBR = \frac{Bi}{P} \times 1000$$

Where, Bi = Live births during the year and
P = Mid-year population of the area.

7. Which continent has the highest growth rate of population? ***(Delhi 2012, 2009)***

Ans. The highest growth rate of population is in Africa.

8. Define the term density of population. ***(Delhi 2012)***

Ans. A ratio between population and land area in a country is called population density. It is calculated by dividing the number of people by area which is usually shown as the number of people per square kilometres.

9. Define the term population growth. ***(All India 2012)***

Ans. Population growth refers to the change in number of inhabitants of a territory during a specific period of time.

10. Define the term 'positive growth of population'. ***(All India 2011)***

Ans. When the birth rate is more than death rate between the two points of time or when people from other countries migrate permanently to a region is called positive growth of population.

3 Marks Questions

1. Study the given figure carefully and answer the questions that follow. ***(CBSE 2023)***

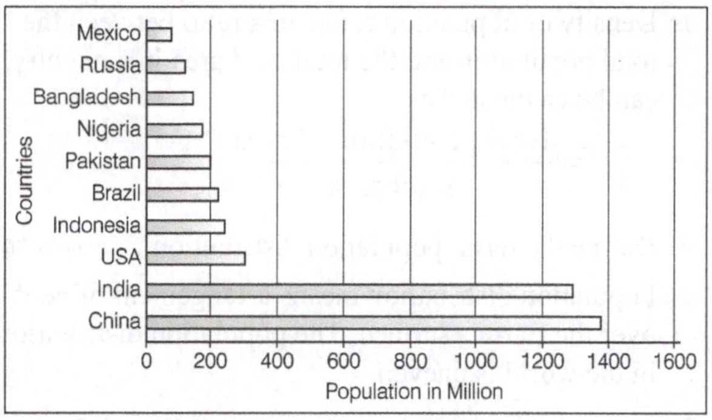

Most Populous Countries

(i) Name the highest populous country.

(ii) How many total countries of Asia continent are shown in the figure?

(iii) How do landforms affect the density of population in Asia?

Ans. (i) China is the highest populous country in the world as per the given graph.

(ii) Six countries of Asia continent are shown in the graph.

(iii) People prefer living on flat plains and gentle slopes. This is because such areas are favourable for the production of crops and to build roads and industries e.g. the Ganga plains in India. The mountainous and hilly areas hinder the development of transport network and hence initially do not favour agricultural and industrial development. So, these areas tend to be less populated e.g. the Himalayas.

2. What is meant by the density of population? Explain with examples the physical and economic factors which affect population distribution. ***(CBSE SQP 2022)***

Ans. The density of population is the ratio between the numbers of people living in a square kilometer of area. It is a measure of human and land relationship. It helps us in getting a better understanding of spatial distribution of population in relation to land.

- Physical factors which affect population distribution include availability of water, terrain, fertile soil and climate. Most of the physical factors influence population distribution indirectly through climatic conditions. For instance, the North India plains, deltas and coastal plains have a higher proportion of population than other regions of the country.
- Economic factors which affect population distribution include industrialisation, urbanisation and development of transport networks causes high concentration of population in urban regions of Delhi, Mumbai, Kolkata, Bangalore, Pune, etc.

3. With the help of a neat and labelled diagram, explain the three stages of the Demographic Transition Theory. ***(CBSE SQP 2022)***

Ans. The Demographic Transition Theory is used to describe and predict the population and its growth in an area. The three stages of the Demographic Transition Theory are explained below with the help of given diagram.

- First stage is characterised by high fertility and high mortality rates. There are increasing deaths due to epidemics and variable food supply and people reproduce more to compensate it.

There is slow growth of population. Life expectancy is low due to epidemics and irregular food supply. This period has high prevalence of illiteracy and lack of technological advancement.

- Second stage is characterised by reduced mortality rate. This is due to an expansion in medical and health facilities and also improvements in sanitation conditions, etc. This is the period of time of population explosion. The fertility remains constantly high in the beginning, but it declines with time. Due to the widening gap between the birth and death rates, population grows at an exceptionally high rate. Thus, during this period net addition of population is high.
- Third stage is characterised by a decline in fertility and mortality rates. Birth rate is nearly equal to death rate and there is little growth in population. In this stage, population becomes more urbanised, literate and has high technical know-how and deliberately controls the family size.

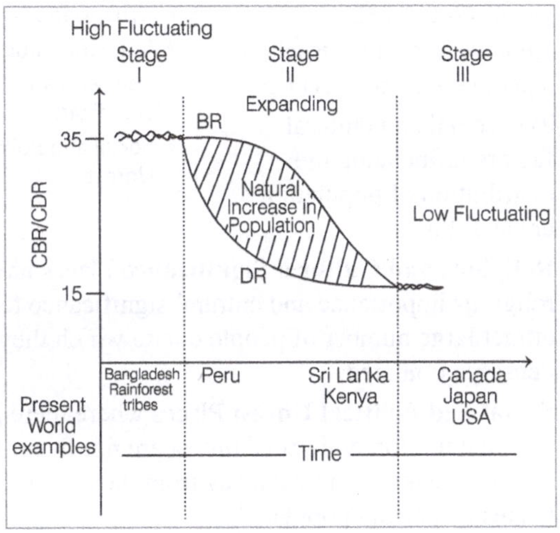

4. Explain any three push and any two pull factors that influence the migrations of population in the world. ***(All India 2016)***

Or How is the mortality rate of a region affected? Explain any four push factors responsible for migration. ***(Delhi 2015)***

Ans. Migration is the displacement of people from one place to another. It can be permanent, temporary or seasonal.

The push factors of migration are

(i) Unemployment
(ii) Poor living conditions
(iii) Political turmoil
(iv) Unpleasant climate

The pull factors of migration are

(i) Better job opportunities
(ii) Better living conditions

The mortality rate of a region is affected by the availability of medical and health facilities, sanitation and provision of nutritious food.

5. Describe any three characteristics of the first stage of 'Demographic Transition Theory'. ***(Delhi 2014)***

Ans. Characteristics of first stage of Demographic Transition Theory are as follows

(i) The first stage has high fertility and high mortality because people reproduce more to compensation for the deaths due to epidemics and variable food supply.
(ii) Most of the people are engaged in agriculture where large families are an asset.
(iii) The population growth is slow.

Additional Info

Other characteristics of the first stage of Demographic Transition Theory are

- Life expectancy is low in this stage. People are mostly illiterate and have low levels of technology.
- Two hundred years ago, all the countries of the world were in this stage.

6. Describe any three characteristics of the last stage of 'Demographic Transition Theory'. ***(All India 2014)***

Ans. Characteristics of last stage of Demographic Transition Theory are as follows

(i) In this stage, both fertility and mortality decline.
(ii) The population is either stable or grows slowly.
(iii) The population becomes urbanised, literate and has high technical know-how.

5 Marks Questions

1. Examine the geographical factors that influence distribution of population in the world. ***(CBSE 2023)***

Other Similar Questions

Or "There are various geographical factors that influence distribution of population in the world." Explain.

Or What are the factors that influence distribution of population in the world?

Ans. The geographical factors that influence distribution of population in the world are

Availablility of Water
Water is considered as life. It has many uses for human beings, such as in activities like drinking, bathing, cooking, for cattle, crops and also for industries and navigation purposes. thus, river valleys are most densely populated areas of the world because of the avilability of fresh water.

Relief Features Relief is the most important physical factor influencing the distribution of population. High mountains, rugged terrain and some of the plateaus restrict human settlements.

Plains River valley have fertile soil. Plain areas provide better living condition. The nature of surface permits wider scope for agriculture, industries, transport and urbanisation.

Climate It has a direct influence on human beings. Man refers to live in normal conditions of temperature and rainfall. Excessive heat, cold, dryness or wetness restrict the human population. Apart from human health, climate affects agriculture also.

Geographical factors that influence distribution of population in the world
- Availability of water
- Relief Features
- Plains
- Climate
- Soil

Asia, North-West Europe and North America are areas of dense population.

Soil It is important factor for the survival of human. Fertile soil support agriculture. High degree of population concentration in South-East Asia is primarily due to fertile soil. Most of the world's fertile soil are found in river valley of Ganga, Indus, Huang Ho, Mississipi, etc.

2. Define the term 'density of population'. Elaborate any four geographical factors that influence the distribution of population in the world. ***(Delhi 2019)***

Or What is the meaning of density of population? Examine the four geographical factors that influence the distribution of population in the world with suitable examples. ***(Delhi 2017)***

Ans. Density of population refers to a ratio between the total population and the total land area in a country. Density of population is an important measure to analyse population distribution.
For geographical factors that influence the distribution of population in the world, refer to Q. 1 of 5 marks questions.

3. Explain the economic and cultural factors that influence the distribution of population in the world. ***(All India 2019)***

Or Explain three economic and two social and cultural factors influencing the distribution of population in the world. ***(All India 2015)***

Or Explain with examples the three economic factors influencing the population distribution in the world. ***(All India 2011, Delhi 2008)***

Ans. Economic and cultural factors that influence the distribution of population in the world are as follows

Minerals Areas with mineral deposits attract not only industries, but also skilled and semi-skilled workers as they generate huge employment.

Urbanisation Urban centres offer better employment opportunities, education and medical facilities, better means of communication which attract people.

Industrialisation Industrial belts provide job opportunities which attract not only factory workers, but also transport operators, shopkeepers, bank employees, doctors, teachers and other service providers.

Economic and cultural factors influencing distribution of population
- Minerals
- Urbanisation
- Industrialisation
- Religious and Cultural significance
- Social and Political Unrest

Two social and cultural factors influencing the distribution of population are as follows

Religious and Cultural Significance Places having religious importance and cultural significance tend to attract large number of people due to which they are densely populated.

Social and Political Unrest Places where there is political turmoil and social unrest are not fit for living and people tend to move away from those areas. This makes it sparsely populated.

4. "90 per cent of the world population lives in about 10 per cent of its total land area, whereas remaining 10 per cent population resides in the 90 per cent of its land area". Support the statement with suitable examples. ***(Delhi 2017)***

Ans. It is true that 90 per cent of the world population lives in about 10 per cent of its total land area, whereas remaining 10 per cent population resides in the 90 per cent of its land area. The factor which affect the distribution of population in the world are

Cultural Factors Traditions and culture of a place includes the distribution of population. People like to migrates in areas where common tradition and culture are found.

Physical Factors Relief, climate, soil and mineral are the physical factors which determine the population of any place. Tibet is the region of very less population, whereas Indo-Gangetic plain is over populated.

Means of Transport Regions with better facilities of means of transport lead to better economic condition. This lead to thick population. Mumbai-Pune Industrial region is the best example.

Factors which affect the distribution of population in the world
- Cultural Factors
- Physical Factors
- Means of Transport
- Economic Condition

Economic Condition Industrial and agriculture regions of the world are thickly populated. Industrial regions of India, USA, Japan, UK are the examples.

5. What is 'demographic cycle'? Describe three stages of Demographic Transition Theory? *(Delhi 2016)*

Other Similar Questions

Or Briefly explain the different stages of Demographic Transition Theory.

Or "The changes in a population occur in three stages that is collectively called Demographic Transition Theory." Discuss the three stages.

Ans. Demographic cycle represents the changes in the population of a region as it moves from high births and high deaths to low births and low deaths as that region/society progresses from rural, agrarian and illiterate to urban, industrial and literate society.

These changes occur in three stages that is collectively called Demographic Transition Theory.

The three stages are as follows

First Stage This stage is marked by high fertility and high mortality. The death rate is also high due to epidemics and variable food supply. Therefore, the population growth is slow and life expectancy is low. People are mostly illiterate and engaged in agriculture due to which large families are preferred. Level of technology is also low.

Second Stage In this stage, the expansion of population remains high because the death rate reduces due to the improvement in sanitation and health conditions but the fertility rate remains high. Though at the later stage it declines with time. The mortality rate also decreases. The net addition to population in this stage is high.

Third Stage In the last stage, both fertility and mortality declines considerably and population either stablises or grows slowly.

The family size is deliberately controlled as the population becomes urbanised and literate. There is high level of technical know-how in this stage. High technical knowledge contributes deliberately in controlling the family size.

6. When does positive population growth takes place? Explain the geographical factors that influence the distribution of population in the world. *(Delhi 2015)*

Ans. When the birth rate is more than death rate between the two points of time or when people from other countries migrate permanently to a region is called positive growth of population.

For geographical factors, refer to Q. 1 of 5 marks questions.

7. Explain the three components of population change in the world. Analyse the impacts of population change. *(Delhi 2014)*

Ans. The three components of population change in the world are

(i) **Crude Birth Rate** It is referred to as a number of live births in a year per thousand of population. It increases the population.

(ii) **Crude Death Rate** It is referred to as number of deaths in a particular year per thousand of population in a particular region. It decreases the population.

(iii) **Migration** It is a displacement of people from place of origin to place of destination. In-migration increases the population. Out-migration decreases the population.

Components of population change in the world
- Crude Birth Rate
- Crude Death Rate
- Migration

Impacts of population change are as follows

(i) If the population change results in high population growth then, it puts pressure on the resources leading to scarcity and other problems.

(ii) Population change resulting in decline of population shows that the available resources are not sufficient to maintain the population.

CHAPTER TEST

01 Mark Questions

1 Which of the following formula correctly depicts natural growth of population?
(a) Births – Deaths
(b) Births – Deaths-In Migration + Out Migration
(c) Births – Deaths + In Migration -Out Migration
(d) Births – Deaths + In Migration

2 Arrange the following stages of Demographic transition in a chronological order and choose the correct option.
I. High fertility, high mortality
II. Birth rate equal to death rate
III. Population explosion

Codes
(a) I, II, III
(b) I, III, II
(c) III, II, I
(d) II, III, I

3 Consider the following about the later colonial period and choose the correct answer.
I The period from 1901-1921 is referred to as a period of nant or stationary phase of growth of population in India.
II. During this period, both the birth and death rates were high.

Codes
(a) Only statement I is correct
(b) Both the statements are true and statement II correctly present the reason for statement I
(c) Only statement II is correct
(d) Both the statements I and II are incorrect

4 **Assertion** (A) The Kobe-Osaka region of Japan is thickly populated.

Reason (R) The Kobe-Osaka region is an industrial area which has a number of industries.

Codes
(a) Both A and R are true and R is the correct explanation of A
(b) Both A and R are true, but R is not the correct explanation of A
(c) A is true, but R is false
(d) A is false, but R is true

5 Which of the following pairs is/are correctly matched?

Stages of Demographic Transition	Features
(a) The first stage	– High fertility and high mortality
(b) The second stage	– Fertility remains high
(c) The third stage	– Both fertility and mortality decline considerably

(d) All of the above

Answers

1. (a) | 2. (b) | 3. (b) | 4. (a) | 5. (d)

03 Marks Questions

6 Distinguish between birth rate and death rate. Write any three points of difference.

7 Mention the reasons, why there are a number of areas with high population density in the world?

8 Despite having a magnetic effect, city life is considered very difficult to live. State important reasons for this.

05 Marks Questions

9 Define the demographic cycle. Also, discuss about the three stages of Demographic Transition Theory.

10 Define density of population. Discuss about the four geographical factors that influence the distribution of population in the world.

11 Which areas have high density of population in the world? Also, mention the factors responsible for high population density in these areas.

03

Human Development

TREND ANALYSIS 3 YEARS

TOPIC 01 Human Development

Average No. of Questions Across all Sets

Types of Questions	2023	2020	2019
1 Mark	4	1	3
3 Marks	2	2	2
5 Marks	2	–	–

The word development or growth is familiar to us, as we see around us almost everything grow whether plants, cities, nations, relationship or even ourselves.

Growth and Development

- Growth and development refers to changes over a period of time but the difference between growth and development is that growth is quantitative but development is qualitative. Therefore, development is always positive.
- Development cannot take place unless there is an increment or addition to the existing conditions, but growth can be positive, negative or neutral, positive growth does not always led to development.
- Development occurs when there is a positive change in qualities. Earlier economic growth and development of country was seen as one but now they are studied separately.

Human Development

- This concept was introduced by **Dr Mahbub-ul-Haq** in 1990. Human development is described as that which enlarges people's choices and improves their lives, thus creating conditions where people can lead meaningful lives.
- This means that people develop talent, participate in society and be free to achieve their goals. According to **Prof. Amartya Sen,** the main objective of development is an increase in freedom. Freedom to make choices brings development, and social and political institutions play a major role in increasing freedom.
- Building people capabilities in health, education and equal access to resources increases freedom and enlarges choices.

Four Pillars of Human Development

The idea of human development is supported by the concepts of the following four pillars of development

Equity It refers to equal access to opportunities available to everybody irrespective to their gender, race, income and caste.

Sustainability It means continuity in the availability of opportunities so that future generations can even use the present resources.

Productivity It means human labour which must be enriched by building capabilities in people.

Empowerment It means having the power to make choices which is possible by increasing freedom and capability.

Approaches to Human Development

There are four ways of looking at or approach the problems of human development. Some of the important approaches are

Income Approach This approach links the development to incomes as it believes that income determines the level of freedom that one enjoys.

Welfare Approach Under this approach, government is responsible for providing basic facilities like health, education and amenities to people.

Basic Needs Approach In this approach, emphasis is on providing six basic needs i.e. health, education, food, water supply, sanitation and housing.

Capability Approach This approach is associated with Prof. Amartya Sen and aims to build human capabilities in health, education and access to resources in order to increase human development.

Measuring Human Development

Following are the ways of measuring human development

Human Development Index

- Human development is measured through Human Development Index (HDI) which ranks the countries between 0 to 1 based on their performance in the key areas of health, education and access to resources.
- It is the sum total of the weights assigned to health, education and access to resources. Indicator to access health is life expectancy at birth, to access knowledge it is adult literacy rate and gross enrollment ratio and resources are measured in terms of purchasing power.

Human Poverty Index

This index measures the shortfall in human development. The index is based on the probability of not surviving till 40, adult literacy rate, people not having access to clean drinking water and number of underweight children.

United Nations Development Programme

The United Nations Development Programme (UNDP) since 1990, publishes the Human Development Report by measuring the Human Development Index and Human Poverty Index.

Gross National Happiness

This is Gross National Happiness (GNH) which is another measure of accessing human development and **Bhutan** is the only country in the world to measure the country's progress through GNH. The GNH encourages the qualitative aspect of development.

International Comparisons

- On comparing the human development of different countries, it is revealed that the size of the territory and per capita income are not directly related to human development.
- For comparisons, the countries are classified into four groups on the basis of human development scores earned by them.

Very High Level of Human Development

- The countries scoring above 0.802 are categorised under it. There are 49 countries in this group.
- Top ten countries with very high value index are Norway, Australia, Netherlands, United States, New Zealand, Canada, Ireland, Liechtenstein, Germany and Sweden.
- The countries in this group provide education and healthcare which is an important government priority as well as invest a lot in the social sector.

High Level of Human Development

- Countries scoring between 0.702 and 0.801 are grouped under it. They are 56 in number.
- Good governance and lot of investment in social sector has led to high level of human development in these countries.

Medium Level of Human Development

- Countries scoring between 0.555 and 0.701 are grouped under it and there are 39 countries in this group.
- Many of these countries were former colonies and are facing political instability as well as high social diversity.

Low Level of Human Development

- Countries scoring below 0.554 are grouped under it and there are 44 countries in it. These countries are going through political turmoil, social instability, civil war, famine or high incidence of diseases.
- Internal comparisons reveal that the culture, religion or community are non-determinants of human development. Rather, pattern of government expenditure on the social sector, political environment, amount of freedom people have and the distribution of resources play a decisive role in the level of human development.

PYQs Previous Years' Questions

1 Mark Questions

Multiple Choice Questions

1. Which one of the following approaches was initially proposed by the International Labour Organisation (ILO)? *(CBSE 2023)*
   (a) Income Approach (b) Welfare Approach
   (c) Basic Needs Approach (d) Capability Approach

Ans. (c) Basic Needs Approach

2. Which of the following is not a key area in human development? *(CBSE 2023)*
   (a) Access to resources (b) Long and healthy life
   (c) Education (d) Economic disadvantage

Ans. (d) Economic disadvantage

3. Who among the following economists created the Human Development Index in the year 1990? *(CBSE 2023)*
   (a) Prof Amartya Sen (b) Dr Manmohan Singh
   (c) Dr Mahbub-ul-Haq (d) Ellen C Semple

Ans. (c) Dr Mahbub-ul-Haq

4. Which one of the following countries comes under very high category in 'Human Development Index'? *(CBSE 2023)*
   (a) Mexico (b) Singapore
   (c) China (d) Colombia

Ans. (b) Singapore

5. Which of the following best describes 'development'? *(CBSE SQP Term I 2019, 2020, 2021)*
   (a) An increase in size
   (b) A constant in size
   (c) A positive change in quality
   (d) A simple change in quality

Ans. (c) A positive change in quality

6. Which of the following pairs is not correctly matched? *(CBSE SQP Term I 2021)*

Pillars of Human Development		Indicators
(a) Equity	–	Making equal access to opportunities available to everybody
(b) Sustainability	–	Continuity in the availability of opportunities
(c) Productivity	–	Resources must be used keeping in mind the future
(d) Empowerment	–	To have the power to make choices

Ans. (c) Productivity – Resources must be used keeping in mind the future

7. Who among the following developed the concept of 'human development'? *(CBSE SQP Term I 2021)*
   (a) Ellen C Semple (b) Dr Mahbub-ul-Haq
   (c) Kanwar Sen (d) Griffith Taylor

Ans. (b) Dr Mahbub-ul-Haq

8. Who among the following is related to 'capability approach'? *(CBSE SQP Term I 2021)*
   (a) Dr Mahbub-ul-Haq
   (b) Prof Amartya Sen
   (c) Malthus
   (d) Ratzel

Ans. (b) Prof Amartya Sen

9. Which among the following explains the 'equity concept of development'? *(CBSE Term I 2021)*
   (a) Equal access to opportunities
   (b) Capabilities building in people
   (c) Power to make choice
   (d) Opportunities for future generation

Ans. (a) Equal access to opportunities

10. Which of the following approaches looks at human beings as beneficiaries? *(CBSE Term I 2021)*
    (a) Income approach (b) Welfare approach
    (c) Basic need approach (d) Capability approach

Ans. (b) Welfare approach

11. Which of the following countries has the highest ranking in 'Human Development Index'? *(CBSE Term I 2021)*
    (a) Belgium (b) Iceland
    (c) Norway (d) Canada

Ans. (c) Norway

12. Choose the correct pair out of the following. *(CBSE Term I 2021)*

Level of Human Development Index		Countries
(a) Very High	–	Australian, Switzerland, Ireland
(b) High	–	Singapore, Germany, Denmark
(c) Medium	–	Sweden, Korea, Japan
(d) Low	–	Qatar, Brazil, Peru

Ans. (a) Very High-Australian, Switzerland, Ireland

13. The term 'growth' is ....
(a) quantitative (b) value neutral
(c) both positive or negative (d) All of these

Ans. (d) All of these

14. Development is ....
(a) a qualitative change (b) value positive
(c) both positive and negative (d) Both (a) and (b)

Ans. (d) Both (a) and (b)

15. Which of the following is/are central to all development under the concept of human development ?
(a) Economy (b) People
(c) Assets (d) Resources

Ans. (b) People

16. Under the concept of human development 'a meaningful life' means
(a) people must be healthy.
(b) people must be able to develop their talents.
(c) people must participate in society.
(d) All of the above

Ans. (d) All of the above

17. Which of the following is the most important aspect of human development?
(a) Leading a long and healthy life.
(b) Being able to gain knowledge.
(c) Having enough means to be able to live a decent life.
(d) All of the above

Ans. (d) All of the above

18. Which of the following is the pillar of human development ?
(a) Equity (b) Sustainability
(c) Productivity (d) All of these

Ans. (d) All of these

19. Which of the following is the earliest approach to human development ?
(a) Welfare approach (b) Income approach
(c) Basic needs approach (d) Capabilities approach

Ans. (b) Income approach

20. Arrange the following countries in sequence according to their rank in HDI-2018 from high HDI value to low HDI value.
I. Switzerland II. Norway
III. Australia IV. Ireland

Codes
(a) I, II, III, IV (b) IV, III, II, I
(c) II, I, III, IV (d) IV, III, I, II

Ans. (c) II, I, III, IV

Very Short Answer Questions

1. Differentiate between 'growth' and 'development'. ***(Delhi 2019)***

Ans. Growth and development both refer to changes over a period of time. Growth is quantitative and value neutral while development means a qualitative change which is always value positive.

2. Examine the concept of 'human development' as introduced by Mahbub-ul-Haq. ***(All India 2019)***

Or Define the concept of human development. ***(All India 2016)***

Ans. Dr Mahbub-ul-Haq has described human development as development that enlarges people's choices and improves their lives. Under this concept, people are considered to occupy a central position.

3. Why has Chhattisgarh recorded the lowest level in the Human Development Index (HDI)? ***(All India 2019)***

Ans. Chhattisgarh has recorded the lowest level in the HDI due to the following reasons
- Having low Per Capita Income (less than ₹ 2000 per year).
- The poverty ratio in Chhattisgarh is also very high.

4. "Leading a long and healthy life is an important aspect of human development." Give an argument to support this statement. ***(Delhi 2016)***

Ans. A life is meaningful when people are healthy, able to develop their talents, participate in society and be free to achieve their goals. This kind of life is an important aspect of human development.

5. Which country has proclaimed 'Gross National Happiness' as the measure of a country's progress? ***(All India 2014)***

Ans. The country to proclaim Gross National Happiness (GNH) as the measure of a country's progress is Bhutan.

6. Which state of India has the highest rank in Human Development Index (HDI) value? ***(All India 2014)***

Ans. Kerala state has the highest rank in HDI.

7. Mention any two key areas of measuring human development. ***(Delhi 2013)***

Ans. The two key areas of measuring human development are
(i) Health (ii) Education

8. Which is the most significant aspect of human development? ***(Delhi 2012)***

Ans. Education, healthy life and resources are the most significant aspects of human development.

3 Marks Questions

1. Explain the concept of 'human development' introduced by Dr Mahbub-ul-Haq. ***(CBSE 2023)***

Ans. The concept of human development was introduced by Dr Mahbub-ul-Haq (Pakistani Economist) who described it as development that enlarges people's choices and improves their lives. These choices of the people keep on changing. This concept gives people a central position in the idea of development.

Mahbub-ul-Haq created the Human Development Index in 1990. Since 1990, the concept of human development has been used by United Nations Development Programme to publish the Human Development Report (HDR) annually. This report provides a rank-wise list of all member countries according to level of human development.

2. Explain the welfare approach of human development. ***(CBSE 2023)***

Or Explain any three features of welfare approach of human development. ***(CBSE SQP 2018, All India 2012)***

Or Explain three characteristics of welfare approach of human development. ***(CBSE SQP 2018)***

Or Explain any three characteristics of 'welfare approach' of human development in the world. ***(Delhi 2010)***

Ans. The characteristics of welfare approach are as follows

(i) The welfare approach of human development is an approach which looks at human beings as beneficiaries or targets of all development activities. According to this approach, the government is responsible for increasing levels of human development.

(ii) It increases expenditure on welfare such as on education, health, housing, sanitation, etc.

(iii) In this approach, people are passive recipients of the beneficiaries of human development, while the government is the provider of those beneficiaries.

3. "Some countries of the world have a high Human Development Index". Try to find out reasons for such a scenario. ***(CBSE SQP 2020)***

Ans. The reasons why some countries of the world have a high Human Development Index are

(i) Pattern of government expenditure on the social sector, that is, how much is being spent on the welfare of the people in the society than on defence sector. These countries spend more on the social sectors such as health and education. Mostly these countries represent the industrialised Western world.

(ii) These countries have a much better political environment, that is, there is stability of the government or the form of government, freedom of the people, rights of the people including the right to vote, Equitable distribution of resources among the people.

(iii) Many of these countries have been the former imperial powers. The degree of social diversity in these countries is not very high. There are no civil uprisings, political turmoil or instability. Providing education and healthcare is an important government priority and hence people have a much better standard of living.

4. Explain any three approaches to study Human Development in the world. ***(CBSE SQP 2020)***

Ans. There are many ways of looking at the problem of human development

- **Income Approach** It is the oldest approach, human development is seen as being linked to income. The idea is that the level of income reflects the level of freedom an individual enjoys. Higher the level of income, the higher is the level of human development.
- **Welfare Approach** This approach looks at human beings as beneficiaries of all development activities. The approach argues for higher government expenditure on education, health, social secondary and amenities. People are not participants in development but only passive recipients. The government is responsible for increasing levels of human development by maximising expenditure on welfare.

Approaches to Study Human Development in the World
- Income Approach
- Welfare Approach
- Basic Need Approach
- Capability Approach

- **Basic Needs Approach proposed by ILO** Six basic needs i.e health, education, food, water supply, sanitation, and housing were identified. The question of human choices is ignored and the emphasis is on the provision of basic needs of defined section.
- **Capability Approach** This approach is associated with Prof Amartya Sen. Building human capabilities in the areas of health, education and access to resources is the key to increasing human development.

5. 'Development has direct bearings on the deteriorating human conditions'. How are poor people more affected in this process? **(CBSE SQP 2019)**

> **HINT** *Dear students, this question simply ask you to explain the impact of development on the condition of poor people.*

Ans. Development has a direct bearing on the deteriorating human conditions due to environmental degradation and the ecological crisis. Air, soil, water and noise pollution, which are the direct consequences of development, have threatened our existence.

Consequently, the poor are subjected to three inter-related processes of declining capabilities as given below

(i) Social capabilities are reduced due to displacement and weakening of social ties.

(ii) Environmental capabilities have been reduced due to pollution.

(iii) Personal capabilities have declined due to increasing incidence of diseases and accidents.

This has adverse effects on their quality of life and human development of the poor.

6. Describe the concept of Human Development as defined by United Nations Development Programme (UNDP). **(CBSE SQP 2019)**

Ans. As per the World Human Development Report, "Human Development is a process of enlarging the range of people's choices, increasing their opportunities for education, healthcare, income and empowerment and covering the full range of human choices from a sound environment to economic, social and political freedom."

Thus, enlarging the range of people's choices is the most significant aspect of human development. It is just opposite to the Western or Euro-centric view of development. People should be able to live a long and healthy life.

They should be educated and have access to resources needed for a decent standard of living. These are necessary and non-negotiable aspects of human development.

7. Explain any three human values which are required to empower socially and economically disadvantaged people. **(Delhi 2013)**

Or "Equity is one of the most important pillars of human development." Explain any three human values that are required to give equal access to opportunities to everybody. **(All India 2013)**

Ans. Equity means availability of equal opportunities to everyone. If everybody have equal access to available opportunities, then a quality life is possible.

The three human values required to give equal access to everybody are as follows

(i) Providing equal opportunities without any discrimination of caste or race.

(ii) Equal opportunities should be available irrespective of gender.

(iii) Equal opportunities without any discrimination of income or class.

8. "Development is a qualitative change, which is always value positive." Support this statement with any three suitable arguments. **(Delhi 2012)**

Ans. Development means a qualitative change which is always value positive. This means that development cannot take place unless there is an increment or addition to the existing conditions. Development occurs when positive growth takes place.

The given statement can be supported by the following three arguments

(i) The term 'development' refers to qualitative shift that is always value positive. It occurs when there is a positive change in quality over a time frame. Although development is always influenced by growth but only in the case of positive and qualitative growth, e.g. if a child grows by height but is not mentally able, then growth is not accompanied with development.

(ii) Countries with better economic conditions are more developed while poor nations are less developed. But in many cases the benefit of economic growth does not reach the common man. Quality of life of the people of a country, the opportunities they have, freedom of living, etc are important aspects of development.

(iii) Dr Mahbub-ul-Haq described human development as development that enlarges people's choice and improves their lives. He believed that people are central to all development and the main aim of development is to create a situation and environment where people get meaningful lives. The meaningful life means a life that must be full of objectivity, that includes health, participation in societal helm of affairs and focus on people's goals.

9. Explain the key areas of human development. *(Delhi 2012)*

Or Explain the three main areas of measuring human development. *(All India 2008)*

Ans. The key areas of human development are health, housing and access to resources.

They are explained as follows

Key areas of human development
- Health Indicator
- Education Indicator
- Access to Resources

Health Indicator Indicator of health is measured through life expectancy at birth, that shows if people have longer and healthier lives.

Education Indicator Level of education is seen through gross enrollment ratio and adult literacy rate that represents access to knowledge.

Access to Resources The indicator of access to resources is purchasing power in terms of US dollars.

10. Differentiate between 'growth and development' with an example. *(All India 2012)*

Ans. Growth refers to quantitative changes. Its value can be neutral, positive or negative.

Development refers to qualitative changes and its value is always positive. This is because development cannot take place unless there is an increase or a raise in existing conditions thus leading to positive changes. For e.g. the population of a city increases from 1 lakh to 2 lakh over a period of time. This is growth as the number has increased.

However, if the basic necessities like food, housing, education and sanitation facilities remain constant, then the growth is not accompanied by development.

11. Explain the concept of 'equity' and 'sustainability' as the pillars of human development. *(Delhi 2011)*

Ans. Just as any building is supported by pillars, the idea of human development is supported by the concepts of equity and sustainability. Both are explained below

- **Equity** It means availability of equal opportunities to an individual. The available opportunities have equal access without any discrimination on the ground of gender, race, income and caste. A quality life is possible if access to resources is provided on the basis of being a human.
- **Sustainability** It refers to continuity in availability of opportunities. Human development is possible when opportunities are available to the present and future generations of a country. It must be ensured that equal access to resource should be available to next generation.

12. Explain the 'basic needs approach' to human development in the world. *(Delhi 2010)*

Ans. The basic needs approach to human development in the world was initially proposed by International Labour Organisation (ILO). In this approach, the question of human choices is ignored as the main emphasis is laid on the provision of basic needs. These basic needs are the necessity that enables a person to survive and fulfil the essential requirements. There are six basic needs identified in this approach. They are as follows

- **Health** Proper health required to maintain a healthy weight.
- **Education** Provision of schools and colleges.
- **Food** Nutritious food to fulfil daily requirements.
- **Water Supply** Provision of clean drinking water.
- **Sanitation** Proper sanitation facility to maintain hygiene.
- **Housing** Proper dwelling place with basic facilities.

5 Marks Questions

1. Explain balance of trade with example and examine the role of World Trade Organisation (WTO) in international trade. *(CBSE 2023)*

Ans. **Balance of Trade** The volume of goods and services imported and exported by a country to other countries is known as balance of trade. A country's economy is affected by its balance of trade. If a country spends more on buying goods then it can earn by selling the goods produced by it, it will lead to exhaustion of the country's financial resources.

Balance of trade can either be favourable or even unfavourable. It is discussed below

(i) **Negative or Unfavourable Balance of Trade** When the value of a country's imports is more than the value of that country's exports, then there is a negative or unfavourable balance of trade.

(ii) **Positive or Favourable Balance of Trade** When the value of a country's exports is more than the value of that country's imports, then there is a positive or favourable balance of trade.

WTO is the only international organisation dealing with the global rules of trade between nations. The main functions of this organisation are to set rules for the global trading system and resolve disputes between its member nations. It also covers trade in services, e.g. telecommunication and banking and other issues including intellectual rights.

2. Examine any five basis of International trade. ***(CBSE 2023)***

Ans. The five basis of international trade are

(i) **Difference in National Resources**

The world's national resources are found unevenly over the space. This is due to differences in their physical structure i.e. geology, relief, soil and climate

- **Geological Structure** Different geological structures determine the mineral resource base and topographical difference ensure diversity of crops and animals raised. Agricultural activities are more common in lowlands, while tourism flourishes in the mountainous areas.
- **Mineral Resources** Different regions have different types of minerals in different proportions. The availability of minerals provides the basis of industrial development.
- **Climate** It has a clear impact on the varieties of flora and fauna in a particular region. Diversity in the range of various products is also ensured by climate. For example, wool production takes place in cold regions whereas bananas, rubber and cocoa grow in tropical regions.

(ii) **Population Factors**

The size, distribution and diversity of people between countries affect the type and volume of goods traded between the countries

- **Cultural Factors** Different cultures are denoted by distinctive forms of art and craft which are famous all over the world. For example, China produces the finest porcelains and brocades. Iran is famous for its carpets, North Africa is famous for leather work and Indonesia is famous for batik cloth.
- **Size of Population** Countries having dense population are dominated by large volume of internal trade and little external trade. This is due to the fact that most of the agricultural and industrial production is consumed in the local markets.
- The demand for better quality imported products is determined by the standard of living of the population. For example, with low standard of living only a few people can afford to buy costly imported goods.

(iii) **Stage of Economic Development**

The nature of commodities changes at different stages of economic development of countries. In non-industrialised nations, agriculture is important sector. These countries export agro-products to the industrialised nations and import machinery and finished products from them. The industrialised nations exports machinery and finished products and imports food grains and raw materials from developing countries.

(iv) **Extent of Foreign Investment**

Developing countries which lack in capital required for the development of mining, oil drilling, heavy engineering, lumbering and plantation agriculture boosts their trade by foreign investment. By investing in these countries in different sectors, the industrial nations can ensure import of food stuffs, minerals and create markets for their finished products. This entire cycle increases the volume of trade between nations.

Five Basis of International Trade

- Difference in National Resource
- Population Factors
- Stage of Economic Development
- Extent of Foreign Investment
- Transport

(v) **Transport**

Before the development of modern means of transport, the trade was restricted to local areas. For example, only high value items like gems, silk and spices were traded over long distances. With the expansion of rail, ocean and air transport, better means of refrigeration and preservation, there was expansion in trade.

3. How have good governance and people-oriented policies with reference to the pillars of human development, increased the values of freedom and capabilities? ***(CBSE SQP 2022)***

HINT *Dear students, this question simply ask you to explain the role of good governance in increasing value of freedom and capabilities in people.*

Ans. Good governance and various policies with people -oriented policies, have increased the values of freedom and capabilities. These policies and governance were in regard to the major pillars of human development. These pillars are equity, sustainability, productivity and empowerment. The ways in which they have increased the value of freedom are as follows

- **Equity** It means that equal access to opportunity should be given to all without any discrimination on the basis of gender, race, income, caste and creed. For example, in any country, it will be interesting to note that dropouts from school belong to which community or group and what might be the reasons for this situation.

In India, a large number of girls and persons belonging to socially and educationally backward groups dropout of schools. This indicates how the choices of these groups are limited by not having equal access to knowledge.

- **Sustainability** It refers to continuity in the availability of opportunities. To achieve sustainable human development, it is must to give equal opportunities to all generations without any misuse of natural resources and environment. All the resources such as environmental, financial and human resources should be used keeping in mind the future generation.

Pillars of Human Development
- Equity
- Sustainability
- Productivity
- Empowerment

- **Productivity** It refers to productivity of human labour or productivity in terms of human work. So, this productivity must be continuously enriched by building capabilities in people, as people are considered the real wealth of nations. Thus, for better work efficiency, it is important to put efforts to increase their knowledge or provide better health facilities.
- **Empowerment** It refers to having power that enables people to make choices. The increasing freedom and capability give such power. The government should provide good governance and people oriented policies to empower people. The government should give special emphasis on socially and economically disadvantage groups to empower them.

4. The ways to measure human development are constantly being redefined. Evaluate this statement keeping in mind the attainments and shortfall in human development. ***(CBSE SQP 2022)***

Ans. The ways to measure human development are constantly being redefined because understanding and measuring human development has complexities and the measurement of qualitative changes is difficult. Many ways were evolved to look at the problem and measurement of human development. Some important approaches in this regard are as follows

(i) **Welfare Approach** This approach puts human beings at a central position where he/she is the beneficiary of all the developmental activities. Here, people do not participate in the process of development but they are only passive recepients. The government is responsible for providing health, education and social services.

(ii) **Income Approach** In this approach, human development is linked to income. The level of income decides the level of freedom an individual enjoys. It is believed that if a nation has higher level of income, it leads to higher level of human development.

(iii) **Minimum Needs Approach** It was proposed by the International Labour Organisation. It considers six basic needs as most important for development of human beings-health, education, food, water supply, sanitation and housing.

(iv) **Capabilities Approach** This approach emphasises upon building human capabilities in areas of health, education and access to resources for their human development.

5. ''The size of a territory and per capita income are not directly related to human development.'' Support the statement with examples. ***(All India 2017)***

Ans. "The size of a territory and per capita income are not directly related to human development". This statement can be supported by the following examples

- There are many smaller countries and regions which have developed tremendously as compared to the largest countries.
- In terms of Human Development Index, certain relatively poorer countries have been ranked better than many. For example, Sri Lanka, Trinidad and Tobago have a higher rank than India in the Human Development Index despite having smaller economies.
- Similarly with India , Kerla performs much better than Punjab and Gujarat in human development desire having lower per capita income.

6. What is human development? Analyse the four pillars of human development. ***(All India 2017)***

Or What is 'human development'? Explain the four pillars of human development. ***(Delhi 2015)***

Or Explain the concept of 'human development'. Elaborate how the idea of human development is supported by concepts of equity, sustainability, productivity and empowerment.

Ans. For definition of human development, refer to Q. 1 of 3 marks questions.

For the pillars of human development, refer to Q. 3 of 5 marks questions.

CHAPTER TEST

01 Mark Questions

1 According to Dr Mahbub-ul-Haq which of the following best describes human development?
(a) Development which increase people's incomes.
(b) Development which makes people smart.
(c) Development which enlarges people's choices.
(d) Development which makes people strong.

2 Which of the following pairs is/are incorrectly matched?
(a) Health – Life expectancy
(b) Education – Adult literacy rate
(c) Access to resources – Purchasing power parity
(d) All of the above

3 Consider the following about the later colonial period and choose the correct answer.
I. An uneducated child cannot make the choice to be a teacher.
II. His/her choice has got limited by her lack of education.

Codes
(a) Only statement I is correct
(b) Both statements are true and statement II correctly present the reason for statement I
(c) Only statement II is correct
(d) Both statements I and II are incorrect

4 **Assertion** (A) Development means a qualitative change which is always value positive.
Reason (R) Development cannot take place unless there is an increment or addition to the existing conditions.

Codes
(a) Both A and R are true and R is the correct explanation of A
(b) Both A and R are true, but R is not the correct explanation of A
(c) A is true, but R is false
(d) A is false, but R is true

Answers
1. (c) | 2. (c) | 3. (b) | 4. (a)

03 Marks Questions

5 What are the three basic areas of human development?

6 State any three characteristics of welfare approach of human development in the world.

7 What do you understand by the term HDI? How have the countries been divided according to their HDI values?

05 Marks Questions

8 The size of a territory and per capita income are not directly related to human development. Analyse the given statement.

9 Discuss the four approaches of human development in brief.

10 People usually blame the culture or religion for low human development of a country. Justify the statement and write the real reasons for low and high human development in a country.

04

Primary Activities

TREND ANALYSIS 3 YEARS

Average No. of Questions Across all Sets

Topic	Types of Questions	2023	2020	2019
TOPIC 01 Archaeological Evidences of The Harappan Civilisation	1 Mark	3	–	2
	2 Marks	–	–	–
	3 Marks	2	–	–
	5 Marks	1	–	–
TOPIC 02 The End of Harappan Civilisation	1 Mark	3	2	5
	2 Marks	–	–	–
	3 Marks	–	–	–
	5 Marks	1	–	–

Human activities that generates income are called as economic activities. These are grouped as primary, secondary, tertiary and quaternary activities. Primary activities are the activities that are directly dependent on environment.

There is a greater utilisation of Earth's resources in these activities such as land, water, minerals, vegetation, etc. Hunting and gathering, pastoral activity, fishing, forestry, agriculture, mining and quarrying all are examples of primary activity. People engaged in primary activities are known as red collar workers.

Hunting and Gathering

- Hunting and gathering are the oldest primitive activities of man. Early man lived in forests and sustained his life by hunting animals. He has also been gathering various products from the forests to satisfy his needs in early days. Thus, early men sustained on animals, plants which they hunted and edible plants which they gathered from the forests.
- Early human beings practiced these activities with the help of primitive tools, made of stones, twigs or arrows, so the number of animals killed was limited. But now modern equipments led to the widespread poaching of animals due to which hunting is declared illegal.
- Gathering is practiced in high latitude zones of North Canada, Northern Eurasia and Southern Chile, low latitude zones of Amazon Basin, tropical Africa, interiors of South-East Asia. This activity requires small capital investment and low level of technology. Valuable plants, leaves, bark, etc are collected and after simple processing they are sold in local markets. These products cannot compete the world market as synthetic products are lower in price and of better quality.

Pastoralism

- This means domestication and rearing of animals on pastures. This is carried either at subsistence level known as nomadic herding or at commercial level known as **commercial livestock rearing**.

Nomadic Herding

- Nomadic herding is also called **pastoral nomadism**, it is a primitive activity where herders move with their livestock from one place to another in search of food and water. They rely on animals for food, clothing, shelter, tools and transport.
- Depending on geographical factors different animals are reared in different regions like cattle in tropical Africa, sheep, goat and camel in Sahara, Asiatic deserts, Yak, Ilamas in Tibet and Andes, reindeer in Arctic and Sub-Arctic areas. Other areas include Mongolia, Central China, Eurasia, South-West Africa and Madagascar.

Transhumance

This is the process of migration from plain areas to mountains during summers and from mountains to plain areas during winters. The tribes of Bakarwals, Gaddis, Bhotiyas, Gujjars of Himalayas and nomadic herders of Tundra region do transhumance.

Commercial Livestock Rearing

- This practice is associated with Western culture, it is more organised and capital intensive. This activity is done on vast ranches that are permanent.
- Modern scientific technology with emphasis on breeding, genetic improvement, disease control and health care is done. Production of meat, wool, hides is done and exported to different world markets.
- Sheep, cattle, goat and horses are reared in the ranches. Australia, New Zealand, Argentina, Uruguay, South-West Africa, Western United States and Central Asia are major centers of commercial livestock rearing.

Agriculture

Agriculture is practiced under multiple combinations of physical and socio- economic conditions, which gives rise to different types of agriculture systems. Based on methods of farming, different type of crops are grown and livestock raised. The following are the main agricultural systems

Subsistence Agriculture

- In this type of agriculture, farmers consume all or nearly all of the produce as the size of the farm is very small.
- It can be divided into primitive subsistence agriculture and intensive subsistence agriculture.

Primitive Subsistence Agriculture

- This is widely practiced in tropical areas of Africa, South, Central America and South-East Asia.
- Different names are given to it in different places like milpa, jhuming, ladang. It is also called **slash and burn agriculture** or **shifting agriculture**.
- Cultivation is done through primitive tools by clearing a patch of land. After 3 to 5 years, when the soil loses its fertility, then new land is cleared for cultivation.

Intensive Subsistence Agriculture

- This type of agriculture is practiced in densely populated regions of monsoon Asia.
- This type of cultivation is either dominated by wet paddy cultivation or crops other than paddy.
- The field per unit area is high but per labour productivity is low as land holdings are small due to high density of population, less use of machines, family labour involved and farm yard manures are used.
- Crops other than paddy are wheat, soybean, barley, sorghum grown in Northern China, Manchuria, North Korea and Japan.
- In India, it is practiced in Indo-Gangetic plains, dry parts of Western and Southern India.

Plantation Agriculture

- This type of agriculture was introduced by the Europeans like **cocoa** and **coffee** in West Africa by French, tea in India and Sri Lanka, rubber in Malaysia, sugarcane and banana in West Indies by British, coconut, sugarcane in Philippines by Spanish, etc.
- Here, agriculture is done on large estates or plantations, requires huge capital investment and scientific methods of cultivation.

Extensive Commercial Grain Cultivation

- This is practiced in the interiors of semi-arid parts of mid latitudes like Eurasian steppes, Canadian and American Prairies, pampas of Argentina, velds of South Africa, Australian Downs and Canterbury plains of New Zealand.
- Crops like wheat, corn, barley, oats and rye are grown. Agriculture is mechanised as farms are very large. There is low yield per acre but high yield per person.

Mixed Farming

- This is practiced in North-Western Europe, Eastern-North America, parts of Eurasia and temperate latitudes of Southern continents. Here, crop cultivation alongwith animal husbandry is practiced.

- Crops like wheat, barley, oats, rye, maize, fodder and root crops alongwith the rearing of farm animals like cattle, sheep, pig, poultry is done to provide extra income.
- There is crop rotation and inter-cropping along with high capital expenditure on farm inputs.

Mediterranean Agriculture

- It is practised on either side of Mediterranean in Europe, North Africa from Tunisia to Atlantic coast, Southern-California, some parts of Chile, South-Western parts of South Africa and South-Western parts of Australia. It is highly specialised commercial agriculture and important supplier of citrus fruits.

Dairy Farming

- It is practiced near urban and industrial centers of North-Western Europe, Canada, South-Eastern Australia, New Zealand and Tasmania. It is highly capital intensive due to cost of feeding, milching machines, animal sheds, storage facilities, veterinary services, etc.
- It is also labour intensive as rigorous care of animals is also needed. There is no off season during the year as in case of crop raising.

Viticulture

- This refers to cultivation of grapes in the Mediterranean regions. Inferior **grapes** are made into raisins and currants while superior grapes are processed into wines. Figs and olives are also cultivated.

Market Gardening and Horticulture

- It is practiced in highly developed and industrial regions of North-West Europe, North-East United States and Mediterranean regions. Netherlands specialises in cultivation of **Tulip flowers**.
- This type of cultivation refers to high value crops like vegetables, fruits and flowers solely for urban markets. Farms are small and mechanised. It is both capital and labour intensive.

Truck Farming

- This refers to the specialisation in the cultivation of vegetables only. The distance between the farms and urban markets can be covered through trucks overnight, hence its name is known as 'truck farming'.

Factory Farming

- This refers to livestock rearing mainly poultry and cattle. This is capital intensive, requires maintenance, supervisation and scientific breeding. It is practiced in industrial regions of Europe and North America.

Co-operative Farming

- Under this farming, group of farmers form a co-operative society by pooling their resources voluntarily for more efficient and profitable farming.
- There is help from societies in buying and selling farm products. Individual farms remain intact. It is practiced in Denmark, Netherlands, Belgium, Sweden and Italy.

Collective Farming

- It is based on social ownership of the means of production and collective labour. On other words, it is a type of agricultural production in which multiple farmers run their holdings as a joint enterprise. Here farmers share their resources, though they are allowed to keep a small part with themselves for their livelihood.
- Produce is sold to state at prefixed prices. Members paid according to the nature of work done. It was first practiced in the erstwhile Soviet Union here it was known as **KolKhoz** collective farm.
- It was introduced to boost agricultural production for self-sufficiency.

Mining

It refers to the extraction of mineral resources from the Earth. Its development began with the Industrial Revolution.

Factors affecting the Mining Activity

There are two factors that affect the mining activity.

These are

(i) **Physical factors** related to size, grade and mode of occurrence of the deposits.

(ii) **Economic factors** related to demand for mineral, technology, capital to develop infrastructure, labour and transport cost.

Methods of Mining

It is of two types i.e. **surface** and **underground mining.** Surface or open cast mining occurs close to the surface, it is easiest and cheapest. The other is underground mining in which minerals are extracted from very deep mines using vertical shafts. It requires lifts, drills and very efficient technology.

The developed economies are retreating from mining due to high labour cost while developing economies are becoming major exporters of minerals due to their large labour force and striving for better standard of living.

PYQs Previous Years' Questions

1 Mark Questions

Multiple Choice Questions

1. Fodder crops are an important component of which among the following types of agriculture? **(CBSE 2023)**
(a) Mixed (b) Mediterranean
(c) Co-operative (d) Collective

Ans. (a) Mixed

2. Which among the following is the largest region of 'commercial dairy farming'? **(CBSE 2023)**
(a) North-Western Europe
(b) Canada region
(c) New-Zealand region
(d) South-Eastern Australia

Ans. (a) North-Western Europe

3. Which one of the following is an important region for subsistence gathering? **(CBSE 2023)**
(a) South Africa (b) Amazon Basin
(c) Indonesia (d) Mexico

Ans. (c) Indonesia

4. Which among the following countries is related to 'Ladang'? **(CBSE 2023)**
(a) Malaysia (b) Mexico (c) India (d) Brazil

Ans. (a) Malaysia

5. Which one of the following features is correct regarding nomadic herding? **(CBSE 2023)**
(a) Nomadism is a modern commercial activity.
(b) It is practiced on permanent pastures.
(c) A wide variety of cattle are reared in different regions.
(d) Nomadism is associated with modern technology.

Ans. (c) A wide variety of cattle are reared in different regions.

6. Identify the feature of mixed farming from the following. **(CBSE 2023)**
(a) It is most advanced and efficient type of rearing milch animals.
(b) Equal emphasis is laid on crop cultivation and animal husbandry.
(c) It was introduced by the Europeans in colonies.
(d) The regions where farmers specialised in vegetables only.

Ans. (b) Equal emphasis is laid on crop cultivation and animal husbandry.

7. "Each community occupies a well-identified territory as a matter of tradition". **(CBSE SQP Term I 2021)**
Above mentioned line is an important characteristic of which of the following activities?
(a) Subsistence agriculture (b) Nomadic herding
(c) Plantation agriculture (d) Collective farming

Ans. (b) Nomadic herding

8. Which of the following colonial super power had monopoly over sugarcane plantation in Indonesia? **(CBSE SQP Term I 2021)**
(a) British (b) French
(c) Dutch (d) Americans

Ans. (c) Dutch

9. Which one of the following is not a method of mining? **(CBSE SQP Term I 2021, CBSE SQP 2020, 2019)**
(a) Shaft mining (b) Opencast mining
(c) Underground mining (d) Refining

Ans. (d) Refining

10. Which one of the following is not a plantation crop? **(CBSE 2021)**
(a) Coffee (b) Sugarcane
(c) Rubber (d) Wheat

Ans. (d) Wheat

11. Coffee plantations in Brazil are known as **(CBSE SQP Term I 2021)**
(a) downs (b) campos
(c) fazendas (d) pampas

Ans. (c) fazendas

12. In Himalayan regions, which of the following tribes are linked with the activity of transhumance? **(CBSE SQP Term I 2021)**
(a) Bhils (b) Gonds
(c) Bakarwals (d) Santhals

Ans. (c) Bakarwals

13. Which of the following pairs is not correctly matched? **(CBSE SQP Term I 2021)**

	Activity	Characteristics
(a)	Truck farming	Growing of vegetables
(b)	Factory farming	Rearing of poultry and cattle
(c)	Market gardening	Growing of flowers
(d)	Viticulture	Rearing of fish

Ans. (d)

14. Consider the following statements and choose the correct option. *(CBSE SQP Term I 2021)*

I. Grape cultivation is the speciality of the Mediterranean agriculture.

II. Wines are produced from high quality grapes and the inferior grapes are dried into raisins and currants.

Codes

(a) Only I is correct (b) Both I and II are correct
(c) Only II is correct (d) Neither I nor II

Ans. (b) Both I and II are correct

15. Consider the following statements and choose correct option from the given options. *(CBSE SQP Term I 2021)*

I. Many species now have become extinct or endangered due to illegal hunting.

II. The early hunters used primitive tools made of stones, twigs or arrows so the number of animals killed were limited.

Codes

(a) Only I is correct (b) Only II is correct
(c) Both I and II are correct (d) Neither I nor II

Ans. (c) Both I and II are correct

16. Which of the following groups comes under the category of 'Transhumance nomadic herding'? *(CBSE Term I 2021)*

(a) Bakarwal (b) Tharu
(c) Santhal (d) Bhil

Ans. (a) Bakarwal

17. In which of the following countries is milpa known as primitive subsistence agriculture? *(CBSE Term I 2021)*

(a) Mexico (b) Malaysia
(c) India (d) Indonesia

Ans. (d) Indonesia

18. Which of the following is known as a major cash crop? *(CBSE Term I 2021)*

(a) Maize (b) Wheat
(c) Rice (d) Sugarcane

Ans. (d) Sugarcane

19. Why are the developed economies retreating from mining, processing and refining stages of production? *(CBSE Term I 2021)*

(a) Low labour cost
(b) High labour cost
(c) More opportunities of employment
(d) Lack of labour force

Ans. (b) High labour cost

20. Which is not a characteristic of shaft method of mining? *(CBSE Term I 2021)*

(a) Cheapest way of mining
(b) Vertical shafts have to be sunk
(c) Specially designed lifts drills used
(d) Gases, fires and floods lend to total accidents

Ans. (a) Cheapest way of mining

21. Which of the following crops are mainly grown in 'Mediterranean agriculture'? *(CBSE Term I 2021)*

(a) Grape, figs, olives
(b) Wheat, barley, ragi
(c) Jowar, bajra, maize
(d) Rubber, cotton, sugarcane

Ans. (a) Grape, figs, olives

22. Which of the following is not a feature of mixed agriculture? *(CBSE Term I 2021)*

(a) Mixed farms are big in size
(b) Fodder crops are an important component of mixed farming
(c) Equal emphasis is laid on crop cultivation and animal husbandry
(d) Crop rotation and inter-cropping play an important role in maintaining soil fertility

Ans. (a) Mixed farms are big in size

23. Read the following statements regarding primitive subsistence agriculture and choose the correct option. *(CBSE Term I 2021)*

I. The vegetation is usually cleared by fire, and the ashes add to the fertility of the soil.

II. The cultivated patches are very small.

III. Machineries and chemical fertilisers are used to increase production.

Codes

(a) Only I and III are correct
(b) Only II and III are correct
(c) Only I and II are correct
(d) I, II and III are correct

Ans. (c) Only I and II are correct

24. In which part of the world is 'slash and burn' agriculture known as 'Jhuming'? *(CBSE Compartment 2020)*

(a) Hokkaido region of Japan
(b) Central America
(c) North-Eastern States of India
(d) Eastern Indonesia

Ans. (c) North-Eastern States of India

25. Which one of the following is a feature of 'Shaft Mining'? *(CBSE Compartment 2020)*

(a) It is the easiest and cheapest way of mining.
(b) Minerals occur close to the surface.
(c) Extracted minerals are transported to the surface through tunnels.
(d) Cost of safety precautions and equipment is relatively low.

Ans. (c) Extracted minerals are transported to the surface through tunnels.

26. Which one of the following types of cultivation was developed by European colonists? *(CBSE SQP 2019)*

(a) Kolkhoz (b) Mixed farming
(c) Viticulture (d) Plantation

Ans. (d) Plantation

27. Which one of the following does not follow monoculture? *(CBSE SQP 2019)*

(a) Commercial grain farming (b) Plantation agriculture
(c) Mixed farming (d) Dairy farming

Ans. (c) Mixed farming

28. Which of the following is/are the oldest economic activity ?

(a) Gathering (b) Hunting
(c) Manufacturing (d) Both (a) and (b)

Ans. (d) Both (a) and (b)

29. Gathering is still practiced in which of the following areas ?

(a) Canada (b) Northern Eurasia
(c) Amazon Basin (d) All of these

Ans. (d) All of these

30. In Sahara and Asiatic deserts which of the following animals is/are reared by the nomads ?

(a) Sheep (b) Goats
(c) Camels (d) All of these

Ans. (d) All of these

31. In the Arctic and sub-Arctic areas, which of the following animals is/are reared by the nomads?

(a) Yak (b) Reindeer
(c) Llaimas (d) Horde

Ans. (b) Reindeer

32. Seasonal migration of herders from plains to mountains and vice-versa is known as......... .

(a) nomadic herding (b) pastoral grazing
(c) transhumance (d) livestock rearing

Ans. (d) livestock rearing

33. In which of the following countries commercial livestock rearing is practiced ?

(a) New Zealand (b) Australia
(c) Argentina (d) All of these

Ans. (d) All of these

34. Intensive subsistence agriculture dominated by crops other than paddy is practiced in which of the following regions ?

(a) China (b) Manchuria
(c) North Korea (d) All of these

Ans. (d) All of these

35. Viticulture is speciality of which of the following type of agriculture ?

(a) Dairy farming
(b) Mediterranean agriculture
(c) Extensive commercial grain agriculture
(d) Intensive subsistence agriculture

Ans. (b) Mediterranean agriculture

36. Complete the following table.

Name of Primitive Subsistence Agriculture	Countries
Jhuming	North Eastern states of India
Milpa	(A) – ?
Ladang	Indonesia

Ans. (a) Central America and Mexico

37. Arrange the following activities in sequence (from oldest to modern)

I. Factory farming
II. Gathering
III. Primitive subsistence agriculture

Codes

(a) II, III, I (b) I, II, III
(c) III, II, I (d) II, I, III

Ans. (a) II, III, I

Very Short Answer Questions

1. State the two groups of factors which affect the profitability of mining. *(All India 2017)*

Ans. The profitability of mining depends on two main factors

(i) Physical factors include the size, grade and the mode of occurrence of the deposits.
(ii) Economic factors such as the demand for the mineral, technology available and used.

2. "Agri-business farms are mechanised and large in size." Examine the statement. *(Delhi 2016)*

Ans. Agri-business farms are large farms where large scale production takes place. Therefore, these farms are mechanised as per latest scientific technology. The production in these farms is done for commercial purposes.

3. What are economic activities? *(Delhi 2015)*

Ans. Human activities that generate income are called economic activities. They are grouped under primary, secondary, tertiary and quaternary activities.

4. Who are called red collar workers? *(All India 2015)*

Ans. People who are engaged in primary activities are called red collar workers due to the outdoor nature of their work.

5. What is truck farming? *(Delhi 2014)*

Ans. Truck farming specialises in the cultivation of vegetables. It constitutes growing of vegetables around the urban centers to meet the daily requirement of urban areas.

6. Name the two activities on which the earliest human beings were dependent for their subsistence. *(Delhi 2011, All India 2008)*

Ans. The two activities are gathering and hunting.

7. What is nomadic herding? *(All India 2011)*

Ans. Nomadic herding is also called pastoral nomadism. It is basically primitive subsistence activity in which herders depend upon animals for food, clothing, shelter, tools and transport.

8. Name any two areas of high latitudes in the world, where gathering economic activity is practiced. *(All India 2010)*

Ans. Two areas of high latitudes where gathering is practiced is Northern Canada and Northern Eurasia.

9. Name the country where practically every farmer is a member of cooperative society. *(Delhi 2008)*

Ans. Denmark is a country where every farmer is a member of cooperative society.

3 Marks Questions

1. ''Every January after the harvest season 'Jonbeel Mela' takes place in Jagiroad, 35 kilometres away from Guwahati and it is possibly the only fair in India, where 'barter system' is still alive. A big market is organised during this fair and people from various tribes and communities exchange their products.''

   In light of the above paragraph, justify the values of 'barter system' in the lives of the tribal communities. *(Delhi 2018)*

Ans. In primitive societies, barter system was the initial form of trade, where direct exchange of goods took place. For example, a rice cultivator in need of cloth will find a weaver who needs rice. For exchange of goods, a market would be required where different tribes and communities could exchange their goods from other communities as per their needs. According to the given passage, the Jonbeel Mela organised this type of market. Tribal communities met and exchange goods and services. This system is valued as it not only makes trading easier but also help in binding the tribal communities together.

2. Explain any three features of underground mining methods in different countries of the world. *(All India 2010)*

Ans. The three features of underground mining methods in different countries of the world are as follows

(i) It is done when the ore lies deep below the surface. In this method, vertical shafts have to be sunk, from where underground gallaries, radiate to reach the minerals.

(ii) For underground mining, lifts, drills, haulage vehicles, ventilation systems for safety and efficient movement of people and materials are required.

(iii) The method used in underground mining is risky because poisonous gases, fires, floods and caving can lead to fatal accidents.

3. "Dairy farming is the most advanced and efficient type of rearing of milch animals in the world." Analyse the statement with examples. *(All India 2009)*

Ans. It is true that dairy farming is the most advanced and efficient type of rearing of animals for milk in the world. This is because it is highly capital as well as labour intensive. Animal sheds, storage facilities for fodder, feeding and milching machines add to the cost of dairy farming.

Special emphasis is laid on cattle breeding, health care and veterinary services. It is labour intensive also due to the caring, feeding and milking processes involved. The developed means of transportation, refrigeration, pasteurisation and other preservation processes are used to increase the duration of storage of various dairy products.

5 Marks Questions

1. Explain any five features of 'plantation agriculture' in the world. *(CBSE 2023)*

Or Describe any five characteristics of plantation agriculture in the world. *(All India 2016, 2009)*

Or Name any six crops of plantation agriculture of the world. Describe any four characteristics of plantation agriculture. *(All India 2008)*

Ans. Six crops of plantation agriculture are tea, coffee, rubber, cotton, sugarcane and bananas. Characteristics of plantation agriculture are as follows

(i) This kind of agriculture was introduced by Europeans in colonies situated in tropics, e.g. the French established cocoa and coffee plantation in West Africa. British set-up large tea gardens in India and Sri Lanka and rubber plantations in Malaysia and banana plantations in West Indies.

(ii) It needs large estates of plantations; large investment and managerial support.

(iii) Technical support and scientific methods of cultivation are required.

(iv) It needs single crop specialisation, cheap, labour and good system of transportation which connects plantations to factories and factories to markets.

2. Explain any five features of 'market gardening and horticulture' in the world. *(CBSE 2023)*

Or What is the meaning of market gardening and horticulture. Describe any four characteristics of this type of agriculture of the world. *(All India 2008)*

Ans. Market gardening and horticulture is a type of agriculture which specialises in the production of high value crops such as vegetables, fruits and flowers, solely devoted to the urban markets. These farms are located near urban areas.

Features of market gardening and horticulture are as follows

(i) Farms are small in size and located near urban centers where good transportation facilities are available.

(ii) It is both labour and capital intensive and lays emphasis on the use of irrigation, HYV seeds, fertilisers, insecticides, greenhouses and artificial heating systems in colder regions.

(iii) The regions where farmers specialise in cultivation of vegetables only is known as truck farming as the distance between the urban market and farms can be covered overnight by trucks.

(iv) This type of agriculture is practiced in well developed and densely populated regions of North-West Europe, North-Eastern USA and the Mediterranean regions. The Netherlands is specialised in growing flower and horticultural crops, especially tulips.

3. Describe the main characteristics of intensive subsistence agriculture. In which parts of the world this type of agriculture is practiced? *(CBSE SQP 2022)*

Other Similar Questions

Or Classify intensive subsistence agriculture into two categories practiced in the world. How are they different from each other? Explain.

Or Where is intensive subsistence agriculture practiced in the world? What are its two types? Describe any two characteristics of each types.

Ans. Intensive subsistence agriculture is largely found in densely populated regions of monsoon Asia. There are two categories practiced in the world

(i) Intensive subsistence agriculture dominated by wet paddy cultivation.

(ii) Intensive subsistence agriculture dominated by crops other than paddy.

Characteristics of intensive subsistence dominated by wet paddy cultivation are

(i) It is characterised by dominance of rice crop. Land holding are very small due to the high density of population.

(ii) Use of machinery is limited and most of the agricultural operations are done by manual labour.

Characteristics of intensive subsistence dominated by crops other than paddy are

(i) Wheat, soybean, barley and sorghum are grown in Northern China Manchuria, North Korea and North Japan. In India, wheat is grown in Western parts of the Indo-Gangetic plains and millets are grown in dry parts of Western and Southern India.

(ii) Irrigation systems are used frequently as this type of agriculture is practiced in dry areas.

4. Highlight the features of commercial livestock rearing, practiced in the developed and developing countries. *(CBSE SQP 2020)*

Or Explain with examples how commercial livestock rearing has become a specialised activity in the world. *(All India 2019)*

Or Define the term commercial livestock rearing. Explain any four characteristics. *(All India 2015)*

Or Describe any five characteristics of 'commercial livestock rearing' practiced in the world. ***(Delhi 2014, 2012)***

Ans. Commercial livestock rearing has become a specialised activity in the world as it is a system in which animals are reared on extensive grasslands with modern scientific methods. This kind of rearing fulfil the demands of milk, meat, wool, etc in worldwide. Animal products are traded at national and international level to earn money.

The characteristics of commercial livestock rearing are as follows

(i) Commercial livestock rearing is totally opposite to the nomadic herding. It is more organised and capital intensive, the commercial livestock rearing is practiced on permanent ranches.

(ii) These ranches are of large size and are divided into parcels which are fenced to regulate the grazing. When one parcel is grazed, then animals are moved to another parcel. All animals are kept according to the carrying capacity of pasture.

(iii) In the pasture, only one type of animals is reared. Some important animals are sheep, goats, horses, etc. They produce meat, wool, skin etc. These products are processed and packed scientifically and exported to different world markets.

(iv) Ranches are managed scientifically and they emphasise on breeding, genetic improvement, disease control and health care of the livestock.

(v) USA, Argentina, New Zealand, Australia and Uruguay are important countries where commercial livestock rearing is practiced.

5. Substantiate the evidence to prove that substitence agriculture is still practiced in different parts of the globe. ***(CBSE SQP 2020)***

Ans. Primitive subsistence agriculture is widely practiced in tropical areas of Africa, South, Central America and South-East Asia. Different names are given to it in different places like milpa, jhuming, ladang. It is also called slash and burn agiculture or shifting agriculture. Cultivation is done through primitive tools by clearing a patch of land. After 3 to 5 years, when the soil loses its fertility, then new land is cleared for cultivation.

6. Compare the features of subsistence and plantation agriculture in five points each. ***(CBSE SQP 2018)***

Ans. The differences between subsistence and plantation agriculture are as follows

Subsistence Agriculture	Plantation Agriculture
Subsistence agriculture is done on small piece of land.	Plantation agriculture is done on a large piece of land / estate / plantation.
The production is consumed by the farmers and his family as the production is in very little quantity.	The produce is done on a large scale so it is for gaining profit.
In this agriculture, primitive methods of farming and tools are utilised.	In this agriculture, modern and scientific methods of farming along with managerial, technical support are utilised.
One or more crops are grown depending on the farmer's needs.	Generally, a single crop is cultivated on a large scale.
Areas included in subsistence agriculture are • **Primitive Subsistence** Malaysia, Indonesia, North-East India • **Intensive Subsistence** – Wet Paddy India, Indonesia, Myanmar – **Other than Paddy** North Korea, Manchuria, North Japan	Areas included in plantation agriculture are • Cocoa and coffee plantations in West Africa • Tea gardens in India and Sri Lanka. • Coconut and sugarcane in Philippines

7. Compare the features of mixed farming and dairy farming in five points each. ***(CBSE SQP 2018)***

Ans. The differences between mixed farming and dairy farming are

Mixed Farming	Dairy Farming
In this farming along with crop cultivation, animal husbandry also has equal importance.	In this type of farming special emphasis is laid on cattle breeding, health care and veterinary services.
Fodder crops along with wheat, barley, oats, rye, maize and root crops are grown.	A number of goods are required like animal sheds, storage facilities, milching machines, etc.
It is characterised by high capital expenditure on farm machinery, building, fertilisers, skill and expertise of the farmers.	It is highly labour intensive as rigorous care of animals are needed. It is also capital intensive.

Mixed Farming	Dairy Farming
Here, crop rotation and inter-cropping maintain the soil fertility.	There is no off season in this type of farming as in the case of crop raising.
It is found in highly developed parts of the world i.e. North-West Europe, North-East America, parts of Eurasia and temperate latitudes of Southern continents.	It is found in North-Western Europe, Canada, South-Eastern Australia, New Zealand and Tasmania.

8. ''Gathering and hunting are the primitive economic activities meant for the subsistence of tribal societies, but in modern times gathering is market oriented and has become commercial.'' Examine the statement. ***(All India 2019)***

Ans. Gathering and hunting are considered as the most primitive or ancient activities. Most of the ancient societies depend on these heavily. In very cold and extremely hot climates people survived by hunting animals. In spite of having modernisation of fishing due to technological progress, still people living in the coastal areas are engaged in catching fishes.

Gathering is the collection of plants and animals for food, shelter and clothing. It is mainly practiced by primitive societies who live in harsh climatic regions. The main features of gathering activity are

- Low capital/skill investment
- Low yield per person
- Non-surplus in production

Gathering is practiced in the following areas

- **High Latitude Zones** It includes Northern Canada, Northern Eurasia and Southern Chile.
- **Low Latitude Zones** It includes the Amazon Basin, Tropical Africa, Northern Fringe of Australia and the interior parts of South-East Asia.

In modern times, gathering is market oriented because gatherers collect valuable plants and other items on a large scale for selling in the market. Gatherers sell products made from valuable plants. They use various parts of the plant, for example, the bark is used for quinine, tannin extract and cork-leaves supply materials for beverages, drugs, cosmetics, fibres and fabrics; nuts for food and oils and tree trunk yield rubber, balata, gums and resins. Gathering has become a major way of earning income so it is has become commercial.

9. Describe the way of life of nomadic herders in the world. ***(All India, 2017)***

Or Define the term nomadic herding. Explain its any four characteristics. ***(Delhi 2015)***

Ans. Nomadic herding is also called pastoral nomadism. It is basically primitive subsistence activity, in which herders depend upon animals for food, clothing, shelter, tools and transport.

Characteristics of nomadic herding are as follows

(i) They move from one place to another place with their livestock for quality of pastures and water. Each nomadic community occupies a well-identified territory as a matter of traditions.

(ii) The variety of animals reared in different regions of the world, e.g. in tropical Africa, cattles are most important livestock; in the hilly areas of Tibet and Andes yak and llamas in Arctic and sub-Arctic areas, reindeer is the most important livestock.

(iii) Movement in search of pastures is undertaken either over vast grassland or mountainous regions.

(iv) Now-a-days number of pastoral nomads have been limited and their areas are also decreased due to imposition of political boundaries and new settlement plans by different countries.

10. Review any five measures adopted to solve the problems of Indian agriculture. ***(All India 2017)***

Ans. Main measures adopted to solve the problems of Indian agriculture are

Irrigation System Earlier Indian agriculture was totally depended on rainfall. But now canals, wells, tubewells were made to decrease the dependence of agriculture on rainfall.

Improvement of Credit Facilities Banks are giving easy credit to the farmer at very low interest rate.

Land Reforms It had changed the distribution of cultivable land and helps in agricultural development.

Commercialisation This helps in increase in the per hectre production increase and also per person production increases.

High Yield Variety Seeds The HYV seeds greatly helps Indian agriculture as these require less water and fertiliser. There seeds increase the production.

Measures to solve the problems of Indian agriculture

- Irrigation System
- Improvement of Credit Facilities
- Land Reforms
- Commercialisation
- High Yielding Variety Seeds

11. Differentiate between nomadic herding and commercial livestock rearing, stating any five points of distinction. *(Delhi 2016)*

Ans. Differences between nomadic herding and commercial livestock rearing are as follows

Nomadic Herding	Commercial Livestock Rearing
Nomadic herding is a primitive subsistence activity where herders move from one place to another along with their livestock.	Commercial livestock rearing is an organised activity that is practiced on permanent ranches.
In nomadic herding, a wide variety of animals are reared.	In commercial livestock, only one type of animal is reared.
Nomads heavily rely on their animals for food, clothing, shelter, tools and transport. Here local needs are fulfilled.	In commercial livestock rearing, animal products like meat, wool, hides, skin are processed, packed scientifically and exported to different world markets.
Nomadic herding is done in open pastures over vast horizontal distances or vertical elevations in hilly areas and mountains using primitive techniques.	Commercial livestock rearing is done on permanent ranches using latest scientific technology.
Nomadic herding is practiced in areas of extreme climatic conditions like in tropical Africa, Asiatic deserts, mountainous regions of Tibet, Arctic and sub-Arctic areas.	Commercial livestock rearing is associated with Western culture and practiced where large areas are available. New Zealand, Australia, Argentina, Uruguay and United States are important countries where it is practiced.

12. Differentiate between cooperative farming and collective farming, stating five points of distinction. *(Delhi 2016)*

Ans. Differences between cooperative farming and collective farming are as follows

Cooperative Farming	Collective Farming
Cooperative farming takes place when farmers pool their resources voluntarily for efficient and profitable farming.	Collective farming takes place when there is collective labour and there is social ownership of means of production.
In cooperative farming, farmers have individual ownership of the resources.	In collective farming, farmers pool all their resources though they are allowed to keep very small plot of land for their own use.
Cooperative societies help farmers in buying farm inputs on favourable terms.	In collective farming all farm inputs are provided by the government.
Cooperative societies also help the farmers in selling the farm products profitably.	In collective farming, farm products are sold to the state at a fixed price.
Cooperative farming has been successful in many European countries and that is why it is practiced in many other countries of the world.	Collective farming was introduced in former Soviet Union but after its disintegration, the system of farming has been modified.

13. Define the term 'mixed farming'. Explain any four characteristics of mixed farming practiced in the world. *(All India 2014)*

Ans. Mixed farming is a type of agricultural farming in which farmers cultivate crops and also rear animals on farm. The four characteristics of mixed farming are as follows

(i) This kind of agriculture is practised in developed parts of the world viz. North-Western Europe, Eastern-North America and parts of Eurasia.

(ii) Mixed farms are moderate in size and usually the crops associated with it are wheat, barley, rye, maize, fodder and root crops. Fodder crops are an important component of mixed farming.

(iii) The rotation and inter-cropping play an important role in maintaining soil fertility, chemical fertilisers and green manures are used extensively to achieve more output.

(iv) Equal emphasis is laid on crop cultivation and animal husbandry so that farm animals like cattle, sheep, pigs, poultry provide income alongwith crops.

14. Explain any five characteristics of extensive commercial grain cultivation practiced in the world. *(All India 2014)*

Ans. The five characteristics of extensive commercial grain cultivation practiced in the world are as follows

(i) Commercial grain cultivation is practiced in the interior parts of semi-arid lands of the mid-latitudes.

(ii) Wheat is the principal crop, though other crops like corn, barley, oats and rye are also grown.
(iii) The size of the farm is very large and often run into hundreds of hectares.
(iv) This is highly mechanised agriculture in which all operations from ploughing to harvesting are done by machines.
(v) Yield per acre is low, but yield per person is high because farms are mechanised and population is sparse.

15. Explain any five characteristics of dairy farming practiced in the world. *(Delhi 2013)*

Ans. The five characteristics of dairy farming practiced in the world are as follows
(i) This kind of agriculture is the most advanced and efficient type of rearing of milch animals.
(ii) It requires huge investment of capital. Animal sheds, storage facilities for fodder, feeding and milching machines add to the cost of dairy farming.
(iii) Focus on health care, cattle breeding and veterinary services.
(iv) Here, labour requirement is high as it is involved in rigorous care in feeding and milching.
(v) It is practiced near urban and industrial regions because these places provide market for milk and dairy products.

16. Describe any five characteristics of the economic activities of hunting and gathering practiced in the world. *(Delhi 2012)*

Ans. Characteristics of hunting and gathering practiced in the world are as follows
(i) Gathering and hunting are the well-known oldest economic activities. These are carried out at different levels with different orientations.
(ii) Gathering is practised in region with harsh climate conditions. It often involves primitive societies, which extract both plants and animals for food, shelter and clothing.
(iii) The early man used stone, tools, twigs or arrows, so animals were hunted in limited number only but now due to excessive and illegal hunting (poaching) many species have become extinct or endangered.
(iv) Gathering leads to collect valuable plant leaves, bark of trees, gatherers also plant the medicinal trees. After simple processing, they sell the products in the markets.
(v) Gathering requires a small amount of capital investment and operates at a very low and little bit technology.

17. What is the importance of dairy farming? Why is it mainly practiced near urban and industrial centers of the world? Explain two reasons. *(Delhi 2011)*

Ans. The importance of dairy farming are as follows
(i) It provides fresh milk and dairy products to us.
(ii) Due to its labour intensiveness, it provides employment to many people as high labour is involved in rigorous care in feeding and milching.
(iii) It provides employment throughout the year, as there is no off season during the year as in the case of crop cultivation.

Dairy farming is mainly practiced near urban and industrial centres because of following reasons
(i) These regions provide neighbourhood markets for fresh milk and dairy products.
(ii) Milk and dairy products are perishable goods and need to be transported soon, so to reduce the time of transportation the farms are located near urban centers.

18. What is subsistence agriculture? Mention any four characteristics of primitive subsistence agriculture. *(All India 2011)*

Ans. Subsistence agriculture means an agriculture in which farmer and his family consume all or nearly all the locally grown products. It can be divided into two categories i.e. primitive subsistence and intensive subsistence agriculture.
Characteristics of primitive subsistence agriculture are as follows
(i) This kind of cultivation is practiced by many tribes in tropics.
(ii) Vegetation is cleared by fire and ashes used in fertility of soil.
(iii) Cultivated fields are small so that people use only primitive tools such as sticks and hoes.
(iv) After 3 to 5 years when the soil loses its fertility, then farmers clear another patch of forest land for cultivation.

Source Based Questions

1. Read the given passage carefully and answer the questions that follow. *(CBSE 2023)*

Methods of Mining

Depending on the mode of occurrence and the nature of the ore, mining is of two types : surface and underground mining. The surface mining also known as open-cast mining is the easiest and the cheapest way of mining minerals that occur close to the surface. Overhead costs such as safety precautions and equipment are relatively low in this method. The output is both large and rapid.

When the ore lies deep below the surface, underground mining method (shaft method) has to be used. In this method, vertical shafts have to be sunk, from where underground galleries radiate to reach the minerals. Minerals are extracted and transported to the surface through these passages. It requires specially designed lifts, drills, haulage vehicles, ventilation system for safety and efficient movement of people and material. This method is risky. Poisonous gases, fires, floods and caving is lead to fatal accidents. Have you ever read about mine fires and flooding of coal mines in India?

The developed economies are retreating from mining, processing and refining stages of production due to high labour costs, while the developing countries with large labour force and striving for higher standard of living are becoming more important. Several countries of Africa and few of South America and Asia have over 50 per cent of the earnings from minerals alone.

(i) Explain the main difference between surface and underground mining.

(ii) Why is open-cast mining the easiest way of mining ?

(iii) Why is shaft mining more risky?

Ans. (i) The main difference between surface and underground mining is that the surface mining is the easiest and the cheapest way of mining minerals that occur close to the surface. On the other hand, when the ore lies deep below the surface, underground mining method (shaft method is used which needs more capital.

(ii) Open-cast mining is an easiest way of mining because excavation through rock is not necessary in this mining method.

(iii) Shaft mining is risky because as it is done underground so there are chances of poisonous gases, fires and floods and caving in leads to fatal accidents.

2. Study the diagram given below and answer the questions that follows. *(Delhi 2008)*

(i) Two types of mining are shown in as A and B. Identify them and give the correct name of each.

(ii) State two characteristics of each type of mining.

Ans. (i) The two types of mining are

A- Surface mining/Open-cast or strip mining

B-Underground mining/Shaft mining

(ii) Characteristics of surface mining are

(a) It is the cheapest and easiest way of mining.

(b) The safety precautions and equipment are relatively low.

Characteristics of underground mining are

(a) It is done when the ore lies deep below the surface.

(b) Lifts, drills, haulage vehicles, ventilation system for safety and efficient movement of people and materials are required.

Map Bases Questions

1. Identify the geographical features shown on the outline map of the world.

A. An area of nomadic herding. ***(Delhi 2016, All India 2011, 2009)***

B. An area of extensive commercial grain farming. ***(Delhi 2013, All India 2014, 2013)***

C. An area of subsistence gathering. ***(Delhi 2014, All India 2012)***

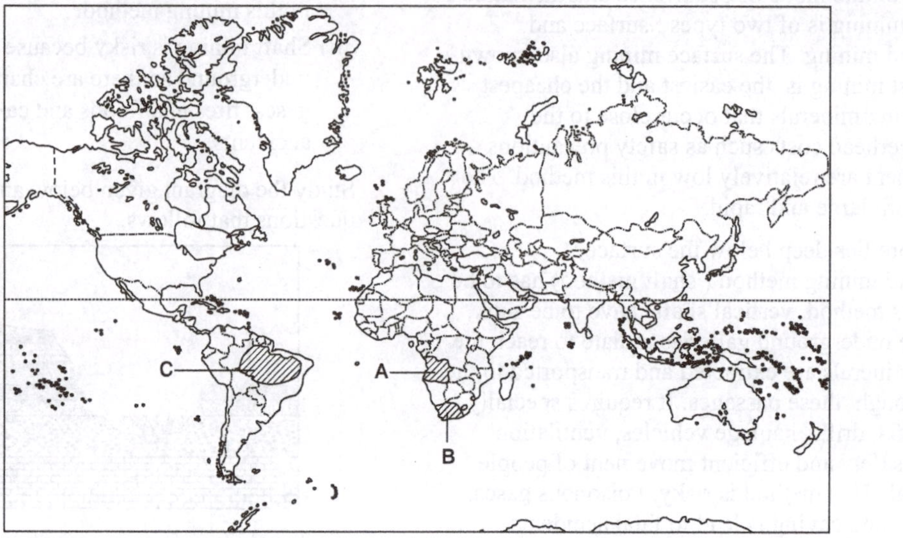

Ans.

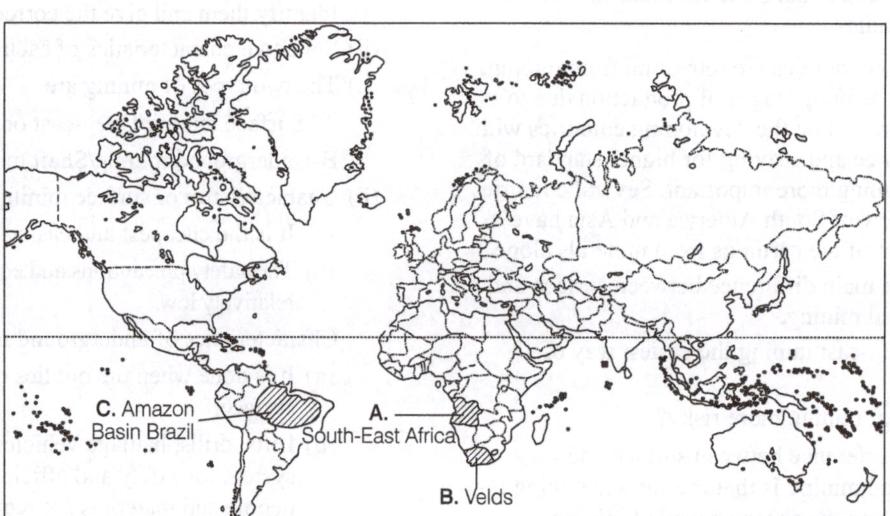

2. Identify the geographical features shown on the outline map of the world.

A. A major area of commercial livestock rearing. *(Delhi 2012, 2011)*

B. An important country of commercial livestock rearing. *(Delhi 2009)*

C. Area of extensive grain farming. *(All India 2008)*

D. Area of extensive commercial grain farming. *(Delhi 2008)*

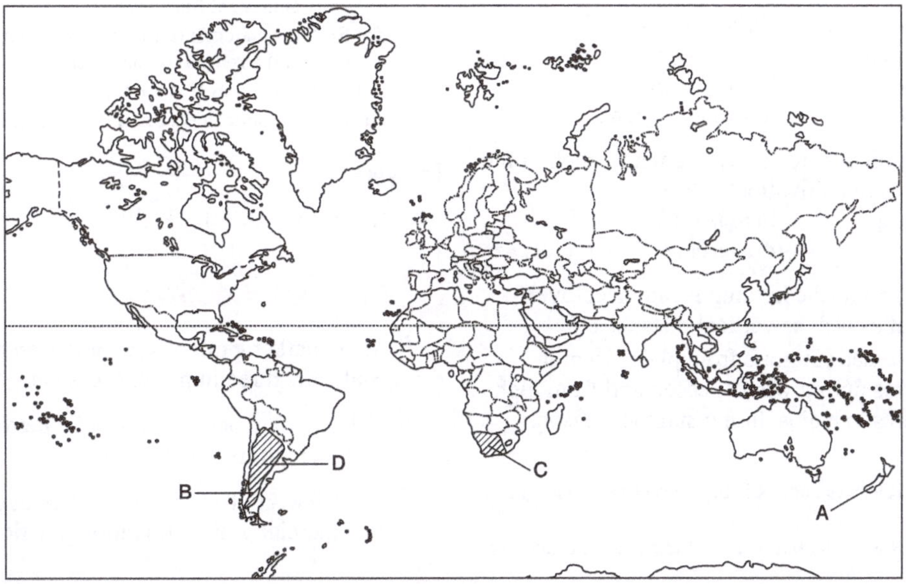

Ans.

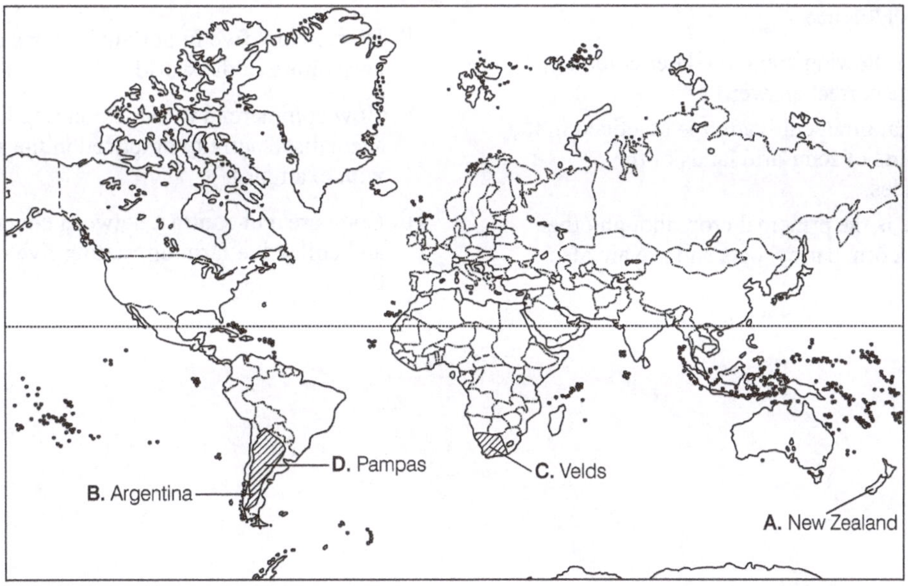

CHAPTER TEST

01 Mark Questions

1 Which term is used for growing of flowers in agricultural practices?
(a) Mixed Farming (b) Floriculture
(c) Truck Farming (d) Factory Farming

2 European colonists were associated with which of the following types of cultivation?
(a) Mixed farming (b) Kolkhoz
(c) Plantation (d) Viticulture

3 **Assertion** (A) Nomadic herding is practiced over vast horizontal as well as vertical distances.
Reason (R) Nomads migrate from plains to high altitude pastures during winter season and from high altitude pastures to plains during summer season.

Codes
(a) Both A and R are true and R is the correct explanation of A
(b) Both A and R are true, but R is not the correct explanation of A
(c) A is true, but R is false
(d) A is false, but R is true

4 Consider the following about the later colonial period and choose the correct answer.
I. Commercial grain cultivation is practiced in the interior parts of semi-arid lands of the mid-latitudes.
II. Sugarcane is the principal crop, though other crops like corn, barley, oats and rye are also grown.

Codes
(a) Only statement I is correct
(b) Both the statements are true and statement II correctly present the reason for statement I
(c) Only statement II is correct
(d) Both the statements I and II are incorrect

Answers
1. (b) | 2. (c) | 3. (b) | 4. (b)

03 Marks Questions

5 Why market gardening is practiced near urban areas? State any three important reasons.

6 Differentiate between nomadic herding and commercial livestock rearing.

7 Describe any five characteristics of extensive commercial grain cultivation practiced in the world.

05 Marks Questions

8 Discuss any five important features of plantation agriculture in the world.

9 How commercial livestock rearing has become a specialised activity practiced in the world? Explain with examples.

10 Compare and contrast between cooperative farming and collective farming, stating five points of distinction.

05

Secondary Activities

TREND ANALYSIS 3 YEARS

TOPIC 01 Manufacturing

Average No. of Questions Across all Sets

Types of Questions	2023	2020	2019
1 Mark	5	–	–
3 Marks	2	–	–
3 Marks	2	–	4

All economic activities like primary, secondary, tertiary and quaternary revolve around obtaining and utilising resources necessary for survival. Whereas, secondary activities are those activities that convert primary products into more useful commodities. Therefore, secondary activities are a type of economic activity that adds value to natural resources.

This is done by transforming, where raw materials are changed into valuable products. For example, transformation of cotton from that plant into yarns, iron-ore into steel, etc. Therefore, secondary activities are concerned with manufacturing, processing and construction (infrastructure) industries.

Manufacturing

The literal meaning of manufacturing is to make by hand, but in the present context, the manufacturing means the conversion of raw material into more useful and valuable fabricated articles with the help of machines.

Manufacturing Industries

These are geographically located manufacturing units that transform raw materials into finished goods of higher value for sale in local or distant markets. The term industry is comprehensive and can also be used in many secondary activities which are not carried on in factories like entertainment industry, tourism industry, etc.

The manufacturing industries are characterised by the following

Specialisation of Skills In industries, one task is done repeatedly that gives specialisation of doing that task. This involves high cost of manufacturing. On the other hand, mass production involves production of large quantity of standardised parts by each worker performing only one task repeatedly.

Mechanisation The industries use automated processes or machines which does the major production. Human thinking is not required in mechanisation.

Technological Innovation Latest technology is used and constant innovation is done to eliminate waste, quality control, combat pollution and bring efficiency.

Organisational Structure and Stratification Modern manufacturing is characterised by complex machine technology, extreme specialisation, division of labour, vast capital, large organisations and executive bureaucracy.

Uneven Geographic Distribution The industries are concentrated in regions that are rich in mineral and other resources. These areas cover less than **10% of the world's land area**. These regions have become the major centres of economic and political power.

Location of Industry

The location of industry at a particular place is governed by a large number of geographical and non-geographical factors. Industries maximise profits by reducing costs. Thus, industries should be located at points where the production costs are minimum. Following factors influence the location of industry at particular places

Access to Market Areas that provide large markets for finished industrial goods like developed areas of Europe, America, Japan, Australia, South Asia have huge concentration of industries.

Access to Sources of Energy Coal, petroleum and hydroelectricity are main sources of energy. Industries using more power are located close to these sources.

Access to Raw Material Industries based on cheap, bulky and weight-losing materials (ores) like steel, sugar are based close to sources of raw materials. Similarly, processing of dairy products, perishable foods and agro based are done near the sources of raw materials.

Access to Labour Supply Industries are located where there is availability of skilled labour. Some types of manufacturing still require skilled labour.

Acccess to Source of Energy Industries which use more power are located nearer to the source of energy supply such as iron and steel industries. Energy is most essential to run machines in industries. The main power resources are coal, petroleum, hydroelectricity, natural gas and nuclear energy.

Access to Transportation and Communication Facilities Industries are located in places that have efficient transportation facilities and communication services for the exchange and management of information.

Access to Agglomeration Economies Agglomeration economies refer to the benefits derived from the linkages that exist between different industries. The small industries or ancillary units like to operate near leader industries to benefit from nearness to big or basic industries.

Government Policy For the balanced economic development, governments promote various regions by setting up industries in a particular link between industrial areas.

Classification of Manufacturing Industries

Industries are classified on the basis of their size, inputs/ raw materials, output/ products and ownership.

Industries Based on Size

Based on amount of capital invested, a number of workers employed and volume of production, industries are classified into the following

Household Industries or Cottage Manufacturing It is the smallest manufacturing unit. Artisans **use local raw materials**, simple tools and production is done with the help of family members. Production is done for local consumption and local markets. There is not much capital needed, e.g. mats, baskets, pottery, jewellery, artefacts and crafts.

Small Scale Manufacturing These type of industries employ semi-skilled labour, operate by power driven machines, use local raw materials and manufacture products in workshops. It provides employment and **raises local purchasing power**. India, China, Indonesia and Brazil have developed labour intensive small scale manufacturing units.

Large Scale Manufacturing Here mass production takes place, involves large market, many raw materials, huge energy requirements, specialised workers, advanced technology and large capital. Large scale manufacturing industries are divided into two parts i.e. **traditional large scale industrial regions** and **high technology large scale industrial regions.**

Industries Based on Inputs/Raw Materials

On the basis of raw materials used, industries are classified as follows

Agro based Industry This involves processing of raw materials from the fields and farms into finished products like sugar, fruit juices, beverages, oils and textiles (cotton, jute, silk), rubber, etc.

Food Processing This is part of agro based industry and includes processes like canning, producing cream, fruit processing, confectionery, drying, fermenting and pickling.

Agri Business This is commercial farming on an industrial scale. The farms are mechanised, very large and highly structured, like tea plantation and tea factories near the plantations.

Mineral based Industry These are industries that use minerals as raw materials such as ferrous like iron and steel and non-ferrous like aluminium, copper, etc. Mineral based non-metallic industries are of cement and pottery.

Chemical based Industry These industries use natural chemical minerals like salts, sulphur, potash, mineral oil in petrochemical industry and chemicals obtained from wood and coal. Synthetic fibre and plastics are other examples of chemical based industry.

Forest based Industry Industries that use forest products such as timber, wood, bamboo, grass, lac, etc come under forest based industry.

Animal based Industry Industries that use animal products such as leather, woollen textiles, ivory are grouped under animal based industry.

Industries based on Output/ Product

This refers to industries based on the finished products or output. These are

Basic Industries These are the industries that produce raw material to be used in other industries such as iron and steel.

Consumer Goods Industries These are the industries which produces what is consumed by consumers directly such as tea, biscuits, toiletries, etc.

Industries based on Ownership

Based on the ownership, the industries are grouped as

Public Sector Industry This refers to industries that are owned and managed by government. In India, it is called public sector undertakings. Socialist economies have all state owned industries.

Private Sector Industry This refers to industries that are owned by private individuals and also managed by them. Capitalist economies have mostly private owned industries.

Joint Sector Industry Industries that are jointly owned and managed by joint stock companies or established by private and government sector are called joint sector industries.

Foot Loose Industries

These industries do not depend on any specific raw material so they can be located at any place. They largely depend on component parts, employ small labour force and produce in small quantity.

High Technology Industry

- Also called **high-tech industry**, it is highly technical and incorporates advanced scientific and engineering research and development strategy.
- The workforce are highly skilled specialists, professionals (known as **white collar**) who outnumber the production labour (**blue collar**).
- Robotics, computer aided design and manufacturing, electronics, new chemicals and pharmaceuticals are examples of these industries.
- High-tech industries that are concentrated regionally, self sustained and highly specialised are called **technopolis**, e.g. Silicon valley near San Francisco and Silicon forest near Seattle.

PYQs Previous Years' Questions

1 Mark Questions

Multiple Choice Questions

1. Modern manufacturing is not characterised by which one of the following? *(CBSE 2023)*
   (a) A complex machine technology
   (b) Vast capital
   (c) Small organisations
   (d) Executive bureaucracy

Ans. (c) Small organisations

2. Which of the following industries produce raw material for other industries? *(CBSE 2023)*
   (a) Small scale industries (b) Basic or key industries
   (c) Household industries (d) Joint sector industries

Ans. (b) Basic or key industries

3. Which of the following is not the feature of small scale industries? *(CBSE 2023)*
   (a) They use simple power driven machines.
   (b) They rely on semi-skilled labour.
   (c) They obtain raw materials locally.
   (d) Their products are sold in international markets.

Ans. (d) Their products are sold in international markets.

4. Which one of the following features is correct about cottage industries? *(CBSE 2023)*
   (a) It is a large manufacturing unit.
   (b) Raw material is imported from outside markets.
   (c) Goods produced by them have low commercial significance.
   (d) Finished products are sold in the open market.

Ans. (c) Goods produced by them have low commercial significance.

5. Read the following (features of Cottage manufacturing) and choose the correct option. *(CBSE 2023)*
   I. Place of manufacturing outside the home
   II. It is the smallest unit of manufacturing
   III. Use local raw materials
   IV. Simple tools are used

   Codes
   (a) Only I, II and III are correct
   (b) Only II, III and IV are correct
   (c) Only, I, II and IV are correct
   (d) Only I, III and IV are correct

Ans. (b) Only II, III and IV are correct

6. Modern manufacturing is characterised by which of the following?
   (a) A complex machine technology
   (b) Vast capital
   (c) Division of labour
   (d) All of the above

Ans. (d) All of the above

7. Which of the following is a factor influencing industrial locations ?
   (a) Access to market
   (b) Access to raw material
   (c) Access to labour supply
   (d) All of the above

Ans. (d) All of the above

8. Foot Lose industries are those industries which
   (a) are not dependent on any specific raw material.
   (b) depend on component parts which can be obtained anywhere.
   (c) produce in small quantity.
   (d) All of the above

Ans. (d) All of the above

9. Which of the following countries practices small scale manufacturing ?
   (a) India (b) China
   (c) Indonesia (d) All of these

Ans. (d) All of these

10. Which of the following regions practices large scale manufacturing?
    (a) North-Eastern USA (b) Europe
    (c) United Kingdom (d) All of these

Ans. (d) All of these

11. Which of the following is a basic industry ?
    (a) Iron Industry (b) Aircraft Industry
    (c) Television Industry (d) All of these

Ans. (a) Iron Industry

12. Which of the following is/are characteristics of technopolis ?
    (a) Regional concentration of high-tech industries.
    (b) Presence of highly specialised industries.
    (c) Presence of self-sustaining industries.
    (d) All of the above

Ans. (d) All of the above

13. Arrange the following industries in sequence as per their size.
I. Large scale manufacturing
II. Small scale manufacturing
III. Cottage manufacturing
Codes
(a) I, II, III (b) III, II, I
(c) II, III, I (d) III, I, II

Ans. (b) III, II, I

Very Short Answer Questions

1. How are large scale industries different from cottage industries? Explain. *(CBSE Term I 2021)*

Ans. In large scale industries, mass production takes place. They use heavy power driven machine and require huge capital investment.

On the other hand, cottage industries are those in which artisans use local raw materials, simple tools and production is done with the help of family members.

2. Why is 'technological innovation' essential for industries? Explain. *(CBSE Term I 2021)*

Ans. Technological innovation is essential for industries because latest technological and constant innovation is uesd to eliminate waste, quality control, combat pollution and bring efficiency.

3. Mention any two factors responsible for the establishment of cotton textile mills in Mumbai. *(Delhi 2018)*

Ans. Two factors responsible for the establishment of cotton textile mills in Mumbai are
(i) Mumbai is very close to the cotton producing areas of Gujarat and Maharashtra.
(ii) Being a large town, it provides huge manpower required for cotton textiles.

4. Define the term technopolies. *(Delhi 2016)*

Ans. Technopolies is the term given to high-tech industries which are regionally concentrated, self-sustained and highly specialised, e.g. Silicon Valley near San Francisco.

5. What is a household industry? *(Delhi 2011)*

Ans. Household industry is the smallest unit of manufacturing, also known as cottage industry. It is basically run by creative individuals or craftsmen who are assisted by their family members in their home.

6. What is the importance of secondary activities in the world? *(All India 2009, Delhi 2009)*

Ans. The importance of secondary activities is that these activities add value to the natural resources by the transformation of raw materials into useful and valuable products.

7. Classify industries into two groups on the basis of metallic minerals. *(All India 2008)*

Ans. Industries classified on the basis of metallic minerals are ferrous and non-ferrous industries.

3 Marks Questions

1. Explain how the 'size of population' and the stage of 'economic development' are the bases of international trade. *(CBSE 2023)*

Ans. The size of population and stage of economic development have become the basis of international trade due to following reasons

Size of population Size of population and capitalistic society provide impetus to international trade. The more the people have purchasing power, the more they demand for goods and as a result trade would flourish. But, densely populated countries have large volume of internal trade and little external trade because most of the agricultural and industrial production is consumed in the local markets. Standard of living of the population determines the demand for better quality imported products because with low standard of living only a few people can afford to buy costly imported goods.

Stage of Economic Development The nature of trade changes with the change in stage of economic development of countries. In developed economies, manufactured goods, machinery are traded for raw materials but in less developed economies, agro products are traded for industrial goods.

2. "Technological innovations through research and development strategy are an important aspect of modern manufacturing." Analyse the statement. *(CBSE 2023)*

Or How are technological innovations an important aspect of modern manufacturing industries? Explain any three aspects in this regard. *(All India 2011)*

Ans. Technological innovations through research and development strategies are an important aspect of modern manufacturing for quality control, eliminating waste and inefficiency and combating pollution.

Three aspects in this regard are as under

(i) Complex machine technology is needed so that high quality goods are produced at less time.

(ii) It requires vast capital so that machines with latest technology can be used in manufacturing.

(iii) Extreme specialisation and division of labour is required, that can work efficiently on the machines.

3. "Speedy and efficient system of transport is essential for the development of industries." Analyse the statement. ***(CBSE 2023)***

> **HINT** *Dear students, this question simply ask you to write the role of speedy and efficient transportation system in the development of industries.*

Ans. Speedy and efficient transport facilities to carry raw materials to the factory and to move finished goods to the market are essential for the development of industries.

The cost of transport plays an important role in the location of industrial units. Western Europe and Eastern North America have a highly developed transport system which has always induced the concentration of industries in these areas.

Modern industry is inseparably tied to transportation systems. Improvements in transportation led to integrated economic development and regional specialisation of manufacturing.

4. Examine the features of cottage manufacturing or household industries. ***(CBSE SQP 2022)***

Or Describe any three characteristics of household industries. ***(Delhi 2014)***

Ans. The features of cottage manufacturing or household industries are

(i) It is the smallest manufacturing unit. In these industries, local raw materials and simple tools are used by the artisans.

(ii) Goods are produced in these industries for everyday use in the homes of artisans with the help of family members. The finished products are used in the same household or sold in the local market.

(iii) Some common examples of products produced in these industries include food stuffs, containers, fabrics, tools, furniture, figurines, jewellery, pottery, etc.

5. Give the meaning of high-tech industry. State any two characteristics of this industry. ***(Delhi 2013)***

Or Explain the concept of 'High Technology Industry' with examples. ***(Delhi 2011)***

Ans. High technology is the latest generation of manufacturing activities. It is best understood as the application of intensive research and development efforts leading to the manufacturing products of an advanced scientific and engineering character.

Characteristics of High-tech industry are

(i) Professional (white collar) workers make-up a large share of the total workforce and greatly outnumber the actual production (blue collar) workers.

(ii) These industries are neatly spaced, low, modern, dispersed, office plant lab buildings rather than massive assembly structures.

6. How do secondary activities add value to natural resources? Explain with three examples. ***(All India 2012)***

Ans. Secondary activities add value to the natural resources by transforming raw materials into valuable products. By various processes, secondary activities add value to the natural products. The examples are as follows

(i) Cotton in the boll has limited use, but after transforming into yarn, it becomes more valuable and can be used for making clothes.

(ii) Iron ore cannot be used directly from the mines but after being converted into steel, it gets its value and can be used for making many valuable machines, tools, etc.

(iii) Materials from the farms, forest products and resources of the sea can be put into greater use by secondary activities.

7. Explain the process of mechanisation in modern large scale manufacturing industry. ***(Delhi 2012)***

Ans. Mechanisation refers to using gadgets which accomplish tasks. The advanced stage of mechanisation is automation that refers to completion of tasks without aid to human thinking during the manufacturing process. These processes are mechanised where the tasks are completed skilfully without any human aid. There are automatic factories with feedback and closed loop computer control systems where machines are developed to think. These kinds of mechanised processing units have sprung up all over the world.

8. Explain any three characteristics of 'foot loose industries.' *(Delhi 2012)*

Ans. The characteristics of foot loose industries are as follows

(i) Foot loose industries can be established at any place, because their location is not affected by any particular raw material, whether it is weight-losing or otherwise. These industries are affected by component parts and they are available at all places.

(ii) These industries produce their products in small numbers and they do not require a large labour force.

(iii) These industries emit less or no pollution. Thus, they are ecofriendly. Road network plays an important role in their location.

9. Classify industries of the world on the basis of ownership into three groups. State the main features of each group. *(All India 2010, 2008)*

Other Similar Questions

Or How industries are classified on the basis of ownership?

Or Explain the classification of industries of the world on the basis of ownership.

Ans. On the basis of ownership, the industries of the world can be classified in following ways

Public Sector Industries In this type, the ownership and management of an industry is in hand of the state. Mainly concerned with social welfare.

Private Sector Industries An individual or a corporate body owns and manages industries that belong to private sector. Mainly concerned with profit.

Joint Sector Industries Industries that are jointly owned and managed by private and government sector are called joint sector industries. Mainly concerned with public sector development.

5 Marks Questions

1. Analyse five main factors affecting location of industries in the world. *(CBSE 2023)*

Or Explain five factors that influence the industrial location in the world. *(Delhi 2015, 2010)*

Or Describe any five factors influencing industrial location in the world? *(Delhi 2010)*

Ans. The five factors influencing the industrial location in the world are as follows

(i) **Access to Market** Market is a place where people, who have demand for goods and the ability to purchase, buy from the sellers, selling their goods at that place. Market affects the location of an industry.

A manufacturing unit is established near the market area. Areas having more population are big markets for manufactured goods, as compared to areas having less population. Apart from it, areas having population with more purchasing power form big markets.

(ii) **Access to Raw Material** Industries that use heavy, bulky and weight-losing raw material are established near the source of raw material. For example, in sugar industries, sugarcane is a perishable and weight-losing raw material. To reduce the transport cost, industries are located near the source of raw material.

Factors influencing industrial locations in the world

- Access to market
- Access to raw material
- Access to sources of energy
- Access to transportation and communication
- Government policies

(iii) **Access to Sources of Energy** Industries using more power and energy are established near the source of energy. For example, aluminium industry.

(iv) **Access to Transportation and Communication** Industries are located in areas that have efficient transport network to get raw material from various regions and supply manufactured goods to market. Communication network is also needed to communicate ideas. Thus, transport and communication are important factors that affect the location of an industry.

(v) **Government Policies** Favourable government policies that promote industrialisation is also important in deciding the location of an industry.

2. Analyse the classification of industries on the basis of raw materials into five heads. *(CBSE 2023)*

Ans. On the basis of inputs or raw materials, industries are classified as

(i) **Agro Based Industries** These industries involves the processing of raw materials of the products which are obtained from agricultural farms and fields. The finished products are sold in the rural and urban markets. These industries include food processing, sugar, pickle, fruit juices, species, textile, etc.

(ii) **Minerals Based Industry** Minerals are used as raw materials in these industries. These include ferrous metallic minerals such as iron and steel industry, non-ferrous metallic minerals such as aluminium, copper, gold, etc and non-metallic minerals based industries like cement industry.

(iii) **Chemical Based Industry** These industries use natural chemical minerals. These include petroleum, salt, sulphur, potash, plastic industries. They also use raw materials obtained from wood and coal.

(iv) **Forest Based Industries** These industries use major and minor forest products such as wood, timber, etc. These include paper industry, furniture industry, lac industry, etc.

Classification of industries on the basis of raw materials
- Agro based industries
- Minerals based industries
- Chemical based industries
- Forest based industries
- Animal based industries

(v) **Animal Based Industries** These industries are based on the products obtained from animals. These include leather industry, woolen, textile industry, etc.

3. Examine the major characteristics of modern large scale manufacturing in the world. **(CBSE 2023)**

Ans. Characteristics of modern large scale manufacturing are discussed below

Specialisation of Skills/Methods of Production Products under craft method are very costly because factories produce only those products which are made-to-order. On the other hand, mass production is related to production of large quantities of standardised parts. In this process, each worker is engaged in only one task and performs that task repeatedly. Thus, the workers are involved in specialised tasks that require specialised skills.

Mechanisation Mechanisation is use of gadgets and machines to accomplish tasks. Automation is the advanced stage of mechanisation in which machines or computer works in all the manufacturing process itself without any human interference or thinking. In the modern world, the automated factories are found almost everywhere. These are operated by feedback and closed loop computer control system which enables the machines to think and work itself.

Technological Innovation Research and development strategy plays a great role in technological innovations, which is considered as an important aspect of modern manufacturing. Technological innovations enables quality control, eliminating waste and inefficiency and combating pollution.

4. "High-tech industry is the latest generation of manufacturing in the world. " Examine the statement. **(CBSE 2023)**

Ans. High-tech industries are the latest generation of manufacturing industries. It involves the application of intensive research and development for manufacturing scientifically advance and engineered products.

These industries have following characteristics

(i) There is production of advanced scientific and engineering products with the use of intensive Research and Development (R and D).

(ii) The workforce in these industries consists of highly skilled specialist workforce. These are professional workers (white collar workers).

(iii) These industries use robotics, computer aided designs, and other highly advanced technologies.

(iv) These industries are self-sustained and highly specialised. Sometimes, they concentrate regionally to form technopolis e.g. Silicon Valley.

5. Explain the main characteristics of 'high-tech industry' in the world. **(CBSE Compartment 2020)**

Or Explain any five characteristics of 'high tech industry' in the world. **(Delhi 2019)**

Ans. Five characteristics of high-tech industries are as follows

(i) It is the latest generation of manufacturing activities.

(ii) It is best understood as the application of intensive Research and Development (R and D) efforts leading to the manufacturing of products of an advanced scientific and engineering character.

(iii) Here professional (white collar) workers makeup a large share of the total workforce and greatly outnumber the actual production (blue collar) workers.

(iv) These industries are neatly spaced, low, modern, dispersed, office-plant-lab buildings rather than massive assembly structures.

(v) Robotics on the assembly line, Computer-Aided Design (CAD) and manufacturing, electronic controls or smelting and refining processes and the constant development of new chemical and pharmaceutical products are notable examples of a high-tech industry.

6. Explain why high-tech industries in many countries are being attracted to the peripheral areas of major metropolitan centres. ***(CBSE SQP 2019)***

Ans. Due to the following reasons, high-tech industries in many countries are being attracted to the peripheral areas of major metropolitan centres

(i) Land is generally cheap in the peripheral areas of the cities and is available in abundance. Single storey buildings can be built.

(ii) The peripheral areas can be well connected with the roadway and railway network used by high-tech industries.

(iii) Cheap and skilled labour is easily available from the nearby areas.

(iv) Highly skilled specialists and professionals are available in major metropolitan centres.

(v) The features of a high-tech industrial landscape are neatly spaced, low, modern, dispersed office plant-laboratory buildings for which the peripheral areas of the cities are most suited.

7. Differentiate between 'small scale manufacturing' and 'large scale manufacturing' in the world. ***(Delhi 2019)***

Or Distinguish between small scale and large scale industries by stating three points of each. ***(All India 2009)***

Ans. The differences between small scale industries and large scale industries are as follows

Small Scale Industries	Large Scale Industries
They use small power driven machines.	They use heavy power driven machine.
A small amount of capital is invested.	Huge capital investment is required.
These industries provide employment in developing countries.	These industries form the parameters of development in developed countries.
These are also stated as 'auxilliary industries' as these provide spare parts to large scale industry.	Large scale industries such as iron and steel industry are known as basic industry.
These require continuous update in technology with semi-skilled labour force.	These require continuous update in technology with highly specialised labour force.

8. Define the term manufacturing. Explain any four features of small scale manufacturing. ***(Delhi 2014)***

Ans. Manufacturing means to make by hand, however now it includes goods made by machines.

It is essentially a process which involves transforming raw materials into finished goods for higher value for sale in local or distant markets. The four features of small scale manufacturing are as follows

(i) It differs from household industries and large scale industries by its production techniques and place.

(ii) This type of manufacturing uses local raw material, simple power driven machines and semi-skilled labour.

(iii) It provides employment and raises local purchasing power.

(iv) These manufacturing units have developed labour intensive techniques in order to provide employment to their population.

9. Define manufacturing. Classify manufacturing industries on the basis of size into three categories and explain the important characteristics of each type. ***(Delhi 2013)***

Ans. For definition and characteristics of manufacturing industries, refer to Q. 8 of 5 marks questions.

On the basis of their size, industries are classified into the following

Classification of industries on the basis of size
- Cottage Manufacturing
- Small Scale Manufacturing
- Large Scale Manufacturing

Cottage Manufacturing It is the smallest manufacturing unit. The artisans use local raw materials. Part time labour or artisan's family members produce everyday goods in their homes with the help of simple tools. Finished goods may be used for consumption in the same household or for sale in the local market.

Small Scale Manufacturing These type of industries employ semi-skilled labour, operate by power driven machines, use local raw materials and manufacture products in workshops. It provides empolyment and raises local purchasing power. India, china, Indonesia and Brazil have developed labour intensive small scale manufacturing units.

Large Scale Manufacturing It requires a large market, enormous energy and various raw materials. It also requires specialised workers, advanced technology, assembly line mass production and huge capital.

10. Explain the role of power and raw material in the location of heavy industries in India. ***(Delhi 2013)***

Ans. All the Industries require energy as they are run by energy such as cotton textile and iron and steel Industries. The role of power is as follows

(i) Power provides the motive force for machines.

(ii) Its supply has to be ensured before the location of any industry.

(iii) Certain industries like aluminium and synthetic nitrogen manufacturing industries tend to be located near sources of power.

Industries are located in those areas where raw material is available near to the industry. The role of raw material is as follows

(i) Industries using weight-losing raw materials are located in the regions where raw material is located.

(ii) Sugar mills, pulp industries, copper smelting and pig iron industries are located near their raw material.

(iii) Most of the iron and steel industries are located near coal fields or near sources of iron ore.

Source Based Questions

1. Read the source given below and answer the following questions by choosing the correct option. ***(CBSE SQP Term II 2021)***

'Manufacturing Industry'

Manufacturing literally means 'to make by hand'. However, now it includes goods 'made by machines'. It is essentially a process which involves transforming raw materials into finished goods of higher value for sale in local or distant markets. Conceptually, an industry is a geographically located manufacturing unit maintaining books of accounts and records under a management system. As the term industry is comprehensive, it is also used as synonymous with 'manufacturing'. When one uses terms like 'steel industry' and 'chemical industry', one thinks of factories and processes. But there are many secondary activities which are not carried on in factories such as what is now called the 'entertainment industry' and 'tourism industry', etc. So for clarity, the longer expression 'manufacturing industry' is used.

(i) What do you understand by the term Manufacturing?

(ii) "Manufacturing involves value addition." Explain with any one suitable example.

(iii) Name two industries which provide services rather than production of goods.

Ans. (i) The conversion of raw material into finished goods through application of power is called manufacturing.

(ii) Manufacturing is a process which involves transforming raw materials into finished goods of higher value. For example, raw cotton is transformed to more valuable threads and then threads are further transformed into more valuable fabric.

(iii) The 'entertainment industry' and 'tourism industry' are two industries which provides services rather than production of goods.

CHAPTER TEST

01 Mark Questions

1 Which of the following types of industries produces raw materials for other industries?

(a) Footloose Industries (b) Cottage Industries
(c) Small-scale Industries (d) Basic Industries

2 Identify the important feature(s) of modern manufacturing units.

(a) Executive bureaucracy
(b) A complex machine technology
(c) Extreme specialisation and division of labour for producing more goods with less effort and low costs
(d) All of the above

3 Which of the following pairs is incorrectly matched?

	Classification of Industries		Examples
(a)	Based on Size	–	Household industries
(b)	Based on Input/Raw materials used	–	Textile industries
(c)	Based on Output	–	Consumer goods
(d)	Based on Ownership	–	Joint Sector industries

4 **Assertion** (A) Agri-business is commercial farming on an industrial scale often financed by business whose main interests lie outside agriculture.

Reason (R) Agri-business farms are mechanised, large in size, highly structured, reliant on chemicals, and may be described as 'agro-factories'.

Codes

(a) Both A and R are true and R is the correct explanation of A
(b) Both A and R are true, but R is not the correct explanation of A
(c) A is true, but R is false
(d) A is false, but R is true

5 Consider the following statements about the later colonial period and choose the correct answer.

I. Small scale manufacturing is as similar as household industries by its production techniques and place of manufacture.

II. This type of manufacturing uses local raw material, simple power -driven machines and semi-skilled labour.

Codes

(a) Only statement I is correct
(b) Both the statements are true and statement II correctly present the reason for statement I
(c) Only statement II is correct
(d) Both the statements I and II are incorrect

Answers

1. (d) | 2. (d) | 3. (a) | 4. (b) | 5. (b)

03 Marks Questions

6 State any three processes through which secondary activities add value to natural resources. Explain with examples.

7 State the importance of manufacturing industries in the economic development of a country.

8 Describe any three characteristics of household industries.

05 Marks Questions

9 Analyse about the major trends of modern industrial activities especially in the developed countries of the world.

10 Why high-tech industries in many countries are being attracted to the peripheral areas of major metropolitan centres? Explain in brief.

11 Differentiate between agro-based industries and mineral based industries in the world.

06

Tertiary and Quaternary Activities

TREND ANALYSIS 3 YEARS

TOPIC 01 Tertiary Activities and Quaternary Activities

TOPIC 02 Quinary Activities

Average No. of Questions Across all Sets

Topic	Types of Questions	2023	2020	2019
TOPIC 01	1 Mark	7	1	–
	2 Marks	–	–	–
	3 Marks	2	–	4
	5 Marks	1	–	–
TOPIC 02	1 Mark	–	–	–
	2 Marks	1	–	–
	3 Marks	–	–	–
	5 Marks	–	–	–

Service sector means providing different services in exchange for payments. This sector is divided into three parts i.e. **tertiary activities, quaternary activities** and **quinary activities**. Trade can be wholesale and retail and can be operated in urban and rural areas. Transport can be through rail network, road network, water and air network.

Tertiary Activities

Tertiary activities are related to the service sector. They involve production and exchange of services instead of goods. These activities facilitate production that is undertaken in the secondary and primary sector. Exchange involves trade, transport and communication facilities.

Health, education, law, governance, recreation, etc are some examples of tertiary sector. These activities are performed by skilled labour, trained experts and consultants, e.g. plumber, doctor, lawyer, etc.

Types of Tertiary Activities

There are four types of tertiary activities. They are trade, transport, communication and services. These include provision of services in exchange of payments.

Trade and Commerce

Trade and commerce is essentially buying and selling of items produced elsewhere. The collection and distribution points where trading takes place are called **trading centres**.

These centres are divided into

Rural Marketing Centres They are quasi urban and cater to local needs and areas. Most of these have mandis (wholesale markets) and retail markets. In rural areas, there are **periodic markets** that may be weekly or bi-weekly and people from the nearby areas meet their demands. These markets are held on specified dates and shopkeepers move from one place to another.

Urban Marketing Centres These markets sell ordinary as well as specialised goods and services, e.g. markets for labour, housing, semi or finished products. Services of educational institutions and professionals like teachers, doctors, lawyers also develop.

Retail Trading In this type of trading, goods are directly sold to consumers. This trading is done through fixed establishments or stores, small shops, consumer cooperatives, big departmental stores and chain stores. The chain stores buy commodities in bulk and then hire skilled specialists for executive tasks. Street peddling, handcarts, trucks, door-to-door, mail order, telephone and Internet are examples of non-store retail trading.

Wholesale Trading Here bulk buying takes place directly from the manufacturer by numerous intermediary merchants. The merchants/ wholesalers extend credit to retailers.

Transport

Transport is a tertiary activity in which people, materials and manufactured goods are physically carried from one place to another.

While selecting the mode of transport, distance, time and cost are seen. Distance can be measured as **km distance**, time taken to travel particular route as **time distance**, expense of travelling on a route as **cost distance.**

Factors Affecting Transport

Demand and routes are two major factors which affect transport services.

Demand Transport depends on the size of population and standard of living of people. The larger the population size, the greater is the demand for transport.

Route It refers to the transport network depends on location of cities, towns, villages, industrial centres, availability of raw materials, nature of landscape, type of climate, availability of funds, etc.

Network

A network is a well developed transport system that is made up of nodes and links. A node is a meeting point of two or more routes and every road that joins any two nodes is called a link.

Communication

Communication services involve the transmission of words, messages, facts and ideas. The development of transport facilitated communication as messages were carried by hand, animals, boat, road, rail and air.

But, new technology has made communication independent of transport, such as mobiles, telephony and satellites. Some of the communication services are discussed below

Telecommunications The development of modern technology has revolutionised communication and it has become direct and instantaneous, e.g. telegraph, morse code and telex in last century and now satellites, mobile, telephony, etc are used.

Mass Media Communication means through which messages could be sent to vast audiences around the world are called mass media. E.g. radio, television, newspapers, etc. The Internet has revolutionised the global communication.

Services

There are different levels at which services are provided and availed. Some are meant for industry, some for people, and some for both industry and people i.e., transport. Services can be divided into three sub-categories. They are

Low Order Services It includes common and widespread services like grocery shops, laundries, etc.

Domestic Services It includes housekeepers, cooks and gardeners which migrate from rural areas in search of employment.

High Order Services These are specialised and less common like accountants, consultants and physicians. Some services are supervised and/or regulated by government like making, maintaining highways, bridges, fire fighting departments, education, healthcare, etc.

Thus, services are present in organised sector that is government owned or big corporations. Some are present in unorganised sector like low order and domestic services. **Mumbai's dabbawala** in India is one such service of unorganised sector.

People Engaged in Tertiary Activities

Earlier more number of people were employed in the primary and secondary sector as these sectors provided more jobs. But, now there has been a shift of jobs to tertiary or service sector. In developed countries, a higher percentage of workers are employed in providing services as compared to less developed countries.

Tourism

Tourism is part of service sector that refers to travel undertaken for purpose of recreation rather than business. This industry generates jobs as people are engaged in providing accommodation, meals, transport, entertainment, infrastructure retail trading and crafts.

Tourist Regions

- Tourism can be seasonal or throughout the year like warmer places around the Mediterranean coast, West coast of India during winters, mountains in summers or winter spots regions found mainly in mountainous areas.
- Historic towns, religious places, heritage sites offer tourism throughout the year.

Tourist Attractions

Tourist attractions are specific features of a place that attract people. These are as follows

Climate In winter holidays, areas having warm sunny weather is preferred like beaches in Southern Europe, so it attracts more number of tourists there.

Landscape Mountains, lakes, spectacular sea coasts and landscapes not completely altered by man are good tourist attractions.

History and Art Ancient or picturesque towns, archaeological sites, historically important places having castles and palaces attract tourists.

Culture and Economy Areas having rich cultures attract people as they go their to experience ethnic and local customs. Places giving economic benefits are also attractions such as cheap home stays in Goa, Madikere and Coorg in Karnataka.

Medical Services for Overseas Patients in India

Medical services or tourism takes place when medical treatment is combined with international tourism activity. People from developed countries like US are visiting India for medical tourism or services. This brings economic benefits to India and other countries where medical tourism is taking place like Thailand, Singapore and Malaysia.

Other medical related activities such as outsourcing of medical tests, data interpretation, reading radiology images, interpreting **Magnetic Resonance Images** (MRIs) and ultrasound tests are taking place in India, Australia and Switzerland.

Quaternary Activities

The activities related to knowledge oriented, involving collection, production and dissemination of information come under quaternary activities. They centre around research development and may involve specialised knowledge and technical skills.

People engaged in Quaternary Activites

Software developers, mutual fund managers, doctors, accounting, brokerage firms are some examples of people engaged in quaternary activities. They can be outsourced even as these are not tied to resources or affected by the environment or markets. This sector has replaced primary and secondary sector and absorbs half of the population in developed economies.

Quinary Activities

The activities that are highly specific and specialised are placed under it. These include high level decision-makers, administrators, government officials, research scientists, etc. They are also known as **gold collar professions**.

Outsourcing

- It means contracting out or giving work to an outside agency to improve efficiency and to reduce cost. It is termed as **off-shoring** when work is transferred to overseas location.
- Outsourcing provides employment in developing countries of India, China, Botswana, etc. Information technology, human resources, customer support, call centres, data processing and other IT related services are examples of outsourcing.

BPO

- BPO stands for **Business Process Outsourcing** which involves customer support services, call centres and similar other processes.
- The developed countries transfer these jobs as overhead costs are much lower making it profitable to get job work carried out.

KPO

- KPO stands for a **Knowledge Process Outsourcing** which involves skilled workers and enables companies to create additional business opportunities, e.g. e-learning, business research, etc.

The Digital Divide

- Development emerging from the information and communication technology is unevenly spread across the globe. Some regions have prospered while others are lagged behind. This is known as digital divide.
- In developing countries, this kind of divide is seen more than developed countries. Here, the metropolitan cities are developed more than rural areas.

PYQs Previous Years' Questions

1 Marks Questions

Multiple Choice Questions

1. Transport activities come under which one of the following sectors? *(CBSE 2023)*
   (a) Primary (b) Secondary
   (c) Tertiary (d) Quarternary

Ans. (c) Tertiary

2. Which of the following is a tertiary activity? *(CBSE 2023)*
   (a) Gathering (b) Hunting
   (c) Nomadic herding (d) Trading

Ans. (d) Trading

3. Which of the following is a quarternary activity? *(CBSE 2023)*
   (a) Catching fish (b) Iron smelting
   (c) Software developing (d) Basket making

Ans. (c) Software developing

4. Which one of the following activities is related to quaternary activities? *(CBSE 2023)*
   (a) Production of information (b) Fishing
   (c) Tourism (d) Trading

Ans. (a) Production of information

5. In a developed economy, the majority of workers get employment in which of the following sectors of economy? *(CBSE 2023)*
   (a) Primary sector (b) Secondary sector
   (c) Tertiary sector (d) Quaternary sector

Ans. (c) Tertiary sector

6. 'Retail trading' under which of the following activities? *(CBSE 2023)*
   (a) Primary (b) Tertiary
   (c) Quarternary (d) Secondary

Ans. (b) Tertiary

7. Which one of the following is not a characteristic of retail trading? *(CBSE 2023)*
   (a) It is concerned with sale of goods directly to the consumers.
   (b) Most of the retail trading takes place in fixed establishments.
   (c) Most of the retail stores procure their supplies from intermediate stores.
   (d) Retail trading constitutes bulk business through numerous intermediary merchants and supply houses.

Ans. (d) Retail trading constitutes bulk business through numerous intermediary merchants and supply houses.

8. Which of the following is not an example of Knowledge Processing Outsourcing (KPO)? *(CBSE SQP 2020)*
   (a) E- Learning
   (b) Intellectual Property
   (c) Collection of Information
   (d) Legal Profession

Ans. (c) Collection of Information

9. Which one of the following is a tertiary activity? *(CBSE Compartment 2020)*
   (a) Farming (b) Fishing (c) Mining (d) Teaching

Ans. (d) Teaching

10. Which one of the following is a Quarternary activity? *(CBSE Compartment 2020)*
   (a) Work of a lawyer
   (b) Collection, production and dissemination of information
   (c) Job of a farmer
   (d) Work of a fisherman

Ans. (b) Collection, production and dissemination of information

11. Which of the following is not a feature of an urban marketing centre?
   (a) They provide specialised services
   (b) The provide specialised markets
   (c) They are organised periodically
   (d) They provide ordinary services

Ans. (c) They are organised periodically

12. Which of the following is the example of tertiary activities?
   (a) Trade (b) Transport
   (c) Communication (d) All of these

Ans. (d) All of these

13. In tertiary activities 'exchange' involves which of the following?
   (a) Trade (b) Transport
   (c) Communication (d) All of these

Ans. (d) All of these

14. Which of the following is the example of non-store retail trading?
   (a) Mail order (b) Trucks
   (c) Internets (d) All of these

Ans. (d) All of these

15. Research and development institutions fall in which of the following category?
(a) Primary activities
(b) Tertiary activities
(c) Quaternary activities
(d) Quinary activities

Ans. (c) Quaternary activities

16. The towns and cities where buying and selling takes place are known as ....
(a) marketing hub (b) trading centre
(c) urban markets (d) outsourced market

Ans. (b) trading centre

17. Complete the following using the options given below.

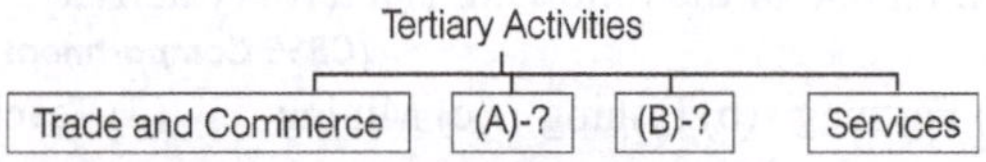

(a) (A) Specialist (B) Insurance
(b) (A) Information based (B) R and D based
(c) (A) Policy makers (B) NGOs
(d) (A) Transport (B) Communication

Ans. (d) (A) Transport (B) Communication

18. Which of the following activities are included under quinary activities?
I. Specialist II. Decision makers
III. Financial banking IV. Retail trade
V. Policy formulations

Codes
(a) I, II and III (b) I, II and V
(c) II, III and V (d) All of these

Ans. (b) I, II and V

19. Arange the following activities in the sequence from the lowest to the highest development stages.
I. Secondary II. Quaternary
III. Tertiary IV. Primary
V. Quinary

Codes
(a) V, II, III, I, IV (b) III, II, V, IV and I
(c) IV, I, III, II and V (d) II, V, IV, I and III

Ans. (c) IV, I, III, II and V

20. Match the following.

List-I (Sector)	**List-II** (Activities)
A. Tertiary	1. Information based
B. Quaternary	2. Policy formulation
C. Quinary	3. Transport

Codes

	A	B	C		A	B	C
(a)	3	1	2	(b)	1	2	3
(c)	2	1	3	(d)	1	3	2

Ans. (a)

Very Short Answer Questions

1. Analyse the development of service sector as an outcome of improvement in transport and communication. ***(CBSE SQP 2018)***

Ans. The service sector consists of services like transport and communication. Improvement in these services play an important role and facilitates economic development and growth for integrated economic development and growth of the country.

2. Write the meaning of 'medical tourism'. ***(Delhi 2019)***

Ans. When medical treatment is combined with international tourism activity, it is known as medical tourism. This kind of tourism brings abundant benefits to developing countries like India.

3. Write the meaning of 'Tourism'. ***(Delhi 2019)***

Or Define the term tourism. ***(Delhi 2012)***

Ans. Travelling with the motive of recreation rather than business is called tourism. It is a business of providing hotels, restaurants, entertainment, etc for people who are travelling.

4. Why is India a popular tourist destination in the world? ***(Delhi 2019)***

Ans. India is a popular destination in the world due to its climate, landscape, history and culture.

5. Evaluate the importance of 'quaternary activities'. ***(Delhi 2019)***

Ans. These activities center around research, development and may be seen as an advanced form of services involving knowledge and technical skills.

6. Give the meaning of digital divide. ***(Delhi 2014)***

Ans. A digital divide is an economic and social inequality arising in the countries due to unequal access and use of knowledge or Information and Communication Technologies (ICT).

7. Define the term 'quaternary activities'. ***(Delhi 2014, All India 2009)***

Ans. Quaternary activities refer to the more intellectual occupations whose task is to think, research and develop ideas. It is concerned with high-order of professional and administrative services, information generation, processing and transmission.

8. Define the term 'tertiary activities'. *(All India 2013)*

Ans. Tertiary activities are the activities related to providing services. They are different from production and do not process or manufacture goods directly. Professionally skilled people and trained labour are required in these activities, e.g. transport, communication, etc.

9. Give any two examples of quaternary activities. *(All India 2013, 2012)*

Ans. Examples of quaternary activities are

(i) Collection of information.

(ii) Production of information.

10. Give the meaning of retail trading services. *(All India 2013, 2011)*

Ans. Retail trading services link the producers with consumers. It is the business activity concerned with the sale of goods directly to consumers. Street peddling, handcarts, trucks, online order, etc are examples of non-store retail trading.

11. Give any two examples of tertiary activities. *(Delhi 2012)*

Ans. Examples of tertiary activities are trade and commerce and transport.

12. Who is an empowered worker? *(Delhi 2012)*

Ans. Empowered workers are people who are engaged in re-arrangement and interpretation and the use and evaluation of new technologies. They come under the category of quinary activities.

3 Marks Questions

1. Define Tertiary Activities. *(CBSE SQP Term II 2021)*

Ans. Tertiary activities involve the commercial output of services rather than the production of tangible goods. Here skilled people are needed who provide services to people against payment of fees. Common examples of tertiary activities are the work of a plumber, electrician, technician, launderer, barber, shopkeeper, driver, cashier, teacher, doctor, lawyer, publisher, etc.

2. Differentiate between retail trading and wholesale trading. *(CBSE SQP Term II 2021)*

Ans. The business activities concerned with the sale of goods directly to the consumers are known as retail trading, while wholesale trading constitutes bulk business through numerous intermediary merchants except retail stores.

3. Differentiate between departmental stores and chain stores. *(CBSE SQP Term II 2021)*

Ans. In departmental system, there is one store with many departments while in chain system, there are several shops and the shops are scattered over several places. Departmental stores deals in a large variety of goods while chain stores deals only in one commodity.

4. ''Transport is an organised industry created to satisfy man's basic need of mobility.'' Support the statement. *(CBSE Term I 2021)*

Ans. Transport is a tertiary activities which facilitates people, material and manufactured goods to be physically carried from one place to another. This is why it can be said "Transport is an organised industry created to satisfy man's basic need of mobility''.

5. ''The quaternary sector along with the tertiary sector has replaced most of the primary and secondary employment.'' Support the statement. *(CBSE Term I 2021)*

Ans. Both tertiary and quaternary sector replaced most employment from primary and secondary sector by providing more jobs and new opportunities. For example, in tourism sector, people are engaged in providing accommodation meals, transport entertainment, infrastructure, etc. On the other hand, quinary activities like outsourcing the work. Most of work is out soured in countries like India and China. It provided job opportunities to many youngsters which shifted from primary and secondary activities.

6. Growth of service sector in modern economies plays a vital role. Derive it's implications for such economies. *(CBSE SQP 2020)*

Ans. Services are an important constituent of modern economic development, which include retailing and sale of goods to the people, education, health and welfare, leisure, recreation and business services. Business services include advertising, recruitment and personal training. Service sector was not given as much attention as was given to the production of goods. But in advanced countries, service-based development has been very rapid. The growing importance of services has now given it an independent status as a productive sector in the economy. Instead of being an accessory to manufacturing or to the people at large, it is a huge contributor to a country's export.

It has generated foreign exchange for these economies. It is also a source of employment in the modern economies which has also resulted in reduced outmigration as people are able to get employment in the home country. It has increased the number of highly skilled workers. Thus, the growth of service sector is vital to these economies.

7. Define outsourcing. Which types of activities are outsourced? ***(CBSE SQP 2018)***

Ans. Outsourcing or contracting out is giving work to an outside agency to improve efficiency and reduce costs. When outsourcing involves transferring work to overseas locations, it is described by the term off-shoring.

The types of activities outsourced are as follows

- Information Technology
- Human Resources
- Customer Support
- Call Centre Services
- Manufacturing and Engineering Services sometimes.

8. Define quinary activities. Describe its features and importance. ***(CBSE SQP 2018)***

Ans. Quinary activities are services that focus on the creation, re-arrangement and interpretation of new and existing ideas; data interpretation and the use and evaluation of new technologies. People who perform quinary activities are highest level decision-makers or policy-makers.

They perform services which focus on the creation, re-arrangement and interpretation of new and existing ideas; data interpretation and the use and evaluation of new technologies. They are often referred to as gold collar professionals representing special and highly paid and skilled senior business executives, government officials, research scientists, financial and legal consultants, etc.

9. Explain any three characteristics of quaternary activities. ***(All India 2011)***

Ans. The three characteristics of quaternary activities are as follows

(i) Quaternary activities centre around research and development and may be seen as an advanced form of services involving specialised knowledge and technical skills.

(ii) Quaternary activities involve the collection, production and dissemination of information.

(iii) Like some of the tertiary functions, quaternary activities can also be outsourced. They are not tied to resources, affected by the environment or necessarily localised by markets.

10. Explain any three characteristics of periodical markets of rural areas in the world. ***(All India 2010)***

Ans. The three characteristics of periodical markets of rural areas in the world are as follows

(i) Periodical markets in rural areas are found where there are no regular markets. Local periodical markets are organised at different intervals.

(ii) These may be weekly, bi-weekly markets and people from the surrounding areas meet their demand.

(iii) These markets are held on specific days and move from one place to another. The shopkeepers thus, remain busy on all the days while a large area is served by them.

11. 'Outsourcing has resulted in opening up a large number of job opportunities in several countries.' Analyse the statement with three suitable examples. ***(Delhi 2009)***

HINT *Dear students, this question simply ask you to describe the role of process of outsourcing in creating more number of jobs worldwide with the help of suitable examples.*

Ans. Outsourcing has resulted in the opening up of a large number of call centres in India, China, Eastern Europe, Israel, Philippines and Costa Rica. It has created new jobs in these countries. Outsourcing is coming to those countries where cheap and skilled workers are available. These are also out-migrating countries. But with the work available in the form of outsourcing, the migration from these countries has come down.

This can be explained through these examples

(i) The Knowledge Processing Outsourcing (KPO) industry includes research and development, e-learning, business research, etc.

(ii) The Business Process Outsourcing (BPO) industry involves highly skilled workers. It is information driven knowledge outsourcing.

(iii) Data processing is another IT related service that employs large number of people in Asian countries.

12. How does the climate of a region attract tourists? Explain with examples from different regions of the world. *(All India 2009)*

Ans. The climatic conditions of any region decide the demand for tourism. The climate of a region attracts tourists in the following ways

(i) People from colder places want to visit warm places as tourist. That's why the Mediterranean lands and Southern Europe, due to their considerable higher temperature, sunny days and less rainfall attract tourists from Europe.

(ii) People from warmer regions love to visit colder places. That's why tourists from Northern plains of India prefer to go to tourist places located in the Himalayan region or other hill stations.

(iii) Climatic conditions of a region also provide some adventurous activities to do and attract tourists, e.g. ice skating and skiing in snowy regions, sea surfing on beaches, etc.

13. Compare the features of rural and urban marketing centres of the world in three points. *(Delhi 2008)*

Ans. Comparison between the features of rural and urban marketing centres is given below

Basis	Rural Marketing Centres	Urban Marketing Centres
Serving area	They provide services to nearby settlements.	They serve needs of a large area as compared to rural marketing centres.
Nature of services	They serve as trading centres of quasi urban type. Personal and professional services are not well-developed here.	They provide specialised urban services. They provide ordinary goods and services as well as many of the specialised goods and services.
Types of services	They are local collecting and distributing centres. Most of these have mandis (wholesale markets) and also retailing areas.	Urban centres offer manufactured goods as well as many specialised markets develop, e.g. markets for labour, housing, semi or finished products, services of educational institutions and professionals such as teachers, lawyers, physicians, etc.

5 Marks Question

1. How do quaternary services differ from tertiary services? Give three reasons why the service sector in developing and developed countries is growing faster than the manufacturing sector? *(CBSE SQP Term II 2022)*

Other Similar Questions

Or How service sector is growing faster than the manufacturing sector in developing and developed countries?

Or What are the reasons for growth of service sector over the manufacturing sector?

Ans. The activities concerning knowledge such as education, information, research and development and more intellectual activities where the major task is to think, research and develop ideas are quaternary activities. For example, as a medical transcription and a CEO of an MNC work under quaternary sector. Tertiary activities are related to service sector.

These activities include the segment of economy that provides services to consumers such as transport, communication, education, health, etc. Here skilled people are needed who provide services to people against payment of fees. Such as doctors, lawyers, publishers, electrician, technician and so on.

The service sector in developing and developed countries is growing faster than the manufacturing sector due to following reasons

(i) The rising per capita income in both, developed and developing countries has generated proportionately larger increase in the many kinds of services such as trade, transport, real estate financial banking etc.

(ii) There is also demand for educational services at all levels with the increase in the demand for literacy and computer skills at the workplace.

(iii) The increasing living standard of people has resulted in rising demand for services such as transport, tourism, sports, etc.

2. "Modern economic development in the world is mainly the result of the development of quaternary services." Explain the statement with suitable examples. *(CBSE SQP 2019)*

Ans. Modern economic development in the world is mainly the result of the development of quaternary activities in the following ways

(i) The quaternary sector along with the teritary sector has replaced most of the primary and secondary employment as the basis for economic growth.

Over half of all workers in developed economies are in the 'Knowledge Sector' and there has been a very high growth in demand for and consumption of information based services from mutual fund managers to tax consultants, software developers and statisticians.

(ii) Personnel working in office buildings, elementary schools and university classrooms, hospitals and doctors' offices, theatres, accounting and brokerage firms all belong to this category of services.

(iii) Like some of the tertiary functions, quaternary activities can also be outsourced. They are not tied to resources, affected by the environment, or necessarily localised by market.

3. What is tourism? Analyse any four tourist attractions in the world. ***(Delhi 2016)***

Or Define the term tourism. Explain any four factors which attract tourists in the world. ***(Delhi 2013)***

Ans. Tourism is travel which is done for the purpose of recreation rather than business. It is one of the largest sectors of tertiary activities in terms of providing employment. It also generates the largest revenue.

The four factors which attract tourists in the world are as follows

Factors that attract tourists in the world
- Climate
- Landscape
- Culture and economy
- History and art

Climate The climatic conditions of any region decide the demand for tourism. People from colder places want to visit warm places and *vice versa*. People from hilly terrain want to visit beaches and people living around sea-shore wish to visit hilly areas, e.g. the Mediterranean lands and Southern Europe, due to their considerable higher temperature during winters attract tourists from Europe.

Landscape Attractive environment like mountains, lakes, spectacular sea coasts and landscapes not completely altered by man are important tourist destinations.

History and Art The archaeological site attracts more people because of its rich past. The area with historical remains like castles, forts, battle fields, palaces, religious monuments, excavation sites are tourist attractions.

Culture and Economy For experiencing ethnic and local customs, tourists like to visit a place. Besides, if a region provides the needs of tourists at a cheap cost, it is likely to become very popular.

4. What is medical tourism? Explain the scope of medical services for overseas patients in India. ***(All India 2015)***

Ans. When medical treatment is combined with international tourism activity, it leads itself to what is commonly known as medical tourism.

The scope of medical tourism for overseas patients in India is as follows

(i) In 2005, about 55,000 patients from USA visited India for treatment. In this way, India has emerged as the leading country of medical tourism in the world.

(ii) It brings foreign currency to India.

(iii) World class hospitals with latest technology are located in metropolitan cities of India. These hospitals cater to patients all over the world.

(iv) This kind of tourism brings abundant benefits to developing countries like India.

Therefore, medical tourism has wide scope in India.

5. 'Services are very important aspect for economic development of a country.' Analyse the statement by explaining five components of a service sector. ***(Delhi 2011)***

Ans. Service sector is very important for the development of economy in the world. It is related to all kinds of services like education, health, welfare, business services, etc in exchange of payments. This sector also provides employment to a large number of people.

The major components of services are

(i) Business services like advertising, legal services, public relations and counselling.

(ii) Finance, insurance and real estate includes banking services.

(iii) Wholesale and retail trading with the producers and consumers.

(iv) Transport and communication such as railway, roadway, shipping, airline services, etc.

(v) Entertainment and mass media such as television, radio, films, magazines and newspapers.

Source Based Questions

1. Read the given passage carefully and answer the questions that follow **(CBSE 2023)**

When you fall ill you go to your family doctor or you call a doctor. sometimes your parents take you to a hospital for treatment. While in school, you are taught by your teachers. In the event of any dispute, legal opinion is obtained from a lawyer. Likewise, (there are many professionals who provide their services against payment of their fee. Thus, all types of services are special skills provided in exchange of payments.) Health education, law, governance and recreation, etc require professional skills.

These services require other theoretical knowledge and practical training. Tertiary activities are related to the service sector. Man power is on important component of the service sector as most of the tertiary activities are performed by skilled labour, professionally trained experts and consultants.

In the initial stages of economic development, larger proportion of people worked in the primary sector. In a developed economy, the majority of workers get employment in tertiary activity and a moderate proportion is employed in the secondary sector.

(i) Explain the main difference between secondary and tertiary activities.

(ii) How have tertiary activities related both production and exchange?

(iii) Mention any two tertiary activities.

Ans. (i) The main difference between secondary and tertiary activities is that the secondary sector includes industries that use basic materials to form new and improved materials. On the other hand, the tertiary sector includes industries that supply the materials made by the secondary industries to the consumers.

(ii) Tertiary activities include both production and exchange. The production involves the 'provision' of services that are 'consumed'. The output is indirectly measured in terms of wages and salaries. Exchange, involves trade, transport and communication facilities that are used to overcome distance.

(iii) Important tertiary activities are Finance, Banking, Administration, Tourism, Trade, Insurance Communication.

CHAPTER TEST

01 Marks Questoins

1 Which one out of the following statements is not true?
(a) Outsourcing reduces costs and increases efficiency.
(b) There may be dissatisfaction among job seekers in the countries that outsource the job.
(c) At times engineering and manufacturing jobs can also be outsourced.
(d) BPOs have better business opportunities as compared to KPOs.

2 **Assertion** (A) India has emerged as the leading country in medical tourism in the world.
Reason (R) There has been a positive growth in the medical facilities in India during the past 30 years.
Codes
(a) Both A and R are true and R is the correct explanation of A
(b) Both A and R are true, but R is not the correct explanation of A
(c) A is true, but R is false
(d) A is false, but R is true

3 Identify the advantage(s) of outsourcing from the following points.
(a) Tax saving (b) Low operating cost
(c) Transfer of technology (d) All of these

4 Which of the following activities are usually outsourced?
(a) Manufacturing (b) Training of personnel
(c) Research (d) Customer support

5 Outsourcing may result in which of the following advantages for developing countries?
(a) Increase in foreign investment
(b) Increase in level of technology
(c) Decrease in out migration
(d) Increase in level of education

Answers
1. (d) | 2. (a) | 3. (d) | 4. (d) | 5. (c)

03 Marks Questions

6 How many types of retail stores are there? Give in brief.

7 Which reasons are responsible for the rise in service sector? Explain in brief.

8 What are quaternary activities? Explain any three characteristics of quaternary activities.

05 Marks Questions

9 Why transport and communication services are significant for a region? Discuss in detail.

10 Explain the term medical tourism. What is the scope of medical services for overseas patients in India?

11 How many types of different marketing centres are there which try to provide services by targeting different markets?

07

Transport and Communication

TREND ANALYSIS 3 YEARS

Average No. of Questions Across all Sets

	Types of Questions	2023	2020	2019
TOPIC 01 Transport	1 Mark	1	–	–
	3 Marks	1	–	–
	5 Marks	5	–	2
TOPIC 02 Communication	1 Mark	–	–	–
	3 Marks	–	–	–
	5 Marks	–	–	–

Natural resources, the economic activities and markets are rarely found in one place. Therefore, transport and communication establish links between producing and consuming centres and also provide the network of routes, channels and carriers through which trade takes place.

Transport

Transport is a facility or a service for the carriage of persons and goods from one place to another using humans, animals and different kinds of vehicles. It is an organised service industry that handles loading, unloading and delivery.

Modes of Transportation

- The main modes of transportation are land, water, air and pipelines. These are used for inter-regional and intra-regional transport, and each one (except pipelines) carries both passengers and goods.
- Several places (nodes) join together by a series of routes (links) to form a pattern is called **transport network**.

Land Transport

This includes movement of goods and services over land i.e. roads and rails. Earlier, humans themselves were carriers such as in palanquin (palki or doli), later **pack animals** such as mules, horses, camels were used. Dogs and reindeers were used in North America.

In India, bullocks were used to pull carts. The revolution came after invention of steam engine in 18th century that started railways and roadways with the invention of internal combustion engines.

Among the **new means of land transport** are pipelines, ropeways and cableways. Rope and cableways are generally found on steep mountain slopes and mines, which are not suitable for building roads.

Roads

It is most economical for short distance and gaining importance for freight transport due to its door to door service. Metalled roads are all weather roads while unmetalled roads are not serviceable in all seasons due to their simple construction. Though heavy rains and floods make both the roads unserviceable. The quality, construction and maintenance of roads are better in developed countries than in developing countries as it requires heavy expenditure.

Road Density

- The total motorable road length of the world is only about 15 million km, in which North America separately accounted 33%. Although, **North America** in compare to Western Europe registered **highest number of vehicles** as well as **highest road density**.
- Road density is the total length of roads per hundred square kilometre of area.

Traffic Flows

- It refers to traffic on roads that has increased dramatically in recent years. As the road network cannot cope with the demands of traffic, so congestion occurs.

Highways

- They are metalled roads connecting distant places for unobstructed vehicular movement. These are 80m wide with separate traffic lanes, bridges, flyovers and dual carriageways.
- In North America, there is dense network of highways. Pacific coast is linked to Atlantic coast, Vancouver is connected to Newfoundland by Trans-Canadian highway and Edmonton is connected to Anchorage through Alaskan highway.
- Trans-continental Stuart highway connects Darwin, Melbourne to Alice springs in Australia. Europe has well developed highway network. Moscow-Vladivostok highway is important for Russia. Highways criss-cross the country in China.
- In India, **National Highway No.7 (NH7)** connecting Varanasi and Kanyakumari is the **longest highway of the country**.
- The golden quadrilateral or super expressway is under construction. (Now, NH-44 became the longest running highway in India. It connects Srinagar to Kanyakumari. NH-7 is renamed as National Highway 44). In Africa, Algiers in North is connected to Guinea and Cairo connected to Capetown in South.

Border Roads

- These are roads laid along international boundaries. These roads help in transport of goods to border areas and military camps.

Railways

Railways are best suited for the transportation of bulky goods and passengers over long distances. Highly industrialised areas, urbanised regions and mineral rich areas are linked to railways for the transportation of ores, grains, timber and machinery. All the continents have dense network while Europe is having the highest density of railways.

The railway network of Africa, Asia and South America connects the mineral rich and fertile areas and is developed primarily to utilise the natural resources.

Trans-Continental Railways

The railway line that runs across the continent and links its two ends is called a trans-continental railway line. They are constructed for economic and political reasons. The following are the most important of these

Trans-Siberian Railway

- It is in Russia and the **longest railway** in the world (9332 km). It runs between St. Petersburg in West to Vladivostok in East, passing through Moscow, Irkutsk, Chita, etc. It links important agro centre with fur centre connecting rail routes to important cities of Asia.

Trans-Canadian Railway

- Constructed in 1886, it is 7050 km long railway in Canada that links Halifax in East to Vancouver in West. It passes through the industrial region connecting the wheat belt of Prairies and the coniferous forest area so it is considered economic artery of Canada. **Wheat** and **meat** are the important exports on this route.

The Union and Pacific Railway

- This rail line connects New York on the Atlantic coast to San Francisco on the Pacific coast passing through Cleveland, Chicago, Omaha, Evans, Ogden and Sacramento. The most valuable exports on this route are ores, grain, paper, chemicals and machinery.

The Australian Trans-Continental Railway

- This rail line runs West-East across the Southern part of the continent from Perth on the West coast to Sydney on the East coast passing through Kalgoorlie, Broken hill and Port Augusta. Another North-South line connects Adelaide and Alice spring and to be joined later to the Darwin-Birdum link.

The Orient Express

- This line runs from Paris to Istanbul passing through Strasbourg, Munich, Vienna, Budapest and Belgrade. It has reduced the 10-day journey to only 4 days. Cheese, wine, bacon, oats, fruits and machinery are chief exports on this rail route.

Water Transport

This is the cheapest mode of transport as no construction cost is there and very little maintenance cost. The linking of oceans have brought greater navigation with ships of various sizes. Water transport is divided into sea routes and inland waterways.

1. Sea Routes

Sea and oceans provide smooth highway traversable in all directions with no maintenance costs. Modern passenger ships and cargo ships are equipped with various navigation aids. The important sea routes are as follows

- **North Atlantic Sea Route** It links North-Eastern USA and North-Western Europe. It is the **busiest in the world** and also called **Big Trunk route.**
- **The Mediterranean Indian Ocean Sea Route** This route passes through the heart of the Old World and serves more countries and people than any other route. Important ports on this sea route are Port Said, Aden, Mumbai, Colombo and Singapore.
- **The Cope of Good Hope Sea Route** This route connects industrialised Western Europe with West Africa, South Africa, South-East Asia, Australia and New Zealand. Natural resources such as gold, diamond, copper, tin, groundnut, oil palm, coffee and fruits are transported through it.
- **The Southern Atlantic Sea Route** This route links West Europe and West African countries with Brazil, Argentina and Uruguay in South America. Traffic is less on this route because the countries falling in this route have similar products and resources.
- **The North Pacific Sea Route** This route connects the ports on the West coast of North America with those of Asia. These are Vancouver, Seattle, Portland, San Francisco and Los Angeles of American side with Yokohama, Kobe, Shanghai, Hong Kong, Manila and Singapore of Asian side.
- **The South Pacific Sea Route** This route is used for reaching Hong Kong, Philippines and Indonesia and also links Western Europe and North America with Australia, New Zealand and Pacific Islands *via* the Panama Canal. Panama is 12000 km far from Sydney. Honolulu is an important port on this route.
- **Coastal Shipping** Coastal shipping is a convenient mode of transportation with long coastlines, e.g. USA, China and India. This type of shipping can reduce congestion on land routes.

Shipping Canals

There are two canals that serve as gateways of commerce for both the Eastern and Western worlds. They are

- **The Suez Canal** Constructed in 1869, it is a man-made canal linking the Mediterranean sea and the Red sea. It is 160 km long and 11-15 m deep without any locks and sea water flows freely through it.
- **The Panama Canal** It is a man-made canal linking Atlantic ocean with Pacific ocean. It is 72 km long and involves a deep cutting for a length of 12 km and has 6 locks. It shortens the distance between New York and San Francisco by 13000 km by sea.

2. Inland Waterways

Rivers, canals, lakes and coastal areas are inland waterways for the transportation of cargo and passengers. The development of inland waterways depends on navigability, water flow and transport technology. The important inland waterways are

- **The Rhine Waterways** This waterway links the industrial areas of Switzerland, Germany, France, Belgium and the Netherlands with the North Atlantic sea routes. The river Rhine flows through Germany and Netherlands. It flows through a rich coal field. **Dusseldorf** is an important port in this region. This waterway is the **world's most heavily used.** More than 20,000 ocean-going ships and 200,000 inland vessels move from this waterways every year.
- **The Danube Waterway** The Danube river which is navigable upto Taurna Severin, emerges in the Black Forest. It is used mainly for the export of wheat, maize, timber and machinery.
- **The Volga Waterway** Volga is one of the developed waterways of Russia. It is navigable upto 11,200 km and drains into the Caspian Sea. It is connected to Moscow region and the Black Sea through Volga-Moscow canal and Volga-Don canal, respectively.
- **The Great Lakes-St Lawrence Seaway** The Great Lakes alongwith estury of St Lawrence river form a waterway in North America. **Duluth** and **Buffalo** are two important ports on this route.

- **The Mississippi Waterways** The Mississippi-Ohio waterway links the interior part of USA with the Gulf of Mexico in the South. Large steamers can move upto Minneapolis.

Air Transport

It is the fastest means of transport but it is very costly. Air transport has brought connectivity revolution in inhospitable deserts, mountainous regions and snow fields where other means of transport are not reachable. Due to high construction and maintenance cost, air transport is more developed in highly industrialised countries. Supersonic aircrafts cover the distance in very short time.

Inter-Continental Air Routes

USA accounts for 60% of airways of the world. Important cities are nodal points where air routes converge or radiate to all continents. Africa, Asiatic part of Russia and South America lack air services, sparser population or limited landmass or low economic development.

Pipelines

These are used to transport water, petroleum, natural gas, liquidified coal for an uninterrupted flow. Milk is supplied through pipelines in New Zealand. USA has dense network of pipelines. **Big Inch** is famous pipeline of USA that transports petroleum from the oil wells of the Gulf of Mexico to the North-Eastern states.

In Europe, Russia, West Asia and India, oil wells are linked to refineries through pipelines.

Communications

Long distance communication in the form of telegraph and telephone are important. In mid-19th century, **American Telegraph and Telephone Company** (AT&T) enjoyed monopoly. In developing countries, the use of cell phones has gained importance for rural connectivity.

Latest technology developments have resulted in **Optical Fibre Cables** (OFC). They allow large quantities of data to be transmitted that are virtually error free.

Now, the telecommunication merged with computers to form integrated networks termed as Internet.

Satellite Communication in India

Artificial satellites are deployed in Earth's orbit to enhance communication and improve connectivity. This is satellite communication which has reduced the per unit cost and time of communication also.

India developed its own satellite **Aryabhatta** and launched it on 19th April, 1979, **Bhaskar-I** in 1979 and **Rohini** in 1980. Bhaskar, Challenger and INSAT-IB satellites are used for long distance communication and weather forecasting.

Cyber Space-Internet

This is the latest technology in which there is instant connectivity by accessing the electronic computerised space. It is called **cyber space** or **Internet** and is encompassed by the World Wide Web (www).

Majority of Internet users are in USA, UK, Germany, Japan, China and India. The social and economic space has expanded through e-mail, e-commerce, e-learning and e-governance.

GPS (Global Positioning System)

GPS is a global navigation satellite system that provides location, velocity and time synchornisation. GPS is everywhere. One can find GPS systems in a car, smartphones and watches. GPS helps us get where we are going, from point A to point B.

Uses of GPS

Global positioning system is used in the following ways

- In finding location means determining a position.
- In navigation means getting from one location to another.
- In tracking means monitoring object or personal movement.
- In mapping means creating maps of the world.
- For timing means bringing precise timing to the world.

PYQs Previous Years' Questions

1 Mark Questions

Multiple Choice Questions

1. Which one of the following sea routes is the busiest in the world? *(CBSE 2023)*
   (a) The North Pacific Sea Route
   (b) The South Pacific Sea Route
   (c) The Northern Atlantic Sea Route
   (d) The Southern Atlantic Sea Route

Ans. (c) The Northern Atlantic Sea Route

2. Which two cities are connected by Channel Tunnel? *(CBSES QP 2022)*
   (a) London with Barcelona (b) London with Berlin
   (c) London with Paris (d) London with Rome

Ans. (c) London with Paris

3. Which of the following modes of transport provide door to door connectivity?
   (a) Airways (b) Railways
   (c) Pipelines (d) Roadways

Ans. (d) Roadways

4. For the transportation of high-value, light and perishable good, which mode of transport is most prefered?
   (a) Roadways (b) Airways
   (c) Waterways (d) Railways

Ans. (b) Airways

5. Where was the first public railway line opened?
   (a) France (b) USA
   (c) England (d) Germany

Ans. (c) England

6. Which Trans-Continental Railway line is longest in the world?
   (a) Trans-Canadian
   (b) The Union and Pacific Railway
   (c) The Orient Express
   (d) Trans-Siberian

Ans. (d) Trans-Siberian

7. The Union and Pacific railway line connects ....
   (a) New York and San Francisco
   (b) Chicago and Omaha
   (c) San Francisco and Chicago
   (d) New York and Cleveland

Ans. (a) New York and San Francisco

8. Which of the following sea routes is most important route in the world in terms of trade?
   (a) The Southern Atlantic Sea Route
   (b) The Cape of Good Hope Sea Route
   (c) The Mediterranean-Indian Ocean Sea Route
   (d) The Northern Atlantic Sea Route

Ans. (d) The Northern Atlantic Sea Route

9. Optical Fiber Cables (OFC) are mainly associated with which of the following activities?
   (a) Transport (b) Communication
   (c) Agriculture (d) All of these

Ans. (b) Communication

10. What is the name of first satellite launched by India in 1979?
   (a) Bhaskar (b) Rohini
   (c) Aryabhata (d) INSAT - IA

Ans. (c) Aryabhata

11. The Panama Canal connects the ....
   (a) Pacific and Arctic Ocean
   (b) Atlantic and Indian Ocean
   (c) Atlantic and Pacific Ocean
   (d) Indian and Pacific Ocean

Ans. (c) Atlantic and Pacific Ocean

12. The Golden Quadrilateral connects which of the following cities?
   I. New Delhi II. Shimla
   III. Mumbai IV. Surat
   V. Kolkata

   Codes
   (a) I, II and III (b) II, III and IV
   (c) I, II and V (d) I, III and V

Ans. (d) I, III and V

13. Which of the following are the advantages offered by water transport?
   I. It does not require any construction and thus reduces costs.
   II. The energy cost is low in water transport.
   III. The oceans are linked and can be navigated in all directions.

   Codes
   (a) I, II and III (b) II and III
   (c) I and III (d) I and II

Ans.(a) I, II and III

14. Match the following.

List I (Railway Gauge)	List II (Length)
A. Broad Gauge	1. 1 meter
B. Standard Gauge	2. 1.5 meter or more
C. Metre Gauge	3. 1.44 meter

Codes

	A	B	C		A	B	C
(a)	3	1	2	(b)	2	1	3
(c)	2	3	1	(d)	1	2	3

Ans. (c)

Very Short Answer Questions

1. Which country of the world has the highest road density? *(All India 2017)*

Ans. Monaco has the highest road density in the world.

2. Why is West Asia the least developed in rail facilities? Explain one reason. *(All India 2017)*

Ans. West Asia is the least developed in rail facilities because of vast deserts and sparsely populated regions.

3. Define the term 'Transport network'. *(Delhi 2015)*

Ans. Several places (nodes) joined together by a series of routes (links) to form a pattern is called transport network.

4. In which country are motorways called 'autobahans'? *(All India 2015)*

Ans. Motorways are called autobahans in Germany.

5. Mention the busiest ocean route of the world. *(Delhi 2014)*

Or Which is the busiest sea route in the world? *(All India 2011)*

Ans. The North Atlantic sea route also called Big Trunk route is the busiest ocean route of the world.

6. Name the seaports on each end of Suez Canal. *(Delhi 2014)*

Ans. In the North, it is Port Said in Mediterranean sea and in the South, it is Port Suez in Red sea.

7. Define the term road density. *(Delhi 2014)*

Ans. Road density is defined as the total length of road per 100 sq km.

8. What is the meaning of cyber space? *(All India 2014)*

Ans. Cyber space is the world of electronic computerised space. It is also called Internet. In other words, it is the means to communicate and access information over computer networks.

9. Name the most important inland waterway of Germany. *(All India 2014)*

Ans. The Rhine waterway is the most important inland waterway of Germany. This waterway is the most heavily used at the world level.

10. Name the terminal stations of 'Australian trans-continental railway.' *(Delhi 2013, 2009)*

Ans. Perth and Sydney are the terminal stations of Australian trans-continental railway.

11. Which highway connects North America and South America? *(All India 2013)*

Ans. The Pan American highway connects the countries of South America, Central America and North America.

12. Name the navigational canal that serves as a gateway of commerce for both the continents of Asia and Europe. *(Delhi 2011)*

Ans. The canal that serves as a gateway is Suez Canal.

13. Give the significance of river St Lawrence as an island waterway. *(Delhi 2011)*

Ans. A unique commercial waterway is formed by the estuary of St Lawrence river and the Great Lakes in the Northern part of North America. The ports on this route are equipped with all facilities of ocean ports. In this way, the inland waterway has become an important commercial waterway.

14. Name the terminal stations of the orient express railway. *(All India 2011)*

Ans. Paris and Istanbul are the two terminal stations of the orient express railway.

15. Name the terminal stations of Australian Trans-continental railway. *(Delhi 2009)*

Ans. The terminal stations of Australian Trans-continental railway are Sydney and Perth.

16. Name the terminal stations of longest railway route in the world. *(All India 2009)*

Ans. The longest railway in the world is Trans-Siberian railway and its terminal stations are Vladivostok and St Petersburg.

17. Which is the famous petroleum pipeline of USA? *(All India 2008)*

Ans. The famous petroleum pipeline of USA is called Big Inch.

3 Marks Questions

1. Explain why all forms of transport are also referred to as lines of communication. *(CBSE 2023)*

Ans. All forms of transport also referred to as lines of communication. It is due to the fact that in ancient times means of transport and communication both were complimentary to each other. In olden periods, when there was no invention of mobile telephony and internet services, the communication was dependent on means of transport alone as written messages were carried by hand, animals, boat, road, rail and air from one place to another place.

With the invention of new technologies in communication like internet, satellite communication, etc this dependence on means of transport is reducing. But all forms of communication are not fully disassociated with transport because of the cheapness of the older systems. Thus, very large volumes of mail continue to be handled by post offices all over the world.

2. Road transport plays a vital role in the promotion of trade and tourism in the world. Support this statement with three suitable arguments. *(CBSE SQP Term II 2022)*

Ans. Road transport plays a vital role in the promotion of trade and tourism in the world. It can be supported with the following examples

(i) Modern society requires speedy and efficient road transport system to assist in the production, distribution and consumption of goods.

(ii) The opening-up of tourist areas has been aided by improvement in transport facilities. Road transport provides link between the origin and destination of tourist places.

(iii) Road transport facilitates the movements of holiday makers, business travellers, people visiting relatives and those undertaking educational and health tourism.

3. Describe any three major problems of road transport in the world. *(Delhi 2018)*

Ans. The three major problems of road transport in the world are as follows

(i) In times of heavy rain, floods seriously damage road networks.

(ii) Construction and maintenance cost of roads is huge which affect the quality of roads greatly, especially in developing countries.

(iii) Traffic jam is another problem associated with road transport. Both developed and developing countries face this problem.

4. What is cyber space? Describe any two advantages of Internet. *(Delhi 2013)*

Ans. Cyberspace is the world of electronic digital space. In other words, it is a digital world used as a means to communicate or access information over computer networks.

Advantages of Internet are as follows

(i) Internet has widened the economic and social space of humans through e-mail, e-commerce, e-learning and e-governance.

(ii) Internet as a modern communication system has made the concept of global village a reality.

5. Mention the famous oil pipeline of the USA. How are pipelines one of the most convenient modes of transport? *(Delhi 2011)*

Ans. There is a dense network of oil pipelines in USA which run from the producing areas to consuming areas. One such famous pipeline called Big Inch carries petroleum from the oil wells of the Gulf of Mexico to the North-Eastern states.

Pipelines are one of the most convenient modes of transport as they are used extensively to transport liquids and gases such as water, petroleum, oil and natural gas. They can carry liquid and gaseous materials for a long distance without any interruption or delays. The pipelines directly link the producing areas to the consuming areas. So they are one of the most convenient modes of transport.

6. Define the term 'transport'. Describe any four features of highways of North America. *(Delhi 2008)*

Ans. Transport is a service or facility for the carriage of persons and goods from one place to the other using different modes. Four features of highways of North America are as follows

(i) There is high density of highways in North America.

(ii) Every place in North America is within a distance of 20 km.

(iii) Cities located on the Pacific coast (West) are well connected with those of the Atlantic coast (East).

(iv) Likewise the cities of Canada in the North are linked with those of Mexico in the South.

5 Marks Questions

1. "Pipelines are used extensively to transport liquids and gases in the world." Support the statement with appropriate arguments. *(CBSE 2023)*

HINT *Dear student, this question simply ask you to describe the importance and uses of pipelines in the world with special reference to transportation of liquids and gases.*

Ans. The means of transport used extensively for carrying water, petroleum, natural gas and other liquids is pipeline transport.

Pipelines are used extensively to transport liquids and gases in the world due to its following characteristics

(i) It is most convenient and efficient means of transporting liquids and gases over long distances.

(ii) Pipelines can also transport solids after converting them into slurry (wet mixture).

(iii) Its initial set up cost is high, but after that, pipelines transport liquids and gases very cheaply.

(iv) It does not require much space.

(v) Pipelines are energy efficient and environment friendly.

Additional Info

Pipeline network can be found in the following regions

- In New Zealand, pipelines are also used to supply milk from farms to factories.
- USA has a dense network of oil pipelines which runs from producing areas to the consuming areas.
- In many parts of the world like Europe, Russia, West Asia and India pipelines are used to connect oil wells to refineries, and to ports or domestic markets. Pipelines are expanding very fast. For example, Turkmenistan in Central Asia has extended pipelines to Iran and also to parts of China.

2. Describe the development of railways in Europe and Russia. *(CBSE 2023)*

Ans. The development of railways in the Europe and Russia are discussed below

- Europe has one of the most dense rail networks in the world. The length of its rail network is 4, 40,000 km and most of which is double or multiple-tracked.
- Belgium has the highest density of 1km of railway for every 6.5 sq kms area. The important rail heads are London, Paris, Brussels, Milan, Berlin and Warsaw.
- Underground railways are important in London and Paris.
- The industrial regions show some of the highest densities in the world. Passenger transport is more important as compared to freight in these countries.
- The Euro Tunnel Group of England operates Channel Tunnel, which connects London with Paris.
- In Russia, railways alone accounts for about 90 per cent of the country's total transport with a very dense network to the West of the Urals.
- Moscow is the most important rail head with major lines extending outwards to different parts of country's vast geographical area. Underground railways and commuter trains are also important in Moscow.

3. Describe the benefits of water transport over railways. *(CBSE 2023)*

Ans. Benefits of water transport over railways are given below

- There is no need to build roads for water transport so, no maintenance cost is needed. Even yet, the cost of building and maintaining canals is much cheaper if they are utilised for purposes other than transportation, such as irrigation.
- While rail transport has very high maintenance costs, water transport has relatively low maintenance costs.
- It has a minimal operating cost, making it the cheapest mode of travel across large distances as compared to railways.
- Ships are the modes of transport that have a higher capacity for transporting a larger amount of goods. This is particularly true when compared to other modes of travel such as rail. Water transport enables the transportation of large and heavy items at a low cost.
- Although it produces very little environmental damage, oil leakage from tanks seems to be the primary issue with this method of transportation at times. If we want a green world with the fewest CO2 emissions, water transport will win since it typically has a lower carbon footprint as compared to railways.

4. Mention the major problems faced by global road transport in mountainous and hot desert areas. *(CBSE 2023)*

Ans. Global road transport plays an important role in the economy of the world. But it also faces major problems in mountainous and hot desert areas. These problems are given below

- **Topography** Mountainous areas pose significant challenges to road transport due to steep slopes, narrow roads, and sharp curves.

Road construction in such areas is costly and difficult, and maintenance can be challenging due to landslides, rock falls, and erosion.

- **Altitude** High altitude areas can cause problems for road transport due to thinner air, which affects engine performance, and extreme weather conditions such as snow and ice.

Major problems faced by global road transport in mountainous and hot desert regions
- Topography
- Altitude
- Extreme Temperatures

- **Extreme Temperatures** Hot desert areas can cause problems for road transport due to extreme temperatures that can damage road surfaces and affect tire performance. Extreme heat can also cause tire blowouts and engine overheating.

5. Explain the advantages and disadvantages of 'Air Transport', in the world. ***(CBSE Compartment 2022)***

Ans. Transportation plays a vital role in the economic growth of any country. It helps to promote trade, tourism and supports imperishable growth all around the world. Air transport is a rapid and sustainable way for moving human and bulky goods.

The advantages of air transport are as follows

Fast speed Air transport is capable of moving bulky cargo and hundreds of people very fast in any part of the world.

Rapid service Air transport is easy, dependable and definitely the fastest way to transport passengers and goods.

Low infrastructure Air transport travels totally on a natural path so it just requires very less investment for its maintenance.

No physical barriers As land routes have so many obstacles or barriers like divided regions need special permission every time which is not applicable while travelling by air.

The disadvantages of air transport are as follows

Costly service As compared to land transport, rail transport and water transport this is relatively more costly for its services.

Limited capacity Air trasnport provides fast means of transportation but it has the drawback of the limited capacity of goods which is better in other modes.

Unfit for cheap and bulky goods Since airways are costly due to numerous conditions, it becomes expensive to move cheap goods and also aircraft are small in size as compared to other modes.

6. What are the modes by which cyber space will expand the contemporary economic and social space of humans? ***(CBSE SQP 2019)***

Ans. Cyber space is very important in today's life. It enables us to communicate or access any information without physical movement of the sender or the receiver. It has brought the inhabitants of the world closer to each other.

One can now communicate with any person in any part of the world. Cyber space can be used in an office, a sailing boat, a flying plane and virtually everywhere.

Cyber space has expanded the contemporary economic and social space of humans through e-mail, e-commerce, e-learning and e-governance. It will be accessible to more and more people cutting across space and time under these circumstances. These modern communication systems have made the concept of the 'Global village' a reality.

7. Which are the major regions of the world having a dense network of airways? ***(CBSE SQP 2019)***

Ans. Airways are the fastest and the most expensive form of public transport. They lessen the travel time for long distances drastically. People who can afford the higher costs prefer to use airways as a time saver and a convenient mode. The importance of airways in commerce, for transportation of valuable cargo has also been growing in the perishable commodities sector.

The airways network is most dense in developed countries of Europe, North America, China, Japan, Australia, Singapore and in a few developing countries of Asia and Africa. Thus, a dense network of airways exists in Eastern USA, Western Europe and South-East Asia. USA alone accounts for 60% of the world's airways.

New York, London, Paris, Amsterdam, Frankfurt, Rome, Moscow, Karachi, New Delhi, Mumbai, Bangkok, Singapore, Tokyo, San Francisco, Los Angeles and Chicago are the nodal points where air route coverage is the maximum.

8. Describe the significance of 'Trans-Siberian Railway'. ***(All India 2019)***

Or Name the longest Trans-Continental railway of the world. Describe its any four features. ***(Delhi 2015)***

Ans. The longest Trans-Continental railway of the world is Trans-Siberian railway. Significance of the Trans-Siberian railways are as follows

- The Trans-Siberian railways runs from St Petersburg in the West to Vladivostok on the Pacific coast in the East. It is Asia's most important route.

- It links the Asian region with the West European market.
- It runs across the Ural mountains where Chita is an agro centre and Irkutsk, a fur centre.
- There are several connecting links to Mongolia, China and North Korea through this railway.
- This railway line covers a distance of 7,050 km running from Halifax in the East to Vancouver on the Pacific coast.

9. Classify means of communication on the basis of scale and quality into two categories. Explain any two characteristics of each category. ***(All India 2017)***

Or How are the means of communication classified on the basis of scale and quality? Mention any two features of each category.

Ans. Communication services involve the transmission of words and messages, facts and ideas.

It means conveyance of information from the place of origin to the place of destination through a channel. On the basis of scale and quality communication services can be divided into following types

Personal Communication Personal means of communication convey information between two people only. For example, postal services, telephone, telegraph and fax services, internet, etc.

Its major characteristics are

(i) It conveys information between two people only.
(ii) It is very fast and efficient way of communication.

Mass Communication Radio and television help to relay news, pictures and information to vast audiences around the world and hence, they are termed as mass media. Its major characteristics are

(i) It conveys information to large audiences.
(ii) They are vital for advertising and entertainment.

10. 'The Suez and the Panama Canal are two vital man-made navigation canals which serve as the gateways of commerce for both the Eastern and Western worlds.' In the light of this statement, explain the economic significance of these two canals. ***(Delhi 2016)***

Or Name the vital man-made shipping canal linking the Mediterranean sea and the Red sea. Write any four characteristics of this canal. ***(All India 2010)***

Ans. The Suez and the Panama Canal are the two vital man-made navigation canals.

Suez Canal links Mediterranean sea and the Red sea. It was constructed in 1869. It is the vital man-made shipping canal which acts as a linkage between Eastern and Western world.

Following are the main characteristics of Suez Canal

(i) Suez Canal links Port Said in the North and Port Suez in the South connecting the Mediterranean sea and Red sea.
(ii) It reduced the sea route distance between Liverpool and Colombo as compared to the Cape of Good Hope route.
(iii) It opens a new route to the Indian Ocean for the Europeans.
(iv) It has no locks.
(v) It is 160 km long.
(vi) The depth of Suez Canal is 10 to 15 m deep.

Panama Canal connects the Atlantic Ocean with the Pacific. It is an artificial 72 km waterway.

Following are the main characteristics of Panama Canal

(i) Panama Canal links Colon on the Atlantic Ocean to the Panama in the Pacific Ocean.
(ii) It shortens the distance between New York and San Francisco by 13,000 km by sea. The distance between Western Europe and West coast of USA is also shortened.
(iii) This canal is about 72 km long and involves a deep cutting for a length of 12 km.
(iv) It has six lock systems and ships cross the different level through these lock systems.

Both the canals are economically significant as they have cut down the sea route by many thousand kilometres. The ships can now reach faster and hence more trade is possible. Though, the economic significance of Panama Canal is less than Suez Canal.

11. 'Trans- Canadian railway line is considered as the economic artery of Canada.' Support the statement with suitable examples. ***(All India 2016)***

Other Similar Questions

Or Why Trans-Canadian railway line is considered significant in Canada? Explain.

Or Explain the economic significance of Trans-Canadian railway line.

Ans. The Trans-Canadian railway line is considered the economic artery of Canada due to the following reasons

(i) This railway line covers a distance of 7,050 km running from Halifax in the East to Vancouver on the Pacific coast.

(ii) It connects important cities of Montreal, Ottawa, Winnipeg and Calgary.

(iii) It connects the Quebec-Montreal industrial region with the wheat belt of the Prairie region, thus gaining economic significance.

(iv) This line also connects the coniferous forest region in the North to Quebec-Montreal and the Prairies. All these regions have become complementary to each other.

(v) A loop line from Winnipeg to Thunder Bay (Lake Superior) connects this rail line with one of the important waterways in the world.

12. "The Rhine waterways is the world's most heavily used island waterway". "In the light of this statement, examine the significance of the waterway." ***(All India 2016)***

Ans. The Rhine waterways is significant in the following ways

(i) It is world's heavily used waterway with more than 20,000 ocean going ships and 200,000 inland vessels exchange their cargo in this route.

(ii) Huge tonnage moves along this stretch of the waterway.

(iii) The river Rhine is navigable for 700 km from Rotterdam in Netherlands to Basel in Switzerland.

(iv) It flows through a rich coal field which has made the whole region prosperous manufacturing area.

(v) The waterway links the industrial areas of Germany, France, Switzerland, Belgium, Netherlands with North Atlantic sea routes.

13. Explain the importance of 'communication services' in the world. ***(All India 2016)***

Ans. The importance of communication services in the world is as follows

(i) Communication connects the people living in different parts of the world, due to which trade is possible.

(ii) Communication through Optic Fibre Cables allows large quantities of data to be transmitted rapidly, securely and are virtually error free.

(iii) Communication through satellites has connected around 1000 million people in more than 100 countries.

(iv) Cyber space or Internet is the latest technology for accessing information over computer networks.

(v) New technologies have connected people and it is very easy to send or receive messages, information. This has made the concept of global village a reality.

14. Describe the journey of development of land transport from the days of humans as carriers and the cableways of today. ***(Delhi 2015)***

Ans. Land transport refers to the movement of goods and services that takes place over land by way of road or rails.

In earlier days, humans themselves were carriers. People were carried on palanquin (palki/doli). Later, animals were used as beasts of burden as on mules, horses and camels. With the invention of wheel, carts and wagons were made that facilitated land transport.

The revolution in transport came about only after the invention of steam engine. The first railway line was started in 1825 in Northern England and railways became the most popular and fastest mode of transportation.

The invention of internal combustion engine revolutionised road transport in terms of road quality and vehicles playing over them. Among the newer development in land transportation are pipelines, ropeways and cableways.

15. Which shipping canal links the Atlantic Ocean and the Pacific ocean? Explain its any four characteristics. ***(All India 2015)***

Ans. The canal that links the Atlantic and Pacific ocean is Panama Canal.

For the characteristics of Panama Canal refer to Q. 10. of 5 marks questions.

16. What is the importance of railways as a mode of land transport? Explain any four main features of the railway network in Europe. ***(All India 2015)***

Or Explain any five characteristics of rail transport in Europe. ***(All India 2012)***

Ans. Railways cover long distances and they are ideal for the transportation of bulky goods. Large number of people also travel by railways. They also form the connecting link between the ocean vessels, barges, boats, motor trucks and pipelines.

Following are the characteristics of rail transport in Europe

(i) Most of the railways in Europe is double or multiple tracked.

(ii) Total length of railway line in Europe is 440,000 km.

(iii) Belgium has highest railway density of 1 km of railway for every 6.5 sq km area.

(iv) In many countries of Europe, passenger transport is more important than freight.

(v) After the development of more flexible system of roadways and airways. The trans-continental railway line has become less important.

17. Which is the longest trans-continental railway of North America? Describe its any four features. ***(All India 2015)***

Ans. The longest Trans-continental railway of North America is Trans-Canadian railway.

For the features of Trans-Canadian railway, refer to Q. 11 of 5 marks questions.

18. State any three characteristics of water transport. Why is traffic far less on the Cape of Good Hope route? ***(Delhi 2012)***

Ans. Three characteristics of water transport are as follows

(i) Water transportation does not require route construction. The oceans are linked with each other and offer smooth routes travelable in all directions with less maintenance costs.

(ii) It is cheaper means of transportation because the friction of water is less than that of the land and energy cost is lower.

(iii) Very heavy cargo like coal, cement, timber and metallic ores can be transported through inland waterways.

The reasons for the less traffic on the Cape of Good Hope route are as follows

(i) There is limited development and population in South America and Africa, so demand is less.

(ii) Both South America and Africa have similar products and resources.

(iii) Large scale industries are only present in South-Eastern Brazil and Plata estuary.

(iv) There is little traffic on the route which links Rio-de Janeiro and Cape Town.

19. Which continent has the highest road density? Why do traffic congestions occur on road? Explain any three measures to solve the problem of traffic congestion. ***(Delhi 2012)***

Ans. North America has the highest road density. About 33% of world's total motorable road length is present in North America. North America also accounts for the highest number of vehicles as compared to Europe.

There is a problem of chronic traffic congestion in most of the cities of the world. The congestion occurs because of the failure of the road networks in meeting the demands of traffic. In recent years, the traffic on roads has substantially increased.

We can see peaks and troughs of traffic flow on roads at different times of the day.

The three measures to solve the problem of traffic congestion are as follows

(i) Mass Rapid Transit (MRT) system should be developed.

(ii) The public bus services should be improved.

(iii) Expressways should be developed to facilitate smooth traffic flow.

20. Explain the merits and demerits of road transport in the world. ***(All India 2012)***

Ans. Merits of road transport are

(i) It is the most economical mode for short distances as compared to railways.

(ii) It offers door-to-door services.

(iii) It is best suited for the transportation of perishable and breakable goods.

Following are the demerits of road transport

(i) Road transport is not sustainable in all seasons.

(ii) Unmetalled roads become unmotorable during rainy season. Metalled ones are also damaged by floods.

(iii) Road construction is very difficult in mountainous or desert areas.

Additional Info

Other merits of road transport are

- Construction of road is comparatively cheaper and easy.
- In road transport, it is very easy to monitor vehicles and goods.

Other demerits of road transport are

- The maintenance of roads requires heavy expenditure.
- Goods are susceptible to damage through careless driving.

21. Explain the significance of each of the transport and communication services available in the world. ***(Delhi 2010)***

Ans. Significance of various transport services are as follows

Road Transport It is cheaper and faster mode of transport over short distances and for door-to-door services.

Railways It is best suited for bulky goods and passengers for long distances.

Water Transport It is the cheapest mode of transport because of less friction of water.

Ocean routes are cheaper for carrying of bulky material from one continent to another.

Air Transport It is the fastest means of transportation. It is best suited for long distance travel and worldwide transportation of valuable cargo.

Pipelines It is used to carry liquids and gases from the producing areas to the consuming areas.

Significance of various communication services are as follows

Satellite Communication In contemporary time, satellites communication has become very important with Internet as the largest electronic network on the planet connecting about 1000 million people in more than 100 countries.

Significance of various transport services
- Road Transport
- Railways
- Water Transport
- Air Transport
- Pipelines
- Satellite Communication
- Cyber Space-Internet

Cyber Space-Internet This electronic network has spread unprecedently the number of users from 400 million in AD 2000 to over two billion in 2010. It has brought people from different parts of world closer to each other.

22. What is the significance of inland waterways? Explain the three factors responsible for the development of inland waterways in the world. *(All India 2010)*

Ans. Inland waterways consist of rivers, lakes, canals and streams linking the coastal areas. They have been used as waterways from time immemorial. Inland waterways are important for domestic and international transport and trade. Many rivers are modified to make inland waterways possible in different developed countries. The significance of inland waterways has been rising.

The three factors responsible for the development of inland waterways in the world are

Navigability This means width and depth of the channel that makes navigation possible.

Water Flow Another factor is continuous flow of water throughout the year so that ships, boats can easily move in the waterways.

Factors responsible for development of inland waterways
- Navigability
- Water flow
- Transport technology

Transport Technology Development of proper technology so that very heavy cargo like coal, timber, metallic ores can also be easily transported through inland waterways.

23. What are highways? Explain the significance of highways with examples from different continents. *(All India 2009)*

Ans. Highways are metalled roads constructed for uninterrupted vehicular movement. Highways link even city and port town in developed countries.

The significance of highways can be explained through the following examples

North America Highways link the cities located on the Pacific coast with those of the Altantic coast. Highway density is very high in North America, about 0.65 km per sq km. The Pan-American Highway connects the countries of South America, Central America and USA.

Europe In Europe, there is a well developed network of highways, but faces competition from railways and waterways.

Russia In Russia, important industrial regions are linked through highways. The Moscow-Vladivostok highway serves the region and it is one of the important highways of Russia.

China All the major cities in China are linked through the highways.

India In India, highways are connecting the major towns and cities. NH7 is the longest in the country which connects Varanasi and Kanyakumari.

Africa In Africa, Algiers in the North is connected to Conakry in Guina and Cairo is connected to Capetown through highways.

24. What is the importance of roads? Explain any three reasons for the existence of good quality roads in the developed countries. *(All India 2009)*

Ans. Roads are an integral part of the transport system of a country. They play a significant role in achieving national development and contributing to the overall performance and social functioning of the community.

Freight transport by road is gaining importance because it offers door-to-door service. Road plays a very important role in the socio-economic development of the country and become the backbone of strong economies and dynamic societies.

Therefore, it is legitimate and indispensable to safeguard an industry and plays a crucial role in everyone's life by meeting the demand for the sustainable mobility of both people and goods.

The reasons for the existence of good quality roads in the developed countries are as follows

(i) Road construction and its maintenance requires heavy expenditure. The developed countries have resources to meet this kind of expenditure.

(ii) Developed countries need good quality roads due to their constant requirement of linking long distance transportation in the form of motorways, autobahans, inter-state highways, etc.

(iii) There is greater intensity and need for speedy movement of vehicular traffic.

25. Write any six characteristics of the Suez Canal. **(Delhi 2009)**

Ans. For answer, refer to Q. 10 of 5 marks questions.

26. Describe any three advantages of water transport in the world. **(Delhi 2013)**

Or Mention any six advantages of oceanic routes. **(Delhi 2009)**

Ans. Advantages of water transport/oceanic routes are as follows

(i) There is no need to construct ocean routes so that cost is saved.

(ii) Because of the less friction of water as compared to land, it is much cheaper mode of transport.

(iii) Compared to land and air, ocean transport is a cheaper means for carrying of bulky materials over long distances.

(iv) It does not require maintenance.

(v) Oceans are linked with each other and the ship and cargo of various sizes can easily traversable in all directions.

(vi) Oceans offer smooth traversible highway in all directions.

27. Which is the busiest sea route in the world? Describe its four characteristics. **(Delhi 2008)**

Ans. The Northern Atlantic sea route or Big Trunk route is the busiest sea route in the world.

Four important characteristics of this route are as follows

(i) It connects the two industrially developed regions of the world which are North-Eastern USA and North-Western Europe.

(ii) It accounts for one-fourth of the world's foreign trade.

(iii) Ports on this route are highly advanced and equipped with the modern facilities.

(iv) This route exhibits highly advanced ports and harbour facilities.

28. Define the term 'Trans-Continental railways.' Write four characteristics each of Trans-Siberian railways and Trans-Canadian railways. **(Delhi 2008)**

Ans. Trans-continental railways connect the two ends of a continent while running across it.

For the features of Trans-Siberian railway, refer to Q. 8 of 5 marks questions.

For the features of Trans-Canadian railways, refer to Q. 11 of 5 marks questions.

Map Based Questions

1. Observe the given map and answer the following questions. **(CBSE SQP 2022)**

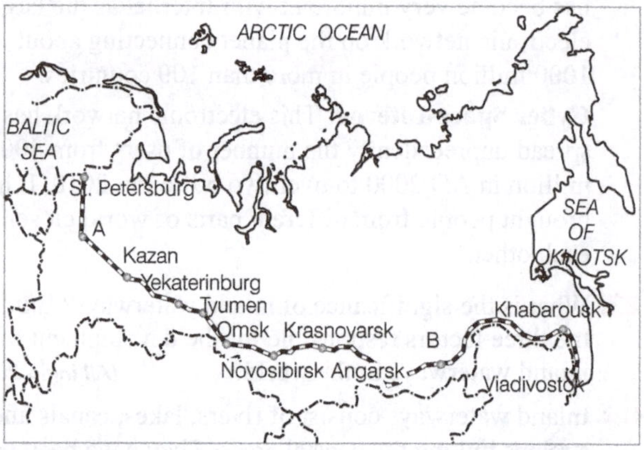

(i) Name the railway line and name the country where it lies.

(ii) Name the stations marked as 'A' and 'B'.

(iii) State two reasons why it is the most important route in Asia.

Ans. (i) The railway line mentioned in the given map is Trans-Siberian Railway line. It is located in Asiatic Russia.

(ii) Here, station 'A' is Moscow, while station 'B' is Chita.

(iii) It is the most important route in Asia due to the following reasons

- It has made it possible to link Asian markets with the European markets. Now, goods can be easily transported between the two continents, which provide a boost to the economies of both continents.
- It connects various commercial centers in Europe and Asia and provides push to trade and commerce. For example, it runs through Ural Mountains and connects Chita (agro centre) to Irkutsk (fur centre) connecting them to Odisa in the South.

2. Study the given map carefully and answer the following questions. ***(CBSE SQP 2018)***

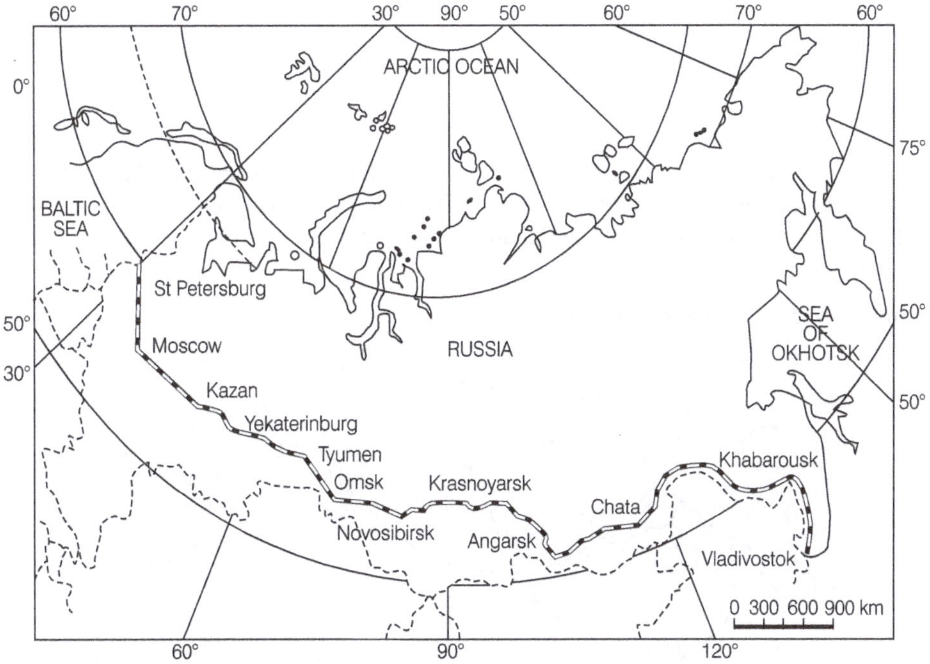

(a) Identify the railway line shown in the map. (b) Which two oceans are connected by this railway line?

(c) Give any one point of significance of this transport line.

Ans. (i) The railway line shown in the map is of Trans-Siberian Railways.

(ii) The two oceans connected by this railway line are the Arctic Ocean and the Pacific Ocean.

(iii) The railway line is very significant. The Siberian part of Russia is agriculturally developed so trade of foodgrains, sugar, etc takes place by this route. The rail route has helped in connecting Europe to Asian countries like Mongolia.

3. Study the following map of the Suez Canal carefully and answer the questions that follow. ***(Delhi 2018)***

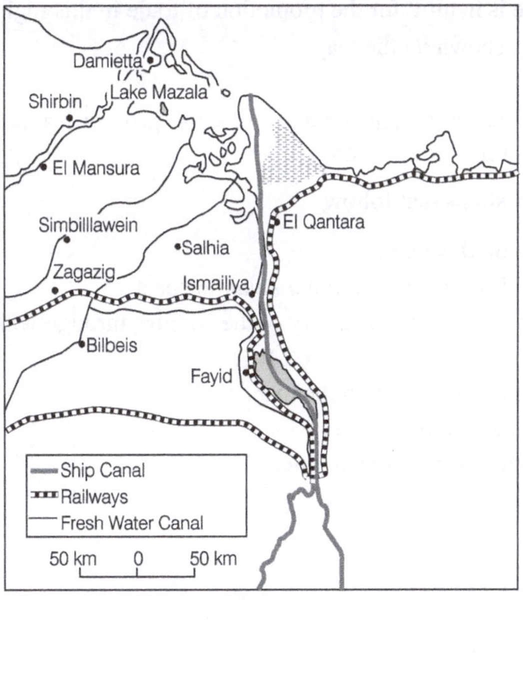

(i) Name the country through which this canal passes.
(ii) Name the seas connected by this canal.
(iii) Why is this canal considered a gateway of Europe to the Indian Ocean?

Ans. (i) Egypt
(ii) Mediterranean Sea and Red Sea.
(iii) Suez Canal was constructed in 1869 in Egypt between Port Said in North and Port Suez in the South. It is a sea level canal without locks and sea water flows freely through it. It is about 160 km and 11 to 15 metre deep. It provides a direct sea route for Europe in the Indian Ocean. Therefore, it is considered as a gateway of Europe to the Indian Ocean.

4. Study the map and answer the questions that follow. ***(All India 2014)***

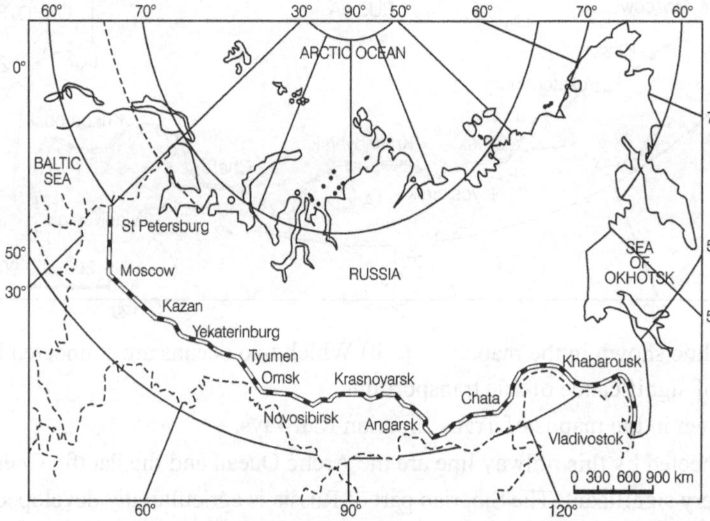

(i) Identify and name the railway line shown on the map.
(ii) Name the continents linked by this rail route.
(iii) Explain how this railway line is helpful for the promotion of trade in this region.

Ans. (i) Trans-Siberian railway line is shown on the map.
(ii) It connects Asia and Europe.
(iii) This railway line runs across the Ural mountain and connects agro centres like Chita and Irkutsk. It also acts as linkage between different manufacturing centres.

5. Study the map and answer the questions that follow. ***(Delhi 2014)***

(i) Name the railway line shown on this map.
(ii) Name the terminal station of this railway along the Atlantic coast.
(iii) Why is this railway line known as economic artery of the country through which it passes?

Or

(i) Name the Trans-continental railway shown in the map.
(ii) Name the terminal stations of this railway line .
(iii) Mention any two characteristics of this railway line.

Ans. (i) Trans-Canadian railway line is shown on this map.

(ii) Halifax is the terminal station of this railway along the Atlantic coast.

(iii) It connects Quebec-Montreal Industrial region with the wheat belt of the Prairie region and the Coniferous forest regions in the North. A loop line from Winnipeg to Thunder Bay connects this line with one of the important waterways. That's why is it called economic artery of Canada.

Or

(i) It is Trans-Canadian railway.

(ii) Halifax and Vancouver are the terminal stations of this railway line

(iii) Two characteristics of this railway line are:

(a) It is 7050 km long rail line in Canada.

(b) It connects the industrial region to wheat belt.

6. Study the given map and answer the questions that follow. ***(All India 2011)***

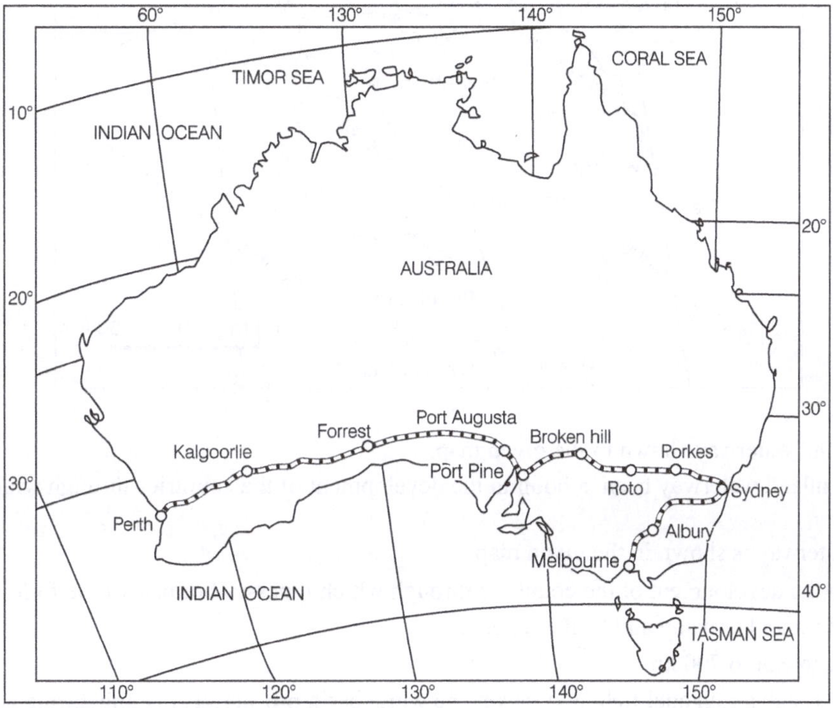

(i) Name the railway line shown in the given map.

(ii) Which are the two terminal stations of this railway line?

(iii) Name the ports located on the coast of Spencer Gulf through which this railway line passes. ***(All India 2009)***

Ans. (i) Australian Trans-Continental railway line is shown in the given map.

(ii) Perth and Sydney are two terminal stations of Australian Trans-Continental railway line.

(iii) Port Augusta and Port Pine are two ports located on the coast of Spencer Gulf through which this railway line passes.

7. Study the given map and answer the questions that follow. ***(All India 2009)***

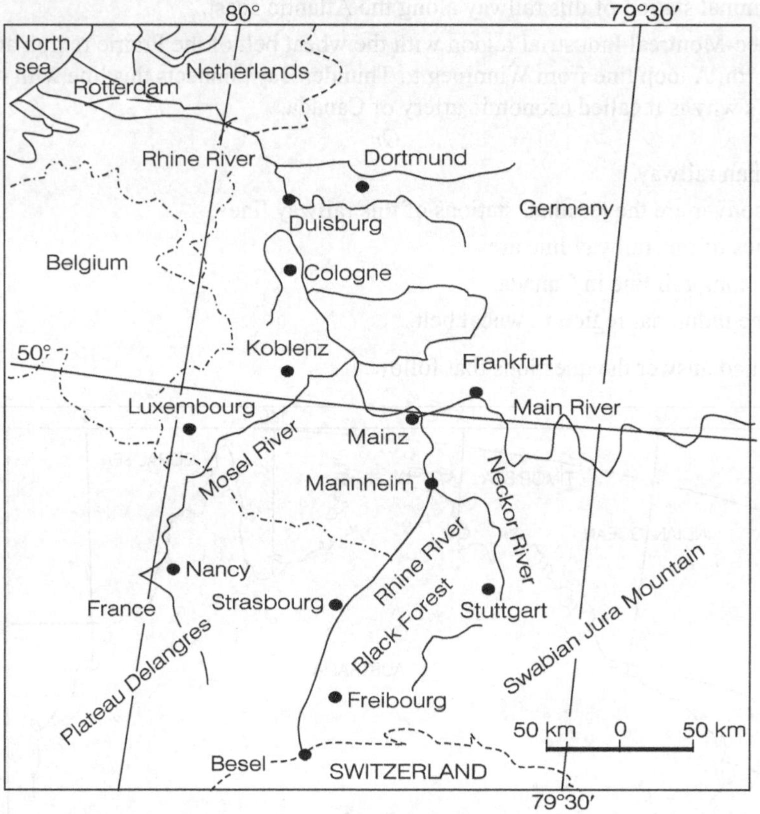

(i) Name the inland waterway shown in the given map.

(ii) How has this inland waterway been a boon in the development of the countries through which it passes? Explain.

Ans. (i) The Rhine waterway is shown in the given map.

(ii) It is a boon in the development of the countries through which it passes because of the following reasons

(a) It flows through Germany and Netherlands.

(b) It is navigable upto 700 km.

(c) It flows through a rich coal field and makes the white basin prosperous manufacturing area.

8. Study the map and answer the questions that follow. ***(All India 2008)***

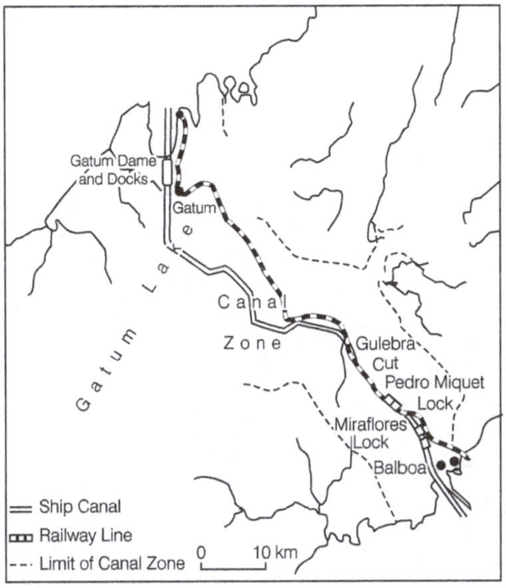

(i) Name the shipping canal shown in the map.
(ii) Name the oceans linked by this canal.
(iii) Name the country which has constructed this canal.
(iv) Why is this canal mostly used by USA?
(v) Why does this canal have lock system?

Ans. (i) The canal shown in the map is Panama canal.
(ii) The oceans linked by this canal are Atlantic ocean and Pacific ocean.
(iii) The United States of America has constructed the Panama Canal.
(iv) This canal is constructed by US Government to shorten the distance between New York and San Francisco which is 12,000 km apart by sea.
(v) The canal is at a higher elevation from sea level and it is made across mountain ranges.

9. Identify the following on the political map of the world.
(i) A major sea port. ***(All India 2016)***
(ii) An international airport. ***(All India 2016)***
(iii) A major sea port. ***(Delhi 2016, 2013, 2011, 2008)***
(iv) An international airport. ***(Delhi 2016)***
(v) A major sea port. ***(All India 2015)***
(vi) A major airport. ***(All India 2015, Delhi 2013)***
(vii) An important airport. ***(Delhi 2015)***
(viii) A major seaport. ***(Delhi 2015, 2014, 2012)***
(ix) A major railway terminal. ***(All India 2015)***

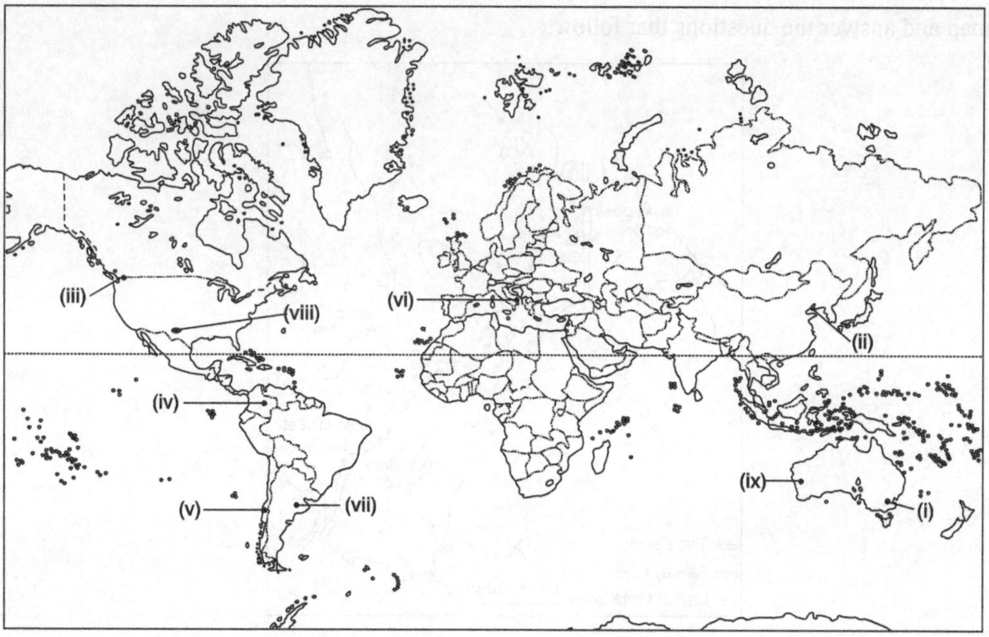
(iii)
(viii)
(vi)
(ii)
(iv)
(ix)
(i)
(v)
(vii)

Ans.

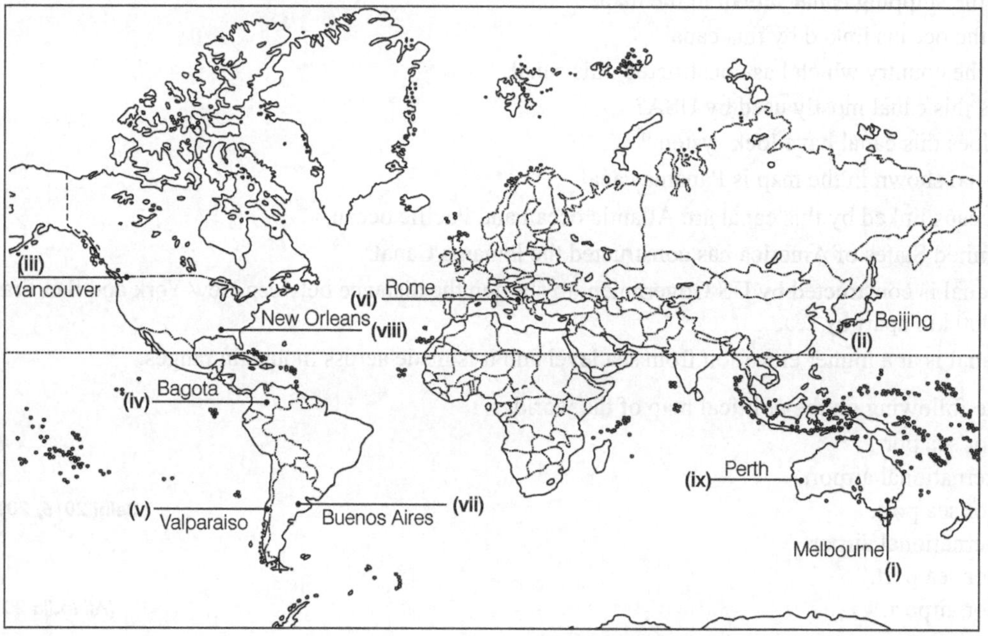
(iii)
Vancouver
Rome
(vi)
New Orleans
(viii)
Beijing
(ii)
Bagota
(iv)
Perth
(ix)
(v)
Valparaiso
Buenos Aires
(vii)
Melbourne
(i)

10. Identify the following in the political map of the world.

(i) Railway terminal station. *(Delhi 2015)*

(ii) A terminal station of Trans-Canadian railway line. *(All India 2014)*

(iii) An important seaport. *(All India 2014)*

(iv) A terminal station of Australian Trans-continental railway. *(Delhi 2014)*

(v) A major sea port. *(Delhi 2013, All India 2011, 2010)*

(vi) A major airport. *(Delhi 2013)*

(vii) Eastern Terminal station of Trans-Siberian railway. *(All India 2012)*

(viii) A major airport. *(All India 2011)*

(ix) A major airport. *(All India 2010)*

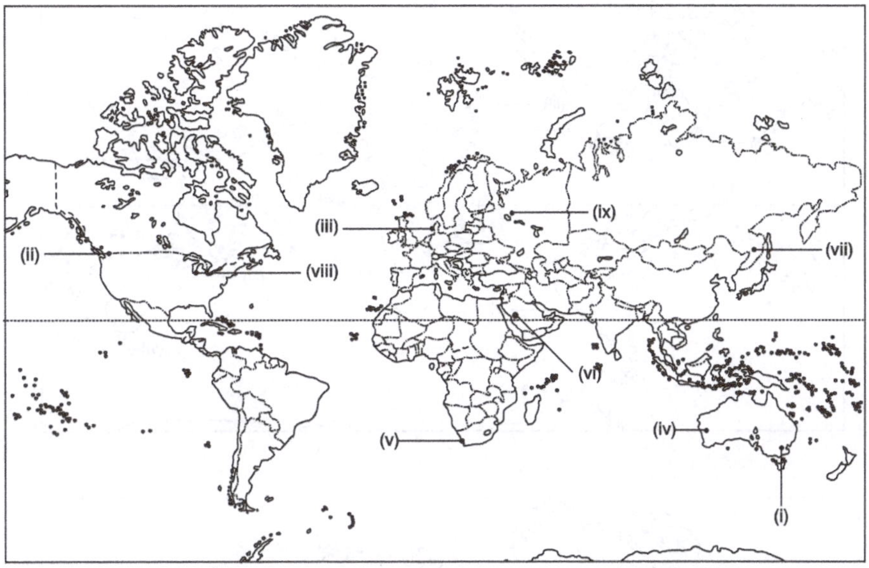

Ans.

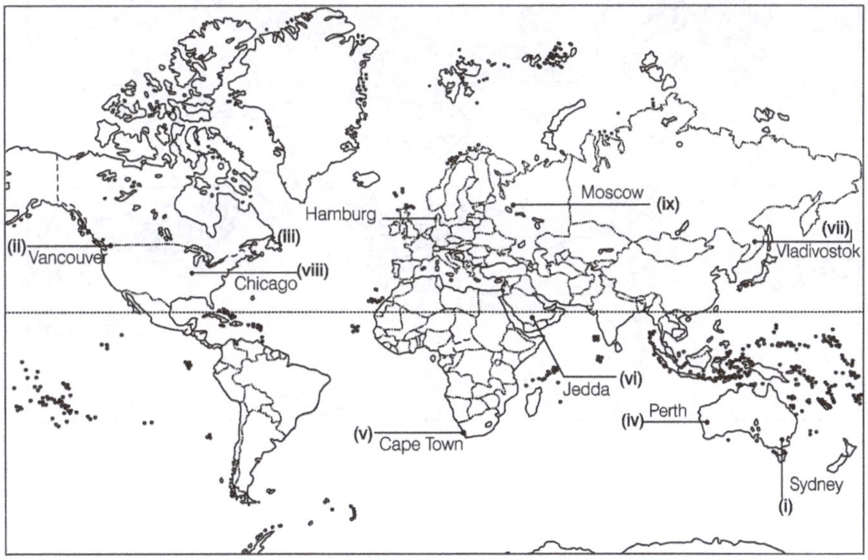

11. Identify the following on the political map of the world.

(i) A major airport. (ii) A major sea port. ***(Delhi 2012)***

(iii) A major sea port. (iv) A major airport. ***(Delhi 2010, All India 2008)***

(v) The important sea port of Brazil. ***(All India 2009)***

Or An important sea port. ***(All India 2008)***

(vi) The important sea port of New Zealand. ***(Delhi 2009)***

(vii) Major airport. ***(Delhi 2008)***

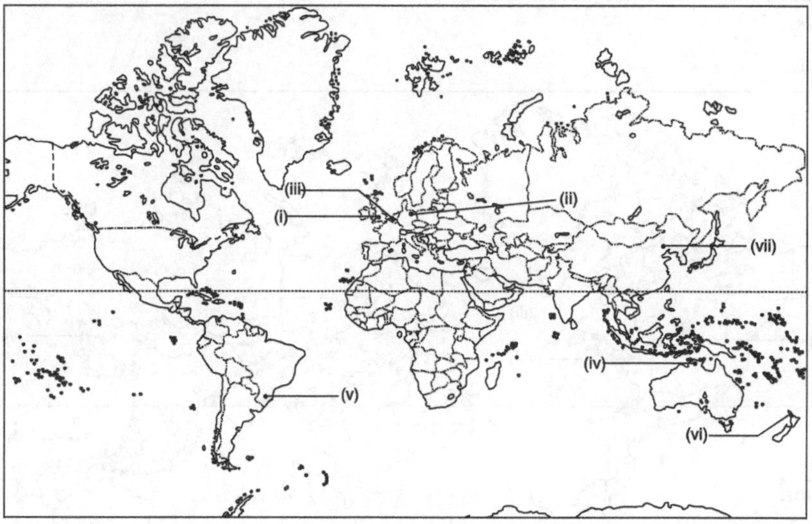

Ans.

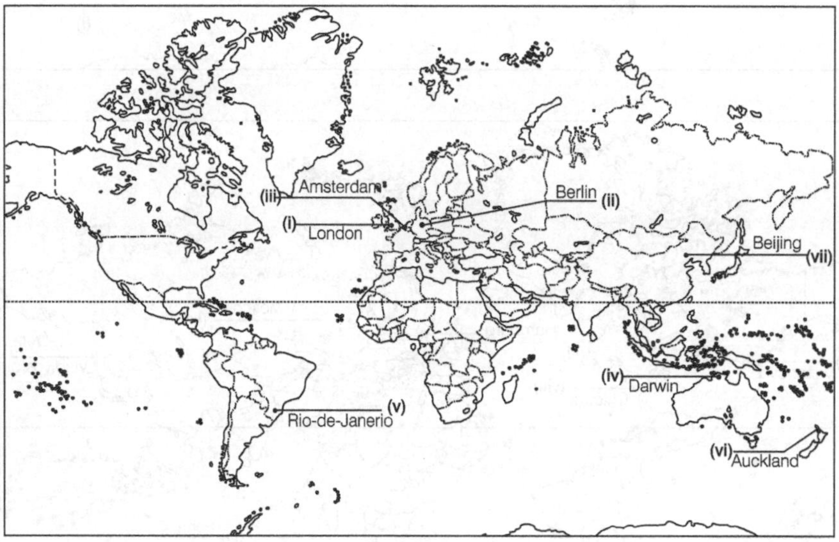

CHAPTER TEST

01 Mark Questions

1 The Trans-Canadian highway connects which of the following places of the world?
(a) Vancouver to Anchorage (b) Edmonton to Anchorage
(c) Vancouver to St John's city (d) Edmonton to Vancouver

2 Identify the highest railway line in the world from the following options.
(a) Nilgiri Rail line (b) Peruvian Railways
(c) Quinghai-Tibet Train (d) Darjeeling Railways

3 Which of the following is/are correctly matched?

Connects		Sea Route
(a) West Europe and West Africa	–	Cape of Good Hope Sea Route
(b) North America and Asia	–	North Pacific Sea Route
(c) N - E USA and N - W Europe	–	North Atlantic Sea Route
(d) All of the above		

4 **Assertion** (A) The first public railway line was opened in 1825 between Stockton and Darlington in northern England.

Reason (R) The revolution in transport came about only after the invention of the steam engine in the 18th century.

Codes
(a) Both A and R are true and R is the correct explanation of A
(b) Both A and R are true, but R is not the correct explanation of A
(c) A is true, but R is false
(d) A is false, but R is true

5 Consider the following statements about the later colonial period and choose the correct answer.
I. Highways are metalled roads connecting distant places.
II. They are constructed in a manner for unobstructed vehicular movement.

Codes
(a) Only statement I is correct
(b) Both the statements are true and statement II correctly present the reason for statement I
(c) Only statement II is correct
(d) Both the statements I and II are incorrect

Answers

1. (b) | 2. (d) | 3. (a) | 4. (a) | 5. (b)

03 Marks Questions

6 State the major problems of road transport in mountainous, and flood prone regions.

7 How railways are an important means of transport? State any four advantages of this mode of transport.

8 Write a short note on the North Atlantic Sea Route and the South Atlantic Sea Route.

05 Marks Questions

9 Explain in brief about the journey of development of land transport from the days of humans as carriers and the cable ways of today.

10 Discuss about the major regions of the world having a dense network of airways.

11 Mention the different modes by which cyber space will expand the contemporary economic and social space of humans.

08

International Trade

TREND ANALYSIS 3 YEARS

		Average No. of Questions Across all Sets			
		Types of Questions	2023	2020	2019
TOPIC 01	History of International Trade	1 Mark	–	–	–
		3 Marks	–	–	–
		5 Marks	–	–	–
TOPIC 02	WTO & Gateways to International Trade	1 Mark	–	–	–
		3 Marks	–	–	–
		5 Marks	–	–	–

Trade means the voluntary exchange of goods and services. Initial form of trade in primitive societies was **barter system**. It is a system in which direct exchange of goods takes place. In India, the **Jon Beel Mela** is held after the harvest season at Jagiroad near Guwahati where the barter system is still practiced.

The difficulties of barter system are overcome by the introduction of money. Before currency, rare objects like flintstones, obsidian, cowrie shells, tiger's paws, whale's teeth, skins, furs, cattle, rice, copper, gold, silver and even salt was used as a mode of payment. Salary word is derived from **salarium** that means **payment by salt**.

History of International Trade

- In ancient times, trade was restricted to local markets. Slowly long distance trade developed; of which **Silk Route** is an example. The route was 6000 km long connecting Rome to China and traders transported Chinese silk, Roman wool, metals, etc through this route. Later, sea and ocean routes were discovered and trade grew.
- The **Slave Trade** emerged in 15th century in which the Portuguese, Dutch, Spaniards and British captured African natives and sold to plantation owners in America. After Industrial Revolution, industrialised nations imported raw materials and exported finished products to non-industrial nations.
- International trade is the result of specialisation in production and division of labour. It is based on the principle of comparative advantage that is mutually beneficial to trading partners.

Basis of International Trade

The factors on which international trade depends are as follows

- **Difference in National Resources** The resources are unevenly distributed in the world. These differences mainly refer to geology, mineral resources and climate.
- **Geological Structure** This means the relief features, type of land such as plains, mountainous, lowlands, that support agriculture, tourism and other activities.

- **Mineral Resources** The regions rich in minerals will support industrial development that leads to trade.
- **Climate** It influences the type of flora and fauna that is found in a region, such as wool production in cold regions. Cocoa, rubber, Bananas can grow in tropical regions.
- **Population Factors** The size, distribution and diversity of population between countries affect the trade in respect of type and volume of goods. Large volume of internal trade than external trade takes place in densely populated areas due to consumption in local markets.
- **Cultural Factors** Distinctive forms of art and craft develop in certain cultures and give rise to trade e.g. porcelain and brocades of China, carpets of Iran, Batik cloth of Indonesia, etc.
- **Stage of Economic Development** Industrialised nations export machinery, finished products and import foodgrains and raw materials. The situation is opposite in agriculturally important countries.
- **Extent of Foreign Investment** Developing countries lack capital so foreign investment can boost trade in developing countries by developing plantation agriculture.
- **Transport** Lack of transport in older time restricted trade only to local areas. The expansion of rail, water and air transport, better means of refrigeration and preservation, trade has experienced spatial expansion.

Types of International Trade

There are two types of international trade

- **Bilateral trade** It is between two countries when they enter into an agreement to trade certain goods in which they are specialised.
- **Multilateral trade** It is conducted with many trading countries at the same time at goods which the countries are specialised in. The country may also grant the status of **Most Favoured Nation** (MNF) on some of trading partners.

Balance of Trade

- It refers to the volume of goods and services imported and exported by one country to other countries. **Favourable balance of trade** means the value of exports is more than its imports.
- **Unfavourable balance of trade** means that imports are more than exports. Balance of payments affects a country's economy as negative balance means country's expenses are more than its income.

Case for Free Trade

- Free trade or trade liberalisation is the act of opening up of economics so that more trade takes place. This is done by bringing down trade barriers like tarrifs. But trade liberalisation causes competition and can cause dumping.
- **Dumping** is the selling of a commodity in two countries at a price that differs for reasons not related to costs. Countries need to be cautious about dumped goods.

World Trade Organisation (WTO)

- **General Agreement for Tariffs and Trade** (GATT) was formed in 1948 to make the world free from tariffs as well as non-tariff barriers.
- On 1st January, 1995, the GATT was transformed into the World Trade Organisation to set up an institution for the promotion of free and fair trade amongst different countries of the world.
- The WTO sets the rules for the global trading system. The headquarters of WTO is located in **Geneva**, Switzerland and 164 countries are its members.
- However, WTO has been criticised and opposed by those who are worried about the effects of free trade and economic globalisation. They argued that free trade is not beneficial to the ordinary people as it is widening the gap between rich and poor.
- They also argued that issues of health, workers' rights, child labour and environment are ignored.

Regional Trade Blocs

- Regional Trade Blocs are set up to encourage trade between countries with geographical closeness, similarity and complementarities in trading items and to keep restrictions on trade of the developing world under control.
- At present, there are 120 regional trade blocs which occupy 52 per cent of the world trade. These trading blocs came into existence due to the failure of the global organisations to speed up intra-regional trade.

Concerns Related to International Trade

This can be summarised as merits and demerits of international trade.

Merits of International Trade International trade is beneficial if it promotes regional specialisation, higher level of production, better standard of living, worldwide availability of goods and services, equalisation of price and wages and diffusion of knowledge and culture.

Demerits of International Trade The demerits are dependence on other countries, uneven levels of development, exploitation and commercial rivalry.

Gateways of International Trade

Harbours and ports are the chief gateways of international trade. These ports facilitate the passage of cargos and travellers as well as provide facilities of docking, loading, unloading and storage.

Types of Ports

Ports are generally, classified according to the types of traffic which they handle.

Types of ports on the basis of cargo handled are

Industrial Ports The ports that handle bulk cargo like grain, ores, oil, chemicals are called industrial ports.

Commercial Ports Ports handling packaged products, manufactured goods, passengers are commercial ports.

Comprehensive Ports Ports that handle bulk and general cargo in large volumes are called comprehensive ports. Most of the world's great ports are classified as comprehensive ports.

Types of Ports on the basis of location are

Inland Ports Ports located away from the sea coasts and linked to the sea through a river or a canal are inland ports, e.g. Mannheim on Rhine river.

Out Ports Ports in deep waters built away from the actual ports and serving big ships are called out ports, e.g. Athens and its out port Piraeus in Greece.

Types of Ports on the basis of specialised functions

Oil Ports Ports that deal in the processing and shipping of oil are known as oil ports. These are tanker ports like Tripoli in Lebanon and refinery ports like Abadon on the Gulf of Persia.

Ports of Call Ports which originally developed as calling points on main sea routes where ships used to anchor for refuelling, watering and taking food items are called ports of call, e.g., Honolulu and Aden.

Packet Station Also known as ferry ports, these are exclusively concerned with the transportation of passengers and mail across water bodies covering short distances, e.g., Dover in England and Calais in France.

Entrepot Ports These are collection centres where the goods are brought from different countries for export, e.g., Singapore is an entrepot for Asia.

Naval Ports These ports serve warships and have repair workshops for them, e.g., Kochi, Karwar in India.

PYQs Previous Years' Questions

1 Marks Questions

Multiple Choice Questions

1. Consider the following statements and choose the correct option from the given options. *(CBSE SQP 2022)*

   I. The WTO however has been criticised and opposed by those who are worried about the effects of free trade and economic globalisation.

   II. Free trade does not make ordinary people's lives more prosperous.

   Codes

   (a) Only statement I is correct
   (b) Both statements are true and statement II correctly present the reason for statement I
   (c) Only statement II is correct
   (d) Both statements I and II are incorrect

Ans. (b) Both statements are true and statement II correctly present the reason for statement I

2. Which of the following pairs is correctly matched? *(CBSE SQP 2022)*

	Name of the country		Oil port
(a)	Tunisia	–	Tripoli
(b)	Lebanon	–	Esskhira
(c)	Venezuela	–	Maracaibo
(d)	Oman	–	Aden

Ans. (c) Venezuela - Maracaibo

3. When two or more countries are involved in trade activity, it is known as

   (a) internal trade (b) external trade
   (c) international trade (d) local trade

Ans. (c) international trade

4. India's International Trade has undergone a huge change in recent years in terms of

   (a) composition (b) volume
   (c) direction (d) All of these

Ans. (d) All of these

5. What is/are the major reason(s) behind the sharp rise in overseas trade of India during 2016-17?

   (a) Momentum picked up by the manufacturing sectors.
   (b) Liberal policies of the Indian Government.
   (c) Diversification of markets
   (d) All of the above

Ans. (d) All of the above

6. Which commodity has maximum share in India's export?

   (a) Ore and minerals
   (b) Agriculture and allied products
   (c) Manufactured goods
   (d) Crude and petroleum products

Ans. (c) Manufactured goods

7. Which commodity has minimum share in India's export?

   (a) Manufactured goods
   (b) Agriculture and allied products
   (c) Ore and minerals
   (d) Crude and petroleum products

Ans. (c) Ore and minerals

8. When import is more than export it is known as

   (a) Positive balance of trade
   (b) Negative balance of trade
   (c) Positive balance of payment
   (d) Negative balance of payment

Ans. (d) Negative balance of payment

9. Green Revolution was introduced in India during

   (a) 1920s (b) 1930s
   (c) 1950s (d) 1970s

Ans. (d) 1970s

10. Which of the following is the biggest port of India?

   (a) Marmagao port
   (b) Mumbai port
   (c) Kandla port
   (d) New Mangalore port

Ans. (b) Mumbai port

11. Arrange the following commodities in sequence in terms of their share in India's import (Highest to lowest).

   I. Food and allied products II. Fuel
   III. Fertilisers IV. Capital goods

   Codes

   (a) I, IV, I, III (b) III, II, I, IV
   (c) IV, III, II, I (d) II, IV, III, I

Ans. (a) II, IV, I, III

Very Short Answer Questions

1. Mention any two ill effects of free trade and economic globalisation. *(Delhi 2019)*

Ans. The two ill effects of free trade and economic globalisation are

(i) It adversely affects the economies of developing countries.

(ii) Imported goods that are being sold at cheaper prices can harm the sale of domestic producers.

2. Examine the functioning of World Trade Organisation (WTO). *(Delhi 2016)*

Or State any two functions of 'World Trade Organisation.' *(Delhi 2013)*

Ans. The two functions of World Trade Organisation (WTO) are

(i) It sets the rules for global trading system.

(ii) It promotes free and fair trade amongst different countries of the world.

3. How is 'barter system' practiced among various tribal communities in the world? *(Delhi 2016)*

Ans. In tribal communities, the barter system is practiced by direct exchange of goods where money is not used.

4. Assess the positive aspect of 'trade liberalisation'. *(All India 2016)*

Ans. Trade liberalisation refers to opening up of economies for trading. It allows goods and services from everywhere to compete with domestic goods and services thereby giving greater choices.

5. How is the favourable balance of trade an indicator of economic development of a country? *(All India 2016)*

Ans. A favourable balance of trade means that the value of exports is more than the value of imports. This means that the country is earning money by selling its goods which is an indicator of economic development of a country.

6. What are naval ports? Give one example of naval port. *(All India 2013)*

Ans. Naval ports are those ports which are strategically important as they serve warships and have repair centres for them. Examples of naval ports are Kochi and Karwar.

7. Name the regional trade bloc of which India is a member. *(Delhi 2010)*

Ans. India is a member of SAFTA (South Asian Free Trade Agreement).

8. Which city is the headquarters of the Organisation of Petroleum Exporting Countries (OPEC)? *(Delhi 2010)*

Ans. The headquarters of OPEC is in Vienna.

9. Name the type of most of the great ports of the world. *(All India 2010)*

Ans. Most of the great ports of the world are comprehensive ports.

10. Categorise the international trade into two types. *(All India 2010)*

Ans. Two types of international trade are

(i) Bilateral trade

(ii) Multilateral trade

11. What was the initial form of trade in the primitive society? *(All India 2009)*

Ans. The initial form of trade in the primitive society was barter system.

12. Name the international organisation dealing with the global rules of trade between nations. *(All India 2008)*

Ans. The international organisation dealing with global rules of trade is World Trade Organisation (WTO).

3 Marks Questions

1. 'The chief gateways of the world of international trade are the harbours and ports'. Justify the statement with examples. *(CBSE SQP 2019)*

HINT *Dear students, this question simply ask you to describe the importance of harbors and ports in International trade.*

Ans. The following examples justify that the chief gateways of the world of international trade are harbours and ports

(i) They provide facilities of docking, loading and unloading of cargo.

(ii) They provide storage facilities for cargo.

(iii) Labour and managerial services are provided at the ports and harbours.

2. Explain with example how 'stage of economic development' and 'foreign investment' become the basis of international trade. *(Delhi 2013)*

Ans. In modern times, trade is the basis of the world's economic organisation and is related to the foreign policy of nations. The stage of economic development and foreign investment have become the basis of international trade due to following reasons

Stage of Economic Development The nature of trade changes with the change in stage of economic development of countries. In developed economies, manufactured goods, machinery are traded for raw materials but in less developed economies, agro products are traded for industrial goods.

Foreign Investment Developing countries lack in capital which is required for the development of mining, oil drilling, heavy engineering, lumbering and plantation agriculture. Foreign investment can boost trade in these countries. Like in India, foreign investment in service sectors has made India one of the leading service provider countries in the world.

3. What is free trade? Give two advantages of free trade. *(All India 2013)*

Ans. The act of opening up economies for trading is known as free trade or trade liberalisation.

Two advantages of free trade are as follows

(i) It makes the economy more open and trading easier by bringing down trade barriers.

(ii) Trade liberalisation or free trade creates the environment of competition between the goods produced globally and the domestic goods.

4. Why are ports called 'gateways of international trade'? Explain any three reasons. *(Delhi 2011)*

Ans. For answer, refer to Q.1 of 3 marks questions.

5. Classify ports of the world into two types on the basis of their location. Explain any two features of each type of ports. *(Delhi 2010)*

Or What are the various types of ports on the basis of location? Discuss any two features of such ports.

Ans. Ports are classified into following two types on the basis of their location

(i) Inland ports (ii) Out ports

Two features of each of these ports are as follows

Inland Ports

(a) These ports are connected to sea through a river or a canal.

(b) They are located away from the sea coast, e.g. Manchester, Memphis, Mannheim and Duisburg; and Kolkata.

Out Ports

(a) These ports serve the parent ports by receiving their large ships.

(b) These are built away from the actual ports in deep water.

6. How is the difference in national resources a basis of international trade? Explain with three examples. *(All India 2010)*

Or Explain how the difference in natural resources becomes one of the basis of international trade. *(Delhi 2009)*

Ans. The difference in national resources is a basis of international trade because these provide basis for development of industries differently in the world. But, the distribution of world's national resources is uneven due to different physical make ups like

Geological Structure Distinct geological structure and topographical differences ensure diversity of crops and animals raised. Like agricultural activity is more in lowland areas, mountains are good for tourism, etc.

Mineral Resources Different regions of the world have different proportion of mineral resources and these mineral resources provide the basis for the development of industries.

Climate It influences flora and fauna of a particular region. It ensures the diversity in the range of various products, e.g. wool production in colder regions, certain cash crops like cocoa, coffee in tropical regions.

5 Marks Questions

1. "In modern times international trade is the basis of the world economy." Support the statement with example. *(All India 2017)*

HINT *Dear students, this question simply ask you to describe the importance of international trade in modern world economy.*

Ans. International trade is the base of the world economy in the modern times. The exchange of surplus goods between different countries is called International trade. It is basis of the world economy because

(i) The resources are unevenly distributed. International trade help in removing these differences.

(ii) International trade lead to foreign investment in developing countries which lack in capital required for the development.

(iii) Export and import help countries to gain foreign exchanges.

(iv) Trade also help to raise the standard of living of the people of the developing countries.

(v) International trade is the index of economic development of a country.

2. Differentiate between bilateral trade and multilateral trade. Explain how ports are helpful in trade. ***(Delhi 2014)***

Ans. Differences between bilateral trade and multilateral trade are as follows

Basis	Bilateral Trade	Multilateral Trade
Involvement of countries	It is the trade between two countries.	It is the trade among different trading partners.
Complementary or Supplementary	In this type of trade, commodities of two countries are complementary.	The trade is not complementary but supplementary.
Variation in Commodities	This type of trade is limited to certain commodities.	This type of trade includes exchange of various types of goods and services.

Ports are helpful in trade because
- (i) Ports are gateways of international trade.
- (ii) They promote international trade.
- (iii) Ports provide facilities of docking, loading, unloading and storage facilities for cargo.
- (iv) Large amount of goods can be taken in by ships.
- (v) The quantity of cargo handled by a port is an indicator of the level of development of its hinterland.

3. Why are ports known as 'gateways of international trade'? Explain any three characteristics of inland ports. ***(All India 2014)***

Ans. For reasons of why ports are known as 'gateways of international trade', refer to Q.1 of 3 marks questions.
Important characteristics of the inland ports are as follows
- (i) Inland ports are located away from the sea coast.
- (ii) They are linked to the sea through a river or a canal, e.g. Manchester is linked with a canal.
- (iii) Such ports are accessible to flat bottom ships or barges.

4. What is the role of 'World Trade Organisation' as an international organisation? Why has the World Trade Organisation been criticised by some countries? Explain the role of World Trade Organisation. ***(Delhi 2014)***

Or Explain any two functions of WTO. Why has this organisation been criticised? Give three arguments in this regard. ***(All India 2011)***

Ans. World Trade Organisation was set up on 1st January, 1995 after transformation of GATT (General Agreement for Tariffs and Trade).
The two functions of WTO are as follows
- (i) It sets the rules for the global trading system.
- (ii) It promotes free and fair trade amongst different countries of the world.

WTO or World Trade Organisation has always been critisised on the following ground
The WTO has been criticised by those who are worried about the effects of free trade and economic globalisation.
- (i) The critique of WTO is based on an argument that free trade is not beneficial to the ordinary people as it is widening the gulf between rich and poor by making rich countries more rich. This is because the influential nations try to satisfy their commercial interests through WTO.
- (ii) In addition, these countries have not fully opened their markets to developing countries.
- (iii) Critics also argue that important issues like health, workers' rights, child labour and environment have been ignored by WTO.

5. Explain the two types of international trade. Examine any three possible negative impacts of globalisation alongwith free trade in the world. ***(Delhi 2013)***

Ans. International trade is the exchange of capital, goods and services across international borders or territories. There are two types of international trade
- (i) **Bilateral Trade** It refers to the trade between two countries. The two countries are specialised in certain commodities and hence, they enter into an agreement to trade specified commodities between them.
- (ii) **Multilateral Trade** It is conducted with many trading countries. The same country can trade with a large number of other countries. The status of the Most Favoured Nation (MFN) can be granted by such country to some of the trading partners.

Three possible negative impacts of globalisation alongwith free trade in the world are as follows
- (i) It does not provide level playing field by imposing unfavourable conditions hence, retard the growth of trade for developing countries.

(ii) Cheaper goods from foreign countries may harm the sell of domestic goods.

(iii) The phenomena of dumping may be visible in the markets of developing countries.

6. Explain any five bases of international trade. ***(Delhi 2012, 2008, All India 2012)***

Or Examine the five bases of international trade which are responsible for promoting international trade. ***(All India 2011)***

Ans. Five bases of international trade are as follows

(i) **Difference in National Resources** The distribution of world's national resources is uneven due to different physical make ups like geology, relief, soil and climate.

(ii) **Population Factors** Type and volume of goods traded between different regions of world are affected by the size, distribution and diversity of people. It includes cultural factors and size of population.

(iii) **Stage of Economic Development** The nature of commodities traded changes with the change in stage of economic development of countries. In less developed countries, agriculture is the most important sector. These countries export agro products to the industrialised nations and import machinery and finished products from them.

Five bases of International Trade
- Difference in National Resources
- Population Factors
- Stage of Economic Development
- Extent of Foreign Investment
- Transport

(iv) **Extent of Foreign Investment** Developing countries lack in capital which is required for the development of mining, oil drilling, heavy engineering, lumbering and plantation agriculture.

(v) **Transport** With the development of modern means of transport and the expansion of rail, ocean and air transport, trade has expanded spatially. In early time, only high value items, e.g. gems, silk and spices were traded over long distances because of the lack of efficient means of transport.

Source Based Questions

1. Study the following table and answer the questions that follow ***(All India 2019)***

World : Imports and Exports (in millions of US $)

Year	Exports Total Merchandise	Imports Total Merchandise
1955	95,000	99,000
1965	1,90,000	1,99,000
1975	8,77,000	9,12,000
1985	19,54,000	20,15,000
1995	51,62,000	52,92,000
2005	1,03,93,000	1,07,53,000
2015	1,55,83,232	1,56,28,204

(i) Which aspect of trade has shown rapid growth?

(ii) Has the total volume of trade increased or decreased?

(iii) Why does import take place? Write any two reasons.

Ans. (i) The imports of total merchandise has shown a rapid growth from 1955 to 2015.

(ii) The given table shows that the total volume of world trade has been steadily rising over the past decades

(iii) Import takes place due to the following reasons:
- When there is lack of some resources or services in a country then import takes place.
- When there is a demand of good quality foreign products then import takes place.

2. Study the table given below carefully and answer the following questions. ***(Delhi 2011)***

World Imports and Exports (in US$)

	Exports Total Merchandise	Imports Total Merchandise
1955	95,000	99,000
1966	19,0000	199,000
1975	877,000	912,000
1985	1,954,000	2,015,000
1995	5,162,000	5,292,000
2005	10,393,000	10,753,000

(i) Which decade shows the highest increase of total value of imports and exports of goods and services?

(ii) How much is the increase in total value of exports during 1955 to 2005?

Ans. (i) 1966-1975 shows the highest increase of total value of imports and exports of goods and services.

(ii) The total value of exports was increased by 10.2 million of US $ during 1955 to 2005.

CHAPTER TEST

01 Mark Questions

1 Name the continent which has the maximum flow of global trade in the world.

(a) Africa
(b) Asia
(c) Europe
(d) North America

2 Identify the statement which best describes the composition of trade.

(a) Destination of exports and imports.
(b) Total value of goods and services.
(c) Nature of goods and services imported and exported.
(d) None of the above

3 Which of the following pairs is/are correctly matched?

Types of Port		Port
(a) Ports of Call	–	Aden
(b) Inland Port	–	Memphis
(c) Tanker Port	–	Tripoli

(d) All of the above

4 **Assertion** (A) Barter system did not promote trade and was very complex.

Reason (R) In primitive societies, it was almost impossible to find people who were in need of the same commodities as one needed to exchange.

Codes

(a) Both A and R are true and R is the correct explanation of A
(b) Both A and R are true, but R is not the correct explanation of A
(c) A is true, but R is false
(d) A is false, but R is true

5 Arrange the following events in the history of international trade in a sequential order.

I. Trade on silk route
II. Trade growth after industrial revolution.
III. Slave trade
IV. Growth of trade between Europe and Asia

Codes

(a) I, II, III, IV
(b) I, III, II, IV
(c) II, I, III, IV
(d) I, IV, III, II

Answers

1. (b) | 2. (c) | 3. (d) | 4. (b) | 5. (b)

03 Marks Questions

6 How a negative balance of payment has serious implications over the financial resources of a country? Explain in your words.

7 Explain in brief about direction of foreign trade.

8 Define balance of trade. When does it become favourable or unfavourable?

05 Marks Questions

9 Which historical events influenced international trade? Explain in brief.

10 What are the five basis of international trade which are responsible for promoting international trade? Discuss in brief.

11 Ports are known as 'gateways of international trade'. Discuss about any three characteristics of inland ports.

01

Population : Distribution, Density, Growth and Composition

TREND ANALYSIS 3 YEARS

Average No. of Questions Across all Sets

Topic	Types of Questions	2023	2020	2019
TOPIC 01 Population : Distribution, Density	1 Mark	–	–	–
	3 Marks	–	–	1
	5 Marks	2	–	–
TOPIC 02 Growth and Composition	1 Mark	–	–	–
	3 Marks	–	–	1
	5 Marks	4	–	–

Population plays a vital role in the development of any country. Inspite of having 7th position in terms of area (2.4%), India is the 2nd largest country in terms of population, after China (having 17.5% population of the world). According to census 2011, India's total population is 1,210 million.

Distribution of Population

Distribution of population means how population is distributed in any given area. In India, spatial pattern of population distribution is very uneven. As some areas are sparsely populated whereas others are densely populated. These states can be categorised into three categories:

- **State with High Population** Uttar Pradesh (highest population), Maharashtra, Bihar, West Bengal, Madhya Pradesh, Tamil Nadu, Rajasthan, Karnataka, Gujarat and Andhra Pradesh. These states together account for 76% of population.
- **States with Moderate Population** Assam, Haryana, Jharkhand, Chhattisgarh, Kerala, Punjab, Goa.
- **States with Low Population** Hilly and tribal areas like Jammu and Kashmir, Uttarakhand, Himachal Pradesh, all North-Eastern state (except Assam) and Union Territories excluding Delhi.

Density of Population

Population density means number of person living in per unit area. According to 2011 census, in India 382 person live in per sq km of area. Over the last 50 years the population density has recorded an increase of about 260 persons per sq km, as ranging from 117 persons/sq km in 1951 to 382 persons/sq km in 2011.

Spatial Pattern of Population Density in India

Spatial pattern of population density is also uneven in India. For example

- **States/UTs having High Density of population**

  States Bihar (1102 highest), West Bengal (1029), Kerala (859), Uttar Pradesh (828),

  UTs Delhi (11297 highest), Chandigrah (9252).

- **States/UTs having Moderate Density of Population** Haryana (573), Tamil Nadu (555), Punjab (550), Jharkhand (414), Assam (397), Goa (394), Maharashtra (365), Tripura (350).

  UTs Dadra and Nagar Haveli (698).

- **States/UTs having Low Density of Population**

  States Arunachal Pradesh (17 Lowest), Mizoram (52), Sikkim (86), Nagaland (119), Jammu and Kashmir (124).

  UTs Andaman and Nicobar islands (46 lowest).

Growth of Population

Growth of population refers to the changes occuring in the number of persons living in a particular area between two points of time. Its rate is expressed in percentage. Two components in population growth are as follows

- **Natural Growth** It means the change occuring by the births and deaths in any area.
- **Induced Growth** It means the changes occurred by the volume of inward and outward movement in an area.

Phases of Population Growth

There are four different phases of population growth

- **Phase-I (1901-1921)** It is stagnant or stationary phase because of very low growth rate.
- **Phase-II (1921-1951)** It is the period of steady population growth.
- **Phase-III (1951-1981)** This period is known as the period of population explosion in India. Rapid fall in death rate and high fertility rate were the main causes of this explosion.
- **Phase-IV (Post 1981 till present)** Growth rate has started down gradually because of downward trend in birth rate. But in developing countries like India, growth rate is still high. According to World Development Report by 2025, Indian population will surpass the figure of 1350 million.

Regional Variation in Population Growth

The spatial pattern of population growth in India is very uneven. It ranges from -0.47% (Negative) in Nagaland to 55.50% in Dadra and Nagar Haveli.

- **States/UTs having High Growth Rate of Population**

  States Meghalaya (27.82%), Arunachal Pradesh (25.92%), Bihar (25.7%), Manipur (18.65%), Jammu and Kashmir (23.71%).

  UTs Dadra and Nagar Haveli (55.50%), Daman and Diu (53.54%), Puducherry (27.72%).

- **States/UTs having Moderate Growth Rate of Population** Chhattisgarh (22.59%), Jharkhand (22.34%), Rajasthan (21.44%), Madhya Pradesh (20.30%), Uttar Pradesh (20.90%).

- **States/UTs having Low Growth Rate of Population**

  States Nagaland (–0.47% lowest), Kerala (4.86%), Goa (8.17%), Andhra Pradesh (11.10%).

  UTs Lakshadweep (6.23%), Andaman and Nicobar islands (6.68%).

Growth of Adolescent Population

The United Nation considers person aged 10-19 year as adolescents population. Since 1971, the proportion of adolescent population has remained around 20.9%. The decadal growth rate of adolescent population of India is 12.5% as per census 2011.

India is on 4th place in adolescent population (10-19 years) after Pakistan, Nigeria and Bangladesh. Adolescent population has increased from 85 million in 1961 to 253.2 million in 2011. Sex-ratio of adolescent population of India is 898 females per 1000 males.

The Government of India has taken many steps by some policies like, National Youth Policy 2014, for channelisation and proper utilisation of adolescents by giving them proper education.

Population Composition

It is a detailed analysis of age and sex, place of residence, ethnic characteristics, tribes, language, religion, marital status, literacy and education, occupational characteristics, etc in population geography.

Rural-Urban Composition

In India, its 68.84% of total population lives in rural villages by 2011. According to census 2011, India has 6,40,867 villages. Percentage of rural population is high in Himachal Pradesh (89.97% highest) and Bihar (88.71%) and low in Goa (37.83%) and Mizoram (47.89%). Delhi has the least rural population (2.50%).

Rural Population in Indian States

- **States having High Proportion of Rural Population** Himachal Pradesh (89.97%) and Bihar (88.71%), Assam (85.90%), Odisha (83.31%).

- **States having Moderate Proportion of Rural Population** Meghalaya (79.93%), Uttar Pradesh (77.73%), Arunachal Pradesh (77.06%), Chhattisgarh (76.76%), Jharkhand (75.95%).
- **States/UTs having Low Proportion of Rural Population States** Goa (37.83%), Mizoram (47.89%), Tamil Nadu (51.60%), Kerala (52.30%).

  UTs Delhi (2.50%), Chandigarh (2.75%).

Urban Population in Indian States

- **Regions having High Degree of Urbanisation States** Goa (62.17%), Mizoram (52.11%), Tamil Nadu (48.40%) Kerala (47.70%).

  UTs Delhi (97.50%), Chandigarh (97.25%), Lakshadweep (78.07%).
- **Regions having Low Degree of Urbanisation** Himachal Pradesh (10.03%), Bihar (11.29%), Assam (14.10%), Odisha (16.69%), Meghalaya (20.07%).

Linguistic Composition

India is a land of linguistic diversity. According to Grierson (Linguistic Survey of India, 1903-1928) there were 179 languages and as many as 544 dialects in India. But now, there are 22 scheduled languages and number of non-scheduled languages.

Linguistic Classification

The speakers of major Indian languages belong to four language families, which have their sub-families and branches or groups.

Language Families

(i) Austric (Nishada-1.38%)
(ii) Dravidian (Dravida-20%)
(iii) Sino-Tibetan (Kirata-0.85%)
(iv) Indo-European (Aryan-73%)

Religious Compositions

All India Religion Census Data 2011

Religion	Percentage	Estimated
All Religion	100.00%	121 Crores
Hindu	79.80%	96.62 Crores
Muslim	14.23%	17.22 Crores
Christian	2.30%	2.78 Crores
Sikh	1.72%	2.08 Crores
Buddhist	0.70%	84.43 Lakhs
Jain	0.4%	44.52 Lakhs
Other Religion	0.7%	79.38 Lakhs
Not stated	0.24%	28.67 Lakhs

Composition of Working Population

The proportion of working population to total population is called **work participation rate**. The population of India according to their economic status is divided into three groups like

- **Main workers** A person who works atleast 183 days in a year.
- **Marginal workers** A person who works for less than 183 days in a year.
- **Non-workers** A person who does not work and depends upon working class. According to 2011 census, it is observed that the proportion of workers (both main and marginal) is only 39.8% leaving a vast majority of about 60% as non-workers.

Occupational Categories

The 2011 census has divided the working population of India into four major categories:

(i) Cultivators
(ii) Agricultural labourers-54.6%
(iii) Household labourers- 3.8%
(iv) Other workers- 41.6% (2011)

Sex Composition

The number of men and women in a country is one of an important characteristics to study the demography of the country.

Sex-ratio

The ratio between the number of women and men in the population is called the sex-ratio. There are different criterias to calculate sex-ratio in the world. These are discussed below

- In some countries it is calculated by using the following formula. $\text{Sex-ratio} = \frac{\text{Male Population}}{\text{Female Population}} \times 100$

  It is expressed as the number of males per thousand females.
- The criteria to calculate sex-ratio is different in India. Here, the sex-ratio is calculated by using the following formula $\text{Sex-ratio} = \frac{\text{Female Population}}{\text{Male Population}} \times 100$

  It is expressed as the number of females per thousand males.
- Ratio above 1000 indicates excess of female over male, those below 1000 indicates a deficit of female.

Sex-ratio in India

According to the 2011 Census, there are 943 females for every 1000 males in India.

PYQs Previous Years' Questions

1 Mark Questions

Multiple Choice Questions

1. Which of the following is the smallest linguistic in India ? *(CBSE 2023)*

(a) Austric (b) Dravidian

(c) Indo- European (d) Sino- Tibetan

Ans. (d) Sino- Tibetan

2. The 2011 Census has divided the working population of India into four major categories. Select the correct option related to the major categories . *(CBSE 2023)*

(a) Cultivators, Agricultural labourers, Household industrial workers and other workers

(b) Agricultural labourers, Household industrial workers, Health workers and other workers

(c) Agricultural labourers, Household industrial workers, Rail workers and other workers

(d) Household industrial workers, Cultivators, Rail workers and other workers

Ans. (a) Cultivators, Agricultural labourers, Household industrial workers and other workers

3. Read the following statements regarding objectives of family planning and choose the correct option. *(CBSE 2023)*

I. Control the birth rate

II. Spacing the birth of children

III. Improving women's health

IV. Reducing the death rate of children

Codes

(a) Only I, II and IV are correct

(b) Only I, II and III are correct

(c) Only II, III and IV are correct

(d) Only I, III and IV are correct

Ans. (b) Only I, II and III are correct

4. Consider the following and choose the correct answer from the given options. *(CBSE SQP Term 2021)*

1. Work participation rate tend to be higher in the areas of lower levels of economic development.

2. Number of manual workers are needed to perform the subsistence or near subsistence economic activities.

Options

(a) Only statement I is correct

(b) Both statements are correct and statement II correctly explains statement I

(c) Only statement II is correct

(d) Both the statements are incorrect

Ans. (b) Both statements are correct and statement II correctly explains statement I

5. In the year 2015, a policy was formulated for the adolescents to give them proper guidance and the better development of their talent. Select the correct answer. *(CBSE SQP Term 2021)*

(a) Skill development and entrepreneurship

(b) Universalisation of education

(c) Rejuvenation of schools

(d) National Youth Policy

Ans. (a) Skill development and entrepreneurship

6. Population of India according to occupation can be categorised into. *(CBSE SQP Term I 2021)*

(a) Main workers, Marginal workers, Non-workers

(b) Marginal workers, Household industrial workers, Non-workers

(c) Agricultural labourers, Marginal workers, Non-workers

(d) Cultivators, Main-workers, Marginal workers

Ans. (a) Main workers, Marginal workers, Non-workers

7. Which one of the following Union Territories has the highest density of population? *(CBSE SQP Term I 2021)*

(a) NCT Delhi

(b) Andaman and Nicobar Island

(c) Chandigarh

(d) Puducherry

Ans. (a) NCT Delhi

8. Which of the following states has the highest percentage of rural population? *(CBSE Term I 2021)*

(a) Himachal Pradesh (b) Bihar

(c) Uttar Pradesh (d) Uttarakhand

Ans. (a) Himachal Pradesh

9. The area of region 'A' is 2500^2 km while total population is 10,00,000 (one million). Density of population of region 'A' will be *(CBSE Term I 2021)*

(a) 500 persons per sq. km

(b) 40 persons per sq. km

(c) 400 persons per sq. km

(d) 4000 persons per sq. km

Ans. (c) 400 persons per sq. km

10. Read statements I and II and choose the correct option.

Statement I The period from 1901-1921 is referred to as a period of stagnant or stationary phase of growth of population in India.

Statement II During this period both the birth and death rates were high

Options *(CBSE Term I 2021)*

(a) Only I is correct
(b) Only II is correct
(c) I and II both are correct and statement II correctly explains statement I
(d) I and II both are correct, but statement II does not correctly explains statement I

Ans. (c) I and II both are correct and statement II correctly explains statement I

11. Study the following facts of density of population in India and choose the correct option.

Statement I Density of population is expressed as number of persons per unit area.

Statement II It helps in getting a better understanding of the spatial distribution of population.

Options *(CBSE Term I 2021)*

(a) Only I is correct
(b) Only II is correct
(c) I and II both are correct and statement II correctly explains statement I
(d) I and II both are correct, but statement II does not correctly explain statementI

Ans. (c) I and II both are correct and statement II correctly explains statement I

12. Population of India according to their economic status is divided into: *(CBSE SQP 2020)*

(a) Main workers, Marginal workers, Non workers
(b) Marginal workers, Household industrial workers, Non workers
(c) Non workers, Agricultural labourers, Marginal workers
(d) Cultivators, Main workers, Marginal workers

Ans. (a) Main workers, Marginal workers, Non workers

13. Which one of the following is the largest linguistic group of India? *(CBSE SQP 2019)*

(a) Sino – Tibetan (b) Indo – Aryan
(c) Austric (d) Dravidian

Ans. (b) Indo-Aryan

14. Which one of the following periods had witnessed rapid growth of population? *(CBSE SQP 2019)*

(a) Before 1921 (b) 1921 - 1951
(c) 1951 – 1981 (d) After 1981

Ans. (c) 1951 - 1981

15. In which year the first population Census was held in India?

(a) 1801 (b) 1847 (c) 1872 (d) 1904

Ans. (c) 1872

16. What is the rank of India in the world in terms of population?

(a) 1st (b) 2nd (c) 4th (d) 5th

Ans. (b) 2nd

17. The people engaged in Primary activities comprise of what% of total workforce in India?

(a) 12.1% (b) 54.6% (c) 89.7% (d) 22.1%

Ans. (b) 54.6%

18. Which of the following is the most populous State of India?

(a) Maharashtra (b) Uttar Pradesh
(c) Bihar (d) West Bengal

Ans. (b) Uttar Pradesh

19. Which of the following largely determines the pattern of the population distribution?

(a) Climate (b) Terrain
(c) Availability of water (d) All of these

Ans. (d) All of these

20. What is the population density of India according to the 2011 census?

(a) 300 persons/sq km (b) 382 persons/sq km
(c) 400 persons/sq km (d) 450 persons/sq km

Ans. (b) 382 persons/sq km

21. The state that has the least population density in India is

(a) Jharkhand (b) Odisha
(c) Bihar (d) Arunachal Pradesh

Ans. (d) Arunachal Pradesh

22. Which period is referred to as the period of population explosion?

(a) 1901-1921 (b) 1921-1951
(c) 1951 - 1981 (d) 1981 till present

Ans. (c) 1951 - 1981

23. Arrange the following states in sequence as per their population (highest to lowest)

1. Bihar 2. Maharashtra
3. Uttar Pradesh 4. West Bengal

Codes

(a) 1, 3, 3, 4 (b) 4, 3, 2, 1
(c) 3, 2, 1, 4 (d) 2, 1, 4, 3

Ans. (c) 3, 2, 1, 4

Very Short Answer Questions

1. What does the proportion of literate population of a country indicate? *(CBSE SQP 2018)*

Ans. The proportion of literate population of a country is an indicator of its socio economic development because it shows the standard of living, status of female population and availability of educational facilities and policies in the country.

2. Name the state of India with largest area. *(Delhi, All India 2016)*

Ans. The largest state of India in terms of area is Rajasthan with an area of about 3, 42,239 sq km.

3. Name the Union Territory of India having lowest density of population as per 2011 census. *(Delhi 2016)*

Ans. As per census 2011, the least densely populated Union Territory of India is Andaman and Nicobar Islands with density of 46 persons/sq km.

4. Define the term 'population distribution.' *(Delhi 2015)*

Ans. Population distribution is the term which means the spread of people across the world, i.e. where do people live.

5. How is density of population of a region calculated? *(All India 2015)*

Or Define the term density of population. *(Delhi 2012)*

Ans. Population density is the ratio of people per unit area. It is usually measured in per sq km or sq mile. Generally, this may be calculated for a country, city, or another territory of the world.

6. Who are the 'marginal workers in India'? *(All India 2014)*

Ans. In India, a marginal worker is referred to as a person who works for less than 183 days in a year and rest of days they have no work.

7. Mention any two causes of the negative growth rate of population in India during (1911-21). *(Delhi 2013)*

Ans. The two causes responsible for the negative growth rate of population are

(i) High birth rate and high death rate.

(ii) Lack of medical facilities, family planning, etc.

8. What is the density of population of India according to 2011 census? *(Delhi 2013)*

Ans. According to census 2011, the density of population of India is 382 persons per sq km.

9. According to census which state of India having the highest density of population and also mention its density. *(Delhi 2009)*

Ans. According to Census 2001, state having highest density of population in India was West Bengal with the average density of 904 persons per sq km. But according to 2011 census, Bihar state having the highest density of population with 1102 sq km, West Bengal stands at second with 1029 sq km of its density.

10. Which age group of population indicates the largest working population? *(All India 2008)*

Ans. Age group of 15-59 years indicates the largest working group of population.

3 Marks Questions

1. "The prime task before any development activity in India is to maintain parity between population and resources." Justify the statements. *(Delhi 2019)*

HINT *Dear students, this question simply ask you to highlight the socio-economic inequality issues faced in India's development.*

Ans. In India, the development is considered as a mixed bag of opportunities and deprivation. A small section of population enjoys all the available modern facilities. On the other hand, the marginalised section include scheduled caste, scheduled tribes, landless agricultural labourers, etc which do not have basic facilities like potable water, education, health.

With the rise in developmental activities, these marginalised sections are becoming even more marginalised and hence are forced to live under poverty and sub-human conditions.

Although, there are sufficient amount of resources but these are unequally distributed. Even today, if all the resources of the country are equally distributed no one will be below poverty line and all will have atleast basic amenities. But rich people have access to avail large resource baskets, while the poors find their resources shrinking.

Thus, it is true that the prime task before any development activity in India is to maintain parity between population and resources.

2. "The period from 1901 to 1921 is referred to as a stagnant phase of India's population growth." Substantiate the statement. *(All India 2019)*

Or Explain any five causes for the stagnant growth of India's population from 1901 to 1921. *(All India 2014, 2011)*

Ans. The period from 1901-1921 is referred to as a period of stagnant or stationary phase of growth of India's population.

The following causes were responsible for the stagnant growth of India's population from 1901 to 1921

(i) High birth rate and high death rate resulted into stationary growth.

(ii) Lack of medical health and sanitation facilities.

(iii) Improper public distribution system.

(iv) Lower level of economic development reduced the migration.

(v) Illiteracy, lack of family planning and social awareness.

3. What is the main thrust of the National Youth Policy of Government of India 2003? ***(All India 2016)***

Or Explain the main aspects of the 'National Youth Policy' of Government of India launched in 2003. ***(All India 2014)***

Ans. The National Youth Policy, 2003 reiterates the commitment of the entire nation to the composite and all-round development of the young sons and daughters of India and seeks to establish an All-India perspective to fulfil their legitimate aspirations. The main thrust of the policy are

(i) To provide the youth with proper educational and training opportunities and to facilitate access to information in respect of employment opportunities and to other services.

(ii) To sustain and reinforce the spirit of volunteerism amongst the youth in order to build up individual character and generate a sense of commitment to the goals of developmental programmes.

4. Which are the two main components of population growth in India? Describe the main feature of each component. ***(Delhi 2009)***

Ans. The two main components of population growth in India are

Natural Growth It refers to the growth in population which is caused by birth rate and death rate. It is estimated by the difference between birth rate and death rate.

Features of natural growth are as under

(i) In India, natural growth is more influential in population growth.

(ii) This growth rate shows the medical, technological and social advancement of a society.

Induced Growth Rate Induced growth refers to the growth in population caused by the migration.

It is measured by the difference between in migrants and out migrants.

Features of induced growth rate are as under

(i) In India, it is more influential in population growth during partition in 1947 and Bangladesh War of 1971.

(ii) This type of growth is caused by the economic advancement of a society that attracts migrants from other areas.

5. Explain the spatial distribution of population density in India. ***(All India 2009)***

Ans. The spatial distribution of population density in India shows a very uneven pattern. It ranges from the lowest 17 persons per sq km in Arunachal Pradesh to 11297 person per sq km in Delhi.

Density of population is very high in states of Northern Plains i.e. Bihar (1102), West Bengal (1029), and Uttar Pradesh (828). Among Southern States, Kerala (859) and Tamil Nadu (555) have higher densities of population.

Some Indian states like Assam, Gujarat, Andhra Pradesh, Haryana, Jharkhand, Odisha and other have moderate densities as compared to other states. Most of the hilly states and regions having extreme climates have low density. Among them, North-Eastern states except Assam are important.

6. Which are the three groups of Indian population according to their economic status? Explain the main characteristics of each group. ***(Delhi 2008)***

Ans. On the basis of economic status India's population is divided into the following three categories

(i) **Main Workers** A person who works for at least 183 days in a year.

Characteristics of main workers are as follows

(a) They are the main contributors in a nation's GDP.

(b) They constitute large proportion of workers in India.

(ii) **Marginal Workers** A person who works for less than 183 days in a year.

Characteristics of marginal workers are as follows

(a) They are mostly engaged in agricultural sector.

(b) They constitute a short proportion of workers in India.

(iii) **Non-Worker** A person who does not work for his livelihood.

Characteristics of non-workers are as follows

(a) They are dependent on working population for their needs.

(b) They represent a larger proportion of Indian population.

This indicates an economic status in which there is a larger proportion of dependent population, further indicating possible existence of large number of unemployed or underemployed people.

5 Marks Questions

1. Why was 'Beti Bachao–Beti Padhao' social campaign launched by the government of India ? Examine. *(CBSE 2023)*

Other Similar Questions

Or Examine the reason for launching 'Beti Bachao-Beti Padhao' compaign by the government of India.

Or What are the objectives of 'Beti Bachao-Beti Padhao' campaign of government of India?

Ans. The social campaign 'Beti Bachao-Beti Padhao' was launched by the government of India in 2015 for the following purposes

(i) The Indian government introduced the Beti Bachao-Beti Padhao (BBBP) scheme to address concerns of gender discrimination and women empowerment in the country.

(ii) The name Beti Bachao-Beti Padhao translates to 'Save the girl child, educate the girl child'. The scheme aims to educate citizens against gender bias and improve efficacy of welfare services for girls.

(iii) It also aims to prevent gender-biased, sex selective elimination.

(iv) It encourages education and participation of the girl child.

(v) It aims to improve the child sex ratio.

(vi) It ensures gender equality and women empowerment.

2. "The proportion of working population of the states shows a variation". Examine the statement with examples. *(CBSE 2023)*

HINT *Dear students, this question simply ask you to write the reasons for the variations in the working populations of Indian States.*

Ans. The proportion of working population of states shows a variation. This can be seen through the following points

(i) The occupational composition of India's population (which actually means engagement of an individual in farming, manufacturing trade, services or any kind of professional activities) shows a large proportion of primary sector workers compared to secondary and tertiary sectors.

(ii) The spatial variation of work participation rate in different sectors in India is very wide.

(iii) For instance, the states like Himachal Pradesh and Nagaland have very large shares of cultivators.

(iv) On the other hand, states like Andhra Pradesh, Chhattisgarh, Odisha, Jharkhand, West Bengal and Madhya Pradesh have higher proportion of agricultural labourers.

(v) The highly urbanised areas like Delhi, Chandigarh and Puducherry have a very large proportion of workers being engaged in other services.

3. Why is Phase II (1921-1951) of growth of population referred to as the period of steady population growth in India ? Explain by giving any three arguments. *(CBSE 2023)*

Ans. The decades 1921-1951 are referred as the period of steady population growth.

The main reasons responsible for this are as follows

(i) There was fall in mortality rate due to improvement in health and sanitation throughout the country.

(ii) At the same time, better transport and communication system improved the distribution system.

(iii) The crude birth rate remained high in this period leading to higher growth rate than the previous phase. This was an excellent achievement in the back drop of Great Economic Depression, 1920s and World War II.

4. Explain the important aspects of population growth with special reference to the growth of adolescents and National Youth Policy, 2014 India *(CBSE 2023)*

Ans. Growth of population is the change in the number of people living in a particular area between two points of time. Its rate is expressed in percentage. The annual growth rate of India's population is 1.64 per cent (2011).

An important aspect of population growth in India is the growth of its adolescents. In 2011 the share of adolescents (age group of 10-19 years) is about 20.9 per cent. Among which male adolescents constitute 52.7 per cent and female adolescents constitute 47.3 per cent.

The adolescent population, though, regarded as the youthful population having high potentials, but at the same time they are quite vulnerable if not guided and channelised properly. There are many challenges for the society as far as these adolescents are concerned, some of which are lower age at marriage, illiteracy – particularly female illiteracy, school dropouts, low intake of nutrients, high rate of maternal mortality of adolescent mothers, high rate of HIV and AIDS infections, physical and mental disability or retardedness, drug abuse and alcoholism, juvenile delinquency and commitence of crimes, etc.

In view of these, the Government of India has undertaken certain policies to impart proper education to the adolescent groups so that their talents are better channelised and properly utilized e.g. the National Youth Policy-2014.

The National Youth Policy (NYP–2014) launched in February, 2014 proposes a holistic 'vision' for the youth of India, which is "To empower the youth of the country to achieve their full potential, and through them enable India to find its rightful place in the community of nations".

5. Explain the various factors affecting density of population in India. ***(CBSE 2023)***

Ans. There are mainly eight factors affecting density of population in India, these are as follow

(i) **Terrain** Terrain of land is a potent factor which influences the concentration and growth of population. The steep slope in mountain areas restrict the availability of land for agriculture, development of transport, industries and other economic activities which may tend to discourage concentration of population and its proper growth.

(ii) **Climate** Climate is as important as terrain in influencing population. Twin elements of rainfall and temperature play the most important role in determining the population of an area. Man cannot go beyond the limits set by climate.

(iii) **Soil** It is an important factor in determining the density of population in an overwhelmingly agricultural country like India.

(iv) **Water Bodies** Availability of water plays a significant role in determining the population of a given area.

(v) **Mineral Resources** Minerals act as preat source of attraction for people from different areas, which results in higher density of population.

(vi) **Industries** Industrial growth offers massive empolyment opportunities and acts as a great magnet to attract people, particularly from the neighbouring areas.

(vii) **Transport** Growth of population is directly proportional to the development of transport facilities.

The Northern plain of India has a dense network of transport routes and is densely populated region.

(viii) **Urbanisation** All the urban centres are marked by high density of population. The minimum density, that an area should have to be designated as urban, is 400 persons per sq km.

6. "The uneven spatial distribution of population suggests a close relationship and physical factors. Analyse the statement. ***(CBSE 2023)***

Or Analyse the causes for the uneven spatial distribution of population in India. ***(CBSE Compartment 2020)***

Or "An uneven distribution of population suggests a close relationship between population and physical and socio-economic factors." Support the statement with suitable examples. ***(All India 2017)***

Or Explain with examples any five factors that affect the population distribution in India. ***(Delhi 2011)***

Ans. The spatial pattern of distribution of population in India is very uneven. The factors responsible for this uneven distribution are physical and economic.

Physical factors that affect the population distribution are

(i) People prefer to live in fertile plain as compared to hilly or mountainous areas. That's why Northern plains, deltas, coastal plains have higher proportion of population than some other parts of the country.

(ii) People usually prefer to live in areas having pleasant climate. Coastal plains are highly preferable place for people to live, for e.g. Southern parts of India. Whereas hilly and desert lands have relatively lower population due to extreme climatic conditions, for e.g. North-Eastern states and Rajasthan desert areas.

(iii) Availability of water is also responsible factor for people to live. Generally, in ancient times most of the civilisaton flourished near river banks. For e.g. Indus Valley Civilisation, Mesopotamian Civilisation.

(iv) Availability of natural resources also attract people to live and develop their livelihood there.

Economic factors that affect the population distribution are

(i) Settled agriculture and agricultural development, pattern of human settlement, all are the main attraction of human being. For e.g. the Northern plains of India are densely populated regions.

(ii) Industrialisation and urbanisation are the pull factors to attract people to move there like, Delhi, Mumbai, Kolkata, Bengaluru, Chennai and Jaipur.

(iii) Good network of transportation also gives rise to population growth in an area which facilitates people to easily move from one place to another.

(iv) Presence of mineral resources are also a factor which attract industrialisation and ultimately urbanisation, for e.g. Chotanagpur Plateau region.

7. Identify the challenges of the adolescent population before the society. Enlist a few measures to overcome these problems. ***(CBSE SQP 2018)***

Ans. In India, the share of adolescents i.e. up to the age group of 10-19 years is about 20.9% as per 2011 census. Among these, male adolescent constitute 52.7% and female adolescent contribute 47.3%.

This youthful population have high potential to utilise in socio-economic and political development of a nation. But this population is highly vulnerable to various challenges like drug addicts, alcoholism, radicalism, etc.

There are many other traditional challenges for the adolescents in the society such as

- Lower age of marriage
- Illiterary among youth particularly in females
- Increasing school dropouts
- Low intake of nutrients
- High rate of maternal mortality of adolescent mothers
- High rate of HIV/AIDS infection

The government of India has undertaken certain policies in this regard to impart proper education to the adolescent group so that their talent are better channelised and properly utilised. These are

(i) The programme like Sabla for adolescent girls and Saksham for adolescent boys are being executed by government to improve the nutrient level and provide skill to youth.

(ii) In National Youth Policy 2011, the government defined youth of age group 15-29 years and identified five well-defined objectives to achieve in the field of education, skill development, employment, entrepreneurship, health, sports and promotion of social values.

(iii) Various efforts are being done by centre and state government to empower the youth and to achieve their full potential under the National Youth Policy.

8. "The decadal and annual growth rates of population in India are both very high and steadily increasing over time." Substantiate the statement. ***(Delhi 2018)***

> **HINT** *Dear students, this question simply ask you to write about the changing and growing pattern of population.*

Ans. Growth of population is the change in the number of people living in a particular area between two points of time. The decadal and annual growth of population in India are very high and steadily increasing over time. In India, the annual and decadal growth rate of population is more than the other developed countries.

The decadal and annual growth rate increased continously in the year 1971 and 1981 respectively, but after the year 1971 and 1981 the decadal and the annual growth rate started declining. At present, the annual growth of India's population is 1.64% (2011). Still, the growth rate of population in India is high as compared to the developed countries. With this increasing rate, it is estimated that India's population will double itself in 30 to 35 years and even surpass population of China in seven years.

9. What is density of population? Describe the spatial variation of population density in India. ***(Delhi 2015)***

Ans. Density of population is referred to as number of persons per unit area. It helps in getting a better understanding of the spatial distribution of population in relation to land.

For spatial variation of population density in India, refer to Q. 6 of 3 marks questions.

10. What is the source of population data in India? Explain the distribution of population in India. ***(Delhi 2015)***

Ans. In India, Population data is collected through census operation which held every 10 years in our country. Spatial pattern of population distribution is very uneven. As some areas are sparsely populated whereas others are dense.

These states can be categorised into three categories

(i) **States with High Population** Uttar Pradesh, (highest population), Maharashtra, Bihar, West Bengal, Andhra Pradesh, Tamil Nadu, Madhya Pradesh, Rajasthan, Karnataka and Gujarat. These states together account for 76% of population.

(ii) **States with Moderate population** Assam, Haryana, Jharkhand, Chhattisgarh, Kerala, Punjab and Goa.

(iii) **States with Low population** Hilly and tribal areas like Jammu and Kashmir, Uttarakhand, all North-Eastern states (except Assam) and Union Territories excluding Delhi.

Source of population in India
- States with high population
- States with moderate population
- States with low population

Population is mainly affected by climate, terrain and availability of water. For example, the North Indian Plains, deltas and coastal plains are densely populated, whereas the mountainous areas and interior areas of central and southern India have relatively low population.

Besides these, evolution of settled and urbanisation are the socio-economic and historical factors of distribution of population.

11. Define the term 'growth of population'. Describe the third (III) phase of growth of population in India. ***(All India 2015)***

Ans. Growth of population refers to the changes occuring in the number of person living in a particular area between two points of time. The growth rate is expressed in percentage.

The third phases of population growth is described below

(i) Its period is from 1951 to 1981.

(ii) This period is well-known for population explosion in the country.

(iii) The situation of population explosion is caused by a rapid fall in mortality rate, but a high fertility rate of population in India.

(iv) In this decade, the average annual growth rate was as high as 2.2%, due to improved and planned developmental activities.

(v) The high growth rate was also a result of increased international migration from countries like Tibet, Bangladesh, Nepal and Pakistan.

12. What is population doubling time? Explain the characteristics of the growth of population in India in phase-I and phase-II. ***(All India 2015)***

Ans. Population doubling time is the time taken by any population to double itself at its current annual growth rate.

Characteristics of the growth of population in India in phase-I are given below

(i) The period of phase-I is from 1901 to 1921.

(ii) This period is considered as stagnant phase of growth.

(iii) During 1911-1921, this period has recorded very low growth rate, even recording a negative growth rate.

(iv) In this period, the rate of increase was low due to both high birth rate and death rate.

Characteristics of the growth of population in India in phase-II are given below

(i) Its period is from 1921 to 1951.

(ii) This period is known for steady population growth.

(iii) In this period, India has recorded an overall improvement in health and sanitation which brought down the mortality rate.

(iv) The crude birth rate remained high in this phase leading to higher growth rate than the previous phase.

13. The decades of 1921-51 are referred to as the period of steady growth of population whereas the decades 1951-81 are referred to as the period of population explosion in India. Explain by giving reasons. ***(Delhi 2014)***

Or Why has population of India been increasing steadily in the period of 1921-51? Explain any three reasons. ***(All India 2012)***

Or Define the terms growth of population. Explain any four causes for the steady growth of population in India during decades of 1921-51. ***(Delhi 2011)***

Ans. Growth of population refers to the change occurring in the number of persons living in an area between two points of time.

The second phase of population growth in India is from 1921 to 1951. This phase is known as steady phase of India's population growth because of the following reasons

(i) High birth rate and declining mortality rate.

(ii) Improvement in medical, sanitation facilities and health services.

(iii) The crude birth rate remained high in this period.

(iv) Better transport system which led to improved distribution system.

The third phase of population growth is from 1951 to 1981 because of the rapid fall in the mortality rate and a high fertility rate or birth rate in the country.

This phase is also known as the phase of population explosion because of the following reasons

(i) The population increased with a high growth rate. The average annual growth rate in this phase was 2.2 percent.

(ii) Population increased because of the starting of developmental activities by centralised planning process that led to the economic development and improvement in the living conditions of the people at large.

(iii) Other reason responsible for population increase was migration from Tibet, Bangladesh, Nepal and Pakistan.

14. "The decades 1951-81 are referred to as the period of population explosion in India." Explain the statement by giving three reasons. ***(All India 2014)***

Or Explain any five causes of the rapid growth of population in India from 1951 to 1981. ***(All India 2011)***

Ans. The decades of 1951-81 are referred to as the period of population explosion in India because of rapid fall in death rate and high birth rate. The main causes of this explosion are as follows

Widening Gap between Birth and Death Rates The average annual birth rate was 42 per thousand population but it came down to 28.7 per thousand in 1981. This shows that the birth rate registered small decline and death rate had gone down rather sharply. This widening gap has increased our population rapidly.

Low Age of Marriage Child marriage have been very common in our country. As per census 1931, 72% marriage in India were performed before 15 and 34% before 10 years of age. The mean age at marriage of females increased from 15.6 in 1951 to 17.6 in 1981.

Reasons for growth of population in 1951-81
- Widening Gap between Birth and Death rates
- Low Age of Marriage
- High Illitracy
- Religious Attitude towards Family Planning
- Other Causes

High Illiteracy During this period (1951-81), the overall literacy rate was very low. Due to this, they would be more orthodox, illogical and religious minded.

Religious Attitude towards Family Planning The religiously orthodox and conservative people are against the use of family planning measures. The women disfavoured family planning on the plea that they cannot go against the wishes of God.

Other Causes Joint family system and lack of responsibility of young couples in these families to bring up their children and lack of recreational facilities, and lack of information or wrong information about the adverse affects of vasectomy, tubectomy are some other causes of the rapid growth of population.

15. Explain with examples the occupational structure of India's population. ***(Delhi 2011)***

Ans. On the basis of economic status India's population is divided into three categories based on occupational structure

(i) **Main Workers** Main worker is a person who works for atleast 183 days in a year.

(ii) **Marginal Workers** Marginal worker is a person who works for less than 183 days in a year.

(iii) **Non-Workers** It is person who does not work for its livelihood.

About 54.6% of total working population are cultivators and agricultural labourers, whereas only 3.8% of workers are engaged in household industries and 41.6% are other workers including non-household industries, trade commerce, construction and repair and other services.

The working proportion is relatively high in Himachal Pradesh, Sikkim, Chhattisgarh, Andhra Pradesh, Karnataka, Arunachal Pradesh, Nagaland, Manipur and Meghalaya.

Work participation rate is higher in economically backward states because large number of people are required subsistence level activity.

It is major characteristic of working population in India that a large number of working population is engaged in agricultural activities. The proportion of female workers is also very low in India.

Data/Source Based Questions

1. Attempt any 3 questions from the following questions 57-60. *(CBSE SQP Term I 2021)*

Table 1.1 Decadal Growth Rates in India, 1901-2011

Census Years	Total Population	Growth Rate	
		Absolute Number	% of Growth
1901	238396327	....	....
1911	252093390	(+) 13697063	(+) 5.75
1921	251321213	(–) 772117	(–) 0.31
1931	278977238	(+) 27656025	(+) 11.60
1941	31866580	(+) 39683342	(+) 14.22
1951	361088090	(+) 42420485	(+) 13.31
1961	439234771	(+) 77682873	(+) 21.51
1971	548159652	(+) 108924881	(+) 24.80
1981	683329097	(+) 135169445	(+) 24.66
1991	846302688	(+) 162973591	(+) 23.85
2001	1028610328	(+) 182307640	(+) 21.54
2011**	1210193422	(+) 181583094	(+) 17.64

*Decadal growth rate: $g = \frac{P_2 - P_1}{P_1} \times 100$

where P_1 = population of the base year

P_2 = population of the present year

**Source : Census of India, 2011 (Provisional)

(i) Which year has seen a negative population growth rate in India?
(a) 1931 (b) 1921 (c) 1911 (d) 1941

(ii) What was the highest recorded growth rate of population in India?
(a) 24.66 (b) 24.80 (c) 23.85 (d) 21.54

(iii) Which year has recorded the highest growth of population in India in terms of absolute numbers?
(a) 2001 (b) 2011 (c) 1991 (d) 1981

(iv) How much population increase has been registered between the census years 1911 to census year 2011?
(a) 900789600 (b) 182307640
(c) 181583094 (d) 971797095

Ans. (i) (b) 1921
(ii) (b) 24.80
(iii) (a) 2001
(iv) (d) 971797095

2. Study the following table and answer the questions that follow. *(Delhi 2019)*

Decadal Growth Rates in India, 1901-2011

Census Years	Total Population	Growth Rate*	
		Absolute Number	% of Growth
1901	238396327	-	-
1911	252093390	(+)13697063	(+)5.75
1921	251321213	(−)772117	(−)0.31
1931	298977238	(+)27656025	(+)11.60
1941	318660580	(+)39683342	(+)14.22
1951	361088090	(+)42420485	(+)13.31
1961	439234771	(+)77682873	(+)21.51
1971	548159652	(+)108924881	(+)24.80
1981	683329097	(+)135169445	(+)24.66
1991	846302688	(+)162973591	(+)23.85
2001	1028610328	(+)182307640	(+)21.54
2011**	1210193422	(+)181583094	(+)17.64

(i) Which decade has shown the negative trend of growth rate of population?

(ii) Mention any two decades in which the percentage decadal growth has shown the regular downward trend.

(iii) Explain any two reasons for the declining trend in the population growth rate.

Ans. (i) The period from 1911 to 1921 shows a negative trend of growth of population.

(ii) The decades 1981 and 1991 have shown a regular downward trend in the population growth in India.

(iii) The decades after 1981 marked the slow growth rate of population due to low birth rate and low death rate. Following are the factors which cause the declining trend in the population growth.

- The fall in crude birth rate due to family planning is responsible for such population growth.
- The progressive social development and increase in mean age of marriage lower down the birth rate in the country. The improved quality of life particularly education of female and increasing economic progress helped to reduce the growth rate of population.

3. Read the following source and answer the questions given below it.

Regional Variation in Population Growth

The growth rate of population during 1991-2001 in Indian States and Union Territories shows very obvious pattern.

The States like Kerala, Karnataka, Tamil Nadu, Andhra Pradesh, Odisha, Puducherry and Goa show a low rate of growth not exceeding 20 per cent over the decade. Kerala registered the lowest growth rate (9-4) not only in this group of states, but also in the country as a whole. A continuous belt of states from West to East in the North-West, North and North Central parts of the country has relatively high growth rate than the Southern states. It is in this belt comprising Gujarat, Maharashtra, Rajasthan, Punjab, Haryana, Uttar Pradesh, Uttarakhand, Madhya Pradesh, Sikkim, Assam, West Bengal, Bihar, Chhattisgarh and Jharkhand, the growth rate on the average remained 20-25 per cent.

During 2001-2011, the growth rates of almost all States and Union Territories have registered a lower figure compared to the previous decade, namely, 1991-2001. The percentage decadal growth rates of the six most populous States, namely, Uttar Pradesh, Maharashtra, Bihar, West Bengal,

Andhra Pradesh and Madhya Pradesh have all fallen during 2001-2011 compared to 1991-2001, the fall being the lowest for Andhra Pradesh (3.5 percentage points) and highest for Maharashtra (6.7 percentage points). Tamil Nadu (3.9 percentage points) and Puducherry (7.1 percentage points) have registered some increase during 2001-2011 over the previous decade.

(*i*) Which of the following States has the largest population?

(a) Bihar (b) Uttar Pradesh
(c) Maharashtra (d) Tamil Nadu

(*ii*) Which of the following States has the highest decrease in population growth rate during the 2001-2011?

(a) Maharashtra (b) Bihar
(c) Uttar Pradesh (d) Tamil Nadu

(iii) Which of the following States has registered increase in population growth rate during 2001-2011?

(a) Tamil Nadu
(b) Andhra Pradesh
(c) Madhya Pradesh
(d) Bihar

(iv) Which one of the following is the correct formula to know the natural growth of population?

(a) Birth - Death
(b) Birth + Death
(c) Birth - Death + Immigration
(d) Birth - Death - Immigration

Ans. (i) (b) Uttar Pradesh
(ii) (a) Maharashtra
(iii) (d) Bihar
(iv) (a) Birth - Death

Map Based Question

1. Locate and label the following on the given political outline map of India with appropriate symbols.

(i) The state having the highest density of population. ***(All India 2011, All India 2008)***

(ii) The state with lowest density of population. ***(All India 2016, Delhi 2011)***

Ans.

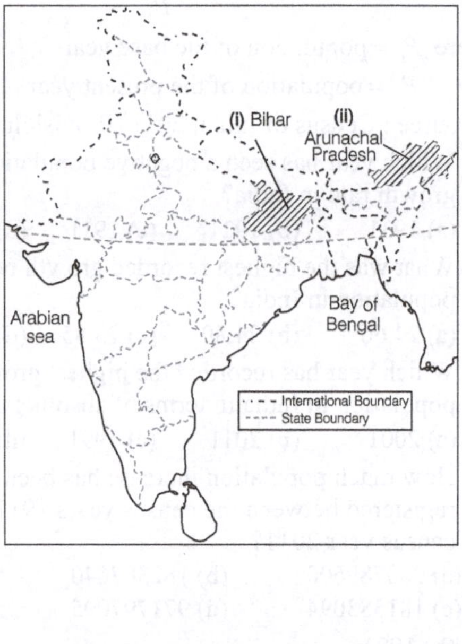

CHAPTER TEST

01 Mark Questions

1 Which one of the following has the lowest density of population in India?

(a) Uttar Pradesh (b) West Bengal
(c) Arunachal Pradesh (d) Bihar

2 Identify the largest linguistic group of India.

(a) Dravidian (b) Sino-Tibetan
(c) Indo-Aryan (d) Austric

3 Which of the following pairs is incorrectly matched?

(a) State having the highest population – Uttar Pradesh
(b) State having the highest percentage of rural population - Rajasthan
(c) State having the highest literacy rate – Kerala
(d) State having the highest percentage of urban population – Goa

4 **Assertion** (A) The Government of India formulated the National Policy for Skill Development and Entrepreneurship in 2015.

Reason (R) The aim of this policy is to provide an umbrella framework to all skilling activities being carried out within the country, and to align these to common standards and link skilling with demand centres.

Codes

(a) Both A and R are true and R is the correct explanation of A
(b) Both A and R are true, but R is not the correct explanation of A
(c) A is true, but R is false
(d) A is false, but R is true

5 Consider the following about the later colonial period and choose the correct answer.

I. Socio-economic factors affect the distribution of population in India.

II. Climate is one of the important socio-economic factors.

Codes

(a) Only statement I is correct
(b) Both the statements are true and statement II correctly present the reason for statement I
(c) Only Statement II is correct
(d) Both the statements I and II are incorrect

Answers

1. (c)	2. (c)	3. (b)	4. (a)	5. (a)

03 Marks Questions

6 What are the physical factors which determine the pattern of population distribution in India? State in brief.

7 Give any three reasons due to which the growth rate of population in Phase IV slowed down in India.

8 Write about the status of adolescent population in India. Also state its challenges.

05 Marks Questions

9 Discuss about the occupational structure of India's population along with suitable examples.

10 What do you understand by density of population? Discuss the spatial pattern of density of population in India.

11 What do you understand by population doubling time? State the main characteristics of the growth of population in India in Phase-I and Phase-II.

02

Human Settlement

TREND ANALYSIS 3 YEARS

Average No. of Questions Across all Sets

Topic	Types of Questions	2023	2020	2019
TOPIC 01 Rural Settlement	1 Mark	–	–	–
	3 Marks	–	1	1
	5 Marks	–	–	–
TOPIC 02 Urban Settlement	1 Mark	–	–	–
	3 Marks	–	–	–
	5 Marks	1	–	–
TOPIC 03 Urbanisation	1 Mark	–	–	–
	3 Marks	–	–	3
	5 Marks	–	–	–

Human settlement refers to the cluster or group of human houses. To earn livelihood, people build houses and other structures and make their control over some areas and resources. The process of settlement involves gathering of people, building houses, controlling a specific territory for resource base.

Each settlement differs from others in size and type. This may be a **hamlet** (smallest settlement) or a **metropolitan city** (largest settlement). When a settlement grows in its size, its social structure, ecology and technology also changes. Settlements could be small and sparsely spaced, they may also be large and closely spaced.

Rural Settlements

They are mainly smaller in size and poorly spaced. The people of these settlements are mainly engaged in primary activities like, agriculture, fishing, mining, etc, e.g. people surviving in hamlets and villages.

Factors Determining the Rural Settlements

There are various factors and conditions responsible for having different types of rural settlements in India. These are

Physical Features These include nature of terrain, altitude, climate and availability of water.

Cultural and Ethnic Factors These include social structure, caste and religion.

Security Factors These include defence against thefts and robberies.

Types of Rural Settlements

Types of the rural settlements are determined by the above determinants as well as by the extent of the built up area and inter-house distance.

In India, Rural settlements can broadly divided into four types

(i) Clustered, agglomerated or nucleated
(ii) Semi-clustered or fragmented
(iii) Hamleted, and
(iv) Dispersed or isolated

Clustered Settlements

- The houses in this settlement are **closely spaced** or have no space between houses.
- The living place is distinct and separated from the surrounding farms, barns and pastures.
- The settlement sometimes present distinct patterns or geometrical shapes like rectangular, radial, linear, etc which are recognisable in fertile alluvial plains and North-Eastern states.
- This type of settlement is built due to various reasons, e.g. in Bundelkhand and Nagaland, people live in these settlements for defence and security purposes, in Rajasthan these settlements are built around/ near water resources due to water scarcity.

Semi-Clustered Settlements

- This type of settlement develops by the concentration of houses in a restricted area of a dispersed settlement or develop due to segregation or fragmentation of a large compact village.
- Here, a dominant community captures the most important part in main village and force other communities to live away. For example, plains of Gujarat and Rajasthan.

Hamleted Settlement

- This type of settlement is formed due to **social** or **ethnic factors** and thus known for different identity and name, like, panna, para, nagla, dhani etc.
- Each hamlet is a unit and has a number of houses.
- Several units of hamlets collectively form a village. For e.g. middle and lower Ganga plain, Chhattisgarh and lower valleys of Himalayas.

Dispersed Settlements

- Isolated huts or hamlets of few huts in remote jungles or on small hills with farms or pastures are characteristics of dispersed type of settlement.
- These houses may be of temporary use. It is found in Meghalaya, Uttaranchal, Himachal Pradesh, Kerala, etc.

Urban Settlements

- Unlike rural settlement, urban settlement are usually more dense, compact and larger in size.
- Here, people are mostly engaged in non-agricultural activities i.e. industries, services, administrative functions, etc.
- Cities and towns both are connected directly or indirectly with villages and also with each other and exchange goods, services and also commute.

Evolution of Towns in India

The evolution of towns started in India from prehistoric times, e.g. Harappa, Mohenjodaro towns, European colonies of modern period, etc.

Indian towns may be classified into three groups on the basis of their evolution in different periods

Ancient Towns

- These towns were developed over 2000 years ago by the various kings as religious and cultural centres, e.g. Varanasi, Prayag (Allahabad), Pataliputra (Patna), Madurai, etc.

Medieval Towns

- These towns were developed as headquarters of principalities and kingdoms by medieval kings and Sultans of India.
- These towns are about 100 in numbers and were generally fort towns which came up on the ruins of ancient towns. For example, Delhi, Hyderabad, Jaipur, Lucknow, Agra and Nagpur.

Modern Towns

These towns were developed by the Britishers and other Europeans in India. These are further divided into the following groups

- **Port Towns** These are located on the coastal areas of India i.e. Surat, Daman, Goa, Puducherry, etc.
- **Administrative Towns** These were developed for the administrative purposes, e.g. Mumbai (Bombay), Chennai (Madras) and Kolkata (Calcutta).
- **Industrial Towns** After 1850, these towns were developed like Jamshedpur.
- **Some other Towns of European Styles** These towns include hill stations for summer resorts, military towns and small towns for administrative purposes.

Towns after Independence

After Independence, some towns were also developed like

- **Administrative Headquarters or Capital of States** These towns include Chandigarh, Bhubaneshwar, Gandhinagar and Dispur etc.
- **Industrial Towns/Centres** These towns include Durgapur Bhilai, Sindri, Barani, etc.

- **Satellite Towns** These were old towns which developed around metropolitan cities such as Ghaziabad, Rohtak, Gurgaon (Gurugram), etc.
- **Medium and Small towns** These are developed due to increasing investment in rural areas.

Urbanisation in India

- Urbanisation is the transition of rural population into urban population.
- It is measured by the percentage of urban population into total population. In India, the **level of urbanisation** is very low, as it was just 31.16% in 2011.
- Developed countries have a higher level of urbanisation than India.
- Although, urbanisation in India is increasing with high rate, as it increased 11 times during twentieth century, but this process is comparatively slow during recent two decades.

Functional Classification of Towns

Apart from population size, Indian towns and cities can be classified into the following heads on the basis of their functions (dominant economic activity)

- **Administrative towns and cities** These towns work as headquarter for surrounding region. Government offices and departments, etc are mainly concentrated in these cities. For example, Chandigarh, New Delhi, Bhopal, Shilong, Guwahati, Imphal, Srinagar, Gandhinagar, Jaipur and Chennai, etc.
- **Industrial Towns** These towns/ cities mainly dominated by industries. For example, Jamshedpur, Bhilai, Durgapur, Madurai, Mumbai, etc.
- **Transport Cities** Transportation is the main function of these cities. Port towns are examples of these towns that are always busy in transporting commodities to other cities. For example, Kandla, Kochchi, Kozhikode, Vishakhapatnam, etc.

  There are some cities which are hubs of inland transport such as Agra, Dhulia, Mughal Sarai, Itarsi, Katni, etc.
- **Commercial Towns** The important functions of these towns are trade and commerce. For example, Kolkata, Saharanpur, Satna, etc.
- **Mining Towns** These towns have developed in mineral rich areas. For example, Raniganj, Jharia, Digboi, Ankaleshwar, Singrauli, etc.
- **Garrison Cantonment Towns** These towns are meant for the army or defence purpose. For example, Ambala, Jalandhar, Mhow, Babina, Udhampur, etc.
- **Educational Towns** Initially these towns were important education centres, but later they emerged as major campus towns. For example, Roorkee, Varanasi, Aligarh, Pilani, Allahabad, etc.
- **Religious and Cultural Towns** These towns are famous for pilgrimage, religious worship or old cultures. For example, Varanasi, Mathura, Amritsar, Madurai, Pune, Ajmer, Tirupati, Kurukshetra, Haridwar, Ujjain, etc.
- **Tourists Towns** These towns are famous for attracting wide range of tourists from India and all over the world. For example, Nainital, Mussoorie, Shimla, Pachmarhi, Jodhpur, Jaisalmer, Udagamandalam (Ooty), Mount Abu, etc.

The functions of these cities are not fix and change with the time as cities are dynamic in nature. With increase in population, cities become etropolis and multi-functional i.e. industry, business, administration, transport, etc. Thus, classification of these cities on the basis of specialised function is impossible as all the functions are interlinked.

PYQs Previous Years' Questions

1 Mark Questions (MCQ)

Multiple Choice Questions

1. Which one of the following is the feature of clustered settlements ? *(CBSE 2023)*
   (a) They are fragmented
   (b) They are isolated
   (c) Closely built up area of houses
   (d) Units are known as panna, para palli, etc

Ans. (c) Closely built up area of houses

2. Which of the following ia an example of ancient town? *(CBSE 2023)*
   (a) Hyderabad (b) Chennai
   (c) Prayag (d) Lucknow

Ans. (c) Prayag

3. Choose the correct pair from the following
   (a) Industrial town – Vishakhapatnam
   (b) Transport twon – Satna
   (c) Commercial town – Bhilai
   (d) Administrative – Bhopal

Ans. (d) Administrative town –Bhopal

4. Match Column I with column II and choose the correct option. *(CBSE 2023)*

Column I	Column II
A. Transport city	I. Jaipur
B. Mining town	II. Ambala
C. Garrison town	III. Itarsi
D. Administrative town	IV. Sangraul

Codes

	A	B	C	D		A	B	C	D
(a)	4	3	2	1	(b)	1	2	3	4
(c)	3	4	2	1	(d)	2	1	4	3

Ans. (c)

5. Which of the following are the features of Urban Settlements in India? *(CBSE SQP 2022)*
   (a) Complex way of life, manufacturing of finished goods, nodes of economic growth.
   (b) Intimate social relations, mainly primary economic activities, people are less mobile.
   (c) Economy mainly based on primary activities, providing food and raw materials and social relations are formal.
   (d) Provide a variety of services, poor transport networks, social relations are intimate.

Ans. (a) Complex way of life, manufacturing of finished goods, nodes of economic growth.

6. According to Census 2011, which of the following depicts the percentage of the level of urbanisation in India? *(CBSE SQP Term I 2021)*
   (a) 31.16 % (b) 28 % (c) 33.16 % (d) 26 %

Ans. (a) 31.16 %

7. Which of the following is a good example of Fort town? *(CBSE SQP Term I 2021)*
   (a) Jaipur (b) Banaras
   (c) Mathura (d) Rameshwaram

Ans. (a) Jaipur

8. Panna, Para, Palli, Nagla and Dhani are examples of which of the following settlements? *(CBSE SQP Term I 2021)*
   (a) Clustered Settlements
   (b) Semi-clustered Settlements
   (c) Dispersed Settlements
   (d) Hamleted Settlements

Ans. (d) Hamleted Settlements

9. Which one of the following is the main feature of rural settlement? *(CBSE SQP Term I 2021)*
   (a) Derive economic needs from primary activities
   (b) Derive economic needs from secondary activities
   (c) Derive economic needs from tertiary activities
   (d) Derive economic needs from quaternary activities

Ans. (a) Derive economic needs from primary activities

10. Which of the following pairs is not matched correctly? *(CBSE SQP Term I 2021)*

	Cities		Basis of Development
(a)	Prayag (Allahabad)	–	On religious and cultural basis
(b)	Lucknow	–	Based on the remnants of ancient cities
(c)	Kolkata	–	On cultural basis
(d)	Mumbai	–	In the form of commercial port

Ans. (c) Kolkata – On cultural basis

11. Match the column I with column II and choose the correct answer with the help of given codes.

(CBSE SQP Term I 2021)

Column I (Cities)	Column II (Types of Cities)
A. Jamshedpur	1. Summer resort
B. Bhuvaneshwar	2. Satellite town
C. Ghaziabad	3. Industrial town
D. Mussoorie	4. Commercial port
E. Goa	5. Administrative town

Codes

	A	B	C	D	E		A	B	C	D	E
(a)	1	2	3	4	5	(b)	3	5	2	1	4
(c)	5	4	3	2	1	(d)	3	5	4	2	1

Ans. (b)

12. Match the Column I with Column II and choose the correct options with the help of given options.

(CBSE SQP Term I 2021)

Column I (Cities)	Column II (Functional Specification)
A. Ambala	1. Mining town
B. Mughal Sarai	2. Transport town
C. Ankaleshwar	3. Educational town
D. Aligarh	4. Garrison town
E. Shimla	5. Commercial town
F. Saharanpur	6. Tourist town

Codes

	A	B	C	D	E	F		A	B	C	D	E	F
(a)	1	2	3	4	5	6	(b)	4	2	1	3	6	5
(c)	6	5	4	3	2	1	(d)	2	1	4	3	5	6

Ans. (b)

13. Identify the classification of towns on the basis of their evolution in different periods in India.

(CBSE Term I 2021)

(a) First, Second and Third Category
(b) Ancient, Medieval and Modern
(c) Transport, Commercial and Industrial
(d) Cantonment, Religious and Educational

Ans. (b) Ancient, Medieval and Modern

14. Identify the town developed in Medieval period. *(CBSE Term I 2021)*

(a) Delhi (b) Madurai
(c) Mumbai (d) Kolkata

Ans. (a) Delhi

15. Which of the following towns has the largest population? *(CBSE Term I 2021)*

(a) Hyderabad (b) Bengaluru
(c) Chennai (d) Lucknow

Ans. (b) Bengaluru

16. Which of the following types of town is 'Babina'? *(CBSE Term I 2021)*

(a) Garrison (b) Commercial
(c) Transport (d) Industrial

Ans. (a) Garrison

17. Which class of towns has the highest number in India? *(CBSE Term I 2021)*

(a) II (b) III (c) IV (d) V

Ans. (d) V

18. Which one of the following towns has developed as an 'administrative headquarter' after independence? *(CBSE Term I 2021)*

(a) Delhi (b) Chandigarh
(c) Prayagraj (d) Madurai

Ans. (b) Chandigarh

19. Study the following facts regarding urbanisation in India and choose the correct option. *(CBSE Term I 2021)*

I. The level of urbanisation in India in 2011 was 31.15 percent.
II. It is quite low in comparison to developed countries.
III. The growth rate of urbanisation has increased during the last two decades.

Options

(a) Only I and II are correct
(b) Only II and III are correct
(c) Only I and III are correct
(d) I, II and III are correct

Ans. (a) Only I and II are correct

20. Match column I with column II and choose the correct option. *(CBSE Term I 2021)*

Column I	Column II
A. Educational town	1. Jodhpur
B. Tourist town	2. Aligarh
C. Commercial town	3. Kurukshetra
D. Religions and Cultural town	4. Saharanpur

Codes

	A	B	C	D		A	B	C	D
(a)	II	I	IV	III	(b)	I	II	III	IV
(c)	III	IV	II	I	(d)	IV	III	II	I

Ans. (a) II I IV III

21. Which type of rural settlements are largely found in Gujarat plains and in some parts of Rajasthan? *(CBSE Compartment 2020)*
(a) Clustered settlements
(b) Semi-clustered settlements
(c) Hamleted settlements
(d) Dispersed settlements

Ans. (b) Semi-clustered settlements

22. Which type of rural settlements are largely found in Middle and Lower Ganga plains? *(CBSE Compartment 2020)*
(a) Clustered settlements
(b) Semi-clustered settlements
(c) Hamleted settlements
(d) Dispersed settlements

Ans. (b) Semi-clustered settlements

23. Which one of the following is the largest 'Urban Agglomeration' in India? *(CBSE Compartment 2020)*
(a) Kolkata
(b) Greater Mumbai
(c) Delhi
(d) Chennai

Ans. (b) Greater Mumbai

24. Which one of the following types of economic activities dominates in all rural settlements? *(CBSE 2019)*
(a) Primary (b) Tertiary
(c) Secondary (d) Quaternary

Ans. (a) Primary

25. Cluster of dwellings of any type or size where human beings live is known as
(a) Human Development (b) Human Settlement
(c) Human Phenomenon (d) None of these

Ans. (b) Human Settlement

26. The sparsely located small settlements are known as
(a) Hamlet (b) Slums
(c) Village (d) None of these

Ans. (a) Hamlet

27. Which of the following factor(s) is/are responsible for different types of rural settlements in India?
(a) Physical features (b) Cultural and ethnicity
(c) Security (d) All of these

Ans. (d) All of the above

28. Which type of rural settlement is a compact or closely built up area of houses?
(a) Semi-clustered (b) Clustered
(c) Hamleted (d) Dispersed

Ans. (b) Clustered

29. Which settlement is also known as fragmented settlement?
(a) Clustered (b) Dispersed
(c) Hamleted (d) Semi-clustered

Ans. (d) Semi-clustered

30. Which of the following is the example of Ancient town?
(a) Madurai (b) Lucknow
(c) Jaipur (d) Kolkata

Ans. (a) Madurai

31. Which of the following is the example of Modern town?
(a) Goa (b) Daman
(c) Chennai (d) All of these

Ans. (d) All of these

Very Short Answer Questions

1. Name any two modern towns built by the British in modern style? *(CBSE SQP 2018)*

Ans. Two modern towns built by the British in modern style in India are Bombay (Mumbai) and Calcutta (Kolkata).

2. Which town was developed as centre of modern industries after 1850? *(CBSE SQP 2018)*

Ans. The town developed as a centre of modern industries after 1850 was Jamshedpur. Other industrial towns were Bhilai, Durgapur, Madurai, etc.

3. How is the level of urbanisation measured in India? *(Delhi 2015)*

Ans. The level of urbanisation is measured by the percentage of urban population to total population.

4. What two factors mostly helped in the development of ancient towns in India? *(Delhi 2015)*

Ans. The two factors that mostly helped in the development of ancient towns in India are:
(i) Religion (ii) Culture

5. Give any two examples of ancient towns of India. *(Delhi 2014)*

Ans. Varanasi, Pataliputra/Patna, Mathura, Allahabad are examples of ancient towns of India.

6. Give an example of ancient historical towns from Bihar. *(All India 2014)*

Ans. Patna/ Pataliputra, Nalanda, Kaushambi are the examples of ancient historical towns from Bihar.

7. Give any two examples of mining towns in India. *(Delhi 2013)*

Ans. Jharia, Bokaro, Raniganj, Digboi, etc are the examples of mining towns in India.

8. Give the meaning of clustered rural settlement of India. *(Delhi 2013)*

Ans. It is a rural settlement where a number of families live close proximity to each other. This living place is not surrounded by farms, barn or pastures.

9. Give the meaning of human settlement. *(Delhi 2011)*

Or What is the meaning of human settlement? *(Delhi 2008)*

Ans. Human settlement refers to the cluster or group of human houses. These houses may vary from a small hut to a large bungalow or any type or size.

10. What is the meaning of rural settlement? *(All India 2008)*

Ans. Rural settlements are basically related to land based activities. Hamlets and villages are examples of rural settlements. They are scattered and smaller in size. The main activities of the dwellers are primary activities, especially agriculture.

3 Marks Questions

1. What are the basic differences between rural and urban settlements in India? *(CBSE SQP 2020)*

Or What makes rural settlement different from urban settlement in India? Explain. *(Delhi 2015)*

Or Differentiate between rural and urban settlements of India in three points. *(Delhi 2014)*

Ans. The differences between rural and urban settlements are as follows

Basis	Rural Settlement	Urban Settlement
Economic Activities	The major economic activities in rural areas are agriculture and other primary activities.	Urban settlement are specialise in industries and services.
Dependency	They are dependent on natural resources mainly land for their income.	They provide various types of services like transport and communication, etc.
Inter-relation ships	Agricultural and other production in rural areas supports industries of urban area. Rural areas provide raw material to the industries.	On return cities provide manufactured goods to rural areas and also to the people of cities.
social life	Social bonds in rural areas are stronger and life in simple.	Social bonds in urban areas are formal and life is complex, fast and sourrounded eith various problems.

2. Describe the development of medieval towns in India during the Mughal period. *(All India 2019)*

Ans. During the Mughal period, the growth of towns happened at a faster pace which continued upto the middle of 18th century.

The basic features of a town were

- The presence of a market, the qasba is defined as the village with a market.
- There was a hierarchy of towns from the qasba to the district headquarter, to the provincial towns like Agra, Delhi, etc.
- Towns were centers of manufacturing, banking, marketing, etc. Fatehpur Sikri built by Akbar while Shahajanabad by Shah Jahan were a couple of important towns.
- Some of the major towns during medieval period were Delhi, Multan, Patan, Kara, etc.

3. Examine the level of urbanisation in India after independence. *(Delhi 2019)*

Ans. Urbanisation is the transition of rural population into urban population. It is measured by the percentage of urban population into total population. After Independence, in India, the level of urbanisation is very low, as it was just 31.16%. Developed countries have a higher level of urbanisation than India which is a developing country. Although, urbanisation in India is increasing with high rate, as it increased 11 times during twentieth century, but this process is comparatively slow during recent two decades.

4. Many of the modern towns of India were developed during the period of British. Explain in brief. *(Delhi 2016)*

Other Similar Questions

Or Describe the development of modern towns in India during the British period.

Or How have the modern towns developed in India? Explain.

Ans. The British and other Europeans have developed a number of modern towns in India. Starting their foothold on coastal locations, they first developed some trading ports such as Surat, Daman, Goa, Pondicherry (Puducherry), etc. The British later consolidated their hold around three principal nodes i.e. Mumbai, Chennai and Kolkata. Towns based on modern industries also evolved after 1850.

For their domination, they established their administrative centres, hill towns as summer resorts and added administrative and military areas. Railways for their administrative purposes equipped India on the way of modernity.

5. Differentiate between 'Hamleted' and 'Dispersed' rural settlement of India. *(Delhi 2016)*

Or Explain any three characteristics each of hamleted and dispersed rural settlements in India. *(Delhi 2013)*

Ans. The differences between hamleted settlements and dispersed settlements are as follows

Hamleted Settlement	Dispersed Settlement
It is fragmented physical unit of settlement.	It is isolated forms of huts or hamlets in remote jungles.
Units are locally called panna, para, palli, nagla, dhani etc	Caused by extreme fragmentation of terrain and land resources.
Found in the middle and lower Ganga plain, Chhattisgarh and lower valleys of the Himalayas.	Found in the areas of Meghalaya, Uttarakhand, Himachal Pradesh and Kerala.

6. Explain any three physical factors responsible for different types of rural settlements in India. *(Delhi 2015)*

Ans. Physical factors which are responsible for different types of rural settlements in India are

Water Supply Settlements need water, they often locate on wet point sites for this. For example, in Rajasthan, scarcity of water has forced people to live in compact villages for maximum utilisation of available water resources.

Factors responsible for rural settlements
- Water Supply
- Climate
- Nature of Terrain

Climate People usually prefer areas which have favourable climatic conditions. Harsh climate like very hot and cold regions have less or no settlements there. For example, coastal plains have favourable climate thus, are dense populated regions.

Nature of Terrain Nature of terrain plays an important role in determining the shape and size of rural settlements.

For example plain areas have compact and larger settlements with dense population, whereas mountainous areas have scattered and hamleted rural settlements. Meghalaya, Uttarakhand and Himachal Pradesh have such types of rural settlement.

7. Explain any three features of semi-clustered rural settlements of India. *(All India 2015)*

Or Mention any three characteristics of semi-clustered rural settlements of India. *(Delhi 2010)*

Ans. The characteristics of semi-clustered rural settlements in India are as follows

(i) Semi-clustered settlements are developed by the concentration of houses in a special or restricted area of a dispersed settlement.

These settlements can also be developed by the division of a large clustered settlements.

(ii) Semi-lustered settlement can also be developed when a particular group start to live far from the centre or main village. In this condition, the dominant community or land owning community captures the most important part in main village and may force other to live away.

(iii) In India, these types of settlements are mostly found in the plain of Gujarat and Rajasthan.

8. Give the meaning of 'dispersed settlement'. Explain any two reasons for the development of such settlement in India. *(Delhi 2014)*

Ans. Dispersed settlements are such type of settlements where space between the houses is more. There are some scattered houses in this settlements. In India, the dispersed settlements are found in the form of few huts in remote jungles, hills with farms or pastures.

Reasons for the development of such settlements are:

(i) Due to extremely fragmented nature of terrain settlements developed.

(ii) Specially tribal people use to live in these isolated huts as their livelihood is fully dependent on the nature.

9. What are ancient towns ? Give four examples of ancient towns of India. ***(Delhi 2012)***

Ans. Ancient towns of India have historical background of over 2000 years. These towns are emerged during the ancient period and were developed by the important ancient kings. Most of these were temple towns. Later, they had became the hub of religion and cultures. Varanasi, Prayag (Allahabad), Patliputra (Patna), Madurai, etc are some of the ancient towns that emerged in India during ancient period.

10. Explain the evolution of towns in India in three points. ***(All India 2012)***

Or Classify Indian towns on the basis of their evolution in three different periods. Name one town of each period. ***(All India 2009)***

Ans. The towns of India can be classified into the following groups on the basis of their evolution in different periods

(i) **Ancient Towns** These towns of India have historical background of over 2000 years. Varanasi, Prayag (Allahabad), Patliputra (Patna) Madurai, etc were developed by the ancient kings.

(ii) **Medieval Towns** These towns were developed during the medieval period of India by kings and Sultans of India as their headquarter and making their administration strong, e.g. Delhi, Hyderabad, Jaipur, Lucknow, Agra etc.

Evolution of towns in India
- Ancient Towns
- Medieval Towns
- Modern Towns

(iii) **Modern Towns** These towns were developed by the Britishers and other Europeans in India like Surat, Daman and Goa, Kolkata, Mumbai, etc. Later, after independence some towns like Bhilai, Durgapur, Chandigarh, Gandhinagar were established.

11. Explain any three factors that determine the type of rural settlements in India. ***(Delhi 2011)***

Ans. Types of rural settlements in India are determined by the following factors

(i) **Physical Factors** It includes nature of terrain, altitude from sea level, climate and availability of water.

(ii) **Cultural and Ethnic Factors** Among these factors, social structure, caste and religion are important in India.

(iii) **Security Factors** It includes protection from thefts and robbers.

Above factors make Indian, settlements different in the world. Rural settlements can be of few houses in India to thousands of houses.

The form and structure of rural settlement is different in different parts of India.

5 Marks Questions

1. Discuss the problems of slums and urban waste disposal in developing countries like India. ***(CBSE SQP 2023)***

Ans. Slums are those area/colonies which are occupied by those migrants who were forced to migrate from the rural areas to urban areas/centres in search of livelihood but due to high rent and high cost of land, they could not afford proper housing. Thus, they are forced to live in environmentally incompatible and degraded areas.

Problems of slums in India are as follows

- Slums are environmentally incompatible and degraded areas.
- Slums have dilapidated (broken-down) houses where people are forced to live due to poverty or lesser income.
- People of slums face poor hygenic conditions. Thus, they are prone to many diseases and illness.
- The houses in slums have poor ventilation. So, people residing there face suffocation problems.
- Slums have substandard housing or illegal and inadequate building structures.
- Slums are overcrowed having narrow street pattern which is prone to serious hazards, e.g. fire hazards because of congested spaces, which increase the chances of its spread.

Additional Info
- Slums lack in basic amenities like drinking water, light and toilet facilities.
- They are marked by unregulated drainage system and open defecation.
- Besides this, most of the slum dwellers engage in low-paid, high risk-prone unorganised sectors of the urban economy. Due to such situation they are undernourished, prone to different types of illness.

2. Name any three factors that determine the clustered or compact rural settlement in India. ***(All India 2011)***

Ans. The three factors that determine the clustered or compact rural settlement in India are as follows

(i) **Fertile Alluvial Plain** It provides a plain surface where houses can be easily build. Fertile plains provide more agricultural land which attracts people to engage in agriculture. More concentration of population results in a compact or clustered rural settlement pattern.

(ii) **Water** It is another reason that can cause people to live in compact conditions. Scarcity of water forces the people to live together for maximum utilisation of the available water, e.g. compact settlements of Rajasthan.

Factors determining clustered or compact rural settlements
- Fertile Alluvial Plain
- Water
- Security or defence

(iii) **Security or Defence** It is another reason that cause people to live in compact settlements e.g. people of Bundelkhand region and Nagaland live in compact settlements for security reasons.

Data Based Questions

1. Study the given table carefully and answer the questions that follow. *(CBSE 2023)*

India-Trends of Urbanisation 1901-2011

Year	Number of Towns/ UAs	Urban Population (in Thousands)	% of Total Population	Decennial growth (%)
1901	1,827	25,851.9	10.84	–
1911	1,815	25,941.6	10.29	0.35
1921	1,949	28,086.2	11.18	8.27
1931	2,072	33,456.0	11.99	19.12
1941	2,250	44,153.3	13.86	31.97
1951	2,843	62,443.7	17.29	41.42
1961	2,365	78,936.6	17.97	26.41
1971	2,590	1,09,114	19.91	38.23
1981	3,378	1,59,463	23.34	46.14
1991	4,689	2,17,611	25.71	36.47
2001	5,161	2,85,355	27.78	31.13
2011	6,171	3,77,000	31.16	31.08

(i) In which year was the decennial growth of urban population is highest in India

(ii) How much was the total urban population in the year 2001 ?

(iii) How much was the total growth of number of towns between the year 1901 to 2011 in India ?

Ans. (i) In the year 1951, the decennial growth of urban population was the highest in India.

(ii) 285355 was the total urban population in the year 2001.

(iii) 37110 was the total growth of number of towns between the years 1901 to 2011 in India.

2. Study the given table carefully and answer the questions that follow. *(CBSE Term I 2021)*

India - Trends of Urbanisation 1901-2011

Year	Number of Towns/ UAs	Urban Population (in Thousands)	% Total Population	Decennial Growth (%)
1901	1,827	25,851.9	10.84	-
1911	1,815	25,941.6	10.29	0.35
1921	1,949	28,086.2	11.18	8.27
1931	2,072	33,456.0	11.99	19.12
1941	2,250	44,153.3	13.86	31.97
1951	2,843	62,443.7	17.29	41.42
1961	2,365	78,936.6	17.97	26.41
1971	2,590	1,09,114	19.91	38.23
1981	3,378	1,59,463	23.34	46.14
1991	4,689	2,17,611	25.71	36.47
2001	5,161	2,85,355	27.78	31.13
2011	6,171	3,77,000	31.16	31.08

(i) Which of the following decades has the largest decennial growth of towns?
(a) 1941 - 1951 (b) 1931 - 1941
(c) 1911 - 1921 (d) 2001 - 2011

(ii) Which of the following decades has highest growth of urban population?
(a) 1901 - 1911 (b) 1921 - 1931
(c) 1951 - 1961 (d) 1991 - 2001

(iii) In which of the following decades has the number of towns declined?
(a) 1901- 1911 (b) 1971 - 1981
(c) 1991 - 2001 (d) 2001 - 2011

(iv) What is the total growth of urban population from 1901 - 1911?
(a) 89,700 (b) 51,793.5
(c) 97,800 (d) 87,800

Ans. (i) (b) 1931 - 1941
(ii) (d) 1991 - 2001
(iii) (a) 1901 - 1911
(iv) (b) 51,793.5

CHAPTER TEST

01 Mark Questions

1 This is not the part of the definition of a town as per the Census of India. Identify it.

(a) Presence of municipality, corporation, etc.
(b) Population density of 400 persons per sq km.
(c) Population size of more than 5,000 persons.
(d) More than 75% of the population engaged in primary sector.

2 In which one of the following environments does one expect the presence of dispersed rural settlements?

(a) Arid and semi-arid regions of Rajasthan.
(b) Alluvial plains of Ganga.
(c) Forests and hills in North-East.
(d) Lower valleys of Himalayas.

3 Which of the following pairs is correctly matched?

Type		Town
(a) Industrial Town	–	Hughli
(b) Satellite Town	–	Ghaziabad
(c) Tourist Town	–	Pachmarhi
(d) All are correct		

4 **Assertion** (A) Semi-clustered or fragmented settlement is a type of rural settlement.

Reason (R) It may result from tendency of clustering in a restricted area of dispersed settlement.

Codes

(a) Both A and R are true and R is the correct explanation of A
(b) Both A and R are true, but R is not the correct explanation of A
(c) A is true, but R is false
(d) A is false, but R is true

5 Consider the following statements about rural settlements and choose the correct answer.

I Rural settlements are sparsely populated.

II Population of rural settlements is engaged in secondary activities.

Codes

(a) Only statement I is correct
(b) Both the statements are true and statement II correctly present the reason for statement I
(c) Only Statement II is correct
(d) Both the statements I and II are incorrect

Answers

1. (d)	2. (c)	3. (d)	4. (a)	5. (a)

03 Marks Questions

6 Many of the modern towns of India were developed during the British period. Explain in brief.

7 State any three features of semi-clustered rural settlements of India.

8 Explain the main features of Administrative Towns and Industrial Towns.

05 Marks Questions

9 Explain the important features of different types of rural settlements. Also state the factors responsible for the settlement pattern in different physical environments.

10 Explain in brief the functional classification of towns in India.

03

Land Resources and Agriculture

TREND ANALYSIS 3 YEARS

Topic	Types of Questions	2023	2020	2019
TOPIC 01 Types of Farming	1 Mark	–	–	–
	3 Marks	1	–	–
	5 Marks	–	–	–
TOPIC 02 Agricultural Development in India	1 Mark	–	–	–
	3 Marks	–	–	–
	5 Marks	1	–	2

Average No. of Questions Across all Sets

Land is a very important resource. Different types of land are suited to different uses. It is used for different purposes like making building of schools, roads on which we travel, parks in which we play, grounds, agriculture, mining activities and so on. Some are man-made creations while others are natural phenomena.

Land use Categories

Land revenue department is responsible for categorising land and maintaining its records. These records contains reporting area. Under the land revenue records land use categories are as follows:

(i) Forest
(ii) Land put to non-agricultural uses.
(iii) Barren and Wastelands.
(iv) Area under permanent pastures and grazing lands.
(v) Area under miscellaneous tree crops and groves.
(vi) Culturable wastelands
(vii) Current fallow
(viii) Net sown area

Land use Changes in India

Unlike other natural resources, land is fixed, it does not change by size or area. Economic activities are the major causes that affect land use. The three main economic changes that changes the land use are

(i) The size of the economy.
(ii) The composition of an economy (proportion of different sectors).
(iii) Increasing pressure on agricultural lands.

During the period of 1950-51 to 2014-15 some land use changes are worth mentioning which show an increase and decrease in these categories

Area Records Increase in Land Use

- Area under forest.
- Area under non-agricultural use.
- Current fallow lands.
- Net sown area.

Area Records Decrease in Land Use

- Barren and wasteland.
- Area under permanent pastures and tree crops.
- Culturable wasteland
- Fallow other than current fallow.

On the basis of ownership land can be classified into two categories

- **Private Land** Owned by individual or group of individuals.
- **Common Property Resources** (CPRs) Available for all and can be used by any person. It provides fodder for the livestock and fuel for the households. In rural areas, such land is of particular relevance for livelihood of the landless and marginal farmers.

Agricultural Land Use in India

Most of the Indians are dependent on agriculture, directly or indirectly for their subsistence. Agriculture is mainly land-based activity unlike secondary and tertiary sectors. The role of quality of land is important in agriculture.

The more the land is fertile the more it gives output/production. Ownership of land resource is considered as a social status in rural areas.

It is also seen as security for credit, natural hazards or life contingencies. Availability of total resources for agricultural uses is calculated by adding up net sown area, all fallow lands and culturable wastelands.

Cropping Intensity (CI) is calculated as follows

Cropping Intensity in percentage = GCA (Gross Cropped Area)/NSA (Net Sown Area) $\times 100$

Cropping seasons in India

Cropping season	**Major crops cultivated**	
	Northern states	Southern States
Kharif: June-September	Rice, cotton, bajra, maize, jowar, tur	Rice, maize, ragi, jowar, groundnut
Rabi: October-March	Wheat, gram, rapeseeds and mustard, barley	Rice, maize, ragi, groundnut, jowar
Zaid: April-June	Vegetables, fruits, fodder	Rice, vegetables, fodder

Types of Farming

In India farming is classified on the basis of moisture available for crops

- **Irrigated Farming** The main source of moisture for this farming is irrigation by various methods i.e. wells, tubewells, etc. Two types are protective and productive farming.
- **Rainfed Farming** (Barani) The main source of moisture for this farming is rainfall. Two types are dryland farming and wetland farming.
- **Dryland farming** is largely confined to the regions having rainfall less than 75 cm. These regions grows hardy and drought resistant crops such as ragi, bajra, moong, gram and gaur.

  On the other hand, in **wetland farming**, the rainfall is in excess of soil moisture requirement of plants during rainy season. Such regions may face flood and soil erosion hazards. These areas grow various water intensive crops such as rice, jute and sugercane.

Cropping Pattern

Food grains

Foodgrains are important for agriculture economy which constitute about two-third of total cropped area in the country. The foodgrains are classified on the basis of structure of grains:

Cereals

India ranks 3rd in the production of cereals after China and USA. India produces 11% of the world and covers about 54% of the total cropped area in India.

These cereals are

- **Rice** It is the most important food crop of India which feeds more than half of our population. States like West Bengal, Punjab and Uttar Pradesh were major rice producing states in India. In North-Western and in Himalyas regions, it is grown as a Kharif crop, whereas in West Bengal, farmers grow three crops of rice called **aus, aman** and **boro**.
- **Wheat** India share 12.8% of total wheat production of the world. It is cultivated on about 14% of the total cropped area. About 85% of this area comes under the Indo-Gangetic Plain, Malwa Plateau and Himalayas in North and central parts of the country. The major wheat producing states of India are Uttar Pradesh, Punjab, Haryana, Rajasthan, and Madhya Pradesh, Bihar and Jammu and Kashmir.

Coarse Grains

These crops are grown in almost 16.50% of total cropped area in the country. These coarse grains are:

- **Jowar/Sorghum** It is grown in about 5.3% of total cropped area. The major producer of Jowar are central and Southern states i.e. Karnataka, Madhya Pradesh and Andhra Pradesh.
- **Bajra** It is grown in about 5.2% of the total cropped area in the country. The major producers of bajra are Maharashtra, Gujarat, Uttar Pradesh, Rajasthan and Haryana.
- **Maize** It is grown in about 3.6% of total cropped area in the country. There is no particular region under maize. It is sown all over India except Eastern and North Eastern regions. The leading producers are Madhya Pradesh, Andhra Pradesh, Telangana, Karnataka, Rajasthan and Uttar Pradesh.
- **Pulses** Pulses are grown in India on about 11% of the total cropped area. India is one of the largest producers of pulses, as it cultivates about 20% pulses of the world. Pulses are legume crops. These are largely confined to the drylands of Deccan and Central plateaus and North-Western parts of the country.
- **Gram** It is grown in 2.8% of the total cropped area. The major producers are Madhya Pradesh, Uttar Pradesh, **Maharashtra**, Andhra Pradesh and Rajasthan.
- **Tur** (Arhar) This is grown in 2% of the total cropped area of India. It is the second important pulse crop in the country. **Maharashtra** is the leading producer of tur which produces about 75% of tur in India. It is also called as red gram or pigeon pea.
- **Oil seeds** Oil seeds are produced for extracting edible oils. Oil seeds include groundnut (3.6%), rapeseed and mustard (2.5%), soybean, sunflower, etc. These different oilseeds are grown in India about 14% of total cropped area in the country.

  Drylands of Malwa Plateau, Maharashtra, Gujarat, Rajasthan, Telangana and Rayalseema of Andhra Pradesh and Karnataka plateau are leading producers of oilseeds. Soybean and sunflower are other important oil seeds grown in India.

Fibre Crops

Fibre crops are one which provides fibre for preparing cloth. These include

- **Cotton** India grows both short staple (Indian) cotton as well as long staple (American) cotton. India is the second largest producer of cotton after China. Largest producers of cotton in India are Maharashtra, Gujarat, Andhra Pradesh, Punjab and Haryana.
- **Jute** India accounts for about three-fifth 60% of the world's jute production. **West Bengal** (75%) is the largest producer of jute in the country. Other producers are Bihar and Assam.

Other Crops

- **Sugarcane** It is an important cash crop in India. India's sugarcane production is about 19.7% of the world's total production, which makes India the 2nd largest producer after Brazil. Major producers are Uttar Pradesh, Maharashtra, and Gujarat. **Uttar Pradesh** accounts 40 per cent of sugarcane production and secures a position of the largest producer of India.
- **Tea** India is the leading producer of tea and accounts for about 21.22% of total production in the world. **Assam** (53.2%) is the largest producer of tea in India. Other states are West Bengal and Tamil Nadu.
- **Coffee** India is the 8th largest producer of coffee in the world which accounts about 3.17% share. **Karnataka** is the largest producer of coffee that produces more than 66% of India's total coffee.

Agricultural Development in India

Before Independence, Indian agriculture was largely subsistence in nature, this period was frequently witnessed severe droughts, famines and food shortage. About 1/3rd of the irrigated area went to Pakistan.

Consequently, Government took several steps to increase the production of foodgrains. Following three strategies were adopted to achieve this goal

(i) Switching over from cash crops to food crops
(ii) Intensification of cropping over already cultivated land.
(iii) Increasing cultivated area by bringing cultivable and fallow land under plough.

However, Indian agriculture could not progress much, then Government introduced modern technology into agriculture. These were

- High Yielding Variety (HYV) of seeds
- Fertilisers
- Mechanisation
- Improved irrigation and credit marketing facilities.
- Intensive Area Development Programme

All the above inputs were the main components of what is known as **Green Revolution**. This strategy of agricultural development in the country made the country self-reliant in foodgrain production.

But, green revolution was initially confined to irrigated areas only. This led to regional disparities in agricultural development in the country till the seventies. Consequently, **Planning Commission** prepared plans to solve the problems of agriculture in rainfed areas in 1980s. It initiated agro-climate planning in 1988 to induce regional balance.

Growth of Agricultural Output and Technology

- Since independence, there has been improvement in technologies used for agricultural production. As a result, increase in agricultural production has been recorded.
- India is now became a leading producer of pulses and jute and 2nd largest in rice, wheat, groundnut, sugarcane and vegetables.
- New technologies also came up to increase the production of food grains, for example, HYV seeds, chemical fertilisers raised 15 folds since mid 1960s.

Problems of Indian Agriculture

These problems are

Dependence on Erratic Monsoon There is only 33% cultivated area is under irrigation. The nature of South-West monsoon is very fluctuating which causes flood and drought situation in India.

Low Productivity India also lags behind in terms of per hectare production and per person production and also behind at International level. This low productivity is a result of high population which creates a heavy pressure on available land resources.

Constraints of Financial Resources and Indebtedness Lack of money and financial resources are the major constraints to the development of agriculture in India. As majority of farmers are small, marginal and poor, they cannot afford highly expensive inputs to increase their production.

Lack of Land Reforms Lack of land reforms and unequal distribution of land resources led to the worst condition of poor and marginal farmers and also become constraint in the development of agriculture in India.

Small Farm Size and Fragmentation of Landholdings 'Inheritance law' is mainly responsible for small and fragmented farm size.

Lack of Commercialisation As most of the farmers are poor and marginal, farmers practice subsistence agriculture for their living.

Vast Under-employment There is seasonal unemployment in agricultural sector. There is no income during ploughing field to harvesting crops.

Degradation of Cultivable Land After green revolution degradation has started in India. Excessive use of irrigation, chemical fertilisers, etc created problems of water lodging and solemnisation. Fertility of land is also decreasing day by day.

PYQs Previous Years' Questions

1 Mark Questions

Multiple Choice Questions

1. Which of the following is not a feature of dryland farming ? *(CBSE 2023)*
   (a) It is practiced where the annual amount of rainfall is less than 75 cm.
   (b) It is practiced in black soil areas.
   (c) Drought resistant crops are grown.
   (d) Measures are taken to preserve soil moisture.

Ans. (d) Measures are taken to preserve soil moisture.

2. Read the given resources and choose the correct option related to 'community's resources'. *(CBSE 2023)*
   I. Village water bodies
   II. Village agriculture land
   III. Village residential land
   IV. Pasture land
   Codes
   (a) Only I and II are correct
   (b) Only II and III are correct
   (c) Only III and IV are correct
   (d) Only I and IV are correct

Ans. (d) Only I and IV are correct

3. In which one of the following countries is 'cooperative farming' very successful? *(CBSE Compartment 2020)*
   (a) India (b) China
   (c) Denmark (d) Germany

Ans. (c) Denmark

4. In which part of the world is 'slash and burn' agriculture known as 'Jhuming'? *(CBSE Compartment 2020)*
   (a) Hokkaido region of Japan
   (b) Central America
   (c) North-Eastern States of India
   (d) Eastern Indonesia

Ans. (c) North-Eastern States of India

5. South-West monsoon in India coincides with which cropping season? *(CBSE SQP 2019)*
   (a) Kharif
   (b) Rabi
   (c) Zaid
   (d) None of the above

Ans. (a) Kharif

6. Which type of land is owned by the Village panchayat or the Government?
   (a) Land put to Non-agricultural uses
   (b) Forests
   (c) Barren and wastelands
   (d) Area under permanent pastures and grazing lands.

Ans. (d) Area under permanent pastures and grazing lands.

7. The land under orchards and fruit trees are included in which category of land use?
   (a) Land put to Non-agricultural uses
   (b) Forests
   (c) Area under miscellaneous tree crops and groves.
   (d) Current fallow

Ans. (c) Area under miscellaneous tree crops and groves

8. Any land which is left fallow (uncultivated) for more than five years is included in which category of land use?
   (a) Culturable wasteland
   (b) Current fallow
   (c) Fallow other than current fallow
   (d) Net sown area

Ans. (a) Culturable wasteland

9. The physical extent of land on which crops are sown and harvested is known as
   (a) Culturable wasteland (b) Current fallow
   (c) Fallow other than current fallow (d) Net sown area

Ans. (d) Net sown area

10. The increase of which land use category is a recent phenomenon due to use of culturable wasteland?
   (a) Current fallow (b) Forests
   (c) Barren and wasteland (d) New area sown

Ans. (d) New area sown

11. Which of the following is an example of Community Property Resource?
   (a) Community forests (b) Pasture lands
   (c) Village water bodies (d) All of these

Ans. (d) All of these

12. What is the rank of India in the world in terms of production of rice?
   (a) 1st (b) 2nd (c) 3rd (d) 4th

Ans. (b) 2nd

13. Arrange the following states in sequence as per their position in the production of rice.

1. Uttar Pradesh 2. West Bengal
3. Punjab

Codes

(a) 1, 2, 3 (b) 3, 2, 1
(c) 2, 1, 3 (d) 2, 3, 1

Ans. (c) 2, 1, 3

Very Short Answer Questions

1. What is the contribution of India in the production of rice in the world? *(Delhi 2011)*

Ans. India ranked 2nd with the production of 22.07% rice in the world. Only China produced more rice than India.

2. What is the meaning of 'Common Property Resources' (CRP)? *(Delhi 2011)*

Ans. Common Property Resources are not owned by any person or group. They are available for all and can be used by any person. These CPRs provide fodder to the livestock and fuel woods for household uses to villagers.

3. How is the cropping intensity calculated in India? *(Delhi 2009)*

Ans. Cropping intensity is calculated in percentage by using the following formula:

Cropping Intensity (CI) = Gross Cropped Area / Net Sown Area x 100

4. How is the productive irrigation able to achieve high productivity in India? *(All India 2009)*

Ans. In productive irrigation farming, water is used in high amount in per unit cultivated area. The main objective of this type of farming is to produce more and more yield by providing sufficient moisture to soil for cultivation. Thus, this type of farming can help India to achieve high productivity.

3 Marks Questions

1. Explain any three differences between irrigated and rainfed farming in India. *(CBSE 2023)*

Ans. Differences between irrigated and rainfed farming are

Irrigated Farming	Rainfed Farming
In this type of farming, the main source of moisture for a crop is irrigation by various methods like wells, tubewells, etc.	In this type of farming, the main source of moisture for soil and crops is rainfall.
Irrigated farming may be of two types on the basis of objective of farming i.e. productive and protective.	On the basis of adequacy of soil moisture, it is classified into two types such as dryland farming and wetland farming.
Productivity can be enhanced by productive irrigation and crops can be saved from drought by providing them with protective irrigation.	Rainfed farming is done in the areas of drylands and wetlands in India. Drylands are areas which receive an annual rainfall of less than 75 cm. Crops cultivated are drought resistant. Wetlands are areas that receive sufficient rainfall to cultivate crops.

2. Explain the importance of irrigation for agriculture in India. *(Delhi 2016)*

Or Why is irrigation necessary in India? Explain any three reasons. *(Delhi 2008)*

Ans. Irrigation is necessary in India for the following reasons

(i) **To Decrease the Dependency on Monsoon Rainfall** After the decades of independence, India is still dependent on monsoon rainfall for agriculture production. Only 33% of agricultural land is irrigated and rest is dependent on rainfall for soil moisture. To decrease the dependency on monsoon rainfall, irrigation is necessary.

(ii) **To Increase Production** Agricultural production under rainfed areas is low and yield is very low. To increase the agricultural production in India irrigation is necessary.

(iii) **To Maintain Balance between Population and Food Production** Foodgrain production in India is very low as compared to population growth rate. To provide food to increasing population growth, increase in production of foodgrains is required. Thus, irrigation is necessary.

> **Importance of Irrigation**
> - Decrease the dependency on monsoon rainfall
> - Increase production
> - Maintaining balance between population and food production

3. "Land resources are more crucial to the livelihood of the people depending on agriculture." Support this statement with any three suitable arguments. *(Delhi 2015, 2012, 2010)*

Or How is land resource more crucial to the livelihood of the people depending on agriculture in India? Explain. *(All India 2010)*

HINT *Dear students, this question simply ask you to provide reasons for the importance of land resources for livelihood and agriculture.*

Ans. Most of the Indians are dependent on agriculture directly or indirectly for their subsistence. Thus, land resource becomes more important. Importance of land resource in agriculture can be understood by following points

(i) Dependence of agriculture on land resource is high as compared to secondary or tertiary sector.

(ii) Agriculture is directly affected by the quality of land but other sectors such as industry or services are not affected by the quality of land.

(iii) Besides agricultural production, ownership of land resource also indicates a social status in rural areas.

4. Differentiate between protective irrigation and productive irrigation. *(Delhi 2015)*

Ans. Differences between protective irrigation and productive irrigation are as follows

Protective Irrigation	Productive Irrigation
As revealed from the name, protective irrigation aims to protect the crops from adverse effect of soil moisture loss.	In the same way, productive irrigation aims to provide adequate moisture to soil to increase the productivity.
Due to fluctuating situation of rainfall, this irrigation system provides alternative source of water.	The water input per unit area of cultivated land is greater in the irrigation as compare to protective irrigation.
In this system of irrigation, the productivity remains low.	In this irrigation, the productivity remains high.

5. State any two characteristics each of the three distinct cropping seasons of India. *(Delhi 2014)*

Ans. The three distinct cropping seasons of India are

Kharif The characteristics of Kharif season are as follows

(a) Kharif season starts with the onset of South-West monsoon (June-September).

(b) The major crops which are cultivated in this season are rice, jute, cotton, jowar, bajra, tur and other tropical crops.

(ii) **Rabi** The characteristics of Rabi season are as follows

(a) Rabi season in India starts from October-November with onset of winter to March-April.

(b) The crops which are cultivated in this season are wheat, gram, mustard and other temperate and sub-tropical crops because of the low temperature condition.

(iii) **Zaid** The characteristics of Zaid season are as follows

(a) Zaid is a short season between rabi and kharif in India (April-June).

(b) The crops which are cultivated in this season are watermelons, cucumbers, vegetables and fodder crops. Crops are cultivated mainly on irrigation lands.

6. Explain any three features of dryland farming in India. *(Delhi 2013)*

Ans. The three features of dryland farming in India are as follows

(i) It is a type of rainfed farming in which the main source of soil moisture for cultivation is rainfall.

(ii) Dryland farming is done in the areas of rainfall receiving less than 75 cm annually.

(iii) The major crops which are cultivated in these regions are ragi, bajra, moong, gram, gur and other hardy and drought resistant crops.

Additional Info

Other features of dryland farming are

- Dry farming is majorly practiced in districts of Chhattisgarh, Uttar Pradesh, Tamil Nadu and Madhya Pradesh.
- Industrial crops like cotton, groundnuts, oilseeds, pulses and tobacco are the foundation of dryland farming systems.

7. Describe any three characteristics of wetland farming in India. *(Delhi 2013)*

Ans. The three characteristics of wetland farming in India are as follows

(i) It is a type of rainfed farming in which the main source of soil moisture for cultivation is rainfall .

(ii) Wetland farming is done in the areas having sufficient rainfall to provide sufficient moisture to soil for growing crops.

(iii) The main crops which are cultivated in these regions are rice, jute, sugarcane and other water intensive crops.

8. "Land use in a region to a large extent is influenced by the nature of economic activities carried out in that region.'' Support the statement by giving three examples from India. ***(Delhi 2012)***

Or Explain the three types of changes that have affected land use in India. ***(Delhi 2010)***

Ans. Land use in a region to a large extent is influenced by the nature of economic activities carried out in that region.

Following three examples from India support the given statement

(i) **The Size of the Economy** (measured in terms of value for all the goods and services produced in the economy) grows over time as a result of increasing population, change in income levels, available technology and associated factors. As a result, the pressure on land will increase with time and marginal lands would come under use.

(ii) **The Composition of the Economy** It would undergo a change over time. In other words, the secondary and the tertiary sectors usually grow much faster than the primary sector, specifically the agricultural sector. This type of change is common in developing countries, like India. This process would result in a gradual shift of land from agricultural uses to non-agricultural uses.

(iii) **Increasing Pressure on Agricultural Land** Though the contribution of the agricultural activities reduces over time, the pressure on land for agricultural activities does not decline.

9. Mention any six land use categories in India. ***(Delhi 2011)***

Ans. Under the land revenue records land use categories are as follows

(i) **Forest** In land revenue records, forest are the area that are identified and demarcated for forest growth.

(ii) **Land put to Non-agricultural Uses** In this category, all land that is not used in agriculture is included, e.g. settlement, roads, canals, industries, shops, etc.

Land use categories
- Forest
- Land put to non-agricultural uses
- Barren and wastelands
- Area under permanent pastures and grazing lands
- Culturable wasteland
- Current fallow

(iii) **Barren and Wastelands** This category includes all land that is unable to cultivate i.e. unproductive land.

(iv) **Area under Permanent Pastures and Grazing Lands** This type of land is usually found in outer part of rural settlement where villagers graze their animals.

(v) **Culturable Wasteland** Land that can be used to cultivate crops by land reclamation and other land quality improving techniques.

(vi) **Current Fallow** The land where cultivation is not practiced for 1 year or less than 1 year is included under this category.

10. How is the degradation of cultivable land one of the serious problem in India? Explain in any three points. ***(All India 2010)***

Ans. The degradation of cultivable land is one of the serious problems in India as

(i) Intensive use of chemical fertilisers and irrigation have resulted into the degradation of cultivable land. It has reduced the fertility of soil in India.

(ii) Unregulated and over irrigation has created problems of alkalisation and salinisation and water logging in irrigated cultivated areas of India. About 8 million hectare land has lost its fertility due to salinisation and alkalisation and about 7 million hectare land has lost its fertility because of water logging in India.

(iii) The natural fertilisation processes of soil like nitrogen fixation by cultivation of leguminous crops are not adopted because these crops are displaced with the commercial crops such as sugarcane.

11. "Land degradation caused by human made process are more harmful than natural processes in India''. Analyse the statement with three suitable examples. ***(Delhi 2009)***

HINT *Dear students, this question simply ask you to give explanation on how land degradation by human made processes or activities are more harmful than natural processes in India.*

Ans. Human activities are majorly responsible for degradation of land than natural resources. This degradation has started after Green Revolution where new methods and techniques were used intensively, e.g. chemical fertilisers, irrigation, etc. Unregulated and over irrigation has created problems of alkanisation, salinisation and waterlogging in irrigated areas of India.

It is estimated that about 15 million hectare land has lost its fertility due to faulty methods of human. Besides these, shifting cultivation, deforestation, mining activities, etc are human made processes of land degradation whereas erosion by wind, water, glacial and steep sloping land, etc are natural processes of land degradation.

5 Marks Questions

1. Explain any five major problems of Indian agriculture. ***(CBSE 2023)***

Or Analyse any five problems faced by indian farmers in agriculture. ***(CBSE SQP 2022)***

Or Analyse any five major problems of Indian agriculture. ***(All India 2014)***

Or Describe any five major problems related to Indian agriculture. ***(Delhi 2011)***

Or Describe any five major problems of Indian agriculture. ***(Delhi 2008)***

Ans. The major problems faced by Indian farmers in agriculture are

(i) **Dependence on Erratic Monsoon** The crop production in majority of the cultivated land directly depends upon rainfall as irrigation covers only about 33% of the cultivated area in India. A weak South-West monsoon adversly affects the supply of canal water for irrigation due to insufficient flow in the rivers. Rainfall in Rajasthan and other drought prone areas is unreliable and inadequate. Even, the high rainfall regions experience fluctuations. Thus, drought and floods are common phenomenon which affect these regions and also the Indian agriculture. Drought is a common phenomenon in the low rainfall areas, which may also experience occasional floods. For example, the flash floods in dryland region of Maharashtra, Gujarat and Rajasthan in 2006 and 2017.

Major problems of Indian agriculture

- Dependence on erratic monsoon
- Low productivity
- Financial constraints
- Lack of implementation of land reforms
- Small size of land holdings

(ii) **Low Productivity** The yield of crops is low in India as compared to the international levels. Per hectare output of crops like rice, wheat, cotton and oilseeds in India is very low as compared to USA, Russia, Japan, etc. Yields are also low in rainfed drylands which mostly grow coarse cereals, pulses and oilseeds. Labour productivity is also low in India in comparison to international level because of very high pressure on land resources.

(iii) **Financial Constraints** Crop failures and low returns from agriculture force the small and marginal farmers to fall in the trap of indebtedness. As the modern inputs of agriculture are very expensive, it becomes difficult for these farmers to invest in agriculture. They have to take credit from various institutions and moneylenders to buy expensive input resources.

(iv) **Lack of Implementation of Land Reforms** Incomplete land reforms after the independence lead to the unequal distribution of land, which made small land holders poor and big landlord much richer. It also effected the cropping pattern in India.

(v) **Small size of Land Holdings** There are a large number of marginal and small farmers in India. The average size of landholdings is shrinking further under increasing population pressure.

Landholdings in India are mostly fragmented which makes them uneconomical and expensive. There are some states where consolidation of landholdings has not been carried out even once and other states where second consolidation is required as landholdings have fragmented again in the process of division of land among the next generation.

2. On the basis of the main source of moisture for crops, analyse the types of farming in the Indian scenario. ***(CBSE SQP 2022)***

Or Classify Indian farming into two groups on the basis of main source of moisture for crops. Write two feature of each. ***(Delhi 2010)***

Ans. In India, farming is classified into following two groups on the basis of moisture available for crops

(i) **Irrigated Farming** The features of the irrigated are as follows

- In this type of farming, the main source of moisture for crop is irrigation by various methods like wells, tubewells, etc.
- Irrigated farming may be of two types on the basis of objective of farming i.e. productive and protective. Productivity can be enhanced by productive irrigation and crops can be saved from drought by providing them protective irrigation.

(ii) **Rainfed Farming** The features of the rainfed farming are as follows:

- In this type of farming, the main source of moisture for soil and crops is rainfall.
- Rainfed farming is done in the areas of drylands and wetlands in India. Dryland are areas that receive annual rainfall less than 75 cm. Crops cultivated are drought resistant. Wetlands are areas that receive sufficient rainfall to cultivate crops. Main crops are rice, jute, sugarcane and other water intensive crops.

3. Explain with examples how 'modern agricultural technology' has brought a significant increase in agricultural output in India. *(All India 2019)*

Ans. The modern agricultural technology has brought a significant increase in agricultural output in India in following ways

(i) Production and yield of several crops such as rice, wheat, sugarcane, oilseeds, cotton, etc have increased considerably.

(ii) India ranked first in the production of pulses, tea, jute, milk, etc.

(iii) Irrigation facilities have expanded to a great extent. This has helped to use modern agricultural technology like HYV seeds, chemical fertilisers, pesticides and farm machinery.

(iv) Consumption of chemical fertilisers increased from a mere 292 thousand tonnes in 1960-61 to 18398 thousand tonnes in 2004-05.

(v) Since the HYVs are highly susceptible to pests and diseases, the use of pesticides has increased significantly since 1960s.

4. "Lack of land reforms' and 'degradation of cultivable land' are the major problems of Indian agriculture." Substantiate the statement. *(Delhi 2019)*

Other Similar Questions

Or What are the major problems of Indian agriculture? Explain.

Or How lack of land reforms and degradation of cultivable land are threats to Indian agriculture?

Ans. 'Lack of land Reforms' and 'degradation of cultivable land' are the major problems of Indian agriculture.

Lack of Land Reforms (Problems of Small Size of Land Holdings) in India Most of the Indian farmers are small and marginal. About 60% land holdings are smaller than one hectare and about 40% land holdings are smaller than 0.5 hectare. The average size of a farm in India is much smaller than developed countries. This average size of farm is becoming smaller every year because of increasing population pressure. Many farmers have two or more farms of small size. It reduces the effort of farmer in production. Small and fragmented lands are less productive.

For degradation of cultivable land, refers to Q. 10 of 3 marks questions.

5. 'Erratic monsoon' and 'Indebtedness' are the major problems of Indian agriculture. Suggest and explain the measures to overcome these problems. *(Delhi 2016)*

Ans. Measures to overcome problem of erratic monsoon are as follows

(i) Nature of monsoon is very erratic in India. It is true that means of irrigations were developed after independence, but the cultivated area under irrigation is only 33%. So, there should be more stress on developing various means of irrigation especially in unirrigated areas of India.

(ii) Water disputes between states should be ended in order to provide equitable water resources to each cultivable land in India.

(iii) There should be stress on rainwater harvesting technique to improve and recharge ground water table. So that farmers can easily harvest their land with the use of these sources.

(iv) Drought resistant crops should be used more in areas where shortage of water occurs.

Measures to overcome problem of indebtedness are as follows

(i) Encourage co-operative credits in rural areas and private lending should be eliminated.

(ii) Agriculture should be conducted on scientific basis so that the income of the farmers would increase and they could meet the unproductive expenses and would not forced to take any loan.

(iii) Encourage minimum support price policy for all farmers.

(iv) Rural banks and cooperative banks should provide storage facilities at cheap interest rates.

6. "Low productivity and fragmentation of land holding are the major problems of Indian agriculture". Suggest and explain measures to overcome these problems. *(Delhi 2016)*

Ans. Measures to overcome the problems of low productivity are as follows

(i) To aware all the farmers about new technologies like use of improved implements, seeds, chemicals, manures, etc.

(ii) Double cropping, better rotation of crops, fighting plant, diseases and pests, etc should be given due emphasis. Different sources of irrigation should be provided to all farmers.

(iii) Timely soil testing should be done in rural areas by establishing soil testing labs.

(iv) Institutional credit or loan facilities should be provided to all farmers at low interest rates, Kisan credit card scheme.

Measures to overcome the problems of fragmentation of land holdings are as follows

(i) Big areas of land which are lying waste can be reclaimed and made fit for cultivation.

(ii) Co-operative farming can be helpful to check the sub-division and fragmentation of holding. This farming would result in the adoption of modern technology on so called big farms. In this way, agriculture will become profitable occupation through economies of large-scale farming.

(iii) There should be framed new agricultural policy to improve this situation.

(iv) The stress of population on land should be reduced.

7. 'Fragmentation of land holdings' and 'degradation of cultivable land' are the serious problems of Indian agriculture. Suggest and explain measures to overcome these problems. ***(All India 2016)***

Ans. For measures to overcome the problems of fragmentation of land holdings, refer to Q. 6 of 5 marks questions.

Following are some measures for controlling land degradation

(i) Strip farming should be encouraged in which cultivated crops are sown in alternative strips to prevent water movement.

(ii) Crop rotation should be in practice.

(iii) In the hilly regions, contour farming should be done. As it is useful in collecting and diverting the run off to avoid erosion.

(iv) To minimise water logging and salinisation, modern techniques of irrigation in the fields should be adopted.

8. Explain the importance of foodgrains in the Indian agricultural economy. Describe any three characteristics of rice cultivation. ***(All India 2015)***

Ans. Foodgrains acquired special position in agriculture economy of India. The important of foodgrains can be seen through the following points:

(i) Within agriculture foodgrains production is by far the major activity, covering about two-third of the total cropped area in the country.

(ii) It dominates both subsistence and commercial farming all over India.

(iii) Foodgrains provide almost all the calories and proteins consumed by the poor and provide the rural poor with the bulk of their employment and income. Rice, wheat, bajra, maize, pulses (Gram, tur), etc are the examples of foodgrains.

Characteristics of rice cultivation are as follows

(i) For most of the Indians, rice is a staple food.

(ii) About 3000 varieties of rice are grown in various agro-climatic regions of India. India ranked 2nd with the production of 22.07% of rice in the world.

(iii) Because of suitable climate conditions, rice can be cultivated twice and even thrice in an agricultural year in Southern India and West Bengal.

9. Explain the term cropping intensity. Describe the three cropping seasons in India. ***(All India 2014)***

Ans. Cropping intensity refers to raising of a number of crops from the same field during one agriculture year. In this process area is counted twice or thrice depending upon the number of crops.

For three cropping seasons, refer to Q. 5 of 3 marks questions.

10. "Land use in a region to a large extent is influenced by the nature economic activities carried out in that region". Support the statement by giving three examples from India. ***(Delhi 2012)***

Other Similar Questions

Or Why is the area under pastures decreasing in India? How do the changes in the economy affect changes in land use? Explain.

Or Explain the three types of changes that have affected land use in India.

Ans. Increasing population pressure on land is one of the major reasons which is responsible for the decline in land under pasture and grazing area.

There are three types of economic changes that affected the land use in India which are as follows:

(i) As population increases the size of economy also increases. High population pressurises land resources and force people to utilise every piece of land. Thus, marginal lands and barren wastelands would be used to support population.

(ii) When composition of an economy changes it also changes the land uses because different sectors use land for different purposes, e.g. when agricultural area decreases the area under other categories like area under non-agriculture use increases.

(iii) With the compositional change in economy and change in land use, area under agriculture declines, but it does not reduce the population pressure on agriculture land.

11. How the small size of land holdings and degradation of cultivable land are the two major problems of Indian agriculture? Explain both these problems with examples. ***(Delhi 2009)***

Ans. Problems of small size of land holdings in India are as follows:

(i) Most of the Indian farmers are small and marginal. About 60% land holdings are smaller than one hectare and about 40% land holdings are smaller than 0.5 hectare.

(ii) The average size of a farm in India is much smaller than developed countries. This average size of farm is becoming smaller every year, because of increasing population pressure.

(iii) Many farmers have two or more farms of small size. It reduces the effort of farmer in production.

(iv) Small and fragmented lands are less productive.

(v) Government has taken steps to solve this problem by consolidation of holdings, but it has not been implemented successfully.

(vi) In non-irrigated rainfed areas the problem of land degradation also exists. Land degradation in these areas are caused by soil erosion from water and wind. These causes are also increased by human activities in these areas.

For problems of degradation of cultivable land, refer to Q. 4 of 5 marks questions.

Map Based Questions

1. On the given political outline map of India, locate and label the following with appropriate symbols.

(i) The leading tea producing state. ***(Delhi 2015)***

Or The leading state in the production of tea. ***(All India 2014)***

(ii) The leading Jute producing state. ***(Delhi 2015)***

Or The leading state in the production of Jute. ***(Delhi 2014)***

Ans.

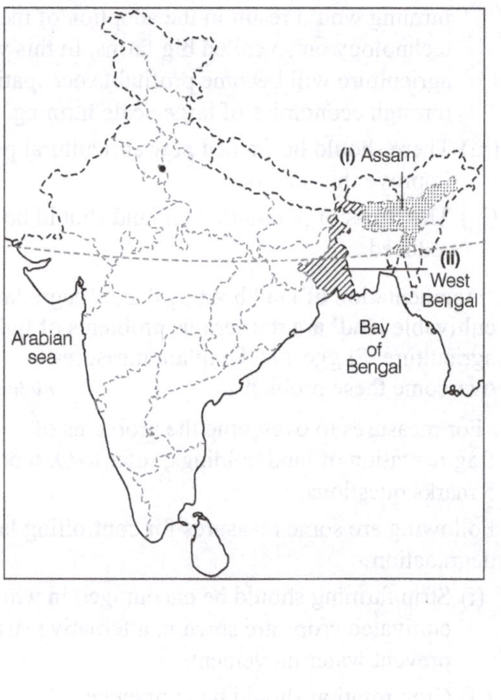

CHAPTER TEST

01 Mark Questions

1 Identify the main reason due to which share of forest has shown an increase in the last forty years.
(a) Better people's participation in managing forest area.
(b) Extensive and efficient efforts of Afforestation.
(c) Increase in community forest land.
(d) Increase in notified area allocated for forest growth.

2 Which one of the following is the main form of degradation in irrigated areas?
(a) Gully erosion
(b) Siltation of land
(c) Wind erosion
(d) Salinisation of soils

3 Arrange the following states in sequence as per their position in the production of wheat.
1. Uttar Pradesh
2. Madhya Pradesh
3. Punjab
4. Haryana

Codes
(a) 1, 2, 3 and 4
(b) 3, 2, 4 and 1
(c) 4, 3, 2 and 1
(d) 2, 4, 3 and 1

4 **Assertion** (A) The rate of increase is the highest in case of area under non-agricultural uses.

Reason (R) This is due to the changing structure of Indian economy, which is increasingly depending on the contribution from industrial and services sectors and expansion of related infrastructural facilities.

Codes
(a) Both A and R are true and R is the correct explanation of A
(b) Both A and R are true, but R is not the correct explanation of A
(c) A is true, but R is false
(d) A is false, but R is true

5 Consider the following statements and choose the correct answer.
I In India the increase in net area sown is a recent phenomenon.
II It is due to use of Culturable waste land for agricultural purpose.

Codes
(a) Only statement I is correct
(b) Both the statements are true and statement II correctly present the reason for statement I
(c) Only statement II is correct
(d) Both the statements I and II are incorrect

Answers

1. (d)	2. (d)	3. (a)	4. (a)	5. (b)

03 Marks Questions

6 State three reasons for the decline of barren and wasteland, Culturable wasteland, area under pastures and tree crops and fallow lands in India.

7 Land resource is important for the livelihood of the people depending on agriculture. Explain in brief.

8 How is wetland farming important in India? State any three reasons.

05 Marks Questions

9 Discuss in brief about different types of environmental problems of land resources in India.

10 Explain the importance of food grains in the Indian agricultural economy. Describe any three characteristics of rice cultivation.

11 The small size of landholdings and degradation of cultivable land are the two major problems of Indian agriculture. How? Explain both these problems with examples.

04

Water Resources

TREND ANALYSIS 3 YEARS

Average No. of Questions Across all Sets

		Types of Questions	2023	2020	2019
TOPIC 01	Water resources	1 Mark	–	–	–
		3 Marks	1	–	–
		5 Marks	–	–	–
TOPIC 02	Water Conservation and Management	1 Mark	–	–	–
		3 Marks	2	–	–
		5 Marks	1	–	–

According to the present scenario, it can be assumed that the coming future, societies would face some changes like demographic transition, geographical shift of population, technological advancement, degradation of environment and the greater one is water scarcity.

With the fast growth of population, the demand of water is increasing, along with its pollution and its over utilisation are creating major problem of water scarcity.

Although more than two-thirds of the Earth surface is filled with water, however **potable** or **fresh water** is only 3%. There is a spatial and temporal variability in the availability of fresh water.

Control over this resource and sharing of water is a major reason for tension and conflict among different communities. Thus, assessment, efficient use and conservation of water are basic requirements to guarantee the sustainable development.

Water Resources of India

- India contributes about 2.45% world's geographical area, the 4% of the world's water resources and about 16% of world population.
- India receives water from annual precipitation i.e. 4000 cubic km, and surface and groundwater sources i.e. 1869 cubic km. But only 60% (1122 cubic km) from these two sources of water are beneficial and usable.

Surface Water Resources

- River, lakes, ponds and tanks are four main sources of surface water resources in India.
- About 10,360 number of river and tributaries existed here and each tributary is more than 1.6 km long.
- The mean annual flow in all the river basin in India is estimated to be 1,869 cubic km. But only about 690 cubic km or 32% of these water can be utilised due to topographical, hydrological and other constraints.
- Size of catchment area/river basin and rainfall in its catchment area control the flow of water in a river. Water availability in rivers is more during monsoon than other seasons in India.

- In India, **Ganga**, **Brahmaputra** and **Indus** have large catchment area. Catchment areas of Ganga and Brahmaputra and Barak rivers fall into the high rainfall receiving area thus, have 60% of total water resources and have only 33% of the surface areas in India, but most of the water is not utilised.
- On the other hand, in the Peninsular rivers like Godavari, Krishna, Kaveri, etc mean annual flow of water is less, but much of their water resources has been utilised.

Groundwater Resources

- There is about 432 cubic km of total replenishable ground water resources available in India. Ganga and Brahmaputra basins have about 46% of the total replenishable groundwater resources.
- The level of groundwater utilisation is relatively high in the river basins of North- Western parts and Southern parts of India.
- States having **very high utilisation** of **groundwater** are Punjab, Haryana, Rajasthan and Tamil Nadu.
- States having **moderate utilisation of ground water** are Gujarat, Uttar Pradesh, Bihar, Tripura and Maharashtsa.
- States having **low Utilisation of groundwater** are Chhattisgarh, Odisha, Kerala, etc.
- It is assumed that if the utilisation of water continue with the present rate, there are chances that it will limit the development and create a situation of social upheaval disruptions.

Lagoons and Backwaters

- Some states of India have indented coastline and thus a number of lagoons and lakes have formed. Examples of such states are Kerala, Odisha and West Bengal.
- Due to brackish water-bodies, these water resources are used for fishing and irrigating certain varieties of paddy crops, coconut, etc.

Water Demand and Utilisation

- Agriculture, being an important part of Indian economy, alone uses about 89% of surface water and 92% of groundwater.
- Most of the developmental projects, river valley projects like the Bhakra-Nangal, Hirakund, Damodar Valley, Nagarjuna Sagar, Indira Gandhi Canal project, etc as well as five year plans were started to provide water to agricultural sector and increase agricultural production.
- Besides this, utilisation of surface and groundwater for domestic purposes are 90% and 3% and for industrial sector are 2% and 5%, respectively.

Demand of Water for Irrigation

- Need for irrigation is very high in India due to the spatial and temporal variation of rainfall.
- As winter and summer season are more or less dry in most parts of India. So, without irrigation agriculture cannot be practised in these parts.
- Some crops like rice, sugarcane, jute and other are water intensive and require more water to grow.
- Irrigation helps to grow multiple crops, gives more agricultural productivity, and along with HYV seeds gives more yield at fast rate. For example, Punjab, Haryana and Western Uttar Pradesh which have more than 85% of net sown area under irrigation.
- Total **net irrigated area** in Punjab under wells and tube wells is 76.1% whereas it is 51.3% in Haryana. These states utilise a large share of their groundwater resources and thus, it is the major cause behind the depletion of these resources.
- Besides these in Rajasthan and Bihar, the concentration of flouride in groundwater is also increasing due to over withdrawal of this resource. Whereas in West Bengal and Bihar, the concentration of arsenic has been increased because of the same reason.

Emerging Water Problems

- Rapid growth in population and pollution from various sources like industries, agriculture, and domestic sources are the major problems which are responsible for declining the availability of potable water.
- The per capita availability of water in India is also decreasing day by day.

Deterioration of Water Quality

- Water quality means water free from unwanted foreign substances that make water polluted i.e. micro-organisms, chemicals, industrial and other wastes.
- These toxic substances are responsible for water pollution by dissolving or lie suspended in lakes, streams, rivers and oceans.
- Sometimes, such pollutants seep down and pollute groundwater. The **most polluted rivers** in India are **Ganga** and **Yamuna**.

Water Conservation and Management

- The conservation and management of water become necessary after decreasing the availability of fresh water and increasing its demand by increasing population.

- For Sustainable development and maintaining the quality of life the government should encourage people to adopt watershed development, rainwater harvesting, recycling and reuse of water, conjunctive use of water for availability of quality water for long time.

Water Scarcity and Prevention of Water Pollution

- Availability of water resources are shrinking with a faster rate. It is seen that hilly areas have less dense population and thus, have high quality of water in their rivers. Whereas plains have dense population and thus have low quality of water in their rivers, and here water is widely used for irrigation, domestic works and industrial works.
- Plains also contribute more in polluting water sources by draining agricultural wastes (chemical fertilisers and insecticides) solid and domestic wastes and industrial wastes.
- During summer, concentration of pollutants in rivers remains high because of low amount of water which unable to flow these pollutants.
- Water quality of national aquatic resources at 507 stations have been monitored by the **Central Pollution Control Board** (CPCB), with the collaboration of State Pollution Control Boards.
- The analysis of data recorded from these stations shows that the major rivers of India are most polluted by the organic and bacterial pollution.
- Yamuna river is most polluted river in the country between Delhi and Etawah. Other severely polluted rivers are the Sabarmati at Ahmedabad, the Gomti at Lucknow, the Kali, the Adyar, the Cooum (at entire stretches), the Vaigai at Madurai, Musi at Hyderabad and the Ganga at Kanpur and Varanasi.
- Ground water is also polluted because of high concentration of heavy toxic metals, flouride nitrates at different parts of the country.

Legislative Provisions and Laws to Prevent River Pollution

- Government has taken various steps to minimise river and water pollution but due to some obstacles, these were proved to be less effective, for e.g. **Water (Prevention and Control of Pollution) Act of 1974,** and **Environment Protection Act of 1986** were unsuccessful as in 1997, 251 polluting factories were established along the rivers and lakes.
- The **Water Cess Act of 1977** which was made to prevent pollution, was also less effective. So there is an urgent need to create awareness in public about the importance of water in life. It will result in reducing the pollutants from agricultural activities and industrial discharge.

Recycle and Reuse of Water

- Recycle and reuse is a simple and best way to conserve fresh water and make it available for all.
- Industries can use water of low quality and their waste water for cooling and fire fighting, which can decrease the cost of water for them and conserve fresh water.
- Water could be collected after bathing and washing utensils, washing clothes and cars can be a better option for gardening.
- Today, reusing and recycling of water is limited to few people but there is enormous scope for replenishing water through recycling.

Watershed Management

Watershed management basically refers to efficient management and conservation of surface water. Watershed management includes

(i) ground water resources.
(ii) prevention of surface runoff.
(iii) storage and recharge of groundwater by different methods such as percolation tanks, recharge wells, etc.
(iv) the conservation, regeneration and judicious use of all natural resources (land, water, plants and animals) and human resources.
(v) create a balance among natural elements as well as in society.
(vi) community participation is a key to success of a Watershed Development Programme.

There are various watershed development and management programmes started by both Central and State Government at national and state level in India like

- **Haryali** It is sponsered by the central government while gram panchayats of different villages execute it with the public participation. This programme enabled people to conserve water for various uses such as drinking, irrigation, fisheries and afforestation.
- **Neeru-Meeru (Water and You)** Programme in Andhra Pradesh and **Arvary Pani Sansad** (in Alwar, Rajasthan)are examples of state initiated watershed development programmes.

Under these two programmes numerous percolation tanks, dug out ponds (**johad**), check dams, etc were constructed for harvesting water with the help of public participation. Tamil Nadu is only state which has made the construction of water harvesting structures compulsory in the houses.

The construction of a building without the structure of water harvesting is not allowed. Despite having such programmes, still most of the people in India are not aware with the benefits of watershed development and managment of water. Thus, there is a need to encourage more people to participate in this programme.

Rain Water Harvesting

Rain water harvesting is a cheap and environmental friendly technique that guides us to store rainwater into bore wells, pits and also recharge groundwater aquifers for different uses. There are various benefits of rainwater harvesting which are as follows

(i) It increases water availability.

(ii) Checks the declining groundwater level.

(iii) It improves the quality of groundwater by dilution of pollutions like fluoride and nitrates.

(iv) It prevents soil erosion and flooding.

(v) It can be used to arrest salt water intrusion in coastal areas, if used to recharge aquifers.

There are numerous methods to harvest rain water in India. In traditional rain water harvesting techniques, water is usually collected in any surface water body i.e. lakes, ponds, irrigation tanks, etc of rural areas.

Another technique is ***kund or tanka*** which is a covered storage under ground tank. This technique is widely used in **Rajasthan**.

Rain water harvesting structure can be made on the roof tops of the houses open spaces and even on the roof tops of the houses and the collected water can be used for domestic use by large number of people and reduce their dependence on ground water.

PYQs Previous Years' Questions

1 Mark Questions

Multiple Choice Questions

1. Which of the following programs sponsored by Central Government aims at enabling the rural population to conserve water for drinking, irrigation, fisheries and afforestation? *(CBSE SQP Term I 2021)*

(a) Arvary Pani Sansad
(b) Haryali
(c) Neeru-Meeru
(d) Narmada Bachao

Ans. (b) Haryali

2. Which of the following programme is launched by the present Union Government for the cleaning of river Ganga? *(CBSE SQP Term I 2021)*

(a) Ganga Action Plan
(b) Namami Gange
(c) Ganga Namami Action Plan
(d) Ganga Cleaning Mission

Ans. (b) Namami Gange

3. Which of the following areas of our country are deficient in rainfall and are drought prone? *(CBSE SQP Term I 2021)*

(a) North- Eastern states (b) Deccan Plateau
(c) Gangetic Plain (d) Brahmaputra valley

Ans. (b) Deccan Plateau

4. Which of the following sectors has used the highest percentage of total water in India? *(CBSE SQP Term I 2021)*

(a) Domestic (b) Commerce
(c) Agriculture (d) Industry

Ans. (c) Agriculture

5. Match the Column I with Column II and choose the correct answer with the help of given codes. *(CBSE SQP Term I 2021)*

	Column I (Rivers)		Column II (Polluted Place)
A.	Yamuna	1.	Hyderabad
B.	Kali	2.	Kanpur and Varanasi
C.	Gomati	3.	Ahmedabad
D.	Sabarmati	4.	Lucknow
E.	Ganga	5.	Muzaffarnagar
F.	Musi	6.	Delhi and Etawah

Codes

	A	B	C	D	E	F
(a)	6	5	4	3	2	1
(b)	1	2	3	4	5	6
(c)	6	5	3	4	1	2
(d)	2	3	1	5	4	6

Ans. (a) 6 5 4 3 2 1

6. In which of the following sectors is the groundwater used the highest? *(CBSE Term I 2021)*

(a) Agriculture (b) Industry
(c) Domestic (d) Commerce

Ans. (a) Agriculture

7. Which of the following states has started the 'Neeru-Meeru' programme? *(CBSE Term I 2021)*

(a) Rajasthan (b) Gujarat
(c) Andhra Pradesh (d) Karnataka

Ans. (c) Andhra Pradesh

8. Which of the following group of states uses the highest amount of ground water? *(CBSE Term I 2021)*

(a) Tripura, Maharashtra, West Bengal
(b) Gujarat, Uttar Pradesh, Bihar
(c) Chhattisgarh, Odisha, Kerala
(d) Punjab, Haryana, Rajasthan

Ans. (d) Punjab, Haryana, Rajasthan

9. Which of the following rivers comes under West flowing group-I? *(CBSE Term I 2021)*

(a) Chambal (b) Yamuna
(c) Sabarmati (d) Periyar

Ans. (c) Sabarmati

10. Which one of the following is not the objective of 'Haryali watershed development project'? *(CBSE Term I 2021)*

(a) Drinking water (b) Irrigation
(c) Fishing (d) Industries

Ans. (d) Industries

11. How much per cent of the Earth's surface is covered by water?

(a) 50% (b) 55% (c) 60% (d) 71%

Ans. (d) 71%

12. India accounts for about how much per cent of the world's surface area?

(a) 1.6% (b) 2.45% (c) 6.5% (d) 7.8%

Ans. (b) 2.45%

13. India accounts for about how much percent of the world's water resources?

(a) 1% (b) 2% (c) 3% (d) 4%

Ans. (d) 4%

14. Which of the following is the major sources of surface water?

(a) Rivers (b) Lakes
(c) Ponds (d) All of these

Ans. (d) All of these

15. Precipitation is relatively high in the catchment areas of which rivers of India?

(a) The Ganga river
(b) The Brahmaputra river
(c) The Barak river
(d) All of the above

Ans. (d) All of the above

16. Groundwater utilisation is very high in which of the following states of India?

(a) Haryana (b) Punjab
(c) Rajasthan (d) All of these

Ans. (d) All of these

17. Which of the following states of India utilises only a small proportion of its ground water potentials?

(a) Chhattisgarh (b) Odisha
(c) Kerala (d) All of these

Ans. (d) All of these

18. In which state the rainwater harvesting structure is known as Kund or Tanka?

(a) Gujarat (b) Rajasthan
(c) Punjab (d) Himachal Pradesh

Ans. (b) Rajasthan

19. Study the following facts and choose the correct option *(CBSE Term I 2021)*

I. These days 'rainwater harvesting' is being taken up on massive scale in many states.
II. Urban areas have benefited from rainwater harvesting.
III. Water demand has been increasing in most of the cities and towns.
IV. There is no benefit of rainwater harvesting for rural areas.

Options

(a) Only I, II and III are correct
(b) Only II, III and IV are correct
(c) Only I, III and IV are correct
(d) I, II, III and IV are correct

Ans. (a) Only I, II and III are correct

20. Arrange the following states in sequence as per their usage of groundwater from very high to low.

1. Punjab 2. Maharashtra
3. Odisha

Codes

(a) 1, 2, 3 (b) 3, 1, 2
(c) 3, 2, 1 (d) 2, 1, 3

Ans. (a) 1, 2, 3

Very Short Answer Questions

1. Mention any two reasons for the deterioration of water quality in India. *(All India 2019)*

Ans. Following are the reasons responsible for deterioration of water quality in India
   (i) Industrial polluted water
   (ii) Agricultural chemicals

2. Mention any two methods for the conservation of water in India. *(All India 2019)*

Ans. Two methods for the conservation of water in India are
   (i) Rainwater harvesting
   (ii) Watershed management

3. Examine the importance of irrigation in the Indian context. *(Delhi 2019)*

Ans. Indian monsoon is insufficient, uncertain and irregular which causes uncertainty in agriculture. The period of rains is restricted to only four months (June to September) when monsoon arrives. Thus, irrigation is very important for agriculture in India.

4. Mention any two sources of water pollution by human beings in India. *(CBSE SQP 2018)*

Or Mention any two sources of water pollutants created. *(Delhi 2015)*

Or Mention any two sources of water pollution in India. *(Delhi 2013)*

Ans. The two sources of water pollution by human being in India are
   (i) Toxic effluents
   (ii) Sewage disposal

5. Define the watershed management. *(All India 2014)*

Ans. Watershed management means the proper management, use and saving of surface and groundwater resources. Prevention of surface runoff and storage and recharge of groundwater by different methods such as percolation tanks, recharge well, etc are done in the watershed.

6. Which is the main source of water borne diseases in India? *(All India 2014, 2009)*

Ans. Water pollution is the main source of water-borne diseases such as
   (i) Diarrhoea (ii) Intestinal worms
   (iii) Hepatitis

7. Name any two natural sources of water pollution. *(Delhi 2012)*

Ans. Two natural sources of water pollution are
   (i) Erosion (ii) Landslides

8. Which river basin of India has the highest percentage of replenishable utilisation of groundwater resources? *(Delhi 2010)*

Ans. Ganga river basin has the highest percentage of replenishable utilisation of groundwater resources.

9. Which sector (economic activity) uses most of the surface and groundwater in India? *(Delhi 2010)*

Ans. Agriculture sector uses most of the surface and groundwater in India.

10. Mention any two cultural activities responsible for water pollution in India. *(Delhi 2009)*

Ans. Cultural activities which are responsible for water pollution in India are
   (i) Pilgrimage (ii) Religious fairs
   (iii) Tourism

11. What is the main reason of degradation of the quality of water in India? *(Delhi 2008)*

Ans. The main reason of degradation of the quality of water in India are
   (i) Domestic waste discharge indiscriminate use of water by increasing population.
   (ii) Industrial waste led to the degradation of the quality of water.

12. Which are the two polluted stretches of river Ganga in Uttar Pardesh and Bihar? *(All India 2008)*

Ans. The Ganga river is polluted in Uttar Pradesh from Kanpur to Varanasi and in Bihar from Varanasi to Patna.

3 Marks Questions

1. Explain the major aspects of India's 'National Water Policy, 2002' *(CBSE 2023)*

Or Describe any three key features of India's National Water Policy, 2002. *(All India 2012)*

Ans. The National Water Policy, 2002 explains water allocation priorities basically in the following order i.e. drinking water, irrigation, hydro-power, navigation, industrial and other uses. The three features of India's National Water Policy, 2002 are
   (i) When there is no source of drinking water, irrigation and multi-purpose projects or dams should invariably include drinking water component.
   (ii) Provide potable water for human being and animals.

(iii) Exploitation of ground water should be stopped and limited by adopting suitable measures.

Additional Info

Other features of India's National Water Policy, 2002 are
- Both surface and groundwater should be regularly monitored for quality.
- Planning, development and management of water resources need to be governed by national perspectives.

2. "There is high demand of water for irrigation in agricultural sector in Indua." Justify the statement. ***(CBSE 2023)***

Or Justify the high demand of water for irrigation in India. ***(CBSE SQP 2020)***

HINT *Dear students, this question simply ask you to provide reasons for the high demand of water for irrigation in India.*

Ans. India has traditionally been an agrarian economy and about 2-3 of its population is dependent on agriculture. Hence, there was a need to construct irrigation methods for productive agriculture. There is high demand for irrigation in India because of the following reasons

(i) Rainfall in India is concentrated only in few months and therefore, irrigation is required in the dry months. Rainfall is uneven and deccan plateau remains dry due to deficient rainfall and agriculture cannot be practiced in the absence of irrigation.

(ii) Water requirement of certain crops such as Jute, Sugarcane and Rice is high which can be met only by means of irrigation.

(iii) Use of HYV seeds, fertilizers and multiple cropping in the fields have made irrigation essential as these methods are only successful when there is assured supply of water through irrigation.

3. "Rainwater harvesting has been practiced through various method by different communication in the country. "Justify the statement".

Or 'Rainwater harvesting is considered as a low cost and eco-friendly technique of preserving water resources." justify. ***(CBSE SQP 2020)***

Ans. Rain water harvesting is a method to capture and store rainwater for various uses. It is also used to recharge groundwater aquifers. It is a low cost and eco-friendly technique for preserving every drop of water by guiding the rain water to bore well, pits and wells.

Rainwater harvesting increases water availability, check the declining ground water table, improves the quality of groundwater through dilution of contaminants like fluorides and nitrates, prevents soil erosion, and flooding and arrests salt water intrusion in coastal areas if used to recharge aquifers.

Rainwater harvesting has been practised in the country by different communities. For example, traditional rainwater harvesting in rural areas is done using surface storage bodies, like lakes, ponds, irrigation tanks, etc.

4. How has rainwater harvesting helped in the development of certain areas of India? Explain with examples. ***(All India 2016)***

Ans. Rainwater harvesting helped in the development of certain areas of India in the following ways:

(i) Rain water harvesting is a cheap and environmental friendly technique that guides to store rain water into bore wells, pits, etc.

(ii) It also recharges groundwater aquifers for different uses.

(iii) It improves the quality of groundwater by dilution of pollutants like fluoride and nitrates.

(iv) It prevents soil erosion and flooding conditions.

(v) It can be used to arrest salt water intrusion in costal areas, if used to recharge aquifers.

5. ''The assessment, efficient use and conservation of water are necessary to ensure development.'' Explain in the light of values regarding conservation of water resources. ***(Delhi 2015)***

Or Why is conservation of water resources necessary? Explain any three reasons. ***(All India 2011)***

Ans. There is need to conserve the water resources due to the following reasons

(i) **Low Availability of Fresh Water** In India fresh water is not available to meet the demand of a large number of population. Increasing population is also shrinking the per capita availability of water. To guarantee the adequate supply of fresh water, we need to create awareness among people for conservation of water resources.

(ii) **To Irrigate Crops** India is an agrarian economy. Most of its population is depended on agriculture. Water is required to irrigate crops and ensure the employment of agrarian workers and development of economy.

Need for conservation of water resources
- Low Availability of Fresh Water
- To Irrigate Crops
- For Sustainable Development

(iii) **For Sustainable Development** Water is a life giving precious resource, if we do not save and conserve it, development cannot be possible.

So, to ensure sustainable development we need to be such a citizen who is responsible to sensitize people with positive cooperation about necessity of water conservation.

6. How do industries pollute India's water bodies? Explain with examples. *(Delhi 2014)*

Ans. Industries pollute India's water bodies in the following ways

(i) Industries discharge chemical wastes comprising substances called effluents in rivers, lakes, streams etc.

(ii) Factories sometimes turn waterways into open sewers by dumping oil, toxic chemicals and other harmful liquids called effluents into them.

(iii) These chemicals not only pollute the water reservoirs but also disturb the natural purification cycle of water carried out by microorganisms.

(iv) Waste from tanneries and other heavy industrial plants contain heavy elements such as Chromium, Lead, and Mercury etc. which pose severe threats to the aquatic life.

(v) Moreover, the fertiliser industries dump nitrogenous and phosphate-containing waste into the rivers, lakes and other reservoirs causing Eutrophication.

7. Analyse the economic and social values of rain water harvesting. *(Delhi 2014)*

Ans. The economic and social values of rain water harvesting are given below

(i) Rain water harvesting technique is environment friendly as well as cost effective for people.

(ii) This technique guides to store rain water into bore wells, pits, etc for future use and in times of scarcity of water.

(iii) It creates sensitivity and awareness among people about benefits of conservation and reuse of water.

(iv) This technique helps to reduce floods like situation and also save life and property.

(v) It helps to reduce conflict among states and communities.

8. Examine any three causes for the deterioration of 'quality of water' in India. *(Delhi 2013)*

Ans. Water quality means water free from unwanted foreign substances or purity of water.

The three causes responsible for the deterioration of quality of water in India are as follows:

(i) The foreign substances like micro-organisms, chemicals, industrial and other wastes make water polluted. Because of these substances, quality of water decreases and it becomes unsuitable for the uses of human beings.

(ii) Toxic substances are responsible for water pollution by dissolving or suspending in lakes, streams, rivers, ocean or other water source. It declines the quality of water and harms aquatic life and systems.

(iii) When toxic substances seep down, they pollute groundwater.

9. Explain watershed management. What is its aim? *(Delhi 2012)*

Ans. Watershed management means the proper management, use and saving of surface and groundwater resources. Prevention of surface runoff and storage and recharge of groundwater by different methods such as percolation tanks, recharge wells, etc are done in the watershed management.

But in the broader terms, the conservation, regeneration and judicious use of all natural resources (land, water, plants and animals) and human resources in a watershed also included in water management.

Major aims of watershed management are as follows:

(i) To create a balance among natural elements as well as in society.

(ii) To enable the villagers to conserve water for various uses such as drinking, irrigation, fisheries and afforestation.

10. Describe any three major problems related to water in India. *(Delhi 2011)*

Or Explain any three major problems related to water in India. *(All India 2008)*

Ans. The three major problems related to water in India are as follows

(i) **Low Availability of Fresh Water** In India, fresh water is not available to meet the demand. Increasing population is also shrinking the per capita availability of water.

(ii) **Water Pollution** It is increased rapidly after independence in India. Industrialisation and urbanisation has more contribution in water pollution in India.

(iii) **Uneven Distribution of Water Resources** Water resources in India is very unevenly distributed. Some regions are facing scarcity of water whereas other areas are facing floods.

11. Why is demand of water for irrigation increasing day by day in India? Explain any three reasons. *(Delhi 2011)*

Ans. The demand of water for irrigation is increasing day by day in India because of the following reasons:

(i) Need for irrigation is very high in India due to the spatial and temporal variation in South-West Monsoon in India. Regions like North-Western India, Deccan plateau and others are drought prone areas and receives very low rainfall in India.

(ii) The variation of rainfall in different season as winter and summer season are more or less dry in most parts of India.
Agriculture can not be practised without irrigation during dry season in these parts of India.

(iii) Some crops like sugarcane, jute, rice, etc are water intensive and require more water to grow. Cultivation of these crops are not possible without irrigation in this condition.

5 Marks Questions

1. Explain with examples how watershed management and rainwater harvesting help in conserving water resources in India. *(CBSE 2023)*

Other Similar Questions

Or "Watershed management and rain water harvesting help in conservation of water resouces." Explain with examples.

Or How the water resources in India can be conserved? Explain with reference to watershed management and rainwater harvesting.

Ans. Watershed management refers to efficient management and conservation of surface and groundwater resources. It include prevention of surface runoff and storage and recharge of groundwater by different methods.

Rainwater harvesting is collection and storage of rain water that runs off from roof tops, parks, roads, open grounds, etc. This water run off can be either stored or recharged into the ground water.

Watershed Management and Rainwater harvesting help in conserving water resources in India through following ways

(i) By reducing soil erosion and flood hazards by collecting rainwater and reducing the flow of stormwater to prevent urban flooding.

(ii) By increasing the groundwater level and improving its quality and also by checking saltwater intrusion in coastal areas.

(iii) By recharging ground water levels and reducing the concentration of containments.

(iv) By mitigating extreme rainfall events without increasing the capacity of existing sewer system, and by mitigating urban heat island problems.

2. Explain any three factors responsible for the depletion of water resources. Examine any two legislative measures for controlling water pollution in India. *(Delhi 2013)*

Ans. The three factors responsible for the depletion of water resources in India are as follow

(i) **Increasing Population** Population in India is increasing with a higher growth rate. This growth is responsible for decreasing the availability of fresh water and per capita availability of water.

(ii) **Industrialisation** It has increased many folds after independence. It created a major problem of water pollution in India as industrial wastes are disposed in water sources.

Factors responsible for depletion of water resources
- Increasing population
- Industrialisation
- Over utilisation of groundwater

(iii) **Over Utillisation of Ground water** India is an agrarian country. Thus, water is required in high amount for irrigation in agriculture. In the irrigated areas, groundwater is used to obtain maximum agriculture output. Over utilisation of groundwater in these areas has led to the declining of groundwater level.

Government has taken some steps to reduce river and water pollution, but some were not effective and some were not implemented successfully.

Two legislative provision are as follows:

(i) Water (Prevention and Control of Pollution) Act of 1974.

(ii) Environment Protection Act (1986).

These acts were unsuccessful as in 1997, 251 polluting factories were established along the rivers and lakes. The Water Cess Act of 1977 was also ineffective. The main reason was that they were unsuccessful in creating awareness about water conservation among people. Generation of awareness in public about the importance of water in life and impacts of water pollution is necessary.

3. Explain how 'watershed management' and 'rainwater harvesting' are the methods of efficient management and conservation of surface water resources in India.

Ans. Watershed management basically refers to efficient management and conservation of surface and groundwater resources.

It includes

(i) Prevention of surface runoff.

(ii) The conservation, regeneration and judicious use of all natural resources.

(iii) Create a balance among natural elements as well as in society.

There are various watershed development and management programmes started by both Central and State Government at national and state level in India like

- **Haryali** is sponsered by the Central Government. This programme enabled people to conserve water for various uses such as drinking, trrigation, fisheries and afforestation.
- **Neeru-Meeru** (Water and You) Programme in Andhra Pradesh and **Arvary Pani Sansad** in Alwar Rajasthan are examples of state initiated watershed development programmes. Under these two programmes, numerous percolation tanks, dug out ponds *(Johad)*, check dams, etc were constructed for harvesting water with the help of public participation.

  Rainwater harvesting is a method to capture and store rainwater for various uses. It is a low cost and eco-friendly technique for preserving every drop of water by guiding the rainwater to bore well, pits and wells. There are numerous methods to harvest rainwater in India. In traditional rainwater harvesting techniques, water is usually collected in any surface water body i.e. lakes, ponds, irrigation tanks, etc of rural areas. Another techniques is kund of tanka which is a covered storage underground tank. This technique is widely used in Rajasthan. Thus, we can conclude that watershed management and rainwater harvesting are the methods of efficient management and conservation of surface water resources in India.

Data/Source Based Questions

1. Study the pie-chart given below and answer the questions that follows.

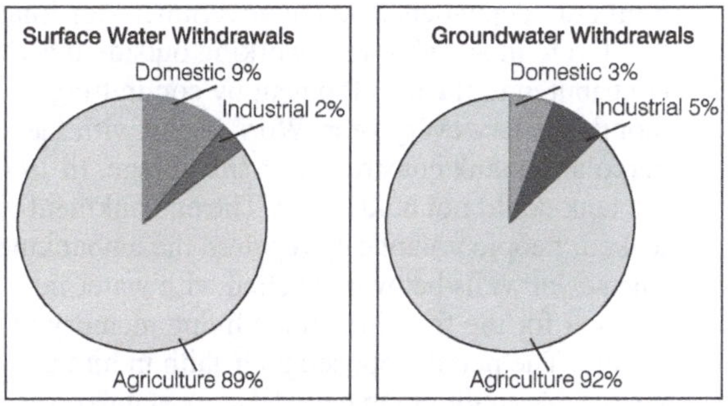

(i) Which sector's share is the maximum in the usage of Surface water and Groundwater?

(ii) What is the percentage of agricultural sector in the usage of Surface water and Groundwater?

(iii) Why the development of irrigation was assigned a very high priority in the Five Years Plans and how? ***(CBSE SQP 2019)***

Ans. (i) The agricultural sector's share is the maximum in the usage of both surfacewater and groundwater.

(ii) The percentage of agricultural sector in the usage of surface water is 89%. In the case of groundwater it is 92%.

(iii) India has traditionally been an agrarian economy with almost two-thirds of its population being dependent on agriculture. Thus, the development of irrigation was assigned a very high priority in the Five Years Plans.

In these plans, irrigation was developed by launching mult-ipurpose river valley projects to meet the irrigation needs of the country.

2. Read the given source and answer the questions that follows.

Ralegan Siddhi is a small village in the district of Ahmednagar, Maharashtra. It has become an example for watershed development throughout the country. In 1975, this village was caught in a web of poverty and illicit liquor trade. The transformation took place when a retired army personnel settled down in the village and took up the task of watershed development. He convinced villagers about the importance of family planning and voluntary labour; preventing open grazing, felling trees and liquor prohibition. Voluntary labour was necessary to ensure minimum dependence on the government for financial aid. Even, those who were working outside the village contributed to the development by committing a month's salary every year. Work began with the percolation tank constructed in the village. In 1975, the tank could not hold water. The embankment wall leaked. People voluntarily repaired the embankment. The seven wells below it swelled with water in summer for the first time in the living memory of the people. The people reposed their faith in him and his visions. A youth group called Tarun Mandal was formed. The group worked to ban the dowry system, caste discrimination and untouchability. Liquor distilling units were removed and prohibition imposed. Open grazing was completely banned with a new emphasis on stallfeeding. The cultivation of water intensive crops like sugarcane was banned. Crops such as pulses, oilseeds and certain cash crops with low water requirements were encouraged.

All elections to local bodies began to be held on the basis of consensus. "It made the community leaders complete representatives of the people." A system of Nyaya Panchayats (informal courts) were also set up. Since then, no case has been referred to the police.

A ₹ 22 lakh school building was constructed using only the resources of the village. No donations were taken. Money, if needed, was borrowed and paid back. The villagers took pride in this self-reliance. A new system of sharing labour grew out of this infusion of pride and voluntary spirit.

People volunteered to help each other in agricultural operations. Landless labourers also gained employment.

(i) Which of the following methods of water conservation brought prosperity in Ralegan Siddhi?
(a) Rainwater harvesting
(b) Watershed development
(c) Groundwater recharge
(d) Construction of dams

Ans. (b) Watershed development

(ii) Which of the following measures were taken to increase democratic participation in the village?
(a) Construction of school
(b) Local body elections
(c) Liquor prohibition
(d) All of the above

Ans. (b) Local body elections

(iii) Which of the following made Ralegan Siddhi independent of government's financial aid?
(a) Prohibition of liquor
(b) Voluntary labour
(c) Local body election
(d) Agriculture

Ans. (b) Voluntary labour

3. Read the given source and answer the questions that follows.

Jal Kranti Abhiyan (2015-16)

Water is a recyclable resource but its availability is limited and the gap between supply and demand will be widening over time. Climate change at the global scale will be creating water stress conditions in many regions of the world. India has a unique situation of high population growth and rapid economic development with high water demand. The Jal Kranti Abhiyan launched by the Government of India in 2015–16 with an aim to ensure water security through per capita availability of water in the country. People in different regions of India had practised the traditional knowledge of water conservation and management to ensure water availability. The Jal Kranti Abhiyan aims at involving local bodies, NGOs and cititzens, at large, in creating awareness regarding its objectives. The following activities have been proposed under the Jal Kranti Abhiyan.

1. Selection of one water stressed village in each 672 districts of the country to create a 'Jal Gram'.

2. Identification of model command area of about 1000 hectares in different parts of the country, for example, UP, Haryana (North), Karnataka, Telangana, Tamil Nadu (South), Rajasthan, Gujarat (West), Odisha (East), Meghalaya (North-East).
3. Abatement of pollution.
   - Water conservation and artificial recharge.
   - Reducing groundwater pollution.
   - Construction of Arsenic-free wells in selected areas of the country.
4. Creating mass awareness through social media, radio, TV, print media, poster and essay writing competitions in schools. Jal Kranti Abhiyan is designed to provide livelihood and food security through water security.

(i) Present day world is experiencing acute water paucity due to
(a) Climate Change
(b) Industrial Pollution
(c) Rising Sea level
(d) Forest Depletion

Ans. (a) Climate Change

(ii) Which of the following is not a characteristic feature of Model Command Area in India?
(a) Water conservation and artificial recharge
(b) Reducing groundwater pollution
(c) Construction of Arsenic-free wells in selected areas of the country
(d) Not concerned with food security and livelihood of the people

Ans. (d) Not concerned with food security and livelihood of the people

(iii) The Objective of the Jal Kranti Abhiyan is achieved through
(a) Using traditional know how
(b) Adopting modern technology
(c) Mixing modern technology with traditional knowledge
(d) Outsource to some other organisation

Ans. (c) Mixing modern technology with traditional knowledge

(iv) The main aim of The Jal Kranti Abhiyan is to ensure water security through
(a) Creating Jal Grams
(b) Reducing ground water pollution
(c) Per capita availability of water
(d) Construction of arsenic free wells

Ans. (c) Per capita availability of water

CHAPTER TEST

01 Mark Questions

1 Which of the following South Indian states has the highest groundwater utilization (in per cent) of its total groundwater potential?

(a) Kerala
(b) Tamil Nadu
(c) Karnataka
(d) Andhra Pradesh

2 **Assertion** (A) Irrigation is needed in India because of spatio-temporal variability of rainfall in the country.

Reason (R) Agriculture accounts for 92% of groundwater utilisation in India.

Codes

(a) Both A and R are true and R is the correct explanation of A
(b) Both A and R are true, but R is not the correct explanation of A
(c) A is true, but R is false
(d) A is false, but R is true

Answers

1. (b) | 2. (b)

03 Marks Questions

3 Write any three major problems related to water in India.

4 What are the important methods of recycling and reusing of water?

5 Why is irrigation more developed in Northern plains than in peninsular India?

05 Marks Questions

6 Give a brief account on the availability of water resources in India and factors that determine its spatial distribution.

7 Explain about watershed management. How does it play an important role in sustainable development?

8 Demand of water for irrigation is increasing in India. Why? Explain with example.

05

Minerals and Energy Resources

TREND ANALYSIS 3 YEARS

		Average No. of Questions Across all Sets			
		Types of Questions	2023	2020	2019
TOPIC 01	Types of Mineral resources	1 Mark	–	–	–
		3 Marks	2	1	1
		5 Marks	–	–	–
TOPIC 02	Types of Energy Resources	1 Mark	–	–	–
		3 Marks	2	–	–
		5 Marks	1	–	3

A naturally occurring substance, which is organic or inorganic in nature and have definite chemical and physical properties is called **mineral**. Minerals are important and provide raw material to different industries and thus support industrial development of a country.

India has a large variation in its geological features. It causes a large and rich deposits of minerals in India. There are areas which have high quantity of valuable minerals like Peninsular plateau region as well as those which have less minerals of economic use like the alluvial plain of North India.

Types of Mineral Resources

Mineral are classified on the basis of their physical and chemical properties which are as follows

Metallic Minerals

These minerals are rich in metals e.g. copper, bauxite, iron, manganese, etc.

These are of two types

- **Ferrous Minerals** These are rich in iron contents and an important source of iron.
- **Non-Ferrous Minerals** These do not have iron content and have highest proportion of other metals, e.g. copper, bauxite, etc.

Non-Metallic Minerals

These minerals do not have contents of metals. They are classified into two groups

- **Organic Minerals** These are made up of organic matter of buried animal and plants, e.g, coal, petroleum.
- **Inorganic Minerals** These are inorganic in nature of origin, e.g. mica, limestone, graphite, etc.

Characteristics of Minerals Resources

The main characteristics of minerals are as follows

(i) Their distribution over the earth surface are uneven.

(ii) There is inverse relationship in quantity and quality of minerals i.e. good quality minerals are less in quantity as compared to low quality minerals.

(iii) Minerals are exhaustible. Once they used can not be replenished immediately at the time of need. So, minerals have to be conserved and used judiciously.

Distribution of Minerals in India

- Most of metallic minerals in India occur in the **Peninsular Plateau region** in the old crystalline rocks.
- River valleys of Damodar, Sone, Mahanadi and Godavari have over 97% of coal reserves in India.
- Sedimentary basins of Assam and offshore region in the Arabian Sea (Gujarat and Mumbai High) are famous for their crude petroleum reserves.
- New reserves of petroleum also have been found in the basins of **Krishna-Godavari** and **Kaveri**.
- Most of the major mineral resources occur to the east of a line linking **Mangalore** and **Kanpur**.
- Minerals are generally concentrated in three broad belts in India. There may be some sporadic occurrences here and there in isolated pockets. These belts are

The North-Eastern Plateau Region

- This belt includes the regions of Chotanagpur (Jharkhand), Odisha Plateau, West Bengal and parts of Chhhattisgarh.
- Important minerals are iron ore, coal, manganese, bauxite and mica.
- Due to availability of these minerals, most of the iron and steel industries are located here.

The South-Western Plateau Region

- This belt extends to lower Karnataka, Goa and contiguous uplands of Tamil Nadu and Kerala.
- Ferrous metals and bauxite are concentrated here along with high grade iron ore, manganese and limestone. This belt lacks in coal deposits except neyveli lignite.
- Neyveli has lignite coal deposit. Deposits of monazite sand and thorium are found in Kerala.
- Mines of iron-ore are located in Goa.

The North-Western Regions

- Minerals of this belt are associated with Dharwar system of rocks which are found in the Rajasthan and parts of Gujarat.
- Major minerals are copper and zinc. Rajasthan is rich in building stones i.e. sandstone, granite, marble, fuller's earth and gypsum.
- Some cement industries are also concentrated here due to availability of dolomite and limestone which are the raw materials of these industries.
- Gujarat is rich in petroleum deposits. Salt is also produced in Gujarat and Rajasthan.

Other Areas/Regions

- Both Eastern and Western parts of the Himalayan belt have minerals like copper, lead, zinc, cobalt and tungsten.
- Assam Valley has mineral oil deposits. Besides, oil resources are also found in off-shore areas near Mumbai Coast (Mumbai High).

Spatial Pattern of Metallic Minerals

Spatial pattern of some of the important minerals are as follows

Ferrous Minerals

- India is well placed in respect of ferrous minerals like iron-ore, manganese, chromite, etc.
- These minerals provide a strong base for the development of metallurgical industries.

Iron ore

India has **largest iron ore reserves in Asia**. Its superior quality of hematite and magnetic iron-ore have a great demand in International market.

Iron ore mines of India are found near the coal fields of North-Eastern Plateau region which is an advantage for iron-ore industries of India.

Few Indian states have about 95% of total iron-ore reserves in India. These states are

- **Odisha** The important mines are located at Sundergarh, Mayurbhanj and Jhar. Gurumahisani, Sulaipet, Badampahar in Mayurbhanj and Kiruburu and Bonai (Sundergarh) have important mines.
- **Jharkhand** It has some of the oldest mines in India. Important mines are Noamundi and Gua in Poorbi and Paschimi Singhbhum districts.
- **Chhattisgarh** The mine belt further extended to Durg, Dantewada, Bailadiala, Dalli and Rajhara.

- **Karnataka** Important mines are Sundar-Hospet area of Bellary district, Bababudan hills and Kundremukh in Chikkamaguluru district and parts of Shivamogga, Chitradurg and Tumkur district .
- **Maharashtra** Important iron-ore deposits are located in Chandrapur, Bhandara and Ratnagiri districts.
- **Andhra Pradesh** Important areas of iron ore are Kurnool, Cuddapah and Anantpur districts.
- **Telangana** : Important areas of non-ore are Karimnagar and Warangal districts.
- **Others** These include Salem and Nilgiris Districts of Tamil Nadu state and Goa state.

Manganese

It is an important raw material which is used in iron and steel industry for smelting of iron-ore and in the manufacturing of ferro alloys.

It is mainly associated with Dharwar system but found almost in all geological formations. Important states are

- **Odisha** It is the **largest manganese producer** of India. The central part of the iron-ore belt of India has most of the manganese mines of Odisha. Important mines are located in the districts of Bonai, Kendujhar, Sundargarh, Gangpur, Koraput, Kalahandi and Bolangir.
- **Karnataka** Dharwar, Bellary, Belgaum, North Canara, Chikkamagaluru, Shivamogga, Chitradurg **and Tumkur** district.
- **Maharashtra** The main disadvantage of its mines are that these are located away from iron and steel plants. Nagpur, Bhandara and Ratnagiri have manganese mines.
- **Madhya Pradesh** Balaghat, Chhindwara, Nimar, Mandla and Jhabua districts have manganese mines.
- **Others** Other producer states of manganese are Telangana, Goa and Jharkhand.

Non-Ferrous Minerals

India has large deposits of bauxite but is lacking behind in other non-ferrous minerals.

Bauxite

It is the ore that used to manufacture aluminum and aluminium products.

It is found in laterite rocks mostly in the plateau or hilly regions of peninsular India and also in the coastal areas. Important states are

- **Odisha** It is the **largest producer of bauxite** and important producing areas are Kalahandi, Sambalpur, Bolangir and Koraput.
- **Jharkhand** Patlands of Jharhand in Lohardaga home rich deposits.
- **Gujarat** Bhavanagar and Jamnagar are important sites of bauxite.
- **Chattisgarh** Amarkanatak plateau region has large deposits of bauxite.
- **Madhya Pradesh** Katni-Jabalpur and Balaghat have important deposits of bauxite.
- **Maharashtra** Kulaba, Thane, Ratnagiri, Satara, Pune and Kolhapur have important deposits of bauxite.
- **Others** Tamil Nadu, Karnataka and Goa are other producers of bauxite.

Copper

It is alloyable, malleable and ductile and an indispensable metal in electrical industry used for making wires, electric motors, transformers and generators.

It is also used to give strength in gold jewelleries. Important copper producing states are

- **Jharkhand** Singbhum district
- **Madhya Pradesh** Balaghat
- **Rajasthan** Jhunjhunu and Alwar
- **Andhra Pradesh** Agnigundala in Guntur district
- **Karnataka** Chitradurg and Hasan
- **Tamil Nadu** South Arcot district

Non-Metallic Minerals

Limestone, dolomite, phosphate and mica are some non-metallic minerals produced in India. Mica is the important among them while others are produced for domestic consumption.

Mica

Mica is mainly used in the electrical/electronic industries which can be split into very thin, strong and flexible sheets.

Due to its resistance quality it is used in electricals and electronic industry. Important producer states are

- **Jharkhand** Hazaribagh plateau produces a high quality of mica.
- **Andhra Pradesh** Nellore district is important producer of mica, it produces best quality mica.
- **Rajasthan** A 320 km long belt from Jaipur to Bhilwara near Udaipur produces mica.
- **Karnataka** Mysore and Hasan are important producers of mica.

- **Others** Coimbatore, Tiruchirapalli, Madurai and Kanniyakumari (Tamil Nadu), Ratnagiri (Maharashtra), Alleppey, (Kerala), Purulia and Bankura (West Bengal) are also known for mica deposits.

Salt

It is a mineral composed of **Sodium Chloride** (NaCl). Salt is used in many industrial processes including the manufacture of polyvinyl chloride, plastics, paper pulp, etc. Rajasthan and Gujarat have rich sources of salt.

Energy Resources

All sectors of economy i.e. agriculture, industry, transport are run by power which comes from mineral fuels whether conventional or non-conventional energy resources.

Conventional Sources of Energy

These are exhaustible in nature e.g. fossil fuels like coal, petroleum and natural gas.

Coal

- It is required in the generation of thermal power and smelting of iron-ore.
- India has about 80% of bituminous coal which is of non-cooking grade.
- It is found in two rock sequences i.e. Gondwana coal fields and tertiary coal fields.

Gondwana Coal Fields

Damodar Valley is the important coal field of India. Jharkhand and West Bengal coal have the entire area of this coal field. Jharia (largest coal field), Raniganj (second largest fields), Bokaro, Giridih, Karanpura are important coal fields of this valley. Other river valleys are Godavari, Mahanadi and Sone.

Tertiary Coal Fields

Important states are

- **Meghalaya** Darangiri, Cherrapunji, Mewlong and Langrin (Meghalaya).
- **Assam** Makum, Jaipur and Nazira in Upper Assam.
- **Arunachal Pradesh** Namchik-Namphurk
- **Jammu and Kashmir** Kalakot
- **Others** Nagaland state

Other Coal Fields

Besides, the brown coal or lignite coal occurs in the coastal areas of Tamil Nadu, Puducherry, Gujarat and Jammu and Kashmir.

Petroleum

Crude petroleum consists of hydrocarbons of liquid and gaseous states varying in chemical composition, colour and specific gravity. It is used as a source of energy in all internal combustion engines of automobiles, railways and aircrafts.

It is also used as a raw material in petrochemical industries to produce fertilizer, synthetic rubber, synthetic fibre, medicines, vaseline, lubricants, wax soap and cosmetics, etc. It is also called **liquid gold** due to the scarcity and different uses. Crude oil is found in sedimentary rocks of tertiary age.

Before independence, Digboi was the only crude oil producing region in India but after independence in 1956, **Oil and Natural Gas Commission** was set up.

Important oil producing regions are

- **Assam** Digboi, Naharkatiya and Moran.
- **Gujarat and Mumbai High** Ankaleshwar, Kalol, Mehasana, Nawagam, Kosamba and Lunej. Krishna, Godavari and Kaveri basin also have Oil and Natural Gas reserves on the East coast of India.

There are two types of oil refineries in India

- **Field Based Refineries** Digboi is an example of field based refinery.
- **Market Based Refineries** Barauni is an example of market based refinery. There are total 23 refineries as on September, 2021.

Natural Gas

- It occurs alongwith oil as well as separately in gas reserves in India.
- These gas reserves are located alongwith Eastern cost of Tamil Nadu, Odisha, Andhra Pradesh, Tripura, Rajasthan, Gujarat and Maharashtra.
- Gujarat and Maharashtra have off-shore wells of natural gas.
- According to a survey report, there are indications of huge gas reserves in Ramathanpuram in Tamil Nadu state.

Hydroelectricity

The process of converting the kinetic energy of water in mechanical energy is termed as hydrologically driven energy. Hydraulic power can be captured when water flows downward from a higher level to a lower level which is then used to turn the turbine, thereby converting the kinetic of water into mechanical energy to drive generator.

Hydropower is the cheapest and cleanest source of energy but there are many environmental and social issues associated with it. Usually problems related to this occurs while constructing big dams projects like Tehri, Narmada etc. Small hydropower stations are free from these problems.

Some major hydropower plants in India are

- Sidrapong Hydroelectric Power Station (West Bengal) was the first power station.
- The **Tehri Hydroelectric Power Plant** (Uttarakhand) is the highest and the tallest power station in India.
- Nathpa Jhakri Hydroelectric Power Plant (Himachal Pradesh) is the biggest underground power project in the country.
- **Sardar Sarovar Dam** (Gujarat) is the world's 2nd largest concrete dam.

Non-Conventional Energy Sources

- Unlike conventional sources of energy, non-conventional energy sources are renewable i.e. solar, wind, hydro-geothermal and biomass and are not threat to natural system.
- Their use ensure sustainable development as these are environment friendly and cheaper energy sources.

Nuclear Energy Sources

- Nuclear energy has emerged as a feasible source in recent times.
- Uranium and thorium are main minerals that are used to generate nuclear energy.

Uranium Deposits in India

It is found in Dharwar rock system. Important regions are

- **Jharkhand** Singbhum (alongwith the copper belt)
- **Rajasthan** Udaipur, Alwar, Jhunjhunu districts.
- **Chhattisgarh** Durg district
- **Maharastra** Bhandara district
- **Himachal Pradesh** Kullu district

Thorium Deposits in India

It is found in very few places in India

- **Kerala** (in monazite and ilmenite beach sands) Plakkad and Kollam districts.
- **Andhra Pradesh** Vishakhapatnam.
- **Odisha** Mahanadi river delta

These three states have world's richest monazite deposits. The development of nuclear energy was started after establishment of **Atomic Energy Institute at Trombay** in 1954 which was renamed as the **Bhabha Atomic Research Centre** in 1967.

Tarapur (Maharashtra), Rawatbhata near Kota (Rajasthan), Kalapakkam (Tamil Nadu), Narora (Uttar Pradesh), Kaiga (Karnataka) and Kakarapara (Gujarat) are other nuclear power sites in India.

Solar Energy

- Sun's energy trapped by two methods i.e. photovoltaic cells and solar thermal technology and convert into electricity is called solar energy.
- Its construction is easy, eco-friendly and cost competitive.
- It is 7% and 10% more effective than coal and oil based plants and nuclear energy, respectively.
- Heaters, dryers, cookers and other heating appliances use solar energy more than others.
- Gujarat, Rajasthan and the Western part of India have higher potential for the development of solar energy.

Wind Energy

- Wind energy is non-polluting and renewable source. Through turbine mechanism, kinetic energy of wind can be directly converted into electrical energy.
- Electricity can be produced by permanent wind systems like trade wind, westerlies or seasonal winds like monsoon winds. Besides, production of electricity can also be done by local winds, land and sea breezes.
- India already has started generating wind energy to lessen the burden of oil import bill.
- **Rajasthan**, **Gujarat**, **Maharashtra** and **Karnataka** have higher potential for the development of wind energy.

Tidal and Wave Energy

- Ocean currents are the store house of infinite energy. Large tidal waves are known to occur along the west coast of India.
- Many efforts for the efficient use of oceanic tides and waves were made since 17th and 18th century.
- But these waves have not yet been utilised properly because of lack of technology.

Geothermal Energy

- Magma that comes over the earth's surface releases vast amount of heat. This heat energy can be converted into electrical energy by tapping it. It is called geothermal energy.

- Main sources of this energy are magma, hot spring (hot water), hot geysers, etc. Geothermal energy is gaining importance and can be used as an alternative to conventional energy sources.
- In India at **Manikaran in Himachal Pradesh**, a geothermal energy plant has been commissioned.

Bio-Energy

- Bio-energy refers to energy derived from biological products which includes agricultural residues, municipal, industrial and other wastes.
- It can be converted into electricity or electrical energy, heat energy or gas for cooking food.
- This can also solve the problem of garbage and waste in urban areas because energy can also be derived from these.
- It can contribute in improving economic life of rural peoples in developing countries, increasing environmental problems like pollution, solid waste management, enhancing self-reliance and reducing pressure on fuel wood.
- A project in **OKHLA** (Delhi) is an example that generates energy from municipal waste.

Conservation of Mineral Resources

There are some methods through which we can conserve mineral resources

(i) Adoption of renewable resources in place of exhaustible resources like solar power, wind, geothermal energy can save our non-renewable resources.

(ii) Use of recycle scrap metals should be encouraged.

(iii) Use of substitutes for scarce metals may also reduce their consumption.

(iv) Export of strategic and scarce minerals must be reduced, so that the existing reserve may be used for a longer period.

PYQs Previous Years' Questions

1 Mark Question

Multiple Choice Questions

1. Which of the following is incorrectly matched? *(CBSE SQP 2022)*

	List I (Name of the State)		List II (Coal mining centre)
(a)	Telangana	–	Singareni
(b)	Maharashtra	–	Korba
(c)	Odisha	–	Talcher
(d)	West Bengal	–	Raniganj

Ans. (b) Maharashtra - Korba

2. Identify the correct order of location from West to East, for the given natural gas reserves of India. *(CBSE SQP 2022)*

(a) Ankaleshwar, Tripura, Jaisalmer, Krishna Godavari basin.

(b) Jaisalmer, Ankaleshwar, Krishna Godavari basin, Tripura.

(c) Tripura, Jaisalmer, Krishna Godavari basin, Ankaleshwar.

(d) Krishna Godavari basin, Ankaleshwar, Tripura, Jaisalmer.

Ans. (b) Jaisalmer, Ankaleshwar, Krishna Godavari basin, Tripura.

3. Arrange the following in correct sequence. Following is the sequence of generating geothermal *(CBSE SQP 2022)*

(i) It is so hot that when it rises to the Earth's surface, it turns into steam.

(ii) Groundwater in such areas (where the geothermal gradient is high) absorbs heat from the rocks and becomes hot.

(iii) This steam is used to drive turbines and generate electricity.

(iv) Geothermal energy exists, because the Earth grows progressively hotter with increasing depth.

Codes

(a) (iv), (ii), (i), (iii) (b) (ii), (i), (iv), (iii)
(c) (i), (iv), (iii), (ii) (d) (iii), (ii), (iv), (i)

Ans. (a) (iv), (ii), (i), (iii)

4. Which one of the following coal fields are located in Odisha State? *(CBSE Compartment 2020)*

(a) Korba (b) Raniganj (c) Talcher (d) Neyveli

Ans. (c) Talcher

5. Which one of the following is a feature of 'Shaft Mining'? *(CBSE Compartment 2022)*

(a) It is the easiest and cheapest way of mining.

(b) Minerals occur close to the surface.

(c) Extracted minerals are transported to the surface through tunnels.
(d) Cost of safety precautions and equipment is relatively low.

Ans. (c) Extracted minerals are transported to the surface through tunnels.

6. Which one of the following states is the largest producer of 'Mica' in India? ***(CBSE Compartment 2020)***
(a) Gujarat (b) Andhra Pradesh
(c) Bihar (d) Jharkhand

Ans. (b) Andhra Pradesh

7. Which one of the following states is the largest producer of 'Bauxite' in India? ***(CBSE Compartment 2020)***
(a) Maharashtra
(b) Rajasthan
(c) Odisha
(d) Andhra Pradesh

Ans. (c) Odisha

8. Which one of the following iron-ore fields is located in Karnataka? ***(CBSE Compartment 2020)***
(a) Bailadila (b) Chitradurga
(c) Mayurbhanj (d) Ratnagiri

Ans. (b) Chitradurga

9. A natural substance of organic or inorganic origin with definite chemical and physical properties is known as
(a) Rock (b) Soil
(c) Mineral (d) Water

Ans. (c) Mineral

10. Metallic minerals include which of the following minerals?
(a) Copper (b) Gold
(c) Iron ore (d) All of these

Ans. (d) All of these

11. Which of the following is an example of inorganic non-metallic minerals?
(a) Mica (b) Limestone
(c) Graphite (d) All of these

Ans. (d) All of these

12. Most of the metallic minerals in India occur in which region?
(a) The Northern Plains
(b) The Valley Region
(c) The Mountainous Region
(d) The Peninsular Plateau Region

Ans. (d) The Peninsular Plateau Region

13. Which of the following is/are a characteristics of mineral resources?
(a) They are exhaustible
(b) Their distribution is uneven
(c) They take long time to replenish
(d) All of the above

Ans. (d) All of the above

14. Petroleum reserves are located in the sedimentary basins of which of the following region?
(a) Assam (b) Gujarat
(c) Mumbai High (d) All of these

Ans. (d) All of these

15. The Himalayan belt consists of which type of minerals?
(a) Lead (b) Zinc
(c) Cobalt (d) All of these

Ans. (d) All of these

16. Noamundi and Gua Iron-ore mines are located in which State of India?
(a) Odisha (b) West Bengal
(c) Jharkhand (d) Chhattisgarh

Ans. (c) Jharkhand

17. Arrange the following states in sequence in terms of production of Bauxite
I. Odisha II. Jharkhand
III. Gujarat IV. Goa

Codes
(a) I, II, III, IV (b) IV, III, II, I
(c) III, II, IV, I (d) III, II, I, IV

Ans. (a) I, II, III, IV

Very Short Answer Questions

1. Classify mineral on the basis of chemical and physical properties. ***(All India 2017)***

Ans. On the basis of chemical properties and physical properties, mineral are classified into the following:
(i) Metallic minerals
(ii) Non-metallic minerals

2. Explain one reason for the import of petroleum and its products in large quantities in India. ***(All India 2016)***

Ans. The import of petroleum and its products in large quantities in India is due to following reasons:
(i) Increased use of diesel for irrigation due to weak monsoon.
(ii) Rising industrialisation.

3. Name any two ferrous minerals other than iron-ore. *(All India 2011)*

Ans. Two ferrous minerals are

(i) Manganese (ii) Nickel

4. Name the place of Maharashtra where an atomic power station is located. *(All India 2010)*

Ans. The atomic power station of Maharashtra is located in Tarapur.

5. Name the river valley where Gondwana coal fields of India are located. *(All India 2008)*

Ans. Gondwana coal-fields are located in Domodar Valley.

6. Which are the two main types of iron-ore found in India? *(All India 2008)*

Ans. The two main types of iron-ore found in India are:

(i) Haematite (ii) Magnetite

3 Marks Questions

1. Mention the main characteristics of the mineral belt of 'South-Western Plateau Region' of India. *(CBSE 2023)*

Ans. The characteristics of mineral belt of 'South-Western Plateau Region' of India are

(i) This belt includes Karnataka, Goa and contiguous uplands of Tamil Nadu and Kerala.

(i) Ferrous metals and bauxite are concentrated here along with high grade iron ore, manganese and limestone.

(iii) Neyveli has lignite coal deposits. Deposits of Monazite sand and thorium are found in Kerala. Mines of iron-ore are located in Goa.

2. Explain why modern society requires speedy and efficient system of transport. *(CBSE 2023)*

Ans. Modern society requires speedy and efficient transport systems for many purposes such as

- Transport is required to assist in the production, distribution and consumption of goods.
- Transport is a service or facility by which persons, manufactured goods, and property are physically carried from one location to another.
- It is an organised industry created to satisfy man's basic need of mobility. At every stage in this complex system, the value of the material is significantly enhanced by transportation.
- Transport activities are essential to carry out trade services.
- Transportation is also essential for defence purpose.
- It links different parts of country with each other and with other countries as well, which increases national and global linkage.
- It also links rural areas with urban areas and helps in ushering development even in rural and backward areas. It makes more places suitable for setting up industries and hence helps, in increasing job opportunities.

3. Explain any three characteristics of non-conventional sources of energy. *(CBSE 2023)*

Ans. The three characteristics of the use of non-conventional sources of energy are

(i) Unlike conventional sources of energy, most of the non-conventional energy sources are cheaper and renewable.

The limitation and scarcity of fossil fuels have given rise to the urgent need for using the alternative energy sources such as renewable non-conventional energy resources.

(ii) Power from non-conventional and renewable sources is must in order to reduce carbon dioxide (CO_2) emissions from the coal-based power plants. Non-conventional resources are environment friendly.

(iii) Locally available non-conventional and renewable power resources like wind and solar can meet local rural energy needs with minimum costs.

Thus, non-conventional energy resources will ensure sustainable development by meeting the needs of the present generation without harming the need of future generation.

4. Mention any four features of non- metallic minerals in India. *(CBSE Term I 2021)*

Ans. Features of non-metallic minerals are

(i) These minerals do not contain metals.

(ii) These are made up of organic matter of burried animals and plants, e.g, coal.

(iii) These are also inorganic in nature of origin, e.g, mica, limestone, graphite etc.

(iv) Most of metallic minerals in India occur in the Peninsular plateau region in the old crystalline rocks.

5. Mention any four features of 'Geothermal energy' in India. *(CBSE Term I 2021)*

Ans. Features of Geothermal energy are

(i) It converts heat energy into electrical energy.

(ii) Sources of this energy are magma, hot spring, hot geysers etc.

(iii) Geothermal energy can be used as an alternative source of energy.

(iv) It is a renewable source of energy.

6. "The promotion of the use of non-conventional sources of energy in India is the need of the hour." Support the statement. *(Delhi 2016)*

> **HINT** *Dear students, this question simply ask you to write the need to promote the use of non-conventional sources of energy in India.*

Ans. It is true that promotion of the use of non-conventional sources of energy in India is the need of the hour due to the following reasons

(i) Unlike conventional sources of energy, most of the non-conventional energy sources are cheaper and renewable. The overall limitation and scarcity of fossil fuels has given rise to the urgent need for exploiting alternative energy sources.

(ii) Power from non-conventional and renewable sources is must in order to reduce carbon dioxide (CO_2) emissions of the coal-based power plants. It is exhaustible in nature and environment friendly.

(iii) Locally available non-conventional and renewable power resources can meet localised rural energy with minimum transportational cost.

7. Explain the significance of bio-energy to humankind in India. *(All India 2016)*

Ans. The significance of bio-energy to humankind can be understood through the following points

(i) Bio-energy is a result of processing of biological products such as agricultural residues, municipal, industrial and other wastes.

(ii) Bio-energy can be used by converting it into electricity or electrical energy, heat energy or gas for cooking food.

(iii) Apart from deriving energy it can also solve the problem of garbage and waste in urban areas because energy can also be derived from these.

(iv) It can improve economic life of rural peoples and also reduce environmental pollution pressure on fuel wood and enhance self-reliance.

8. Explain any three main characteristics of mineral resources of India. *(Delhi 2014)*

Ans. The major characteristics of mineral resources are as follows

(i) Their distribution over the earth surface are uneven i.e. some regions may have rich in minerals whereas others may be lack behind in availability of minerals.

(ii) Minerals of good quality are less in amount and minerals of low quality are more in amount on earth i.e. quality and quantity of minerals have an inverse relationship.

(iii) Minerals are exhaustible, i.e. once used they can't be used again. Minerals take long time to develop geologically and once they exhausted they cannot be available at that time for use.

9. Give two advantages of 'copper'. Mention four copper mining areas of India. *(Delhi 2013)*

Ans. Copper is a non-ferrous mineral found in India. It has various advantages such as

(i) Copper due to its alloyable, malleable and ductile properties mostly use in electrical industry for making wires, electric motors, transformers and generators.

(ii) To give strength, copper is also mixed with gold in making jewelleries.

Four copper producing states of India are

(i) Copper deposits mainly found in Singhbhum district in Jharkhand.

(ii) It is found in Balaghat district of Madhya Pradesh.

(iii) Alwar, Jhunjhunu, Bhilwara and Udaipur districts of Rajasthan are producers of copper.

(iv) Agni Gundala in Guntar district of Andhra Pradesh. Chitradurg and Hassan districts of Karnataka and South Arcot district of Tamil Nadu are other producers of copper ore.

10. Give two advantages of Manganese. Mention four manganese producing states of India. *(Delhi 2013)*

Ans. The two advantages of manganese are as follows

(i) Manganese is a ferrous mineral found in India. It is used as a raw material in iron and steel industry for smelting of iron-ore.

(ii) It is also used in the manufacturing of ferro alloys.

Four manganese producing states of India are

(i) **Odisha** It is the largest manganese producer in India. Important mines are located in the districts of Bonai, Kendujhar, Sundergarh, Gangpur, Koraput, Kalahandi and Bolangir.

(ii) **Karnataka** Important mines are located in Dharwar, Billary, Belgaum, North Canara, Chikkamaguluru, Shivamogga, Chitradurg and Tumkur districts

> **Manganese producing states of India**
> - Odisha
> - Karnataka
> - Maharashtra
> - Madhya Pradesh

(iii) **Maharashtra** Manganese mines are found in Bhandara, Nagpur and Ratnagiri.

(iv) **Madhya Pradesh** Its mines are located in the belt of Balaghat, Chhindwara, Nimar, Mandla and Jhabua districts.

11. Give two advantages of 'wind energy.' Mention four states for India having favourable conditions for the development of wind energy. *(Delhi 2013)*

Ans. Wind energy is another non-conventional source of energy. The two advantages of wind energy are as follows

(i) Wind energy is a clean fuel source. It does not pollute the air as compare to conventional sources.

(ii) Wind power is one of the lowest-cost renewable energy technologies available today. Even without government subsidies, wind power is a low-cost fuel in many areas of the country.

Four wind power producing states of India are

(i) Rajasthan (ii) Gujarat

(iii) Maharashtra (iv) Karnataka

12. Describe the uneven distribution of mineral and energy resources in India by giving suitable examples. *(Delhi 2012)*

Ans. India is a rich country in terms of minerals. Most of the metallic minerals occur in the Peninsular Plateau region in the old crystalline rocks. River valleys of Damodar, Sone, Mahanadi and Godavari have over 97% of coal reserves in India.

Sedimentary basins of Assam and off-shore region in the Aarbian Sea (Gujarat and Mumbai High) are famous for their crude petroleum reserves. The area to the east of a line linking Mangalore and Kanpur has most of the major mineral resources of India. Mineral are mainly concentrated in three broad belts, namely:

(i) The North-Eastern Plateau region

(ii) The South-Western Plateau region

(iii) The North-Western region

13. ''Conservation of minerals is more important than other resources''. Explain by giving three arguments. *(All India 2012)*

Other Similar Questions

Or Why conservation of minerals is more significant then other resources?

Or "Minerals should be conserved more than other resources." Justify the statement.

Ans. Conservation of minerals is more important than other resources due to the following reasons

(i) Minerals are important to conserve as industries and agriculture are dependent completely on minerals and the substance manufactured from them.

(ii) We are rapidly consuming mineral resources that require millions of years to be renewed.

(iii) Workable minerals are in insufficient quantities, for e.g. only 1% of the earth's crust.

(iv) Due to decrease in good quality and they come from greater depths, the costs of mineral extraction is increasing.

(v) Economic and industrial development depends on minerals.

14. Explain any three methods of conservation of minerals resources in India. *(Delhi 2010)*

Ans. There are some methods through which we can conserve mineral resources

(i) Adoption of renewable resources in place of exhaustible resources like solar power, wind, wave, geothermal energy can save our non-renewable resources.

(ii) Use of recycle scrap metals should be encouraged. It can save the mining of newer metals. In India, scope of some scarce metallic minerals like zinc, copper, lead are useful because India is lacking behind in these minerals.

(iii) Substitute for some precious and scarce-metals should be encouraged. It can reduce their consumption.

5 Marks Questions

1. "The challenge of sustainable development requires integration of quest for economic development with environmental concerns" Evaluate the statement in the context of conservation of mineral resources. *(CBSE 2023)*

HINT *Dear students, this question simply ask you to give explanation on why conservation of mineral resources is important for the sustainable development.*

Ans. Conservation of minerals resources is essential for development of India because of multiple reasons. In the last few decades, mismanagement and over exploitations of resources has put India's development at risk.

Their conservation is essential because of following reasons

- In India, mineral resources are unevenly distributed throughout the country, if these resources get extinct, then it will a huge challenge to fulfil domestic requirement.
- Its conservation is important as large number of industries are dependent completely on mineral resources.
- If mineral resources are not conserved, then we have to import them from other countries which will put huge economical pressure.
- The formation of minerals takes number of years. Moreover, they finite and non-renewable. Once finished, they take millions of years for their replenishment.
- Every country has a moral responsibility to conserve resources for the future generation, so that, they can also use them for their development.

Hence, efficient and judicious of minerals is demand of time, if we want ensure development of India.

2. "Coal and petroleum are still essential sources of energy in India." Support the statement.

(CBSE Compartment 2022)

Ans. Fossil fuels, like coal and petroleum are non renewable natural resources. They have an organic origin and are called hydrocarbon fuels. Coal was formed in nature as a solid from the remains of the trees buried deep inside the earth. Petroleum also occurs deep inside the earth's crust, as a liquid, and is formed by the bacterial decomposition of marine plant and animal matter

The use of coal and petroleum and their products are of great importance in the world economy. Coal is an important fuel source as its energy is converted into other forms such as electricity, steam and coal gas. Thermal power stations runs on coal. Coal is used for many industrial applications such as fuel for iron and steel foundries, metal extraction plants and steam based turbines. Coal tar, a black liquid, produces a mixture of carbon compounds which are used to prepare drugs, dyes, paints, explosives, plastics, etc.

It is a source of aromatic hydrocarbon compounds like benzene, toluene, aniline, phenol, naphthalene, anthracene, etc. Petroleum is often referred to as liquid gold, due to its importance as a fuel in transportation (petrol, diesel, kerosene, gas oil, fuel oil) and as a source of over hundred and fifty important petrochemicals used in industrial and consumer applications.

3. Classify minerals into two groups on the basis of chemical and physical properties and give one example of minerals of each group. Mention any two features of the three minerals belts of India.

(CBSE SQP 2020, Delhi 2009)

Ans. Minerals are classified on the basis of their physical properties and chemical properties such as:

(i) **Metallic Minerals** Metallic minerals are those that are rich in metals and a source to procure a variety of metals like copper, gold, iron, etc. Bauxite, iron-ore are some examples of metallic minerals. There are two types of metallic minerals i.e. ferrous and non-ferrous.

(ii) **Non-Metallic Minerals** Non-metallic minerals are those that do not have metal components. For example coal, petroleum, mica etc. Non-metallic minerals can be organic in origin or inorganic in origin.

Features of three mineral belts of India are:

(i) **The North-Eastern Plateau Region** This belt includes the regions of Chotanagpur (Jharkhand), Odisha plateau, West Bengal and parts of Chhattisgarh. Important minerals are iron-ore, coal, manganese, bauxite, mica.

(ii) **The South-Western Plateau Region** This belt includes Karnataka, Goa and contiguous uplands of Tamil Nadu and Kerala. Ferrous metals and bauxite are concentrated here along with high-grade iron-ore, manganese, and limestone. Neyveli has lignite coal deposit. Deposits of Monazite sand and thorium are found in Kerala. Mines of iron-ore are located in Goa.

(iii) **The North-Western Region** Minerals of this belt are associated with the Dharwar system of rocks which are found in the Aravali in Rajasthan and parts of Gujarat. Major minerals are copper and zinc. Rajasthan is rich in building stones i.e. sandstone, granite, marble, fuller's earth, and gypsum.

Mineral Belts of India

- The North-Eastern Plateau Region
- The South-Western Plateau Region
- The North-Western Region

4. "The challenge of sustainable development requires integration of the quest for economic development with environmental concerns." Comprehend the statement in relation to the development of non-conventional sources of energy in India by giving suitable examples. ***(CBSE SQP 2019)***

Ans. Sustainable development is important because it calls for the conservation of resources for future generations. Sustainable energy resources in India are non-conventional sources of energy such as solar energy, wind energy, geothermal energy, biomass energy, tidal energy, etc.

These energy sources are more equitably distributed and are also environment friendly. Thus, these non-conventional energy sources will provide more sustained, eco-friendly and cheaper energy after their initial costs are taken care of. In contrast, traditional energy resources such as coal and petroleum generate pollution when consumed. Thus they do not address environmental concerns. They also generate enormous quantities of waste products. Hence, sustainable development calls for the conservation of resources for the future generations and more use non-conventional sources of energy, as they are also abundantly available in India.

5. "Nuclear energy is replacing the conventional sources in India." Do you think it as a viable energy source of energy in future keeping in view the availability of nuclear minerals in India? ***(CBSE SQP 2019)***

Ans. Nuclear energy has emerged as a viable source in recent times. Important minerals used for the generation of nuclear energy are Uranium and Thorium. Uranium deposits occur in the Dharwar system of rocks. They are found in several locations along the Singhbhum copper belt.

They are also found in Udaipur, Alwar and Jhunjhunu districts of Rajasthan, Durg district of Chhattisgarh, Bhandara district of Maharashtra and Kulu district of Himachal Pradesh. Thorium is mainly obtained from the monazite and limonite in the beach sand along the coasts of Kerala and Tamil Nadu.

The world's richest monazite deposits occur in Palakkad and Kollam districts of Kerala, near Visakhapatnam in Andhra Pradesh and in the Mahanadi river delta in Odisha.

Further the, Atomic Energy Commission of India was established in 1948. Important nuclear power projects which are operational are Tarapur (Maharashtra), Rawatbhata near Kota (Rajasthan), Kalpakkam (Tamil Nadu), Narora (Uttar Pradesh), Kaiga (Karnataka) and Kakrapara (Gujarat). Collaboration with France, Germany, Russia and USA in developing the required technology is a positive step in this direction. Thus, there is adequate availability of nuclear minerals in India to feed these nuclear power plants, making it a viable energy source in future.

6. "The non-conventional sources of energy in India will provide more sustained and environment friendly energy." Examine the statement. ***(All India 2019)***

Or "The non-conventional sources of energy will provide more sustained, eco-friendly and cheaper energy if the initial cost is taken care of." Examine the statement. ***(Delhi 2018)***

Ans. It is true that non-conventional sources of energy in India will provide more sustained and environment friendly energy due to the following reasons

(i) Unlike conventional sources of energy, most of the non-conventional energy sources are cheaper and renewable. The overall limitation and scarcity of fossil fuels has given rise to the urgent need for exploiting alternative energy sources.

(ii) Power from non-conventional and renewable sources is must in order to reduce carbon dioxide (CO_2) emissions of the coal-based power plants. It is exhaustible in nature and environment friendly.

(iii) Locally available non-conventional and renewable power resources can meet localised rural energy with minimum transportational cost.

(iv) The non-conventional energy sources are solar energy, wind energy, geothermal energy, biomass energy etc. These are easily available in the country and can be harnessed with the help of modern technolgoy.

(v) These sources are capable of regeneration. These are renewed along with exploitation and hence, always available for us.

7. What is the use of manganese? Describe the statewise distribution of manganese in India. ***(All India 2009)***

Ans. Manganese is used as follows

(i) It is used as a raw material in iron and steel industry for smelting of iron-ore.

(ii) It is used in the manufacturing of ferro alloys.

Statewise distribution of manganese is as follows

(i) Manganese is found in the rocks of all geological formations in India. But large manganese deposits are found in the rocks of Dharwar system.

(ii) Odisha is the largest manganese producer in India. Central part of the iron-ore belt of India has most of the manganese mines of Odisha. These mines are located in the districts of Bonai, Kendujhar, Sundergarh, Gangpur, Koraput, Kalahandi and Bolangir in Odisha.

(iii) Karnataka is also known for its manganese mines and production. Dharwar, Bellary, Belgaum, North Canara, Chikkamaguluru, Shivamogga, Chitradurg and Tumkur districts having major manganese mines.

(iv) Most of the manganese mines are located in the belt of Balaghat, Chhindwara-Nima, Mandla and Jhabua districts in Madhya Pradesh.

(v) Other producer states of manganese are Telangana, Goa and Jharkhand.

Map Based Questions

1. On the given political outline map of India, locate and label the following Geographical features with appropriate symbols. ***(CBSE Term I 2021)***

(i) Raniganj – Coal mines

(ii) Balaghat – Manganese mines

(iii) Khetri – Copper mines

(iv) Jamnagar – Oil mines

Ans.

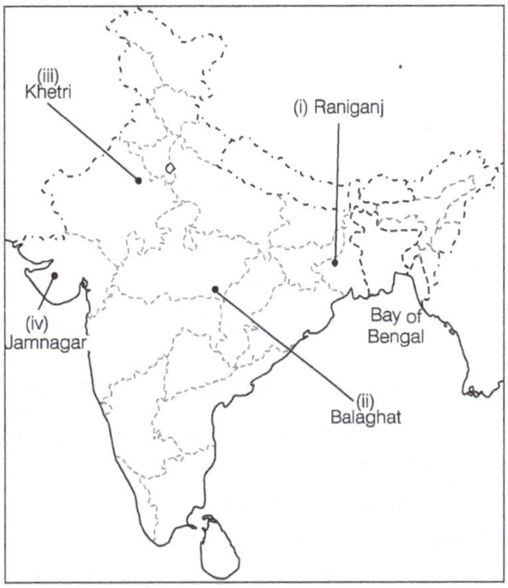

2. Locate and label the following on the given political outline map of India with appropriate symbols.

(i) Mayurbhanj an iron-ore mining area. ***(Delhi 2016, 2013)***

(ii) A copper mining area of Southern Jharkhand. ***(Delhi 2013)***

Ans.

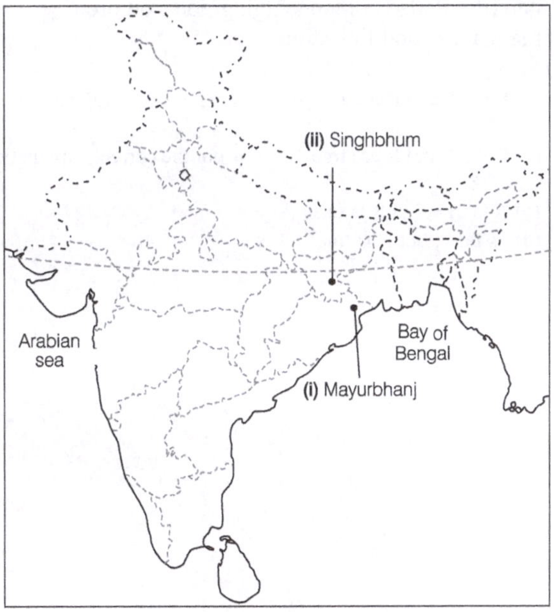

CHAPTER TEST

01 Mark Questions

1 Name the place at which the first atomic power station of India was started.
(a) Narora (b) Kalpakkam
(c) Tarapur (d) Rana Pratap Sagar

2 Which of the following minerals is known as brown diamond?
(a) Iron (b) Mica (c) Lignite (d) Manganese

3 Arrange the following oil refineries in correct order from North to South.
1. Visakhapatnam 2. Haldia
3. Chennai 4. Nagapattinam

Codes
(a) 1234 (b) 2134 (c) 4321 (d) 3124

4 **Assertion** (A) The South-Western Plateau Region mineral belt extends over Karnataka, Goa and contiguous Tamil Nadu uplands and Kerala.
Reason (R) This belt is rich in ferrous metals and bauxite. It also contains high grade iron ore, manganese and limestone.

Codes
(a) Both A and R are true and R is the correct explanation of A
(b) Both A and R are true, but R is not the correct explanation of A
(c) A is true, but R is false
(d) is false, but R is true

5 Which of the following pairs is matched incorrectly?

State		Copper Producing Region
(a) Jharkhand	–	Singhbhum
(b) Madhya Pradesh	–	Balaghat
(c) Odisha	–	Jhunjhunu
(d) Andhra Pradesh	–	Agnigundala

Answers

1. (c)	2. (c)	3. (b)	4. (a)	5. (c)

03 Marks Questions

6 Write about the three major mineral belts of India.

7 Explain the distribution of Bauxite in India.

8 State any two advantages of manganese ore. Mention four manganese producing states of India.

05 Marks Questions

9 Give a brief account on hydel power in India.

10 Which are the two main ferrous minerals found in India? Explain any four characteristics of each.

11 Explain any three characteristics of the solar energy, tidal energy and geothermal energy resources.

06

Planning & Sustainable Development in Indian Context

TREND ANALYSIS 3 YEARS

TOPIC 01 Planning and Sustainable Development

Average No. of Questions Across all Sets

Types of Questions	2023	2020	2019
1 Mark	–	–	–
3 Marks	–	–	–
5 Marks	1	–	2

Planning

The word 'Planning' can be considered as a general term as well as it specifically involves the process of thinking, formulation of a scheme or programme and the implementation of a set of ideas to achieve certain goals.

Approaches of Planning

There are two approaches of planning which are as follows

Sectoral Planning Approach In this approach, the development of various sectors of economy, such as agriculture, irrigation, manufacturing, power, construction, transport, communication, social infrastructure and services, are taken into consideration to which various sets of schemes or programmes are to be formulised and implemented.

Regional Planning Approach In this approach, the main emphasis is on to draw such plans which may help to reduce regional disparities and bring uniform economic development.

Target Area Planning

The core focus of planning process is in promoting economically backward areas. It is important for proper regional development that the resource base should be accompanied by technology and investment simultaneously, because it has been seen that sometimes resource rich regions also remain backward.

After having about one and half decade of planning experience, it has been realised that our economic development is still facing the regional imbalances. In order to encounter both regional and social disparities, the Planning Commission introduced the **target area** and **target group approaches** to planning. Some of the programmes which are directed towards the development of these two approaches are as follows

Target Area Programmes

Target area has the following programmes such as

(i) Command Area Development programme
(ii) Drought Prone Area Development Programme
(iii) Desert Development Programme
(iv) Hill Area Development Programme

Target Group Programmes

Target groups has the following programmes such as

(i) The Small Farmers Development Agency (SFDA)

(ii) Marginal Farmers Development Agency (MFDA)

In the Eighth Five Year Plan, hill areas, North-Eastern states, tribal areas and backward areas were taken into consideration in order to develop special area programmes.

Planning Related to Area Development Programme

Hill Area Development Programme

- It covers 15 districts comprising all the hilly districts of Uttar Pradesh (present Uttarakhand), Mikir hill and North Cachar hills of Assam, Darjiling district of West Bengal and Nilgiri district of Tamil Nadu. It was stated in Fifth Five Year Plan.
- It was recommended in 1981, by the National Committee on the Development of Backward Area, that the hill areas having a height above 600 m and not covered under tribal sub-plan be treated as backward hill areas.
- The aims of Hill Area Development Programmes are as follows
  (i) Development of horticulture, plantation agriculture, animal husbandry, poultry, forestry and small scale and village industry were the main objectives of the programme through which exploitation of local resources may become possible.
  (ii) The detailed plans were based on topographical, ecological, economic and social conditions of the hill areas.

Drought Prone Area Programme (DPAP)

This programme was started during the Fourth Five Year Plan. The main objectives of Drought Prone Area Programme are as follows

- This plan mainly emphasised on generating employment opportunities to the people of drought prone areas along with creating productive assets.
- Besides, irrigation projects, land development programmes, afforestation, grassland development and creation of basic rural infrastructure such as rural electrification, roads, market, credit and services were also its main priorities.
- The National Committee on Development of Backward Areas found that this programme was mostly confined to the development of agriculture and allied sectors along with restoration of ecological balance.
- The society due to burden of population was bound to utilise the marginal lands for agriculture and as a result led ecological degradation.

Thus, it was observed that there is an urgent need to generate alternative employment opportunities in these regions.

Drought Prone Regions

- There are 67 districts (entire or partly) in India identified by planning commission (1967) as drought prone regions.
- Irrigation commission (1972), demarcated the drought affected areas and also introduced the criterion of 30% irrigated land.
- These areas are semi-arid and arid tract of Rajasthan, Gujarat, Western Madhya Pradesh, Marathwada, region of Maharashtra, Rayalseema and Telangana plateaus of Andhra Pradesh, Karnataka plateau and Higlands and interior parts of Tamil Nadu.

Due to the advancement in irrigation facilities, Haryana, Punjab and Northern Rajasthan have become protected regions.

Integrated Tribal Development Project in Bharmaur Region

- The region lies between 32° 11′ N and 32° 41′ N latitudes and 76° 22′ E and 76° 53′ E longitudes. Spread over an area of about 1818 sq km, the region mostly lies between 1500 m to 3700 m above the mean sea level.
- This region popularly known as the **homeland of Gaddis** and is surrounded by lofty mountains on all sides. It has Pir Panjal in the North and Dhaula Dhar in the South. In the East, the extension of Dhaula Dhar converges with Pir Panjal near Rohtang pass.
- The river Ravi and its tributaries, the Budhil and the Tundahen, drain this territory and carve out deep gorges.
- These rivers divide the region into four physiographic divisions called Holi, Khani, Kugti and Tundah areas. Bharmaurs experiences freezing weather conditions and snowfall in winter. It means monthly temperature in January remains 4°C and in July 26°C.

Area and Life of People in Bharmaur

The area and life of people of Bharmaur region are discussed below

- The tribal area covers Bharmaur and Holi tehsils of Chamba district of Himachal Pradesh.
- It is one of the most backward area economically as well as socially in Himachal Pradesh and also a notified tribal region since 21st November, 1975.

- The area is occupied by a tribal group of community named 'Gaddi', who practised transhumance and speak 'Gaddiali' dialect.
- According to 2001 census, the total population of the area was 39113 i.e. 21 persons per sq km.
- People of the area face major problems as the economy is mostly affected by its harsh climate, low resource base and fragile environment.

Economy in the Area of Bharmaur

- Traditionally, subsistence agriculture-cum-pastoral activities such as growing food grains and animal husbandry like sheep and goat are the main activities of these people.

Integrated Tribal Development Project (ITDP)

- In 1970s, Gaddis were included in the list of scheduled tribes and in the same period the development process of tribal area of this region started.
- Later in 1974 under the Fifth Five Year Plan, the tribal sub-plan was introduced and Bharmaur was designed as one of the five **Integrated Tribal Development Project** (ITDP) in Himachal Pradesh.
- Aims and priorities of the Intergrated Tribal Development Project are as follows
  - (i) Improving the quality of life of the Gaddis.
  - (ii) Narrowing the gap in the level of development between Bharmaur and other districts of Himachal Pradesh.
  - (iii) The highest priority was on development of transport and communications, agriculture and allied activities as well as social and community services.

The main achievements of the tribal sub-plan are as follows

Infrastructural Facilities

Infrastructural facilities of tribal sub-plan are as follows

- Development of infrastructure i.e schools, health care facilities, potable water, roads, communications and electricity supply.
- Villages located along the river Ravi in Holi and Khani areas are main beneficiaries infrastructural development.

Social Benefits

Social benefits of tribal sub-plan are as follows

- There are tremendous increase in literacy rate, e.g, the female literacy rate in the region increased from 1.88% in 1971 to 65% in 2011.
- Decline in gender inequality i.e. between male and female literacy rate.
- Improvement in sex-ratio.
- Decline in child marriage.

Economic Benefits

As the Gaddis had practiced traditionally, subsistence agriculture cum-pastroral economy, later on during the last three decades of 20th century, pulses and other cash crops became one of the main crops of the region.

Some Shortcomings to ITDP

- In terms of infrastructural facilities, the remote villages in Tundah and Kugti areas are still remained unaffected.
- The technology is still traditional in nature.
- The importance of pastoralism has been decreasing day-by-day as only about one tenth of the total households practice transhumance.

Overview of Planning Perspective in India

India has centralised planning and the Planning Commission has been assigned to administer the functions of planning in India.

Being a statutory body, Planning Commission is headed by the Prime Minister and has a Deputy Chairman and members. Five Year Plans are responsible to carry out the planning in India which are as follows

- The First Five Year Plan launched in 1951 and covered the period, 1951-52 to 1955-56.
- Second and Third Five Year Plans covered the period from 1956-57 to 1960-61 and 1961-62 to 1965-1966, respectively.
- Two successive droughts during mid sixties (1965-66 and 1966-67) and war with Pakistan in 1965 forced plan Holiday in 1966-67 and 1968-69. This period was covered by annual plans which are also termed as rolling plans.
- The Fourth Five Year Plan began in 1969-70 and ended in 1973-74.
- Following this the Fifth Five Year Plan began in 1974-75, but it was terminated by the government one year earlier i.e. in 1977-78.
- The Sixth Five Year Plan took off in 1980.
- The Seventh Five Year Plan covered the period between 1985 and 1990.
- Once again, due to the political instability and initiation of liberalisation policy, the Eighth Five Year Plan got delayed. It covered the period from 1997 to 2002.
- The Tenth Five Year Plan began in 2002 and ended in 2007.

- The Eleventh Five Year Plan started in 2007 and ended in 2012. It was entitled " Towards faster and more inclusive growth".
- The Twelfth Five Year Plan in 2012 and it is still in progress. It will come to an end in 2017.

Sustainable Development

- In the 1960, this was the period when people throughout the world were much concerned about the environmental issues because of undesirable effects of industrial development and thus, the concept of sustainable development emerged in Western world.
- This level of fear among environmentalists and common people reached at its peak with the publication of **The population Bomb** by Ehrlich in 1968 and **The Limits to Growth** by Meadows and others in 1972.

Aims of Sustainable Development

- The main aim of sustainable development is to take care of economic, social and ecological spheres of development during the present times as well as conserve all the resources in such a manner that these can be retain for future generations.
- So, there is a need of changing our attitude towards nature as well as economic development.

Concept of Development

- Development is a dynamic concept and has evolved in the second half of twentieth century, used to describe the state of particular societies and the process of changes experienced by them.
- In early human history, the main criteria of determination of a society's state was the interaction process between human societies and their bio-physical environment.
- Societies helped in the development of various levels of technology and institutions upon which human-environment process depend.
- These have helped in increasing the pace of human environment interaction, therefore, the momentum generated and festinated technological progress and transformation and creation of institutions.
- After the period of World War II, the two important terms i.e. **development** and **economic growth** considered as one concept. But due to unequal distribution, a faster rate of growth in poverty is experienced by even the developed nations having high economic growth.
- Then, redistribution with growth and 'growth and equity' broaden the term development in 1970s. Now, the concept of development not only restricted to economic sphere alone, but also incorporates balance and equality among people in term of welfare and quality of life of people, health education and other facilities, equal opportunity to all and ensuring political and civil rights.
- Hence, the concept of development has become multi-dimensional and stands for positive, irreversible transformation of the economy, society and environment.

World Commission on Environment and Development (WCED)

- The United Nations established a World Commission on Environment and Development (WCED), after concerning the opinion of world community on the environmental issues.
- The WCED was headed by the Norwegian Prime Minister, **Gro Harlem Brundtland.** The commission gave its report entitled 'Our Common Future' in 1987, also known as **Brundtland Report**.
- In Brundtland and Report, 'sustainable development' took into consideration and defined as 'A development that meets the needs of the present without compromising the ability of future generations to meet their own needs'.

Measures for Promotion of Sustainable Development

As we have seen that this project has affected the ecological sustainablity and physical environment of the region badly. So, attaining the goal of sustainable development in command area requires such measures that can achieve ecological, social and economic sustainabality, simultaneously.

Hence, five of the seven measures have been proposed in this respect such as

(i) Rigorous implementation of water management policy is the first and foremost requirement of this project.

Stage I and Stage II comprising of protective irrigation and extensive irrigation for crops and pasture development, respectively according to the canal project.

(ii) By and large water intensive crops shall be avoided and plantation crops such as fruits shall be encouraged by folks.

(iii) In order to reduce the conveyance loss of water, few important programmes shall be taken into account such as the CAD (Command Area Development) programmes i.e.

(a) Lining of water courses.
(b) Land development and levelling.
(c) Warabandi system (means equal distribution of canal water in the command area of outlet).

(iv) The areas should be reclaimed that got affected by water logging and soil salinity.

(v) The eco-development is a must, especially in the fragile environment of Stage II, through afforestation, shelterbelt, plantation and pasture development activities.

(vi) By providing a decent financial and institutional support for cultivation of the land, allottees who have poor economic background, can be prove a positive step towards achieving the social sustainability in the region.

(vii) The economic sustainability can be attained through expanding the economic sector which must include agriculture and allied activities along with other economic sectors, as a whole. Hence, we will then find diversification of economic base and establishment of functional linkages between basic villages, agro-service centres and market centres.

Promotion of Sustainable Development in Indira Gandhi Canal Command Area

- It is one of the largest canal systems in India, conceived by **Kanwar Sain** in 1948. This project was launched on 31st March, 1958 that transformed a desert into greenland.
- The origin place of the canal is at Harike barrage in Punjab state and goes parallel to Pakistan Border at an average distance of 40 km in Thar Desert of Rajasthan (Marusthali).
- 9060 km is the total planned length of the system catering to the irrigation needs of a total culturable command area of 19.63 lakh hectares.
- The canal has two irrigation system such as **flow system** and **lift system**. Around 70% land of the command area is irrigated by flow system and rest 30% land by lift system.

There are two stages through which the construction work of the canal system has been done such as

Stage I of Indra Gandhi Canal Command Area

- This command area covers Ganganagar, Hanumangarh and Northern part of Bikaner districts.
- Its culturable command area is 5.53 lakh hectares along with gentle undulating topography.
- In this stage, the irrigation system was introduced in early 1960s.

Stage II of Indira Gandhi Canal Command Area

This stage covers 14.10 lakh hectares cultarable area of Bikaner, Jaisalmer, Barmer, Jodhpur, Nagpur and Churu districts.

The main characteristics of the area are:

(i) Hot desert with shifting sands dunes.
(ii) Summer temperature upto 50°C.

Irrigation system was introduced in this stage in mid-1980s. In the lift canal, water is lifted up to make it to flow against the slope of the land. All the lift canals of this system originate at the left bank of main canal while all the canals on the right bank of main canal are flow channels.

Effects of Indira Gandhi Canal Irrigation

There are various effects of Indira Gandhi Canal irrigation on environment and on agricultural economy

Effects on Environment

The environment of the areas is influenced by this project both positively and negatively

- **Positive Effect** Now, there is sufficient soil moisture availability for a longer duration. Various afforestation and pasture development programme came into being. A considerable reduction in wind erosion and siltation of canal systems have also been recorded.
- **Negative Effect** Due to intensive irrigation and excessive use of water, an alarming rate of water logging and soil salinity have been recorded.

Effects on Agriculture

There are some positive and negative effect on agriculture

- **Positive Effect** This canal irrigation led to increase in cultivated land and intensity of cropping. Main commercial crops i.e. wheat, rice, cotton, groundnut replaced the drought resistant crops like gram, bajra, and Jowar.
- **Negative Effect** Intensive irrigation has also became a cause of water logging and soil salinity. So, in the near future it may hampers the sustainability of agriculture.

PYQs Previous Years' Questions

1 Mark Questions (MCQ)

Multiple Choice Questions

1. Which of the following commissions replaced 'Planning Commission'? ***(CBSE 2023)***
   (a) Election Commission
   (b) NITI Aayog
   (c) Law Commission
   (d) Education Commission

Ans. (b) NITI Aayog

2. Which of the following statements is not true regarding Indira Gandhi Canal? ***(CBSE 2023)***
   (a) It was previously known as Rajasthan canal.
   (b) It originates at Harika barrage in Punjab.
   (c) The canal runs almost parallel to Pakistan border.
   (d) Rajasthan is least benefitted by this canal.

Ans. (d) Rajasthan is least benefitted by this canal.

3. Which one of the following is not true about Bharmaur tribal region? ***(CBSE 2023)***
   (a) This region comprises of Bharmaur and Holi tehsil of Chamba district.
   (b) It is not a notified tribal area.
   (c) It is manly inhabited by Gaddi tribal community.
   (d) The tribals practice transhumance.

Ans. (b) It is not a notified tribal area

4. 'Planning' involves which of the following?
   (a) The process of thinking
   (b) Formulation of a scheme
   (c) Implementation of a set of actions
   (d) All of the above

Ans. (d) All of the above

5. Which of the following is/are an approach of planning?
   (a) Sectoral planning (b) Regional planning
   (c) Genetic planning (d) Both (a) and (b)

Ans. (d) Both (a) and (b)

6. Sectoral planning is used to plan for which of the following sectors?
   (a) Agriculture (b) Irrigation
   (c) Transport (d) All of these

Ans. (d) All of these

7. Which of the following programmes is the example of Target Area Planning?
   (a) Command Area Development Programme
   (b) Desert Development Programme
   (c) Hill Area Development Programme
   (d) All of the above

Ans. (d) All of the above

8. In which Five Year Plan, special area programmes were designed to develop infrastructure in hill areas, North-Eastern states, tribal area and backward areas?
   (a) 1st Five Year Plan (b) 2nd Five Year Plan
   (c) 7th Five Year Plan (d) 8th Five Year Plan

Ans. (d) 8th Five Year Plan

9. In which Five Year Plan, Hill Area Development Programmes were initiated?
   (a) 1st Five Year Plan
   (b) 3rd Five Year Plan
   (c) 5th Five Year Plan
   (d) 7th Five Year Plan

Ans. (c) 5th Five Year Plan

10. Hilly districts of which states were covered under Hill Area Development Programme?
    (a) West Bengal (b) Uttar Pradesh
    (c) Assam (d) All of these

Ans. (d) All of these

11. The Planning Commission of India identified how many districts of India which were prone to drought?
    (a) 67 (b) 80
    (c) 90 (d) 100

Ans. (a) 67

12. Arrange the following events in sequence as per their date of occurrence.
    I. Notion of Sustainable Development
    II. Publication of 'the Population Bomb '
    III. Publication of 'the limits to Growth '
    IV. Report 'Our Common Future'

    Codes
    (a) I, II, III, IV (b) IV, III, II, I
    (c) I, II, IV, III (d) III, II, I, IV

Ans. (a) I, II, III, IV

Very Short Answer Questions

1. Examine the concept of 'regional planning(Delhi 2018)

Ans. In this approach, the main emphasis is on to make such plans which may help to reduce regional disparities and bring uniform economic development.

2. Examine the twin environmental problems that have emerged in the 'Indira Gandhi Canal Command Area'. *(All India 2017)*

Ans. Environmental problems that have emerged in the 'Indira Gandhi Canal Command Area' are

(i) Water logging (ii) Soil salinity

3. What is 'sectoral planning'? *(Delhi 2013)*

Ans. In sectoral planning approach, the development of various sectors such as agriculture, irrigation, manufacturing, power, construction, transport, communication, social infrastructure and services take into consideration to which various sets of schemes or programmes are formalised and implemented.

4. How has the Gaddi tribal community of Bharmaur region maintained a distinct identity? *(All India 2013)*

Ans. The Gaddi tribal community of Bharmaur region maintained a distinct identity as they practised transhumance and conversed through Gaddiali dialect.

5. What is the main objective to implement the Fourth Five Year Plan for the people in drought prone areas? *(Delhi 2009)*

Ans. The main objectives to implement the Fourth Five Year Plan for the people in drought prone areas are to provide employment and create productive assets.

6. In which Five Year Plan of India were Hill Area Development Programmes initiated? *(All India 2009)*

Ans. Hill Area Development Programmes were initiated in the Fifth Five Year Plan of India.

3 Marks Questions

1. Explain the main aims of Bharmaur Tribal Area Development plan. *(Delhi 2014)*

Ans. The main aims and priorities of this project are as follows

(i) Improving the quality of life of the Gaddis.

(ii) Narrowing the gap in the level of development between Bharmaur and other districts of Himachal Pradesh.

(iii) The highest priority was on development of transport and communications, agriculture and allied activities as well as social and community services.

2. How has the introduction of Indira Gandhi Canal irrigation in the drylands of Rajasthan influenced the environmental conditions of the region positively? Explain in any three points. *(All India 2012)*

Ans. The positive impacts of Indira Gandhi canal irrigation on the environmental conditions of the dryland area of Rajasthan are as follow

(i) CAD programmes (Command Area Development) i.e. afforestation and pastures programs developed the desertic area into greenland.

(ii) An increase in agriculture, livestock productivity and intensity of cropping also has been recorded.

(iii) Commercial crops i.e. wheat, rice, cotton, groundnut replaced the drought resistant crops like gram, bajra and jowar.

3. Write in brief about the physical setting of Bharmaur region. *(Delhi 2008)*

Ans. Bharmaur region lies between 32°11′ N and 32°41 ′N latitudes and 76°22′ E and 76°53′ E longitudes. It is spread over an area of about 1818 sq km. This region is the homeland of Gaddi tribal community and surrounded by lofty mountains on all sides.

It has Pir Panjal in the North and Dhaula Dhar in the South. In the East, the extension of Dhaula converges with Pir Panjal near Rohtang Pass. The river Ravi and its tributaries, the Budhil and Tundahen, carve out deep gorges here and divide the region into the four Physiographic divisions such as

(i) Holi (ii) Khani

(iii) Kugti (iv) Tundah areas

Bharmaur experiences freezing weather conditions and snowfall in winter. Its mean monthly temperature in January remains 4°C and in July 26°C.

4. Give a brief account on the two stages of Indira Gandhi Canal Project. *(All India 2008)*

Ans. Two stages of Indira Gandhi Canal Project are as follows

(i) **Stage I of Indira Gandhi Canal Command Area** This command area covers Ganganagar, Hanumangarh and Northern part of Bikaner districts. Its culturable command area is 5.53 lakh hectares along with gentle undulating topography. Irrigation system was introduced in this stage in early 1960s.

(ii) **State II of Indira Gandhi Canal Command Area** This stage II covers 14.10 lakh hectares culturable land of Bikaner, Jaisalmer, Barmer, Jodhpur, Nagaur and Churu districts.
Hot desert with shifting sand dunes and temperature soaring to 50° C in summers are the main characteristics of the region.

5. How would you define ecological, social and economic sustainabilities? Explain in brief. ***(All India 2008)***

Ans. Ecological, social and economic sustainabilities are as follows

- **Ecological Sustainability** It means using our natural resources wisely in the short term so that these resources are available in the long term.
- **Social Sustainability** The ability of a community to develop processes and structures which not only meet the needs of its current members, but also support the ability of future generations to maintain a healthy community.
- **Economic Sustainability** The use of various strategies for employing existing resources optimally, so that a responsible and beneficial balance can be achieved over the longer period of time.

5 Marks Questions

1. Describe the concepts of sustainability and productivity in the context of human development. ***(CBSE 2023)***

Ans. The concepts of sustainability and productivity are pillars of human development. These are

Sustainability It refers to continuity in the availability of opportunities. To achieve sustainable human development, it is must to give equal opportunities to all generations without any misuse of natural resources and environment.

All the resources such as environmental, financial and human resources should be used keeping in mind the future generation.

For example, if a society is not in favour of girl's education, it may severely affect the other aspects of girls lives as it would curtail their career choices and many opportunities will be lost when they grow up. Thus, it is the responsibility of the society to provide equal opportunities and choices to its future generations.

Productivity It refers to productivity of human labour productivity in terms of human work. So, this productivity must be continuously enriched by building capabilities in people, as people are considered the real wealth of nations.

Thus, for better work efficiency, it is important to put efforts to increase their knowledge or provide better health facilities.

2. Justify the tremendous growth of the service sector in developed and developing countries than the manufacturing sector? Explain giving suitable examples. ***(CBSE SQP 2022)***

Ans. Tertiary sector is a skilled and knowledge oriented sector, which works on the components of skilled man power. This sector includes both production and exchange of services, trading, transportation, tourism, etc. It is providing a strong base to modern economic development in the world. In both developed and developing countries, the tertiary sector is contributing more than manufacturing and agriculture sector. Over 50% of all the workforce in developed countries is involved in the tertiary sector.

There has been very high growth in demand and consumption of transportation, trading, tourism and other services. These include both technical and non-technical services. Many services were also outsourced which resulted in growth of this sector beyond national boundaries to interaction regions.

One of the major example of expanding contribution of tertiary sector is tourism. It is the world's largest tertiary activity, with total registered jobs around 250 million and total revenue about 40 per cent of total GDP. Besides many local persons, are employed to provide services like transport, catering accommodation, entertainment, etc. Tourism fasters the growth of infrastructure industries, retail trading and craft industries.

3. Critically analyse the measures to promote sustainability in Indira Gandhi Canal Command Area. ***(CBSE SQP 2022)***

Or Examine the measures to be taken to achieve ecological sustainability in the 'Indira Gandhi Canal Command Area'. ***(CBSE Compartment 2022)***

Or Attaining sustainable development in the command area requires major thrust upon the measures to achieve ecological sustainability. Highlight the measures proposed to promote sustainable development in the command area of Indira Gandhi Rajasthan Canal. ***(CBSE SQP Term II 2021)***

Or Explain any five measures necessary for the promotion of sustainable development in 'Indira Gandhi Canal Command Area'. ***(All India 2009)***

Or Describe any five measures needed for the promotion of sustainable development in the 'Indira Gandhi Canal Command Area'. ***(Delhi 2008)***

Ans. Measures for promotion of sustainability in 'Indira Gandhi Canal Command Area' are as follows

(i) Rigorous implementation of water management policy is the first and foremost requirement of this project.

(ii) Adoption of plantation crops such as citrus fruits, instead of water intensive crops.

(iii) In order to reduce the conveyance loss of water, few important programmes shall be taken into account such as the CAD (Command Area Development) programmes i.e.

(a) lining of water courses.

(b) land development and levelling.

(c) Warabandi system (means equal distribution of canal water in the command area of outlet).

(iv) The areas should be reclaimed that got affected by water logging and soil salinity.

(v) Promoting eco-development in the fragile environment especially in stage-II command area through afforestation, shelter belt, plantation and pasture development activities.

Additional Info

Other measures for promotion of sustainability in Indira Gandhi Canal Command Area are

- To promote social sustainability by providing financial and institutional support for land cultivation to the land allottees of poor background.
- Other sectors of economy in addition to agriculture, animal husbandry and allied activities should be encouraged for attaining economic sustainability.

4. Critically analyse the socio-economic benefits that are being experienced by implementation of Integrated Tribal Development Project in Bharmaur district of Himachal Pradesh. ***(CBSE SQP 2020)***

Or Examine the advantages of Tribal Development Project launched in Bharmaur region of Himachal Pradesh. ***(CBSE Compartment 2022)***

Ans. Under the Fifth Five Year plan, the tribal sub-plan was introduced in 1974 and Bharmaur was designated as one of the five Integrated Tribal Development Projects (ITDP) in Himachal Pradesh. Various social and economic benefits are being experienced by this region in the following ways

(i) This project drastically improved the life of the Gaddis and narrowed the gap in the level of development between Bharmaur and other areas of Himachal Pradesh.

(ii) A lot of development was made in the field of transport and communication, agriculture and allied activities and social and community services.

(iii) The most significant contribution of the ITDP in the region is the development of infrastructure in terms of schools, healthcare facilities, potable water, roads, electricity and communication network. The villages located along river Ravi in Holi and Khani areas are the main beneficiaries of infrastructural development.

(iv) The social benefits from ITDP are the tremendous increase in literacy rate, improvement in sex-ratio and decline in child marriages.

(v) The cultivation of pulses and other cash crops has increased in Bharmaur region. In addition to this, now only ten per cent of the total households practice transhumance.

5. "The restoration of ecological balance between water, soil, plants, human and animal population should be a basic consideration in the strategy of development of drought prone areas in India". Explain the statement with suitable facts. ***(CBSE SQP 2018)***

Ans. In India, almost one-sixth area with 12% of the population is drought-prone; the areas that receive an annual rainfall up to 60 cm are the most prone. Most of the drought-prone areas are found in arid, sem-arid and sub-humid regions of the country. There is need for the strategy of development of drought prone areas in India because of following reasons

(i) The drought-prone areas form a significant proportion of the country's area.

(ii) These areas are characterised by low productivity which is a major cause of regional imbalances.

(iii) These areas are a strain on the country's financial resources.

The restoration of ecological balance between water, soil, plants, human and animal population in the drought prone areas will mitigate adverse effects of droughts on production of crops and productivity of land, water, livestock and human resources through an integrated development of natural resource base of the area and it will create additional employment in these areas.

Therefore, the restoration of ecological balance between water, soil, plants, human, and animal population should be a basic consideration in the strategy of development of drought prone areas in India.

6. Development is a multi-dimensional concept and signifies the positive, irreversible transformation of the economy, society and environment.
Support the statement with suitable arguments from India. *(Delhi 2010)*

Value Points

For getting maximum marks, following value points can be included in the answer

- Concept of development
- Role of societies in development
- Development after World War II and now

Ans. Development is a dynamic concept that used to describe the state of particular societies and the process of changes experienced by them. In early human history, the main criteria of determination of a society's state were the interaction processes between human societies and their bio-physical environment.

Societies helped in the development of various levels of technology and institutions upon which human environment processes depend. These have helped in increasing the pace of human environment interaction, therefore the momentum generated and festinated technological progress and transformation and creation of institution.

After the period of World War II, development and economic growth considered as one concept. But due to unequal distribution, a faster rate of growth in poverty is experienced by even the developed nations having high economic growth. Then redistribution with growth and equity broaden the term development in 1970.

Now, the concept of development not only restricted to the economic sphere alone, but also incorporates balance and equality among people in term of welfare and quality of life of people health, education and other facilities, equal opportunity to all and ensuring political and civil rights.

Hence, the concept of development has become multi-dimensional and stands for positive, irreversible transformation of the economy, society and environment.

7. ''Hill Area Development Programmes in India were drawn keeping in view their topographical ecological, social and economic conditions''. Support this statement with suitable explanation. *(All India 2010)*

Ans. Yes it is true, that Hill Area Development Programmes in India were drawn keeping in view their topographical, ecological, social and economic conditions because the main objectives of these programmes were on to development of

(i) Horticulture
(ii) Plantation agriculture
(iii) Animal Husbandry
(iv) Poultry
(v) Forestry
(vi) Small scale and village industry.

By this, exploitation of local resources may become possible.

The programme was recommended by the National Commitee on the Development of Backward Area (1981), which set a criterion that the hill areas having a height above 600 m and not covered under tribal sub-plan be treated as backward hill areas. The programme covers all the hilly districts of Uttar Pradesh, Uttarakhand, Mikir Hill and North hills of Assam, Darjeeling district of West Bengal and Nilgiri district of Tamil Nadu . It was started in Fifth Five Year Plan.

8. Describe five main points of the integrated tribal development project implemented in Bharmaur region. *(All India 2008)*

Ans. The main points of the integrated tribal development project implemented in Bharmaur region are

(i) Improving the quality of life of the Gaddis and narrowing the gap in the level of development between Bharmaur and other districts of Himachal Pradesh.

(ii) The highest priority was on development of transport and communications, agriculture and attired activities as well as social and community services.

(iii) Improvement in the basic infrastructure of health care facilities, potable water supply, schools, transport and communication, training, marketing, credit and electricity supply, e.g. villages located along the river Ravi in Holi and Khani areas are main beneficiaries of infrastructural development.

(iv) Employment generation through agricultural allied activities like horticulture, animal husbandry and cottage industry.

(v) The Gaddis had traditionally subsistence agriculture cum-pastorol economy, later on during the last three decades of 20th century, pulses and other cash crops became one of the main crops of this region.

9. Suppose you have given the power to modify the planning process. How would you use this power wisely and what would be your plan? Explain with reason. ***(All India 2008)***

Ans. If I had some power to modify the present planning process, I would have broaden the planning process by adding some important terms such as equity, sustainability and empowerment. These are described below

Equity It means making equal access to opportunities available to everybody. The opportunities available to people must be equal irrespective of their gender, race, income and caste.

Sustainability It refers to continuity in the availability of opportunities. This means that each generation must have the same opportunities, therefore we must use our environmental, financial and human resources in such a way that our future generations are not deprived off these opportunities.

Empowerment It refers to have power to make choices. Such power comes from increasing freedom and capability. Good governance and people oriented polices are required to empower people. The empowerment of social and economically disadvantaged groups are of special importance.

10. Explain in brief the meaning and purpose of Target Area Programme with suitable examples from India. ***(All India 2008)***

Ans. The Target Area Programmes come out from the idea of target area planning approach which focuses on the development of economically backward areas in a targeted way. The target area programmes where made to reduce regional imbalances and development of infrastructure.

The programmes covered by target areas are

(i) Command Area Development Programme
(ii) Drought Prone Area Development Programme
(iii) Desert Development Programme
(iv) Hill Area Development Programme

The examples of Targeted Area Programmes in India are

- **Hill Area Development Programme** It covered 15 districts of hilly region of Uttarakhand, Mikir hill and North Cachar hills of Assam, Darjeeling district of West Bengal, etc. It focused on development of horticulture, plantation, agriculture, animal husbandry, poultry forestry and small scale village industry.
- **Drought Prone Area Programme** It aims to generate employment opportunities in drought prone areas along with creating productive assets. Priority areas in this programmes were afforestation, irrigation projects, grass land development and creation of basic rural infrastructure such as rural electrification, roads, markets, credit services, etc.

Source Based Questions

1. Read the case given below and answer the following questions.

Integrated Tribal Developments Project in Bharmaur Region

Bharmaur tribal area comprises Bharmaur and Holi tehsils of Chamba district of Himachal Pradesh. It is a notified tribal area sine 12th November, 1975, Bharmaur is inhabited by 'Gaddi' a tribal community who have maintained a distincted identity in the Himalayan region as they practiced transhumance and conversed through Gaddiali dialect.

Bharmaur tribal region has harsh climate condition's low resource base and fragile environment. These factors have influenced the society and economy of the region. According to the 2011 census, the total population of Bharmaur sub-division was 39, 113 i.e, 21 persons per sq km. It is one of the most (economically and socially) backward areas of Himachal Pradesh. Historically, the Gaddis have experienced geographical and political isolation and socio-economic deprivation. The economy is largely based on agriculture and allied activities such as sheep and goat rearing.

The process of development of tribal area of Bharmaur started in 1970s when Gaddis were included among 'Scheduled Tribes'. Under the fifth Five Year Plan, the tribal sub-plan was introduced in 1974 and Bharmaur was designated as one of the five Integrated Tribal Development Projects (ITDP) in Himachal Pradesh. This area development plan was aimed at improving the quality of life of the Gaddis. ***(CBSE 2023)***

(i) Bharmaur tribal region belongs to which of the following states ?
(a) Uttarakhand
(b) Himachal Pradesh
(c) Uttar Pradesh
(d) Jammu and Kashmir

(ii) Which of the following tribal communities dominate in Bharmaur region ?
(a) Bakkarwals (b) Bhils
(c) Gonds (d) Gaddis

(iii) What is the major aim of Integrated Tribal Development Project (ITDP) ?
(a) Improving irrigation
(b) Improving sheep rearing
(c) Improving soils of the region
(d) Improving the quality of life of the Gaddis

Ans. (i) (b) Himachal Pradesh
(ii) (d) Gaddis
(iii) (d) Improving the quality of life of the Gaddis

2. Read the case given below and answer the following questions. ***(CBSE 2023)***

Indira Gandhi Canal, previously known as the Rajasthan Canal, is one of the largest canal systems in India. Conceived by Kanwar Sain in 1948, the canal project was launched on 31 March, 1958. The canal originates at Harike barrage in Punjab and runs parallel to Pakistan border at an average distance of 40 km in Thar Desert (Marusthali) of Rajasthan. The total planned length of the system is 9,060 km catering to the irrigation needs of a total culturable command area of 19.63 lakh hectares. Out of the total command area, about 70 per cent was envisaged to be irrigated by flow system and the rest by lift system. The construction work of the canal system has been carried out through two stages. The command area of Stage-I lies in Ganganagar, Hanumangarh and northern part of Bikaner districts. It has a gently undulating topography and its culturable command area is 5.53 lakh hectares. The command area of Stage-II is spread over Bikaner, Jaisalmer, Barmer, Jodhpur, Nagaur and Churu districts covering culturable command area of 14.10 lakh ha. It comprises desert land dotted with shifting sand dunes and temperature soaring to 50ºC in summers. In the lift canal, the water is lifted up to make it to flow against the slope of the land. All the lift canals of Indira Gandhi Canal system originate at the left bank of main canal while all the canals on the right bank of main canal are flow channels.

Irrigation in Stage-I command area of the canal was introduced in early 1960s, whereas, the command area of Stage-II began receiving irrigation in mid-1980s. The introduction of canal irrigation in this dry land has transformed its ecology, economy and society. It has influenced the environmental conditions of the region both positively as well as negatively. The availability of soil moisture for a longer period of time and various afforestation and pasture development programmes under CAD have resulted in greening the land. This has also helped in reducing wind erosion and siltation of canal systems. But the intensive irrigation and excessive use of water has led to the emergence of twin environmental problems of water logging and soil salinity.

(i) What is the main objective to construct of Indira Gandhi Canal?
(a) Providing water for irrigation in the command area
(b) Providing water for drinking purpose
(c) Providing water for afforestation
(d) Providing water for industries

(ii) What is the major benefit of this canal in the command area?
(a) Transformation of ecology and economy
(b) Environmental condition slightly changed
(c) People had not settled permanently
(d) Crop production is still at lower level

(iii) What is the negative impact of this canal?
(a) Soils become fertile
(b) Water logging and salinity
(c) Multiple cropping system
(d) Command area becomes green

Ans. (i) (a) Providing water for irrigation in the command area
(ii) (a) Transformation of ecology and economy
(iii) (b) Water logging and salinity

3. Read the given passage carefully and answer the questions that follow.

Bharmaur tribal area comprises Bharmaur and Holi tehsils of Chamba district of Himachal Pradesh. It has been a notified tribal area since 21st November, 1975. Bharmaur is inhabited by 'Gaddi' a tribal community who have maintained a distinct identity in the Himalayan region as they practiced transhumance and conversed through Gaddiyali dialect. Bharmaur tribal region has harsh climate conditions, low resource base and fragile environment. These factors have influenced the society and economy of the region.

According to the 2011 Census, the total population of Bharmaur sub-division was 39,113 i.e., 21 persons per sq km. It is one of the most (economically and socially) backward areas of Himachal Pradesh. Historically, the Gaddis have experienced geographical and political isolation and socio-economic deprivation. The economy is largely based on agriculture and allied activities such as sheep and goat rearing.

The process of development of the tribal area of Bharmaur started in the 1970s, when Gaddis were included among 'Scheduled Tribes'. Under the Fifth Five Years Plan, the tribal sub-plan was introduced in 1974 and Bharmaur was designated as one of the five Integrated Tribal Development Project (ITDP) in Himachal Pradesh.

This area development plan was aimed at improving the quality of life of the Gaddis and narrowing the gap in the level of development between Bharmaur and other areas of Himachal Pradesh. This plan laid the highest priority on development of transport and communications, agriculture and allied activities, and social and community services.

(i) How have the Gaddi tribal community maintained a distinct identity in the Himalayan region?

(ii) Which factors have influenced the society and economy of the region to remain backward?

(iii) Under the Integrated Tribal Development Project, which areas were given the highest priority? ***(CBSE SQP 2022)***

Ans. (i) Gaddi tribal communities have maintained a distinct identity in the Himalayan region because of the following reasons

(a) They practiced transhumance that involves seasonal migration of humans along with their livestock.

(b) They conserved their culture through their Gaddiyali dialect.

(ii) The factors which have influenced the society and economy of the region to remain backward are due to the harsh climatic conditions, low resource base and fragile environment in Bharmaur tribal region. Here, the economy is largely based on agriculture and allied activities such as sheep and goat rearing.

(iii) Under the Integrated Tribal Development Project, the areas which were given the highest priority include development of transport and communications, agriculture and allied activities and social and community services.

4. Study the map given below and answer the questions that follows. ***(CBSE SQP 2019)***

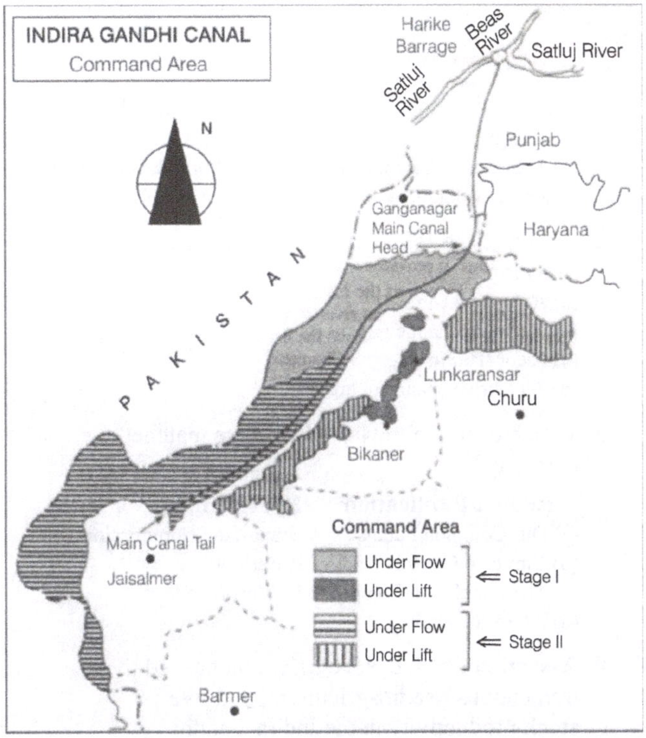

(i) What is the difference between the two areas shown as 'Under Flow' and 'Under Lift' system of irrigation?

(ii) Name the districts that are benefitted by the command area of the canal in Stage I and Stage II.

Ans. (i) The canal has two irrigation systems, which are Flow system (Under flow) and Lift system (Under lift). Around 70% land of the command area is irrigated by the flow system and 30% land by the Lift system. All the lift channels of Indira Gandhi Canal System originate on the left Bank of main canal while the canals on the Right Bank of the main canal are Flow canals.

(ii) The districts benefitted by the command area of the canal are as follows

Stage I Ganganagar, Hanumangarh and Northern parts of Bikaner and Jaisalmer district.

Stage II Bikaner, Jaisalmer, Barmer, Jodhpur, Nagaur and Churu districts.

CHAPTER TEST

01 Mark Questions

1 Identify the most crucial factor for sustainable development in Indira Gandhi Canal Command Area.
(a) Transport development (b) Agricultural development
(c) Eco-development (d) Colonisation of land

2 Which of the following best describes 'development'?
(a) An increase in size
(b) A simple change in quality
(c) A constant in size
(d) A positive change in quality

3 Which of the following pairs is/are matched correctly?

Report/Publication	Published by
(a) Our Common Future	– Brundtland Commission
(b) Limits to Growth	– P. Ehrlich
(c) The Population Bomb	– D. Meadows

(d) All of the above

4 **Assertion** (A) Intensive irrigation has led to tremendous rise in agricultural and live stock productivity in the Indira Gandhi Command Area.

Reason (R) Intensive irrigation has led to excessive water logging and soil salinity.

Codes
(a) Both A and R are true and R is the correct explanation of A
(b) Both A and R are true, but R is not the correct explanation of A
(c) A is true, but R is false
(d) A is false, but R is true

5 Consider the following statements and choose the correct answer.
I. The NITI Aayog reviewed the performance of Drought Prone Area Programme.
II. This programme is largely confined to the development of agriculture and allied sectors with major focus on restoration of ecological balance.

Codes
(a) Only statement I is correct
(b) Both the statements are true and statement II correctly present the reason for statement I
(c) Only Statement II is correct
(d) Both the statements I and II are incorrect

Answers

1. (c) | 2. (d) | 3. (a) | 4. (a) | 5. (c)

03 Marks Questions

6 Explain the main aims and priorities of Bharmaur Tribal Area Development plan.

7 Discuss the social benefits of tribal sub-plan in the Bharmaur Region.

8 Discuss the role of World Commission on Environment and Development (WCED) in promotion of the idea of sustainable development.

05 Marks Questions

9 Write short notes on Drought Prone Area Programme. How does this programme help in the development of dryland agriculture in India?

10 Discuss any five points of the integrated tribal development project implemented in Bharmaur region.

11 Development is a multi-dimensional concept and signifies the positive, irreversible transformation of the economy, society and environment. Support the statement with suitable arguments from India.

07

Transport and Communication

TREND ANALYSIS 3 YEARS

Average No. of Questions Across all Sets

	Types of Questions	2023	2020	2019
TOPIC 01 Means of Transport	1 Mark	–	–	–
	3 Marks	–	–	–
	5 Marks	2	1	3
TOPIC 02 Communication Networks	1 Mark	–	–	–
	3 Marks	–	1	1
	5 Marks	–	–	–

Natural resources, economic activities and market are rarely found in one place. Transport and communication establish links between producing centres and consuming centres.

The means of transport and communication have acquired distinct and specialised forms as compared to the ancient times. The use of transport and communication depends upon our need to move things from place of their availability to the place of their use.

Means of Transport

There are various ways means of transportation by which human beings move goods, commodities, ideas, etc from one place to another place. Major means of transportation are as follows

Land Transport

Transportation of people and goods by road transport is not new in India. Since ancient times, pathways and unmetalled roads have been in use for this purpose.

With the technological advancement, there are now metalled roads, railways, cableways and pipelines for movement of large volume of goods and passengers.

Road Transport

India has its count in countries which is having **largest road networks** worldwide. India has a total road length of 62.16 lakhs km that places it among the countries which has largest road network.

Road transport carries about 85% of passenger and 70% of freight traffic every year. Road transport is preferable for short distance travel. The first attempt to improve and modernise road network was made in 1943 with **Nagpur Plan**. But due to lack of coordination among Princely States and British India, it remained unimplemented.

The second attempt was made after independence with twenty year road plan (1961) to improve the conditions of roads in India, but still roads continue to concentrate in and around urban centres and rural and remote areas remained less connected by road.

For the purpose of construction and maintenance, roads are classified as National Highways (NH), State Highways (SH), Major District Roads and Rural Roads

National Highways

- NH referred to roads which are constructed and maintained by Central Government.
- National Highways are meant for inter-state transport and movement of defence men and material in strategic areas.
- In 2020, total length of National Highways was 1,36,440 km which was 19,700 km in 1951.
- These highways connect the state capitals, major cities, important ports, railways junctions, etc and carry about 40% of the road traffic despite they constitute only 1.67% of total road length.
- The National Highways Authority of India (NHAI - 1995) is an autonomous body, under the Ministry of Surface Transport which is entrusted with the responsibility of development, maintenance, operation and for the improvement of the quality of National Highways.

National Highways Development Projects

- **Golden Quadrilateral** It is 5846 km long 4/6 lane, high . density corridor. It was meant to connect India's four big metro cities of **Delhi-Mumbai-Chennai-Kolkata**. It will deduct the time-distance and cost of movement among the mega cities of India. Its construction help in reducing the time distance and cost of movement among mega cities considerably.
- **North-South and East-West corridors** The North-South corridor is a 4076 km long highway which is meant to connect Srinagar in Jammu and Kashmir with Kanyakumari in Tamil Nadu including Kochchi-Salem Spur. The East-West corridor is 3640 km long road which aims to connect Silchar in Assam with the port town of Porbandar in Gujarat.

State Highways

These roads are connected to the National Highways and join the state capitals with district headquarters and other important towns.

Their share in the total road length is about 4%. State Governments are responsible to construct and maintain these highways.

District Roads

These roads connect district headquarters and other important nodes in the district. They account for 14% of the total road length of the country.

Rural Roads

These roads provide links in the rural areas. About 80% of the total road length in India are categorised as rural roads.

Other Roads

These include Border Roads and International highways

- **Border Roads** These are strategically important roads along the Northern and North-Eastern boundary of the country.
  Border Road Organisation (BRO) is responsible for construction and maintenance of these roads. It was established in May, 1960 with the aim to accelerate economic development and strengthening defence preparedness through rapid and coordinated improvement of strategically important border roads.
  BRO's major achievement is construction of roads in high altitude mountainous terrain joining Chandigarh with Manali (Himachal Pradesh) and Leh (Ladakh). This road is located at the average height of 4270 meters above mean sea level.
  The **total length of border roads** was 40450 km in 2005 which was constructed by BRO. Besides the construction and maintenance of roads in strategically sensitive areas The BRO also undertakes snow clearance in high altitude area.
- **International Highways** They are constructed with the aim to promote harmonious relationship with neighbouring countries and provide an effective connection with India.

Density of Roads

- The distribution of roads is not uniform in the country. Density of roads (length of roads per 100 sq km of area) is the method to compare the network of roads of one area to another area. **The national average road density** is 142.7 km (2011).
- The density of roads is influenced by nature of terrains, and level of economic development. Most of the Northern states and major Southern states have high density of roads (e.g. Uttar Pradesh has **highest road density** of 532.27 km), whereas Himalayan region, North-Eastern region, Madhya Pradesh and Rajasthan have low density of roads (e.g. Jammu and Kashmir has lowest road density of 10.04 km).
- Quality of roads, besides density, is also better in plains as compared to high altitude areas, rainy and forested regions.

Rail Transport

- India has one of the longest railway network in the world. On one hand, it facilitates the movement of freight and passengers and on the other hand, it contributes to the growth of economy. Mahatma Gandhi said, the Indian railways, ''brought people of diverse cultures together to contribute to India's freedom struggle''
- In 1853, the **first Indian railway** was started from Bombay to Thane covering a distance of 34 km.
- Being the largest government undertaking in India, Indian Railways network is 67,956 km long (2019-20).
- To reduce the pressure of this large size railway from a centralised railway management system, Indian Railway system has been divided into sixteen zones.

These are as follows

Railway Zone and Head quarters

1.	Central	Mumbai CST
2.	Eastern	Kolkata
3.	East Central	Hajipur
4.	East Coast	Bhubaneswar
5.	Northern	New Delhi
6.	North-Central	Allahabad
7.	North-Eastern	Gorakhpur
8.	North-East Frontier	Maligaon (Guwahati)
9.	North-Western	Jaipur
10.	Southern	Chennai
11.	South Central	Secunderabad
12.	South-Eastern	Kolkata
13.	South-East Central	Bilaspur
14.	South-Western	Hubli
15.	Western	Mumbai (Church Gate)
16.	West Central	Jabalpur

Gauges in Indian Railways

Indian Railways has been divided into three categories. On the basis of the width of the track of Indian railways as follows

- **Broad Gauge** In broad gauge, the distance between rails is 1.676 metre. The total length of broad gauge lines is 63,950 km in 2019-20.
- **Metre Gauge** In metre gauge, the distance between the rails is 1 metre. The total length of metre gauge is 2402 km in 2019-20.
- **Narrow Gauge** In narrow gauge, the distance between the rails is 0.762 metres or 0.610 metres. The total length of narrow gauge line is 1604 km in 2019-20. This category of railway lines is mostly found in the hilly areas.

Indian Railways has taken major steps to improve the performance of this means of transport like

(i) To convert the metre and narrow gauges to broad gauge.

(ii) Replacement of steam engine by diesel and electric engines which may help in keeping the environment clean.

(iii) Introduction of metro rail in Kolkata and Delhi, etc.

Development of railways in India was started by the Britishers and after the independence, scenario has been changed by extending railway routes to other areas. **Konkan railways** along the Western coast which provide a direct line between Mumbai and Mangalore was a significant development in this regard.

Konkan Railway is one of the important achievements of Indian Railways which was constructed in 1998. It is a 760 km long rail route which connects Roha in Maharashtra to Mangalore in Karnataka. It is considered an engineering marvel.

Railway is still the most important means of transport for the masses. In the hill states, North-Eastern states, central part of India and Rajasthan, railway network is relatively less dense.

Water Transport

Water transport is the cheapest means of transport for carrying heavy and bulky material as well as passenger services. It is a fuel efficient and eco-friendly mode of transport.

The water transport is of two types

(i) Inland Waterways

(ii) Oceanic Waterways

Inland Waterways

Before the introduction of railways, inland waterways was the chief mode of transport. But, now it is losing its significance due to

(i) Tough competition from road and railway transport.

(ii) Diversion of river water for irrigation purposes made them non-navigable in large parts of their courses.

India has 14500 km of navigable waterways which accounts for about 1% of country's transportation.

It includes rivers, canals backwater, creeks, etc. At present, 5,685 km of major rivers are navigable by mechanised flat bottom vessels. Similiarly, out of 4800 km of the network of navigable canal, only 900 km is navigable by mechanised vessels.

The **Inland Waterways Authority** which was setup in 1986 is responsible for the development, maintenance and regulation of national waterways in the country. Currently, there are three inland waterways which are considered as national waterways by the authority. Description of these waterways are as follows

National Waterways of India

Waterways Stretch		Specification	Date of Declaration
NW1	Allahabad- Haldia Stretch (1620 km)	It is one of the most important waterways in India which is navigable by mechanical boats upto Patna and by ordinary boats upto Haridwar. It is divided into three parts for developmental purposes (i) Haldia Farakka (560 km) (ii) Farakka Patna (460 km) (iii) Patna -Allahabad (600 km	27.10.1986
NW2	Sadiya- Dhubri Stretch (891 km)	Brahmaputra is navigable by steamers up to Dibrugarh (1384km), which is shared by India and Bangladesh.	26.10.1988
NW3	Kottapuram-Kollam Stretch (205 km)	It includes 168 km of West coast canal along with Champakara canal (23 km) and Udyogmandal canal (14 km).	01.02.1991
NW 4	Kakinada Puducherry (1078 km)	Stretch of canal and Kalurelly Tank stretches of river Godavari and Krishna.	2008
NW 5	Talcher Dhamra (588 km)	Stretch of river Brahmani, Geonkhali Cherlatia stretch of East coast canal, Chertectia-Dharma, stretch of Matai river alongwith Mahanadi delta river system	2008

Ten other inland waterways have been identified by inland waterways authority. The backwaters (Kadal) of Kerala has special significance which not only provides transport but also attract tourists here. The famous **Nehru Trophy Boat Race** (Vallamkali) is also held in the backwaters.

Oceanic Routes

- These play an important role in the transport sector of India's economy.
- India's vast coastline of about 7,517 km (including islands) easily facilitates this type of transport. There are twelve major and 185 minor ports which provide infrastructural support to these routes.
- About 95% of India's foreign trade by volume and 70% by value moves through ocean routes.
- These routes give international trade service as well as provide transportation between the islands and the rest of the country.

Air Transportation

Air transport facilitates the fastest movement of goods and passengers from one place to another place. It is good for long distances and areas which have uneven terrain and climatic conditions. Air transport in India was started in 1911 with a short distance, (10 km) airmail operation from Allahabad to Naini.

The **Airport Authority of India** is responsible for providing safe, efficient air traffic and aeronautical communication services in the Indian Air space. Now, it manages 125 airports.

There are two corporations, **Air India** and **Indian Airlines** which manage air transport in India. Both corporations were nationalised in 1953. Now many private companies have also started passenger services.

Air India

It is a corporation of India which provides International Air Service for both passengers and cargo traffic. It connects all the continents of the world through its services. It has now been privatised.

Indian Airlines

Indian Airlines, the largest state owned domestic carrier changed its names to 'Indian by dropping' word 'Airlines' in 8th December, 2005. The new brand name 'Indian' now appears on both sides of the fuselage.

The logo depicting IA which was used to be display on orange tail is now replaced by a new logo. New logo is apartly visible blue wheel and is inspired by the Sun Temple at Konark (Odisha), symbolising timeless motion, convergence and divergence. It also represents strength as well as trust that has stood the test of time. It was merged with Air India in 2011.

Pawan Hans Helicopter Service

Pawan Hans is the major organisation in India which provides helicopter services in hilly areas, for tourism in North-Eastern sector and mainly to petroleum sector and tourism.

Oil And Gas Pipelines

Pipelines are convenient and best means of transporting liquids and gases over long distances. These can also transport solids after converting them into slurry. **Oil India Limited** (OIL) is responsible for exploration, production and transportation of crude oil and natural gas.

Its one of the major achievement is the construction of Asia's first cross country pipeline. This pipeline covers a distance of 1157 km from Naharkatiya oil field in Assam to Barauni refinery in Bihar. In 1966, this pipeline was further extended to Kanpur, Uttar Pradesh.

Gail

GAIL India Limited set up as a public sector undertaking to transport, process and market the natural gas.

The first 1700 km long Hazira-Vijaipur-Jagdishpur cross country gas pipeline, constructed by GAIL, linked Mumbai High and Bassin gas fields with various industrial complex.

Over all India's gas infrastructure expanded from 1700 km to 18,500 km of cross country pipeline.

Communication Networks

A number of communication cum-transportation means have been used since human history, e.g. messages were delivered by beating drum or hollow tree trunks, giving indication through smoke or fire or with the help of fast runners.

Development in the field of science and technology brought many revolutionary inventions in means of communication like post office, telegraph, printing press, telephone, satellite, etc.

On the basis of scale and quality, the mode of communication can be divided into following categories

Personal Communication System

- The most advanced and best means among all personal communication system is internet which is widely used in urban cities.
- **E-mail** is the main source through which a user can directly connect with others and can also get access to the world of knowledge and information.
- Use of internet is increasing for e-commerce and carrying out money transactions.
- The internet is like a huge control warehouse of data, with detailed information on various items. It is a cheaper mode of communication which provides an efficient access to information at a comparatively low cost.
- Letters, telephone, fax are also used for personal communication.

Mass Communication System

Radio

- Radio broadcasting was started in 1923 by **Radio Club of Bombay**. Within short time, it gained immense popularity and became a part of every househod in India.
- After seeing its popularity, the government of India, in 1930 took the control of this mode of communication under Indian Broadcasting System.
- It was changed to All India Radio in 1936 and to Akashwani in 1957.
- It broadcasts various programmes related to information, education, entertainment and special news bulletins on special session of Parliament and State Legislature.

Television (TV)

- Television (TV) broadcasting has emerged as the most effective audio-visual medium for disseminating information and educating masses.
- **First television broadcasting** was started in National Capital in 1959. Till 1972, it was the only urban place where TV services were available.
- After 1972, several other centres became operational. In 1976, TV broadcasting services were separated by All India Radio and got a separate identity as Doordarshan (DD).
- Its revolutionary development began after the launch of INSAT-IA (National Television-D1) when Common National Programmes (CNP) were started for the entire network and its services were extended to the backward and remote rural areas.

Satellite Communication

Satellite is an advanced mode of communication. They also regulate the use of other means of communication. From economic and strategic point of view, use of satellite is very vital for the country as these give continuous and synoptic view larger area.

Various operations can be done through satellite images, e.g. weather forcast, monitoring of natural calamities, surveillance of border areas, etc. There are two satellite system in India on the basis of configuration and purposes

(i) **Indian National Satellite System (INSAT)** This was established in 1983. It is a multi-purpose satellite system for telecommunication, meteorological observatioon and for various other data and programmes.

(ii) **Indian Remote Sensing Satellite System (IRS)** The IRS satellite system started in India with the launch of IRS-IA in March, 1988 from Vaikanour in Russia. India has also developed its indigenous launching vehicle PSLV (Polar Satellite Launch Vehicle). These remote sensing satellites collect data in several spectral band and transmit them to ground stations which is very useful in the management of natural resources and other various purposes.

The National Remote Sensing Agency (NRSA) at Hyderabad is responsible for facilitating for acquisition of data and its processing.

PYQs Previous Years' Questions

1 Mark Questions

Multiple Choice Questions

1. Which of the following is not true regarding the development of border roads? *(CBSE 2023)*

(a) Integration of people of remote areas with major cities.
(b) Strengthening defence preparedness.
(c) Helps in transporting goods to border villages.
(d) Help in developing large scale industries

Ans. (d) Help in developing large scale industries

2. Which one of the following is the Easternmost station of the East-West corridor? *(CBSE 2023)*

(a) Guwahati (b) Bhopal
(c) Kolkata (d) Silchar

Ans. (d) Silchar

3. Study the following statements and choose the correct option. *(CBSE 2023)*

Statement I With the digitisation of information, telecommunication slowly merged with computers.

Statement II It resulted in integrated networks termed as Internet.

Codes

(a) Only statement I is correct
(b) Only statement II is correct
(c) Both statements I and II are correct, but statement II is the correct result of statement I
(d) Both statements I and II are correct, statement II is not the correct result of statement I

Ans. (c) Both Statements I and II both are correct, but statement II is the correct result of statement I

4. Match Column I with Column II and choose the correct option. *(CBSE 2023)*

	Column I (Railway zone)		Column II (Headquarter)
A.	North Central	1.	Secunderabad
B.	East Central	2.	Allahabad/Prayagraj
C.	West Central	3.	Hajipur
D.	South Central	4.	Jabalpur

Codes

	A	B	C	D		A	B	C	D
(a)	1	2	3	4	(b)	4	3	2	1
(c)	3	4	1	2	(d)	2	3	4	1

Ans. (d)

5. Which among the following is the Westernmost station of East-West corridor? ***(CBSE 2023)***
(a) Kolkata (b) Guwahati
(c) Porbandar (d) Mumbai

Ans. (c) Porbandar

6. Which of the following features is not true regarding NHAI? ***(CBSE 2023)***
(a) It is an autonomous body under the Ministry of Surface Transport.
(b) It is responsible for constructing and maintaining National Highways.
(c) It also constructs village link roads
(d) NHAI was operationalised in 1995.

Ans. (c) It also constructs village link roads

7. Through which of the following, functional relations establish between rural and urban areas? ***(CBSE SQP Term I 2021)***
(a) Through the means of transport and communications
(b) Through the supply of raw material
(c) Through the exchange of finished products in rural areas
(d) Through the consumption of products produced in rural areas

Ans. (d) Through the means of transport and communications

8. Name the headquarters of Northern Railway Zone of India. ***(CBSE SQP 2019)***
(a) Lucknow (b) Kanpur
(c) New Delhi (d) Chandigarh

Ans. (c) New Delhi

9. Which one of the following is the longest National Highway of India? ***(CBSE SQP 2019)***
(a) NH-1 (b) NH-7
(c) NH-6 (d) NH-8

Ans. (b) NH-7

10. Which of the following is the means of land transport?
(a) Road (b) Railway
(c) Pipeline (d) All of these

Ans. (d) All of these

11. The total length of Road Network in India as per Economic Survey, 2017-18 is
(a) 42 lakh km (b) 49 lakh km
(c) 56 lakh km (d) 60 lakh km

Ans. (c) 56 lakh km

12. About how much per cent of freight traffic is carried by roads every year?
(a) 50% (b) 70%
(c) 90% (d) 91%

Ans. (b) 70%

13. Which of the following transports is relatively suitable for shorter distance travel?
(a) Rail (b) Road
(c) Water (d) Air

Ans. (b) Road

14. When was the 'twenty - year road plan' introduced to improve the conditions of roads in India?
(a) 1930 (b) 1940
(c) 1951 (d) 1961

Ans. (d) 1961

15. The National Highways Authority of India was operationalised in which year?
(a) 1901 (b) 1930
(c) 1947 (d) 1995

Ans. (d) 1995

16. Which of the following is the headquarter of Central Railway zone?
(a) Hajipur (b) Kolkata
(c) Mumbai CST (d) New Delhi

Ans. (c) Mumbai CST

17. India has how many railway zones?
(a) 11 (b) 13
(c) 16 (d) 20

Ans. (c) 16

18. Arrange the following types of roads in sequence as per their percentage share in the total road length in India. (Highest to lowest).
I. National Highways II. State Highways
III. District Roads IV. Rural Roads

Codes
(a) IV, III, II, I (b) I, II, III, IV
(c) IV, III, I, II (d) III, I, IV, II

Ans. (a) IV, III, II, I

Very Short Answer Questions

1. On the basis of configuration and purpose, compare the two satellite systems in India. ***(CBSE SQP 2018)***

Ans. On the basis of configuration and purpose, the two satellite systems in India are Indian National Satellite System (INSAT) and Indian Remote Sensing Satellite System (IRS).

2. State any two advantages of air transport in the international trade. ***(Delhi 2018)***

Ans. The two advantages of air transport are as follows

(i) Air transport has a great advantage of handling high value or perishable goods over long distances.

(ii) It has reduced distances by minimising the travel time, thus, it quickly approaches to its destination point.

3. Why did Sher Shah Suri built the Shahi (Royal) road? ***(Delhi 2015)***

Ans. The main reason behind building the Shahi (Royal) road by Sher Shah was to strengthen and consolidate his empire from the Indus Valley to the Sonar Valley in Bengal.

4. Explain the term 'Golden Quadrilateral'. ***(Delhi 2015)***

Ans. Golden Quadrilateral is a 4 or 6 lane super highway project undertaken by National Highway Authority of India. It is a 5846 km long highway meant to connect India's four big metro cities of Delhi-Mumbai-Chennai-Kolkata. It deducts the time-distance and cost of movement along the mega cities of India.

5. What is satellite communication? ***(All India 2014)***

Ans. Satellite is an advanced mode of communication in themselves. They also regulate the use of other means of communication.

6. Why is the density of rural roads very low in the hilly areas of India? Give one reason. ***(Delhi 2013)***

Ans. Nature of difficult terrain makes construction of roads difficult and comparatively costly that's why density of roads is very low in the hilly areas of India.

7. State the main function of Border Road Organisation. ***(All India 2013)***

Ans. The main function of Border Road Organisation (BRO) are

(i) Construction and maintenance of border roads.

(ii) Clearance of snow in high altitude areas.

8. State the main function of National Highways Authority of India. ***(All India 2013)***

Ans. The National Highways Authority of India (NHAI) is entrusted with the responsibility of development, maintenance and operation of National Highways.

9. What are National Highways? ***(Delhi 2012)***

Ans. The main roads which are constructed and maintained by the Central Government are known as National Highways.

10. Name the headquarters of South Central Railway Zone. ***(Delhi 2012)***

Ans. Secunderabad is the headquarter of 'South Central Railway Zone' of India.

11. Which is the Eastern terminal city of East-West corridor? ***(All India 2012)***

Ans. Silchar in Assam is the Eastern terminal city of East-West corridor.

12. Name the railway line that was constructed between Roha in Maharashtra and Mangalore in Karnataka. ***(All India 2012)***

Ans. Konkan railway line was constructed between Roha in Maharashtra and Mangalore in Karnataka.

13. Name the air services which is widely used in the hilly areas of North-Eastern sector of India. ***(All India 2011)***

Ans. The air services which is widely used in the hilly areas of North-Eastern sector of India is Pawan Hans helicopter service.

14. What was the main aim behind establishing 'Border Road Organisation' in India? ***(Delhi 2008)***

Ans. Border Road Organisation (BRO) was established with the aim to accelerate economic development and strengthening defence preparedness through rapid and coordinated improvement of strategically important border roads.

3 Marks Questions

1. Elucidate any three characteristics of the most effective and advanced personal communication system in India. ***(CBSE SQP 2022)***

Or Which is the most effective and advanced personal communication system in India? Explain any four characteristics of it. ***(Delhi 2009)***

Ans. The most effective and advanced personal communication system in India is internet. It has following characteristics

(i) With the help of internet, users can directly communicate through e-mail and can get access to the world of knowledge and information.

(ii) Use of internet is increasing for e-commerce and carrying out money transactions.

(iii) Communication network through internet and e-mail is a cheaper mode of communication which provides an efficient access to information at a comparatively low cost.

2. Satellites and computers have brought revolutionary changes in the present life of the people. Elaborate the statement with three suitable example. ***(CBSE SQP Term II 2021)***

Ans. Satellites and computers have brought revolutionary changes in the present life of the people in many ways. With the help of satellites and computer, the speed of communication has reached almost lights speed.

Following are the three suitable examples of the importance of satellites and computers

- Every time we use a cell phone to call a friend, send an SMS or watch a popular programme on cable television, we are using satellite communication.
- The contemporary economic and social transactions through ernail, e-commerce, e-Iearning and e-governance.
- Education, healthcare and Entertainment services are now just one click away from the user of computer.

3. Describe any three advantages of satellite communication in India. ***(Delhi 2014)***

Ans. Advantages of satellite communication in India are as follows

(i) Satellites provide a continuous and synoptic view of larger area which is very vital for the country due to the economic and strategic reasons.

(ii) The Indian National Satellite system (INSAT) is a multipurpose satellite system which is very useful in telecommunication meteorological observation and other data and programmes for India.

(iii) The Indian Remote Sensing Satellite System (IRS) is very useful in the management of natural resources, monitoring of natural calamities, surveillance of border, etc in India.

4. Describe any three advantages of pipelines as a means of transport in India. ***(All India 2014)***

Ans. Advantages of pipelines as means of transport in India are as follows

(i) It is most convenient and efficient means of transporting liquids and gases over long distances.

(ii) Pipelines can also transport solids after converting them into slurry.

(iii) Its initial set up cost is high, after it pipelines transport liquids and gases very cheaply.

5. What are the three categories to the track of Indian railways? Write any one feature of each. ***(Delhi 2010)***

Or What are the three categories of Indian Railways on the basis of width of track? Write main feature of each category. ***(All India 2008)***

Ans. Indian railways has been divided into three categories on the basis of the width of the track

(i) **Broad Gauge** In broad gauge, the distance between rails is 1.676 metres.

Characteristics of broad gauge are

(a) Broad gauge line share 94.11 per cent of railway length in the total length of rail routes in the country.

(b) The total length of broad gauge lines is 63950 km.

(ii) **Metre Gauge** In metre gauge, the distance between the rail is one metre.

Characteristics of metre gauge are

(a) It accounts for 3.53% of total route length in the country.

(b) The total length of metre gauge is 2402 km.

(iii) **Narrow Gauge** In narrow gauge, the distance between the rails in 0.762 metres.

Characteristics of narrow gauge are

(a) It accounts for about 2.36 per cent of total route length in the country.

(b) The total length of narrow gauge line is 1604 km.

Categories of Track
- Broad Gauge
- Metre Gauge
- Narrow Gauge

6. Which are the two types of roads included under the category of 'other roads' in India? Write any two features of each. ***(Delhi 2010)***

Ans. Border roads and International Highways are included under the category of 'Other Roads' in India.

These are described below

(i) **Border Roads** These are strategically important roads along the Northern and North- Eastern boundary of the country.

Characteristics of border roads are as follows

(a) The total length of border roads was 60,000 km in 2019 which was constructed by BRO.

(b) These roads are important to accelerate economic development and strengthening defence preparedness.

(ii) **International Highway** These are roads which connect India to neighbouring countries.

Characteristics of International highways are as follows

(a) They aim to promote harmonious relationship with neighbouring countries.

(b) They provide an effective connection to neighbouring countries.

7. Write any six characteristics of road transport in India. ***(Delhi 2009)***

Ans. Characteristics of road transport in India are as follows

(i) With a total length of 62.16 lakh km of roads, India has placed itself among the countries which have a large road network.

(ii) Road transport carries about 85% of passenger and 70% of freight traffic every year.

(iii) Various attempts are made to modernise and improve the condition of roads in India such as Nagpur plan, twenty-year road plan.

(iv) In India, roads are classified on the basis of purpose of construction and maintenance in National Highways (NH), State Highways (SH), Major District Roads and Rural Roads.

(v) Apart from above roads, there are border roads which are constructed for defence purpose and international roads which are constructed to link connection with neighbouring countries.

(vi) Distribution of roads is not even throughout the country. Road density is highest in Uttar Pradesh and lowest in Jammu and Kashmir.

8. Mention any six advantages of oceanic routes. ***(Delhi 2009)***

Ans. Following are the advantages of oceanic routes

(i) These play an important role in the transport section of India's economy.

(ii) India's vast coastline of about 7, 517 km easily facilitates this type of transport.

(iii) There are 12 major and 185 minor ports in India.

(iv) About 95% of India's foreign trade by volume and 70% by value moves through oceanic routes.

(v) These trade gives international trade service.

(vi) It provides transportation between the islands and rest of the country.

9. Describe any three characteristics of State Highways of India. ***(All India 2008)***

Ans. Three characteristics of State Highways of India are as follows

(i) These are the highways which are constructed and maintained by the State Governments.

(ii) They are meant to connect the state capitals with district headquarters and other important towns.

(iii) These roads are further connected to National Highways, so they can connect these areas to other states.

5 Marks Questions

1. "India has one of the second largest road networks in the world". Support the statement. ***(CBSE 2023)***

Or ''Indian railways network is one of the longest networks of the world and has contributed a lot to the growth of the economy.'' Support the statement. ***(All India 2019)***

Ans. India has the second largest road network in the world. The role of roads in economic development is as follows

- Roads connect the remote villages and backward areas with the cities.
- Roads provides opportunity to people living in areas of difficult terrain such as desert and hilly areas.
- It contributes to the economic development of India as about 80% of passenger traffic and 75% of freight in India is carried by roads every year.
- Road transport establishes easy contacts between farms, fields and factories and markets.
- It facilitates easy movement of raw materials as well as finished products across the country.
- The National Highways are used to transport men and materials in the strategic areas. They also connect state capitals, important economic and industrial cities, important ports, railway junctions, etc.

- State Highways connect state capitals with district headquarters and commercial towns.

> **Additional Info**
>
> Other roles of roads in economic development are
> - Border roads accelerate economic development by rapidly improving strategically important roads along North and North-Eastern border of the country.
> - Golden Quadrilateral and North-South economic corridor helps in connecting major urban, industrial centres, promoting growth and development.

2. How are Indian railways contributing to the growth of national economy? Explain with examples. ***(All India 2011)***

Ans. India has one of the longest railway networks in the world. It has contributed to the growth of national economy in following ways

- Indian Railways form the lifeline of India catering to its needs for large scale movement of traffic, both freight and passenger, thereby contributing to economic growth.
- Railways has also helped in promoting national integration. It connects areas having important mineral resources to regions where there are industries.
- It also helps in transporting raw materials and finished products.
- Apart from the passengers and traffic, the freight also increased tremendously. Development in industrial and agricultural sectors has generated high demand for railway transport.
- Major commodities transported by railways include coal, iron and steel ores, petroleum products and essential commodities such as foodgrains, fertilisers, cement, sugar, salt, edible oils, etc.
- Indian railways also contribute in tourism sector by connecting hill stations, religious places and other important tourist places.
- It is the largest government undertaking which provides employment to millions of people in India.

3. ''Pipelines are the most convenient and efficient mode of transporting liquids and gases over long distances in India.'' Examine the statement. ***(CBSE Term I 2021)***

Ans. Pipelines are convenient and best means of transporting liquid and gases over long distances.

Oil India Limited (OIL) is responsible for crude oil and natural gas production and transportation. It has constructed Asia first cross country pipeline. This pipeline covers a distance of 1157 km from Naharkatiya oil field in Assam to Barauni refinery in Bihar.

The pipelines cover whole of India and fulfils the oil and gas requirement of different regions. In Western region, oil constructed extensive network of pipelines i.e, Ankleshwar-Koyali, Mumbai High-Koyal and Hazira- Vijaipur- Jagdispur (HVJ) pipelines. A pipeline is also constructed from Salaya (Gujarat) to Mathura (UP). A pipeline of 660km from Numaligarh to Siliguri is also constructed. These pipelines has become the key source for oil and gas supply in India.

4. ''Waterways is an important mode of transport for both passenger and cargo traffic in India.'' Support the statement with examples. ***(Delhi 2019)***

Ans. Waterways is important mode of transport for both passengers and cargo traffic in India in the following ways

(i) Waterways provide cheapest and most suitable transportation for heavy and bulky material.
(ii) It is a fuel efficient and eco-friendly means of transport.
(iii) The risk of accidents breakdowns in this form of transport are minimum as compared to any other form of transport.
(iv) It provides much more flexible service than railways and can be adjusted to individual requirements.

5. Analyse any five points of importance of 'pipelines' as means of transportation. ***(Delhi 2019)***

Ans. Advantages of pipelines as means of transport in India are as follows

(i) It is most convenient and efficient means of transporting liquids and gases over long distances.
(ii) Pipelines can also transport solids after converting them into slurry.
(iii) Its initial set up cost is high, but after it, pipelines transport liquids and gases very cheaply.
(iv) It does not require much space.
(v) Pipelines are energy efficient and environment friendly.

6. Analyse the three factors that affect the development of inland waterways. ***(Delhi 2019)***

Ans. Inland waterways consist of rivers, lakes, canals and streams linking the coastal areas. They have been used as waterways from time immemorial. Inland waterways are important for domestic and international transport and trade. Many rivers are modified to make inland waterways possible in different developed countries.

The three factors responsible for the development of inland waterways in the world are

(i) **Navigability** This means width and depth of the channel that makes navigation possible.

(ii) **Water Flow** Another factor is continuous flow of water throughout the year so that ships, boats can easily move in the waterways.

Factors that affect inland waterways
- Navigability
- Water Flow
- Transport Technology

(iii) **Transport Technology** Development of proper technology so that very heavy cargo like coal, timber, metallic ores can also be easily transported through inland waterways.

7. Analyse the importance and declining popularity of water transport in India in recent times. ***(CBSE SQP 2018)***

Ans. India has 14500 km of navigable inland waterways that consist of rivers, canals, back waters and creeks. Indias coastline consist of about 7517 kms and the country has 12 major and 185 minor ports. They provide infrastructural support to India's foreign trade. Importance of waterways are as follows

(i) Waterways are important mode of transport for both passengers and cargo traffic in India.

(ii) An important advantage of water transport is that it does not require route construction.

(iii) It is also an eco friendly way of transport. It also aids in lessening the congestion on inland transport.

(iv) Waterways provide cheapest and most suitable transportation for heavy and bulky material.

(v) It is a fuel efficient and eco-friendly means of transport.

In ancient times, water transport have much importance but now, it is losing its significance due to the following reasons

(i) Competition from railways.

(ii) Lack of water due to diver sion for irrigation.

(iii) Poor maintenance of water bodies.

8. 'The distribution of roads is not uniform in India.' Support this statement with suitable arguments. ***(CBSE SQP 2018, Delhi 2012)***

Or Why is the distribution of roads not uniform in India? Explain with examples. ***(Delhi 2016)***

Ans. The distribution of roads is not uniform in India. For example,

(i) Construction of roads in plains is easily and cheaper than compare to hilly and mountainous areas, that's why Indo-Gangetic plains have high density of roads.

(ii) Difficult terrain, thick forest does not provide suitable conditions for the development of roads. That's the reason for having low density of roads in Himalayan and North-Eastern region.

(iii) Sandy soil is also a restriction in the development of roads, that's the reason for having less density of roads in Western Rajasthan.

(iv) Economic development also affects the density of roads. Karnataka plateau and Maharashtra have density of roads due to high concentration of industries and urbanisation in these areas.

(v) High density of 50-100 km (per 100 sq km) of area is also found in Punjab, Haryana and Uttar Pradesh of Northern plains. This is due to advanced agriculture, industry and urbanisation in these areas.

9. Describe any five characteristics of National Highways of India. ***(Delhi 2018)***

Ans. Characteristics of National Highways of India are as follows

(i) These roads are constructed and maintained by Central Government. They are made for inter-state transport and movement.

(ii) These highways connect the state capitals, major cities, important ports, railway junctions and extreme places of India.

(iii) They carry about 40% of the road traffic, despite they constitute only 1.67% of total road length.

(iv) The National Highways Authority of India (NHAI-1995) is an autonomous body, under the Ministry of Surface Transport which is assigned for the improvement of the quality of National Highways.

(v) National Highways reduce the time, distance and cost of movement between cities.

10. Which is the apex body in India to improve the quality of National Highways? Examine the significance of National Highways. ***(All India 2016)***

Ans. The National Highways Authority of India (NHAI) is the nodal agency responsible for building, upgrading and maintaining most of the National Highways network. It operates under the the Ministry of Road Transport and Highways.

For the significance of National Highways, refer to Q. 9 of 5 marks questions.

11. Explain why inland water transport is an important mode of transport. *(All India 2016)*

Ans. Inland water transport is an important mode of transport due to following reasons

(i) Inland water transport was the chief mode of transport before the advent of railways.

(ii) These are important mode of transport for both passenger and cargo traffic in India.

(iii) These provide cheapest and most suitable transportation for heavy and bulky material.

(iv) It is fuel efficient and eco-friendly means of transport.

(v) Apart from transportation, Inland waterways is also significant for promotion of tourism, e.g. the famous Nehru Trophy Boat Race (Vallamkali) which held every year in backwaters.

12. What are National Highways? Explain any four uses of National Highways in India. *(Delhi 2013)*

Ans. The main roads which are constructed and maintained by the central government are known as the National Highways.

The main uses of National Highways are

(i) These roads are meant for inter-state and strategic defence movements.

(ii) The National Highways constitute only 1.67% of the total road length but carry 40% of the road traffic.

(iii) National Highways are most important for industrial development. Most of the industries use such a location where National Highways provide good connectivity for the easy movement of goods and commodities from source region to market areas. Thus, National Highways are important as they give good connectivity of distant areas with ease.

(iv) These also connect the state capitals, major cities, important ports, railways junctions, etc.

13. Define the term road density. Explain with examples the two main determinants of road density in India. *(Delhi 2011)*

Or Explain with examples the two main determinants of road density in India. *(Delhi 2011)*

Ans. Density of roads is defined as the length of roads per 100 sq km of surface area. It is a method to compare road network of an area to another area.

The two determinants of road density in India are as follows

(i) **Nature of Terrain** It directly affects the density of roads. The maximum concentration of roads is in the Northern Plains. The surface in plains is even and level. The North-Eastern states don't have good networks of roads due to difficult terrain. Large numbers of rivers due to heavy rainfall makes it necessary to construct a large number to bridges. Construction of roads is easily and comparatively cheaper in plains.

(ii) **Level of Economic Development** Uttar Pradesh has highest density of roads i.e. 532 27 km in 100 sq km area. Density of over 100 km of road length per 100 sq km of areas is also found in Tamil Nadu. Karnataka Plateau and Maharashtra have also high density of 50 to 100 sq km of road length per 100 sq km of area. This is because of high concentration of industries and urbanisation in these areas. Building material is locally available. High density of roads is also found in Punjab and Haryana of Northern plain. This is due to advanced agriculture, industry and urbanisation in these areas. Building material is obtained from the Himalayan region. Large parts of Deccan plateau have moderate density of roads.

14. What is the importance of air transport? Describe any four characteristics of air transport system of India. *(All India 2010)*

Ans. Air transport facilitates the fastest movement of goods and passengers from one place to another place. It has reduced distances and converted the world into one unit. Air transport has a great importance for a vast country like India where distances are large and the terrain and the climatic conditions are uneven throughout the country.

It is also important for our links with other countries. India occupies a central location between Western Europe and Africa on the one hand and South -East and East Asia on the other hand.

Characteristics of air transport system of India are as follows

(i) To provide safe, efficient air traffic and aeronautical communication services in Indian space, there is regulatory body known as Airport Authority of India.

(ii) There are two corporations, Air India and Indian Airlines, which provide air services in India. Air India handles international traffic passengers and cargo whereas Indian Airlines is the major domestic air carrier of the country.

(iii) In addition to Air India and Indian Airlines, there are two private scheduled airlines operating on the domestic network. 38 companies hold non-scheduled air taxi operators permit. The share of the private sector airways has increased very rapidly after liberalistion .

(iv) Union government has launched open sky policy in 1982. Under this policy, foreign airlines or association of exporters can bring any freighters to the country. Its objectives is to help exporters, so that their exports become more competitive in the world.

15. What is the importance of water transport? Describe in brief water transport system of India. ***(All India 2010)***

Ans. For importance of waterways, refer to Q. 4 of 5 marks questions.

There are two types of water transport system in India

(i) **Inland Waterways** India has 14500 km of navigable inland waterways which is used for about 1% of country's total transportation. It includes rivers, canals, backwater, creeks, etc. At present, 3700 km of major rivers and 4300 km of canal network are navigable by mechanised vessels.

The inland waterways authority is responsible for the development, maintenance and regulation of national waterways in the country. Currently, there are three Inland waterways which are considered as national waterways.

(ii) **Oceanic Routes** India's vast coastline of about 7517 km including islands easily facilitate this type of transport. There are 12 major and 185 minor ports, which provide infastructural support to these routes.

About 95% of India's foreign trade by volume and 70% by value moves through oceanic routes. Besides, trade, its development is also necessary for the transportation between the island and mainland of India.

Map Based Questions

1. On the given political outline map of India, locate and label the following with appropriate symbols.

(i) The international airport in Punjab. ***(All India 2015)***

Or The Northern most international airport. ***(Delhi 2014)***

(ii) The international airport in Karnataka. ***(Delhi 2015)***

(iii) The international airport in Tamil Nadu. ***(All India 2014)***

Ans. (i) Amritsar (ii) Bengaluru

(iii) Chennai

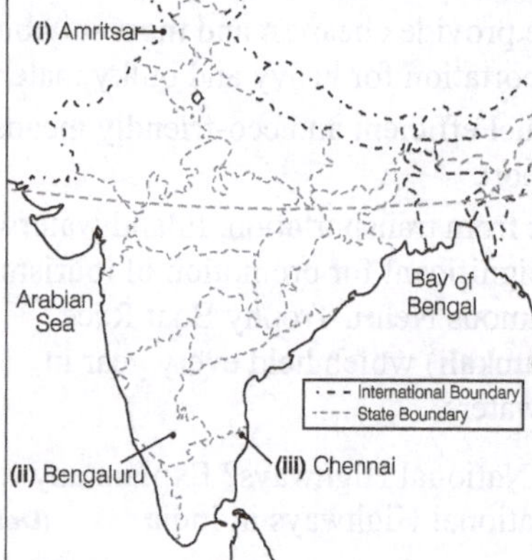

2. On the given political outline map of India provided to you, locate and label the following with appropriate symbols.

(i) The Southernmost international airport. ***(All India 2008)***

(ii) The Easternmost international airport. ***(Delhi 2008)***

Ans. (i) Thiruvananthapuram

(ii) Guwahati

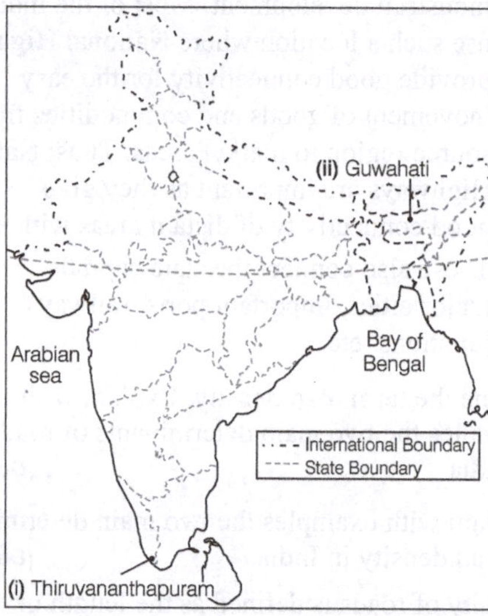

CHAPTER TEST

01 Mark Questions

1 Which of the following is responsible for the construction and maintenance of Border Roads?
(a) Ministry of Road Transport and Highways
(b) Border Road Organisation
(c) Ministry of Home Affairs
(d) Ministry of Defence

2 ....connects the National Highway and join the state capitals with districts headquarter and other important towns.
(a) Rural Roads
(b) State Highway
(c) Golden Quadrilateral
(d) District Roads

3 .... is the cheapest mode of transport for carrying heavy and bulky materials as well as passenger service.
(a) Waterways
(b) Railways
(c) Roadways
(d) Airways

4 Identify the incorrectly matched pair.

	Railway Zones		Headquarters
(a)	Central	–	Mumbai CST
(b)	Northern	–	New Delhi
(c)	Southern	–	Kolkata
(d)	Western	–	Mumbai Church Gate

5 The National Waterway 1 connects the region of .... with ....
(a) Sadiya- Dhubri
(b) Kottapuram- Kollam Stretch
(c) Talcher- Dhamra
(d) Allahabad- Haldia

Answers

1. (d) | 2. (c) | 3. (a) | 4. (c) | 5. (d)

03 Marks Questions

6 What are the advantages of road transport in India? How does it contribute in an Indian economic development?

7 Indian railways brought people of diverse cultures together." Support this statement with suitable examples.

8 The distribution of roads in India is not uniform. Examine the statement by giving three reasons.

05 Marks Questions

9 What is the importance of air transport? Describe any four characteristics of the air transport system of India.

10 Define the term road density. Explain with examples the two main determinants of road density in India.

11 What are National Highways? Explain any four uses of National Highways in India.

08

International Trade

TREND ANALYSIS 3 YEARS

		Average No. of Questions Across all Sets			
		Types of Questions	2023	2020	2019
TOPIC 01	Changing patterns of India's export and import	1 Mark	–	–	–
		3 Marks	–	–	1
		5 Marks	1	–	–
TOPIC 02	Major Ports of India	1 Mark	–	–	–
		3 Marks	–	–	–
		5 Marks	1	–	–

International trade is the need of every nation as no country is self sufficient. According to recent study, India's international trade has transformed in terms of volume, composition and direction.

Despite contributing as low as 1% of total volume in world trade, India plays a significant role in the world economy. India's **external** or **foreign trade** is increasing.

Various reasons are responsible for this sharp rise in foreign trade i.e. the momentum picked up by the manufacturing sectors, the liberal policies of the government and the diversification of markets.

The nature of India's foreign trade has changed over the years. Although, the total volume of export and import has been increased but the value of import is still higher than exports. **Trade deficit** has also been increased during recent years which is result of the price rise of crude petroleum which is a major commodity of import in India.

Changing Patterns of the Composition of India's Exports

- During recent years, a change has been recorded in the composition of commodities in India's international trade. There is a decline in the share of agriculture and allied products whereas shares of petroleum and crude products and other commodities have increased. The share of petroleum products has increased mainly because of the rise in petroleum prices and increase in the petroleum refining capacity of India.
- A huge decline is registered in the export of traditional items like, coffee, spices, tea, pulses, etc due to the tough international competition. Though an increase has been registered in floricultural products, fresh fruits, marine products and sugar, etc. But manufacturing sector alone accounted for 73.6% of India's total value of export in 2016-17.

- The major competitors of India are China and other East Asian countries. Apart from this, the gems and jewellery are other commodities that have larger share in India's international trade.

Changing Patterns of the Composition of India's Import

- During 1950s and 1960s, India faced serious food shortage, thus, the country had to import food grain, capital goods, machinery and equipments at large scale.
- The balance of payment was adverse as imports were more than export inspite of all the efforts of imports substitution.
- After 1970s, the **success of Green Revolution** discontinued the food grain import. But the energy crises of 1973 replaced the import of foodgrains by fertilisers and petroleum as the prices of petroleum had been raised.
- Besides, other imported goods were machine and equipment, special steel, edible oil and chemicals.
- According to economic survey 2016-17, petroleum products have registered a rapid increase in import goods.
- It is a raw material for petrochemical industries and also used as fuel. The increase signifies the tempo of rising industrialisation and improvement in standard of living.
- Periodic price rise of petroleum in the international market may be another reason for this increase.
- Import of **capital goods** like non-electrical machinery, transport equipment, manufactures of metals and machine tools registered a steady increase. This increase could be because of increasing demand in the export oriented industrial and domestic sectors.
- Import of food and allied products registered a decrease because of a sudden decline in imports of edible oils.
- Pearls and semi-precious stones, gold and silver, metalliferrous ores and metal scrap, non-ferrous metals, electronic goods, etc are other important items of India's import.

Direction of Trade

- India is a trading partner with most of the countries and major trading blocks of the world.
- India has goal to double its share in international trade within the next 5 years. To achieve this objective, India has started to adopt suitable measures which includes import liberalisation, reduction in import duties, de-licensing and change from process to product patents.
- India has created an example in terms of percentage of Asia and ASEAN (Association of South-East Asian Nations) in total trade of world has increased.
- There is a growth in trade with Europe and USA as compared to 2011-12 in 2016-17.
- Trade with African countries also seen an upsurge. Trade with latin American countries is also increasing.
- Indian foreign trade is mainly carried through air and sea routes. However, a small portion of trade is also carried through land route to neighbouring countries like Nepal, Bhutan, Bangladesh and Pakistan.

Sea ports as Gateways of International Trade

- India has a long history of international trade via sea ports as it has long coastline and is opened to sea from three sides. Water provides smooth surface and cheap transport without any hinderance.
- India has developed many ports on its coast. These ports are named with suffix **pattan** meaning port. It is interesting to know that India has more sea ports on West coast than its East coast.
- After coming of the European traders and colonisation of the country by the British, the Indian ports have emerged as gateways of international trade.
- There are some parts which have very vast area of influence and some have limited area of influence.

Major and Minor ports

- At present, India has **12 major** and **200 minor or intermediate ports**. For major ports, Central Government is responsible for deciding the policies and regulate their functions and for minor ports, State Government is responsible for the same functions stated above.
- A larger share of total traffic is handled by major ports.
- The Britishers used these ports to export natural resources of India; particularly from their hinterland but this trend was discontinued after 1947.
- The India lost its two very important ports i.e. **Karachi port** to Pakistan and **Chittagong port** to Bangladesh (erstwhile East-Pakistan). But India recovered successfully from this loss by opening many new ports, for instance, Kandla in the West and the Diamond Harbour near Kolkata on river Hugli in the East.

- Today, large volumes of domestic and international trade are handled by these Indian ports. Most of the ports are equipped with modern infrastructure.
- Previously, it was expected that government agencies are responsible for the development and modernisation of Indian ports. But it was considered that there is a need to increase the functions and bring these ports at par with the international ports. Thus, private entrepreneurs have been invited for the modernisation of ports in the country.
- The **cargo handling capacity** of Indian ports increased from 20 million tonnes in 1951 to more than 837 million tonnes in 2016.

Important Ports

Some of the Indian ports along with their hinterlands are as follows

Kandla Port

- This port is situated at the head of Gulf of Kuchchh. The main objectives of this major port are to serve the needs of Western and North-Western parts of the country and also to reduce the pressure at Mumbai port.
- This port is mainly designed to receive large quantities of petroleum and petroleum products and fertilisers.
- To reduce the pressure at Kandla port, an offshore terminal named **Vadinar** has also been developed.
- Due to confusion in demarcation of the boundary, hinterland of one port may overlap with that of the other.

Mumbai Port

- This is a **natural harbour** and the **biggest port** of India.
- The location of this port is closer to the general routes from the countries of Middle East, Mediterranean countries, North Africa, North America and Europe, where the major share of country's overseas trade is carried out.
- This port is extended over a large area with the length of 20 km and width of 6-10 km with 54 berths and has the country's largest oil terminal.
- The main **hinterlands** of this port are Madhya Pradesh, Maharashtra, Gujarat, Uttar Pradesh and some parts of Rajasthan.

Jawaharlal Nehru Port

- This **satellite port** is located at Nhava Sheva. It was developed to relieve the pressure at the Mumbai port.
- It is the **largest container port** in India.

Marmagao Port

- It is located at the entrance of the Zuari estuary which is a **natural harbour** in Goa. It gained significance after its remodelling in 1961 to handle iron-ore exports to Japan.
- Construction of Konkan railway extended its hinterland, e.g. Karnataka, Goa, Southern Maharashtra constitute its hinterland.

New Mangalore Port

- It is mainly used to export iron-ore and iron concentrates, and other commodities like fertilisers, petroleum products, edible oils, coffee, tea, wood pulp, yarn, granite stone, molasses, etc.
- It is located in Karnataka which is its major hinterland.

Kochchi Port

- This port is popularly known as **Queen of the Arabian Sea.**
- It is a natural harbour and situated at the head of Vembanad Kayal.
- Kochchi port is located close to the Suez-Colombo route.
- It serves the needs of Kerala, Southern- Karnataka and South-Western Tamil Nadu.

Kolkata Port

- It is located on the Hugli river 128 km inland from the Bay of Bengal. This port was developed by the British as it was once the capital of British India.
- The port has lost its significance considerably on account of the diversion of exports to the other ports such as Vishakhapatnam, Paradwip and satellite port, Haldia.
- It is also facing the problem of silt accumulation in the Hugli river, which hinders the link to the sea.
- Its hinterland covers Uttar Pradesh, Bihar, Jharkhand, West Bengal, Sikkim and the North-Eastern states.
- It also provides port facilities to our neighbouring **land-locked countries** such as **Nepal** and **Bhutan**.

Haldia Port

- It is located 105 km downstream from Kolkata.
- It has been constructed to reduce the congestion at Kolkata port.

- It handles bulk cargo like iron-ore, coal, petroleum, petroleum products and fertilisers, jute, jute products, cotton, and cotton yarn, etc.

Paradwip Port

- The port is located in the Mahanadi delta and it is about 100 km far from Cuttack.
- It has advantage of having the **deepest harbour**, thus it is best suited to handle very large vessels.
- It mainly handles large scale export of iron-ore.
- Odisha, Chhattisgarh and Jharkhand constitute its hinterland.

Vishakhapatnam Port

- It is a **land locked harbour** situated in Andhra Pradesh.
- It is connected to the sea by a channel which is cut through solid rock and sand.
- To handle various commodities like iron-ore, petroleum and general cargo an outer harbour has been developed.
- Andhra Pradesh is the main hinterland for this port.

Chennai Port

- The **artificial harbour** of Chennai is one of the oldest port on the Eastern coast. It was built in 1859.
- Because of the shallow water near the coast, it is not suitable for large ships.
- Tamil Nadu and Puducherry constitute its hinterland.

Ennore Port

- This newly developed port, is situated 25 km North of Chennai.
- It was developed to minimise the pressure at Chennai port.

Tuticorin Port

- It is another port which was developed to relieve the pressure of Chennai port.
- This port handles a number of commodities like coal, salt, food grains, edible oils, sugar, chemicals and petroleum products.

Airports

Air transport plays a significant role in the international trade of a nation.

The advantages are follows

(i) Air transport is very useful for handling high value or perishable goods over long distance.

(ii) It takes less time to transport cargo.

The disadvantages are as follows

(i) Air transportation is very costly.

(ii) It is not suitable for the transportation of heavy and bulky commodities.

Thus, having these disadvantages air transport is not/less preferred for international trade as compared to oceanic routes.

There were **25 major airports** in India according to Annual Report, 2016-17. They are Ahmedabad, Bengaluru, Chennai, Delhi, Goa, Guwahati, Hyderabad, Kochi, Kolkata, Mumbai, Thiruvananthapuram, Srinagar, Jaipur, Calicut, Nagpur, Coimbatore, Lucknow, Pune, Chandigarh, Mangaluru, Vishakhapatnam, Indore, Patna, Bhubaneshwar and Kannur. Apart from these, there are 112 domestic airports in India.

PYQs Previous Years' Questions

1 Mark Questions

Multiple Choice Questions

1. Which of the following sea ports located on Mahanadi delta? ***(CBSE 2023)***
   (a) Haldia (b) Ennore
   (c) Paradi (d) Vishakhapatnam

Ans. (c) Paradip

2. Why has Kolkata port minimised its significance? ***(CBSE 2023)***
   (a) It has a vast hinterland.
   (b) Accumulation of silt in Hugli river.
   (c) Diversion of exports to other ports.
   (d) Passenger traffic is very low.

Ans. (b) Accumulation of silt in Hugli river.

3. India's foreign trade is largely carried out by which of the following routes? ***(CBSE 2023)***
   (a) Land and air routes (b) Land and sea routes
   (c) Air and sea routes (d) Only sea routes

Ans. (b) Land and sea routes

4. The port designed to receive petroleum, petroleum products and fertiliser is .... ***(CBSE 2023)***
   (a) New Mangaluru (b) Haldia
   (c) Kandla (d) Tuticorin

Ans. (c) Kandla

5. What is the major export from New Mangalore ports? ***(CBSE SQP 2022)***
   (a) Coal (b) Iron-ore
   (c) Copper (d) Mica

Ans. (b) Iron-ore

6. Which of the following is a feature of Kandla port? ***(CBSE SQP 2022)***
   (a) It is the biggest port of the country.
   (b) Its harbour is situated at Zuari estuary.
   (c) It is situated at the head of Gulf of Kuchchh.
   (d) It is the oldest port of India.

Ans. (c) It is situated at the head of Gulf of Kuchchh.

7. Which one of the following is a landlocked harbour? ***(CBSE SQP 2019)***
   (a) Vishakhapatnam (b) Mumbai
   (c) Ennore (d) Haldia

Ans. (a) Vishakhapatnam

8. What is/are the main basis of Modern International Trade?
   (a) Geological structure (b) Size of population
   (c) Climate (d) All of these

Ans. (d) All of the above

9. Which of the following describes composition of trade?
   (a) Total value of goods and services.
   (b) Nature of goods and services imported and exported.
   (c) Destination of exports and imports.
   (d) None of the above

Ans. (b) Nature of goods and services imported and exported.

10. If the value of exports is more than the value of import then there is a .... balance of trade.
    (a) equal (b) negative
    (c) positive (d) None of these

Ans. (c) positive

11. The international trade can be categorised into how many types?
    (a) One (b) Two
    (c) Three (d) Four

Ans. (b) Two

12. What do you understand by the term dumping in International Trade?
    (a) Selling same commodity in two countries at different price.
    (b) Trade on large scale.
    (c) Breaking off trade relations.
    (d) None of the above

Ans. (a) Selling same commodity in two countries at different price.

Very Short Answer Questions

1. Identify the Indian sea port which provides port facilities to its land locked neighbour counties. Name any one such country. ***(CBSE SQP 2018)***

Or Which one of the Indian sea port provides port facilities to its land locked neighbouring countries? Name any one such country. ***(Delhi 2009)***

Ans. Kolkata port provides port facilities to its land locked neighbouring countries i.e. Nepal and Bhutan.

2. State the major problem being faced by Kolkata sea port. ***(Delhi 2018)***

Ans. The port of Kolkata is a reverine port in the city of Kolkata. The major problem of silt accumulation is being faced by Kolkata sea port.

3. Which major sea port on the Eastern coast of India has a land locked harbour? *(Delhi 2016)*

Ans. Vishakhapatnam is major sea port on the Eastern coast of India which has a land locked harbour.

4. Name the major sea ports which have been developed to relieve the pressure at Chennai sea port. *(Delhi 2016, All India 2011)*

Ans. Tuticorin and Ennore are the major sea ports which have been developed to relieve the pressure at Chennai sea port.

5. Name the two countries which are the largest trading partners of India as per economic survey report of 2011-12. *(All India 2016)*

Ans. UAE and China are the largest trading partners of India as per economic survey report of 2011-12.

6. Name the sea port which was constructed to reduce the congestion of Kolkata port. *(Delhi 2014)*

Or Which port has been constructed to reduce congestion of Kolkata port? *(Delhi 2010)*

Ans. Haldia port was constructed to reduce the congestion at Kolkata port.

7. Name the major sea port which was developed just after independence on the Western coast of India. *(Delhi 2014)*

Or Name the first major sea port of India developed after independence. *(Delhi 2011)*

Ans. Kandla port was developed just after independence on the Western coast of India.

8. Name the port developed as a satellite port to relieve the pressure at Mumbai port. *(Delhi 2014)*

Ans. Jawaharlal Nehru port was developed as a satellite port to relieve the pressure at Mumbai port.

9. Give the meaning of the term 'hinterland'. *(Delhi 2013)*

Ans. Hinterland is the area which lies behind the sea port and serves the sea port for imports and exports.

10. Name the major sea port located on Hugli river. *(All India 2013)*

Ans. Kolkata port is located on the Hugli river.

11. Which is the principle import commodity of India? *(Delhi 2010)*

Ans. Crude petroleum and petroleum products are principle import commodities of India.

12. Which export commodity of India has the highest value? *(All India 2010)*

Ans. Manufactured goods and agriculture and allied products have the highest value in the India's export.

13. Name the oldest artificial sea port of India. *(All India 2009)*

Ans. The oldest artificial sea port of India is Chennai port.

14. Name the biggest sea port of India. *(Delhi, All India 2008)*

Ans. The biggest sea port of India is Mumbai port.

3 Marks Questions

1. Explain the Characteristics of India's foreign trade. *(Compartment 2020)*

Or Compare with examples, the hinterland, the cargo handled and significance of Kandla sea port and Haldia Sea port. *(CBSE 2022)*

Ans. The following are the characterstics of India's international trade

(i) It helped India in increasing its productivity and improving the quality of its products and then exporting the manufactured goods.

(ii) India exports agriculture and allied products, ores and minerals, gems and jewelry, chemical and allied products, enginerring goods, and petroleum products.

(iii) Technical know-how can be imported.

(iv) Surplus production can be exported.

(v) Development of new ports and thereby increasing the empolyment rate in India.

2. Describe the importance of sea routes in handling India's foreign trade. *(Delhi 2019)*

Or ''Most of India's foreign trade is carried through sea routes''. Explain the statement giving three reasons. *(All India 2014)*

Ans. The importance of sea routes in handling India's foreign trade is as follows

(i) **Long Coastline** India has a long coastline of 7511 km. It provides India to connect with other countries easily by sea route.

(ii) **Open to Sea from Three Sides** India's peninsular plate is opened to sea from three sides. This strategic situation in Indian ocean provides a great advantage for India's international trade.

Importance of Sea Routes
- Long coastline
- Open to sea from three sides
- Cheapest means of transport

(iii) **Cheapest Means of Transport** Water transport is a cheap means of transport as it does not require any investment, provides a smooth surface and zero turbulance.

5 Marks Questions

1. Examine the role of air transport in the promotion of international trade. *(CBSE 2023)*

Ans. The role of air transport in the promotion of international trade can be seen through the following points

(i) Air transport is the fastest means of transportation thus, it plays an important role in international trade.

(ii) Valuable cargo can be moved rapidly on a worldwide scale. It is the only means to reach inaccessible areas. Air transport has brought about a connectivity revolution in the world.

(iii) The frictions created by mountainous snow fields or inhospitable desert terrains have been overcome and the accessibility has increased. The aeroplane brings varied articles to the Eskimos in Northern Canada.

(iv) Travel by air can now be measured by hours. Frequent air services are available to many parts of the world. United Kingdom pioneered the use of commercial jet transport.

(v) The underdeveloped countries are also taking part in the global trade with the help of fast delivery of cargos through air transport.

2. Why are sea ports known as gateways of international trade in India's? Explain. *(CBSE 2023)*

Ans. Waterways are the cheapest and easiest way of carrying bulky goods over long distances. With a long coastline of 7,516.6 km, India is dotted with 12 major and 187 minor ports. These major ports handle 95 per cent of India's foreign trade, thus waterways are the gateway to international trade in India.

The following are the major ports which make waterways the gateway of international trade

- **Kandla Port (Kuchchh)** It was the first port to be developed immediately after independence. Its main aim was to reduce the volume of trade through the Mumbai port that had increased due to the loss of Karachi port to Pakistan after the partition. It mainly focuses on the exports and imports from the fertile lands and industrial belt that stretches across Jammu and Kashmir, Himachal Pradesh, Punjab, Haryana, Rajasthan and Gujarat.
- **Mumbai Port** It is the biggest port in the country. It also caters to the export and import requirements of the Mumbai-Pune industrial belt. The Jawaharlal Nehru port was scheduled to reduce the trade load of the Mumbai port and to be established as the core port for the region.
- **Marmagao Port (Goa)** It concentrates on the export of iron-ore from the country. Nearly 50% of the iron ore export of the country is enabled from this port.
- **New Mangalore Port (Karnataka)** It concentrates on the export of iron-ore from the country. It enables the export of iron-ore procured from the Kudremukh mines.

3. Explain how international trade can prove to be detrimental to the nations. *(Compartment 2022)*

Ans. International trade can prove to be detrimental to the nations through following points

(i) International trade can prove to be detrimental nations as trade of dependence on other countries, uneven levels of development, exploitation and commercial rivalry leading to wars.

(ii) Global trade affects may aspects of life, it can impact everthing from the environment to health and well-being of the people around the world.

(iii) As countries compete to trade more production and the use of natural resources spiral up, resources get used up faster than they can be replenished. As a result, marine life is also depleting fase, forests are being cut down and river basins sold off to private drinking water companies.

4. "Despite the set back caused by the partition, Indian ports continued to grow after the independence". Support the statement with examples. *(Delhi 2012)*

> **HINT** *Dear students, this question simply ask you to write about the ports before the partition during British rule and the development of ports after the partition.*

Ans. India has a long history of international trade via sea ports. These ports emerged as gateways of international trade after the coming of European traders and colonisation of India by British. These ports linked the local market to regional markets, regional to national and national to international markets. This process was continued till independence.

But, India faced a huge loss when Karachi and Chittagong ports were lost with the partition of the country. Karachi port went to Pakistan and Chittagong port went to East-Pakistan (now Bangladesh).

To recover from this loss, many new ports were developed.

For instance, Kandla in the West and Diamond Harbour in the East near Kolkata on river Hugli. India recovered successfully from this loss and continued the growth of Indian ports.

Today, large volumes of domestic and international trades are handled by these Indian ports. Modern infrastructure facilities are available in most of the Indian ports. Many private entrepreneurs have been invited for the modernisation of ports in the country. The cargo handling capacity of Indian ports has increased from 20 million tonnes in 1951 to more than 837 million tonnes in 2016.

Currently, there are 12 major ports and 200 minor or intermediate ports. A larger part of total traffic is carried through major ports.

5. Describe in brief the changing nature of export items in the international trade of India. ***(All India 2009)***

Or Explain with examples, the changing pattern of the composition of India's exports. ***(All India 2008)***

Ans. The changing pattern of the composition of India's exports can be understood through the following points

(i) There is a decrease in the share of agriculture and allied products.

(ii) The share of petroleum products has increased mainly because of the rise in petroleum prices and increase in the petroleum refining capacity of India.

(iii) A huge decline is registered in the exports of traditional items like, coffee, spices, tea, pulses, etc due to the tough international competition.

(iv) Increase has been registered in floricultural products, fresh fruits, marine products and sugar, etc.

(v) Gems and jewellery are other commodities that have larger share in India's international trade.

5. Describe any five features of changing patterns of the composition of India's import. ***(Delhi 2008)***

Ans. The changing pattern of the composition of India's import is discussed below

(i) During 1950s and 1960s, India faced serious food shortage, thus the country had to import food grains, capital goods, machinery and equipments at large scale.

(ii) After 1970, when the success of Green Revolution took place, it resulted in discontinuation of the food grain import.

(iii) The energy crises of 1973 raised the import prices of petroleum and fertilisers along with machine and equipment, special steel, edible oil and chemicals.

(iv) Import of capital goods like non-electrical machinery, transport equipment, manufactures of metals and machine tools registered a steady increase. This increase could be because of increasing demand in the export oriented industrial and domestic sectors.

(v) Pearls and semi-precious stones, gold and silver, metallic ferrous ores and metal scrap non-ferrous metals, electronic goods, etc are other important items of India's import.

Data Based Question

1. Study the given graph and answer the question that follow.

Changing pattern of the Composition of India's Exports

Extent of gap between Export and Import in India's Foreign Trade During 2012-13 to-2016-17

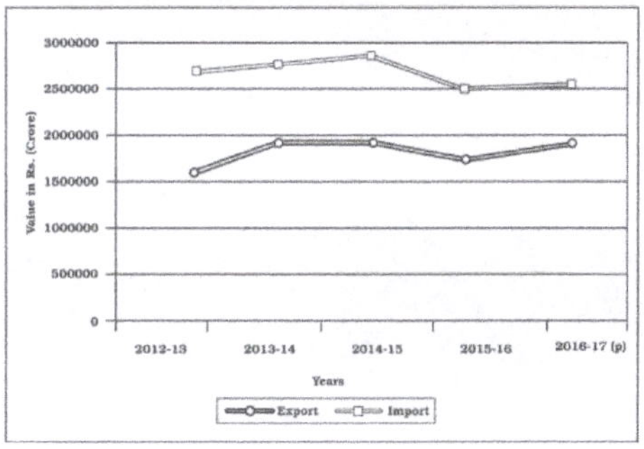

Source : Economic Survey 2016-17

(i) In which year was the gap between imports and exports maximum?

(ii) When was the gap between imports and exports minimum?

(iii) In which year had India's exports shown highest upward trend?

Ans. (i) In the year 2012-13, the gap between import and export was maximum.

(ii) In the year 2016-17, the gap between import and export was minimum.

(iii) In the year 2013-14, India's export had shown highest upward trend.

Map Based Questions

1. In the given political outline map of India, locate and label the following with appropriate symbols.
   (i) The major sea port located in Goa. *(Delhi 2011)*
   (ii) The Southernmost major sea port of India. *(All India 2011)*

Ans. (i) Marmagao (ii) Tuticorin

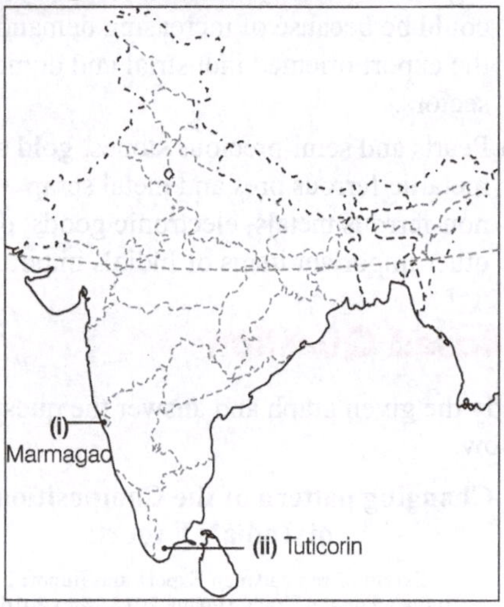

2. In the given political map of India, locate and label the following with appropriate symbols.
   (i) The major sea port located in Odisha. *(Delhi 2010)*
   (ii) The major sea port located in Kerala. *(All India 2010, 09)*

Ans. (i) Paradwip sea port (ii) Kochi sea port

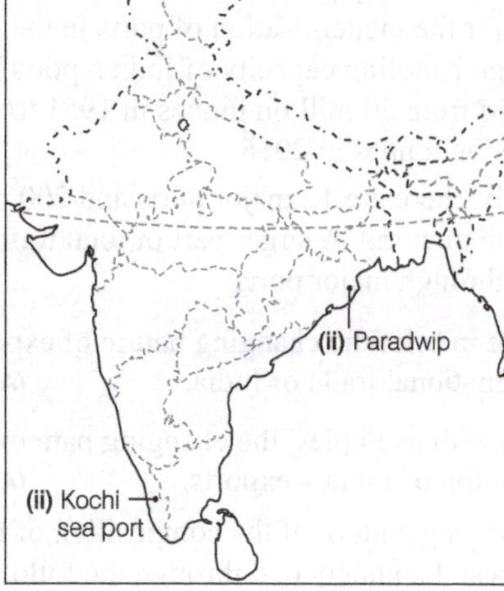

CHAPTER TEST

01 Mark Questions

1 ……….. is a natural harbour and the biggest port of India.

(a) Mangalore port (b) Kochchi port
(c) Kolkata port (d) Mumbai port

2 Which of the following ports is popularly known as 'Queen of the Arabian Sea'?

(a) Kochchi port (b) Kandla port
(c) Haldia port (d) Chennai port

3 The term 'Dumping' in international relations is related to ………….

(a) free trade agreement
(b) trade on large scale
(c) selling same commodity in two countries at different price.
(d) breaking off trade relations

4 ………. is the largest container port in India.

(a) Jawaharlal Nehru port (b) Paradwip port
(c) Vishakhapatnam port (d) Tuticorn port

5 Which of the following ports belongs to the state of West Bengal?

(a) Kandla port (b) Haldia port
(c) Jawaharlal Nehru port (d) Ennore Port

Answers

1. (d) | 2. (a) | 3. (c) | 4. (a) | 5. (c)

03 Marks Questions

6 Describe about the three significant ports of Tamil Nadu.

7 Describe the changes that have taken place in India's foreign trade after independence.

8 Define balance of trade. When the balance of trade is called favourable or unfavourable?

05 Marks Questions

9 "In modern times, international trade is the basis of the world economy." Support the statement with example.

10 Differentiate between bilateral trade and multilateral trade. Explain how ports are helpful in trade.

11 Examine the five bases of international trade which are responsible for promoting international trade.

09

Geographical Perspective on Selected Issues and Problems

TREND ANALYSIS 3 YEARS

TOPIC 01 Environmental Pollution

TOPIC 02 Land Degradation/Slums

Average No. of Questions Across all Sets

Topic	Types of Questions	2023	2020	2019
TOPIC 01 Environmental Pollution	1 Mark	–	–	2
	3 Marks	–	–	1
	5 Marks	–	–	1
TOPIC 02 Land Degradation/Slums	1 Mark	–	–	–
	3 Marks	–	–	–
	5 Marks	1	–	1

The environmental problems in India are growing rapidly. **Over exploitation of resources** of the country has resulted in the environmental degradation of resources. Environmental pollution is one of the most serious problems faced by the human beings and other life forms.

Environmental Pollution

Environmental pollution is the release of substances and energy from waste products of human activities. It is of various types. Thus, they are classified on the basis of medium through which pollutants are transported and diffused. The classification of pollution are as follows

(i) Water pollution
(ii) Air pollution
(iii) Noise pollution
(iv) Land pollution

Water Pollution

Quality of water is majorly degraded by a number of factors i.e. indiscriminate use of water by fast growing population and expansion of industries.

No surface water is found in pure form in rivers, canals, lakes, etc as all the water sources contain small quantities of suspended particles, organic and inorganic substances.

Water becomes polluted, when quantity of these substances increases in it. It becomes unsuitable for human uses and its self purifying capacity declines.

There are two sources of water pollution

(i) **Natural** Erosion, landslides, decay and decomposition of plants and animals, etc are natural sources that make water polluted.

(ii) **Human** Industrial, agricultural and cultural activities of human beings make water polluted.

Water pollution created from human beings are major problem in modern times. Industrial activities of human beings are important in polluting water. It is a major source of water pollution.

Most of the industrial wastes, e.g. polluted waste water, poisonous gases, chemical residuals numerous heavy metals, dust, smoke, etc are disposed off in running water, lakes, reservoirs, rivers and other water bodies and thus, destroy the bio-system of these waters. Major culprits are leather, pulp and paper, textiles and chemicals industries.

Today use of **various types of chemicals** like inorganic fertilisers, pesticides and herbicides are common in agriculture. These chemicals pollute surface water such as rivers, lakes, tanks as well as groundwater by infiltrating into the soil.

These fertilisers increase the amount of nitrate content of surface waters. Besides this, **cultural activities** such as pilgrimage, religious fairs, tourism, etc also cause water pollution. In India, almost all surface water sources are contaminated and unfit for human consumption.

Use of polluted water can harm human health and can cause various water borne diseases, e.g. diarrhoea, intestinal worms, hepatitis, etc. World Health Organisation (WHO) shows that about one-fourth of the communicable diseases in India are water borne.

Source of Pollution in the Ganga and the Yamuna Rivers

River and State	Polluted Stretches	Nature of Pollution	Main Polluters
Ganga (Uttar Pradesh, Bihar and West Bengal)	Downstream of Kanpur	Industrial pollution from towns like Kanpur.	Cities of Kanpur, Allahabad, Varanasi, Patna and Kolkata, release domestic wastes into the river.
	Downstream of Varanasi	Domestic wastes from urban centres.	
	Farrakka Barrage	Dumping of carcasses in river.	
Yamuna (Delhi and Uttar Pradesh)	Delhi to confluence with chambal	Extraction of water by Haryana and Uttar Pradesh for irrigation.	Delhi dumping its domestic waste.
	Mathura and Agra	Agricultural runoff resulting in high levels of micro-pollutants in the Yamuna. Domestic and industrial waste of Delhi flowing into the river.	

Air Pollution

A larger proportion of contaminants like dust, fumes, gas, fog, odour, smoke or vapour in air for a long duration is known as air pollution.

It may be harmful to flora and fauna and to property. There is an increase in emission of poisonous gases into the atmosphere because of increasing use of various fuels for energy in various sectors, thus resulting in the pollution of air.

The **main sources of air pollution** are combustion of fossil fuels, mining and industries which release oxides of sulphur, and nitrogen, hydrocarbons, carbon dioxide, carbon monoxide, lead and asbestos.

Effects of Air Pollution

The effects of air pollution are as follows

(i) Air pollution is responsible for many diseases related to our respiratory, nervous and circulatory systems.

(ii) Air pollution is responsible for creating smoky fog over cities which is known as **urban smog**. It has negative effects on human health.

(iii) Air pollution is also responsible for **acid rain**. First rain after summer in urban areas always shows high acidic nature of rain water i.e. it shows lower pH level than the subsequent rain.

Noise Pollution

Noise pollution refers to a noise that causes a condition which is unbearable and uncomfortable to human beings. This noise can be from various sources. It is a recent phenomenon which became a serious concern only after a variety of technological innovations. The level of steady noise is measured by sound level expressed in terms of decibels (dB).

Factories, mechanised construction and demolition works, automobiles and aircrafts are major sources of noise that cause noise pollution.

Apart from these, there are also some periodic sources of noise pollution such as sirens, loudspeakers in different festivals and programmes and other activities of different communities.

Noise produced by traffic is a major source of noise pollution. It creates a huge inconvenience to the people. Intensity and nature of noise made by traffic is dependent on various factors such as type of vehicle (aircraft, train vehicle, etc), condition of road and condition of vehicle (in case of automobiles).

In sea traffic, the noise pollution is limited to the harbour because of loading and unloading activities of containers. Noise pollution from industries is also a serious problem but its intensity varies because of some factors such as type of industry, types of machines and tools, etc.

The intensity of noise pollution decreases as distance from source of pollution (Industrial areas, arteries of transportation, airport, etc) increases. Thus, noise pollution is **location specific**.

Effects of Noise Pollution

Noise pollution is a major cause of anxiety, tension and some other mental problems and disorders among people in many metropolitan and big cities in India.

Urban Waste Disposal

Overcrowding, congestion, increasing population, improper infrastructure and facilities to support this population, lack of sanitation, foul air, etc are some features of urban areas. Mismanagement of solid wastes and environmental pollution caused by them has now become a major problem.

Solid wastes are a variety of old and used articles, e.g. stained small pieces of metals, broken glasswares, plastic containers, polythene bags, ashes, floppies, CDs, etc dumped at different places.

These discarded materials are also known as refuses, garbage and rubbish, etc and are disposed off from two sources i.e. household or domestic establishments and industrial or commercial establishments.

Public lands or private contractor's sites are used to disposed off household or domestic wastes. Low lying public grounds (landfill areas) are used to disposed off industrial solid wastes by public (municipal) facilities. Industries, thermal power houses and building constructions and demolitions are contributing with more turn out of ashes and debris in solid wastes.

Disposal of industrial wastes has increased because of the concentration of industrial units in and around urban centres. Urban waste is a bigger problem in small towns and cities than metropolitan cities in the country.

About 90% of solid waste is collected and disposed off successfully in Mumbai, Kolkata, Chennai, Bengaluru and other metropolitan cities. About 30-50% solid wastes in other towns and cities in country is not collected and disposed off properly.

It is a major problem because it accumulates on streets, in open spaces between houses and in wastelands and can cause various health problems.

Impacts of Improper Management of Solid Wastes

Improper management of solid wastes has following impacts

(i) Solid wastes are threat to human health and can cause various diseases. It creates foul smell and it harbours flies and rodents that can cause typhoid, diphtheria, diarrhoea, malaria, cholera and other diseases.

(ii) Solid waste can create inconvenience rapidly if they are not properly handled. Wind and rain water can splitted it and cause a discomfort to people.

(iii) Industrial solid waste can cause water pollution by dumping it into water bodies. Drains carrying untreated sewage also result into various health problems.

(iv) Untreated waste release various poisonous biogases such as methane in air by slow **fermentation process**. These wastes are resources as energy can be generated from them. By compositing these wastes, problem of energy could be solved as well as its management in urban areas.

Rural-Urban Migration

Movement of people from rural area to urban area is caused by various factors such as high demand for labour in urban areas, low job opportunities in rural areas and disparities in terms of development in rural and urban areas.

Smaller and medium cities provide low opportunities which force people to bypass these small cities and directly come to the mega cities for their livelihood. Mostly daily wage workers like, welders, carpenter, etc move to another cities for work, periodically and provide remittances to their families for daily consumption, health care, schooling of children, etc. This has improved their early abject situation into a better one. Simultaneously, due to temporary and transferable job situation, these labourers and their families bear the pain of separation of their near and dear ones. Sometimes these workers also face difficulty in assimilation to the new culture and environment.

Due to these menial jobs at low wages in informal sector in urban areas, the spouses are left behind in rural areas to look after children and elderly people. Thus, the rural-urban migration stream is dominated by the males.

Trend of Urbanisation in the World

Currently, about 54% of the world's 7 billion (2011) population lives in urban areas of world. This proportion of urban population will increase in future.

It is estimated that between 2025 to 2030, this percentage would be grown with 1.44% per year. This high urban population will pressurise governments to optimise infrastructure facilities in urban areas for giving a standard quality of life.

It is estimated that by 2050, about two-thirds of the world's population will live in urban areas. It would create a high pressure on existing infrastructure and sanitation, health, crime problems and urban poverty.

There are various factors responsible for growth of urban population

(i) When high birth rate and low morality rate increase.

(ii) Net in-migration or movement of people from other areas.

(iii) Reclassification of urban areas to encompass formerly rural settlements.

In India, there is a estimation that about 60% India's urban population has increased after 1961. About 29% of this growth has been caused by rural-urban migration.

Problems of Slums

- Settlement geography differentiate the two concepts namely urban or urban centres and rural. They are also defined differently in different countries.
- These two are differentiated by their functions but sometimes interdependent on each other. These two concepts are also divided in terms of their separate cultural, economic and technological aspects.
- According to 2011 census, about 69% of India's population is rural. Most of these rural areas are still in poor conditions and perform primary activities.
- According to Mahatma Gandhi, villages are ideal republics. These work as supplement to the core urban centre forming its hinterland.
- Urban areas are more developed in terms of the socio-economic, politico-cultural, etc than other areas.
- Urban areas have farm house, high income of people and their localities, wide roads, street lights, water and sanitation facilities, lawns, well developed green belts, parks, playgrounds and other facilities, provisions for individual security and right of privacy.
- Apart from these attractions urban areas also have slums, *'jhuggi jhopari'* clusters and colonies of shanty-structures.
- These are environmentally incompatible and degraded areas of the cities. These are occupied by the migrants who were forced to migrate from rural areas to urban areas for employment and livelihood. But because of high rent and high costs of land, they could not afford proper housing and start to live in these areas.

Characteristics of Slums

Slums have following characteristics

(i) Slums are **least choice residential areas** that have broken down house, bad hygienic conditions, poor ventilation and does not have basic facilities like drinking water, light and toilet facilities, etc.

(ii) Slums are over crowded with people and have many narrow street patterns prone to serious hazards from fire.

(iv) Most of the slum dwellers works for low wages, high risk-prone and unorganised sectors of the urban economy.

(v) They face various health related problems such as malnutrition, illness and prone to various diseases. They are not able to send their children school to provide them education because of low level of income.

(vi) Dwellers are vulnerable to drug abuse, alcoholism, crime, vandalism, escapism, apathy and social exclusion because of poverty.

Land Degradation

The limited availability and deterioration of quality of land, both are responsible to exert pressure on agricultural land. Soil erosion, water logging, salinisation and alkalinisation of land lead to land degradation which declines productivity of land.

In simple words, temporary or permanent decline in productive capacity of the land is known as land degradation.

All degraded land may not be considered as wasteland. But if process of degradation is not checked, then a degraded land may be converted into **wasteland**. Natural and man-made processes, both degrade the quality of land.

Classification of Wastelands

- **National Remote Sensing Agency (NRSA)** It is an organisation responsible for classification of wastelands in India. It classifies wastelands by using remote sensing techniques on the basis of the processes that have created them.

- **Wasteland Caused by Natural Agents** Gullied/ ravinous land, desertic or coastal sand, barren rocky areas, steep sloping land, glacial areas, etc are types of wastelands caused by the natural agents.
- **Wasteland Caused by Natural as well as Human Factors** Water logged and marshy areas, land affected by salinity and alkalinity and land with and without scrubs which are degraded by the natural as well as human factors are included in this category.
- **Wastelands Caused by Man-made Processes** Shifting cultivation area, degraded land under plantation crops, degraded forests, degraded pastures and mining and industrial wastelands are some types of wastelands that are degraded because of human actions.

PYQs Previous Years' Questions

1 Mark Questions

Multiple Choice Questions

1. Which of the following is not the cause of land pollution? *(CBSE 2023)*
(a) Disposal of untreated industrial waste (b) Use of pesticides and chemical fertilisers
(c) Improper human activities (d) Organic farming

Ans. (d) Organic farming

2. Which one of the following rivers is highly polluted? *(CBSE 2023)*
(a) Kosi (b) Ravi
(c) Narmada (d) Yamuna

Ans. (d) Yamuna

3. Which one of the following is not a significant factor in creating noise pollution? *(CBSE 2023)*
(a) Mechanised construction (b) Automobiles
(c) Fodder cutting machine (d) Variety of industries

Ans. (c) Fodder cutting machine

4. Which one of the following is a major polluting industry? *(CBSE 2023)*
(a) Food processing industry (b) Cottage industry
(c) Chemical industry (d) Food loose industry

Ans. (c) Chemical industry

5. Which one of the following is the cause of acid rainfall? *(CBSE Compartment 2020)*
(a) Water pollution (b) Air pollution
(c) Land pollution (d) Noise population

Ans. (b) Air pollution

6. Land degradation in irrigated areas is caused by which of following reasons? *(CBSE SQP 2019)*
(a) Gully erosion (b) Wind erosion
(c) Salinisation of soil (d) Siltation of land

Ans. (c) Salinisation of soil

7. Which of the following is/are an example of source of surface water?
(a) Lakes (b) Rivers
(c) Canals (d) All of these

Ans. (d) All of these

8. Which of the following natural sources is/are responsible for water pollution?
(a) Erosion
(b) Landslides
(c) Decay and decomposition of plants and animals
(d) All of the above

Ans. (d) All of the above

9. Which of the following activities is the most significant contributor to water pollution?
(a) Industrial activities
(b) Agricultural activities
(c) Cultural activities
(d) None of the above

Ans. (a) Industrial activities

10. Which of the following cities is the main contributor to the pollution of Ganga River?
(a) Kanpur (b) Varanasi
(c) Patna (d) All of these

Ans. (d) All of these

11. Industries produce which type of undesirable products?
(a) Poisonous gases (b) Polluted waste water
(c) Chemical residuals (d) All of these

Ans. (d) All of these

12. Which of the following industries is the major water polluting industry in India?
(a) Leather industry (b) Pulp industry
(c) Paper industry (d) All of these

Ans. (d) All of these

13. Which of the following is the main source of air pollution?
(a) Combustion of fossil fuels (b) Mining
(c) Industry (d) All of these

Ans. (d) All of these

14. Jhabua district is located in which state of India?
(a) Maharashtra (b) Madhya Pradesh
(c) Tamil Nadu (d) Karnataka

Ans. (b) Madhya Pradesh

15. Arrange the following wastelands in sequence in terms of their share in the total geographical area of India.
I. Barren and Uncultivable wasteland
II. Man - made Degraded Culturable wasteland
III. Natural and Man - made Culturable wasteland
IV. Natural Degraded Culturable wasteland

Codes
(a) III, II, IV, I (b) IV, III, II, I
(c) II, I, IV, III (d) I, II, III, IV

Ans. (a) III, II, IV, I

Very Short Answer Questions

1. Why is urban waste a serious problem in India? Explain one reason. *(All India 2019)*

Ans. Urban waste is a serious problem in India because it poses a health hazard through creation of obnoxious smell and harbouring of flies and rodents, which act as carriers of diseases such as typhoid, diphtheria, diarrhoea, malaria, cholera, etc.

2. Why is air pollution a serious problem in India? Explain one reason. *(All India 2019)*

Ans. Air pollution is a serious problem in India because it causes various diseases related to the respiratory, nervous and circulatory systems.

3. What is criterion for the classification of pollution? *(Delhi 2016)*

Ans. Types of pollution are classified on the basis of medium through which pollutants are transported and diffused.

4. Mention any two sources of water pollutants created by humans. *(Delhi 2015)*

Ans. Two sources of water pollutants created by humans are
(i) Sewage disposal
(ii) Toxic effluents from industries.

5. Mention any two diseases caused by contaminated water. *(All India 2014)*

Ans. The two diseases caused by the contaminated water are
(i) Diarrhoea
(ii) Hepatitis

6. Mention any two sources of land pollution in India. *(All India 2013)*

Ans. Two sources of land pollution in India are as follows
(i) Increasing use of chemicals like fertilisers and pesticides in agriculture.
(ii) Increasing industrial activities.

7. Name any two natural sources of water pollution. *(Delhi 2012)*

Ans. Landslides and decay and decomposition of plants and animals are natural sources of water pollution.

8. Name any two diseases that are caused by air pollution. *(All India 2012)*

Ans. Lung cancer and asthama are two diseases caused by air pollution.

9. Mention the root cause of 'acid rains'.

Or Which source of pollution is responsible for acid rains. *(Delhi 2011)*

Ans. Air pollution is responsible for acid rains. It is caused by a chemical reaction that begins when compound like sulphur dioxide and nitrogen oxides are released into the air in atmosphere. They mix and react with water molecules and oxygen to form acidic rain.

10. Name two metropolitan cities which are the main polluters of river Ganga before it reaches Varanasi. *(Delhi 2011)*

Ans. Kanpur and Allahabad are the two metropolitan cities which are the main polluters of river Ganga before it reaches Varanasi.

11. Which city is the main polluter of river Yamuna? *(Delhi 2010)*

Ans. The city which is the main polluter of river Yamuna is Delhi.

12. Which is the main source of environmental pollution in India? *(All India 2010)*

Ans. Industries are the main source of environmental pollution in India.

13. Mention any two cultural activities responsible for water pollution in India. ***(Delhi 2009)***

Ans. The two cultural activities of human beings that make water polluted are

(i) Pilgrimage (ii) Religious fairs

14. Which is the main source of water borne diseases in India? Name any one water borne disease. ***(All India 2009)***

Ans. Water pollution is the main source of water borne diseases in India. The main water borne diseases are

(i) Diarrhoea (ii) Intestinal worms

3 Marks Questions

1. Explain the reasons for the coming up of slums in developing countries like India with suitable examples. ***(CBSE SQP 2018)***

Ans. Slums *(jhuggi-jhopari)* are the clusters and colonies of small house structures. Slums are occupied by those migrants who were forced to migrate from the rural areas to the urban centres in search of livelihood. But due to high rent and high cost of land, they could not afford proper housing and compelled to live in slums. Slums are the residential areas of least choice, which have the following characteristics

(i) Dillapidated (broken-down) houses

(ii) Poor hygienic conditions

(iii) Poor ventilation

(iv) Lack of basic amenities like drinking water, light and toilet facilities

Developing countries like India face the problem of slums on a large scale. India has a predominance of rural population that migrates to urban areas in search of jobs. This increases the population in urban areas. The illiterate and unskilled rural population end up living in drenched housings in slum areas. For example, Dharavi slum of Central Mumbai is Asia's largest slum.

2. Explain the causes and consequences of Rural-Urban migration in India with suitable examples. ***(CBSE SQP 2018)***

Ans. There can be many reasons for migration. These reasons can be put into two broad categories

(i) **Push Factors** These are factors which forces people to leave their place of residence or origin. Some of them are as follows

(a) Natural disaster like flood, drought, cyclonic storms, earthquake, Tsunami, etc.

(b) Political/local conflicts like war, insurgency, riots, etc.

(ii) **Pull factors** These refer to factors which attract the people from different places. Some of them are as follows

(a) Better opportunities for education

(b) Better health facilities

Migration also creates major consequences on people's life. These consequences can be both negative and positive, such as

(i) Remittances (allowance) are important for economy of a country as migrants sent remittances to their family members for food, repayment of loans, etc. Remittance from the international migrants are one of the major sources of foreign exchange. Among the states, Kerala, Andhra Pradesh, Tamil Nadu and Punjab receive maximum remittances.

(ii) Migration leads to the redistribution of the population within a country. The process of urbanisation is dependent on rural-urban migration.

(iii) Migration creates social gap and feeling of depression among individuals due to separation from family and home and loneliness, etc. This feeling ultimately results in anti-social activities such as crime, drug abuse, theft, etc.

(iv) Pressure of overcrowding of people put pressure on existing social and physical infrastructure.

3. How does air pollution affect human health? ***(All India 2019)***

Other Similar Questions

Or Explain any three consequences of air pollution.

Or Explain any three effects of air pollution on human life.

Ans. The main consequences of air pollution are as follows

(i) Air pollution is responsible for many diseases that cause harm to our respiratory, nervous and circulatory systems.

(ii) Air pollution is responsible for creating smoky fog over cities which is known as urban smog. It also has negative effects on human health.

(iii) Air pollution is also responsible for acid rains. First rain after summers in urban area always show acidic nature of rain water i.e. it shows lower pH level than the subsequent rain.

(iv) Air pollution may be harmful to flora and fauna and to property.

4. How does noise pollution affect human health? *(All India 2019)*

Ans. Noise pollution affects human health in the following ways

(i) Noise may permanently damage hearing. A sudden loud noise can cause severe damage to the eardrum.

(ii) Noise increases the chances of occurrence of diseases such as headache, blood pressure, heart failure, etc.

5. ''Indiscriminate use of water by increasing population and industrial expansion has led to degradation of the quality of water considerably.'' Evaluate the statement. *(Delhi 2018)*

HINT *Dear students, this question simply ask you to explain how indiscriminate use of water by increasing population and industrial expansion has led to the degradation of the quality of water.*

Ans. The quality of water is degraded by indiscriminate use of water by increasing population and industrial expansion. It can be explained through the following points

(i) Sewage, garbage and liquid waste of households and industries are discharged into lakes and rivers. These wastes contain harmful chemicals and toxins which make the water polluted.

(ii) The use of various types of chemical fertilisers like inorganic fertilisers, pesticides and herbicides, etc also pollute groundwater, as they infiltrate the soil to reach the groundwater.

(iii) Due to rapid increase in population, huge amount of waste is disposed in the water sources which degrades the quality of water.

6. ''Indiscriminate use of water by increasing population and industrial expansion has led to degradation of the water quality considerably in India''. Explain the values that can help in maintaining the quality of water. *(All India 2017)*

Ans. Following values will help in maintaining the quality of water

Creating Awareness Creating awareness towards our environment is very important. Government should try to make people aware about importance of water.

Values maintaining the quality of water
- Creating Awareness
- Participation of Community
- Use of New Techniques

Participation of Community By creating awareness and making community participate in saving water will help in maintaining quality of water.

Use of New Techniques It will also maintain quality of water.

7. Examine the success of watershed management programme implemented in Jhabua district of Madhya Pradesh. *(All India 2016)*

Ans. The success of Watershed Management programme in Jhabua district can be examined through the following points

(i) Through watershed management programme the degradation of land in Jhabua district has controlled in a significant manner.

(ii) This programme also helped to improve soil quality in the district.

(iii) About 20% of the total area under Jhabua district has treated by the watershed programmes.

(iv) They planted fodder grass on the pasture land and adopted social fencing of these lands for at least two years.

8. Define the term air pollution. Explain any two harmful effects of air pollution. *(Delhi 2015)*

Ans. A larger proportion of contaminants like dust fumes, gas, fog, odour, smoke or vapour to air for a long duration is known as air pollution. It may be harmful to flora and fauna and to property.

For harmful effects of air pollution, refer to Q. 3 of 3 marks questions.

9. How is environment pollution caused? Mention four types of pollution responsible for the environmental degradation. *(Delhi 2015)*

Ans. Pollution is the contamination of the environment by introduction of contaminants that can cause damage to environment and harm or discomfort to humans or other living species. It is the addition of another form of any substance or form of energy to the environment at a faster rate than that the environment can accommodate it by dispersion, breakdown recycling or shortage in some harmless form.

The four types of pollution which are responsible for the environmental degradation are as follows

(i) Water pollution (ii) Air pollution

(iii) Land pollution (iv) Noise pollution

10. How do industries pollute India's water bodies? Explain with examples. *(Delhi 2015)*

Ans. Waste water, poisonous gases, chemical residuals, numerous heavy metals, dust, smoke, etc from industries contribute to water pollution. During the last fifty years, the number of industries in India has grown rapidly.

But water pollution is concentrated within a few sub-sections, mainly in the form of toxic wastes and organic pollutants.

Most of these defaulting industries are leather, pulp and paper, textiles, chemicals, sugar mills, distilleries and thermal power stations. Not all industries have treatment facilities for industrial affluents. As small scale industries cannot afford enormous investments in pollution control equipment as their profit margin is very slender.

11. What is noise pollution? Explain any four sources of noise. ***(All India 2015)***

Other Similar Questions

Or Describe three main sources of noise pollution in India.

Or How has noise pollution become hazardous in many big cities of India? Explain with examples.

Ans. Noise pollution refers to a noise that causes a condition which is unbearable and uncomfortable to human beings. After technological innovations, it has become a serious problem especially in urban areas. The noise can be from various sources such as

(i) Factories, mechanised construction and demolition works, aircrafts, automobiles loudspeaker, siren, etc.

(ii) Noise produced by traffic is a major source of noise pollution. It creates a huge inconvenience to the people. Intensity and nature of noise made by traffic is dependent on various factors such as type of vehicle, (aircraft, train, etc) condition of road and condition of vehicle (in case of automobiles).

(iii) In sea traffic, the noise pollution is limited to the harbour because of loading and unloading activities of containers.

(iv) Noise pollution from industries is also a serious problem, but its intensity varies because of some factors such as types of industry, types of machines and tools, etc.

12. Why is the urban waste disposal a serious problem in India? Explain any three reasons. ***(Delhi 2014)***

Or Urban waste disposal has become a serious problem in India." Support the statement. ***(CBSE Compartment 2020)***

Other Similar Questions

Or Analyse three problems arising as a result of urban waste disposal.

Or Explain any three major problems associated with urban waste disposal in India.

Or Explain with examples any three major problems associated with urban waste disposal in India.

Ans. Mismanagement and environmental problem related to solid waste has now become a major problem due to the following reasons

Impacts of improper management of solid wastes are

(i) Solid wastes are threat to human health and can cause various diseases. It creates foul smell and it harbours flies and rodents that can cause typhoid, diptheria, diarrhoea, malaria, cholera and other diseases.

(ii) Solid waste can create inconvenience rapidly if they are not properly handled, wind and rain water can splitted it and cause a discomfort to people.

(iii) Industrial solid waste can cause water pollution by dumping it into water bodies. Drains carrying untreated sewage also result into various health problems.

13. Describe any three major problems of slums in India. ***(Delhi 2014)***

Or Analyse any three major problems of slum dweller in India. ***(Delhi 2013)***

Or Explain any three problems faced by slum dwellers in India. ***(All India 2012)***

Or How do slums develop in India. Explain any four miserable condition of the residents of slum areas. ***(All India 2010)***

Ans. Slums are environmentally incompatible and degraded areas of the cities. These are occupied by the migrants who were forced to migrate from rural areas to urban areas for employment and livelihood.

Problems faced by the residents of slums are as follows

(i) Slums are least choice residential areas that have broken down houses, bad hygienic conditions, poor ventilation and does not have basic facilities like drinking water, light and toilet, etc.

(ii) They face various health related problems such as malnutrition, illness and prone to various diseases. They are not able to send their children school to provide them education, because of low level of income.

(iii) Dwellers are vulnerable to drug abuse, alcoholism, crime, vandalism, escapism, apathy and social exclusion because of poverty.

14. How is the degradation of cultivable land one of the serious problems in India? Explain in any three points. *(Delhi 2010)*

Ans. Degradation of cultivable land is one of the serious problem in India because

(i) The limited availability and deterioration of quality of land, both are responsible to exert pressure on agricultural land.

(ii) Soil erosion, water logging, salinisation and alkalinisation of land lead to land degradation which decline productivity of land.

(iii) Natural and man-made processes, both degrade the quality of land.

15. State any two major sources of air pollution in India. How is air pollution harmful to human health? Explain. *(Delhi 2008)*

Ans. The main sources of air pollution are release of various gases such as oxides of sulphur and nitrogens, hydrocarbons, carbon dioxide, carbon monoxide, lead and asbestos by combustion of fossil fuels, mining and industries.

For the effects of air pollution, refer to Q. 3 of 3 marks questions.

5 Marks Questions

1. Slums are residential areas of serious health and socio-environmental hazards. Support the statement. *(CBSE 2023)*

Ans. Slums are those area/colonies which are occupied by those migrants who were forced to migrate from the rural areas to urban areas/centres in search of livelihood but due to high rent and high cost of land, they could not afford proper housing.

The Problems of slums in India are as follows

- Slums are environmentally incompatible and degraded areas.
- Slums have dilapidated (broken-down) houses where people are forced to live due to poverty or lesser income.
- People of slums face poor hygenic conditions. Thus, they are prone to many diseases and illness.
- The houses in slums have poor ventilation. So, people residing there face suffocation problems.
- Slums have substandard housing or illegal and inadequate building structures.
- Slums are overcrowed having narrow street pattern which is prone to serious hazards, e.g. Fire hazards because of congested spaces, which increase the chances of its spread.
- Slums lack in basic amenities like drinking water, light and toilet facilities.
- They are marked by unregulated drainage system and open defecation.
- Besides this, most of the slum dwellers engage in low-paid, high risk-prone unorganised sectors of the urban economy. Because of such situation they are undernourished, prone to different types of illness.
- Due to poverty, slum dwellers are unable to give proper education to their children.
- Poverty has also made these people vulnerable to drug abuse, alcoholism, crime, vandalism, escapism, apathy and ultimately social exclusion.

2. How is the use of plastic bags harmful for environmental degradation? Evaluate it by citing suitable reasons. *(CBSE SQP Term II 2021)*

Ans. Use of plastic bags is harmful for environmental degradation in the following ways

(i) The major impact of plastic bags on the environment is that it takes many years to for them to decompose.

(ii) Waste from plastic bags poses serious environmental danger to human and animal health. If plastic bags are not properly disposed of, they can impact the environment by causing littering and stormwater drain blockages.

(iii) Animals often confuse the plastic bags for food and consume them, therefore blocking their digestive processes.

(iv) Plastic buried deep in landfills can drain harmful chemicals that spread into groundwater.

(v) If plastic bags are burned, they release a toxic substance into the air causing ambient air pollution.

3. The disposal of urban waste has become a serious concern for the local authorities. Analyse the statement with suitable examples. *(CBSE SQP Term II 2021)*

Ans. The disposal of urban waste has become a serious concern for the local authorities in the following ways

(i) Tons of waste come out daily in metropolitan cities and are burnt. The smoke released from the waste pollutes the air.

(ii) Lack of sewers or other means to dispose of human excretes safely and the inadequacy of garbage collection sources adds to water pollution.

(iii) The concentration of industrial units in and around urban centres gives rise to a series of environmental problems.

(iv) Dumping of industrial waste into rivers is the major cause of water pollution. The solid waste generation continues to increase in both absolute and per capita in cities.

(v) The improper disposal of solid waste attracts rodents and flies which spread diseases. The thermal plants release a lot of smoke and ash in the air. For example, a plant producing 500MW electricity releases 2000 tons of ash which is difficult to manage.

4. "Land degradation caused by human made processes is more harmful than natural processes in India." Analyse the statement with suitable examples.

(CBSE SQP 2019)

Ans. Land degradation is generally understood either as a temporary or a permanent decline in productive capacity of the land.

The causes or factors responsible for land degradation in India are given below

(i) Soil erosion
(ii) Waterlogging
(iii) Salinisation
(iv) Alkalinisation of land

Land is constantly used without managing its fertility, it is degraded and its productivity declines. Deforestation, overgrazing, mining and quarrying too are responsible for land degradation in India. Thus, land degradation caused by human processes is more harmful than natural processes in India.

Man-made degraded wastelands such as degraded shifting cultivation areas, degraded land under plantation crops, degraded forest, mining and industrial wasteland are 5.8% of the total geographical area of the country.

In states, such as Jharkhand, Chhattisgarh, Madhya Pradesh and Odisha, deforestation due to mining has, caused severe land degradation.

In states, such as Gujarat, Rajasthan, Madhya Pradesh and Maharashtra overgrazing is one of the main reasons for land degradation.

Source Based Questions

1. Read the following source and answer the questions

Jhabua district is located in the westernmost agro-climatic zone in Madhya Pradesh. It is, in fact, one of the five most backward districts of the country. It is characterised by high concentration of tribal population (mostly Bhils). The people suffer due to poverty which has been accentuated by the high rate of resource degradation, both forest and land. The watershed management programmes funded by both the ministries of "Rural Development" and "Agriculture", Government of India, have been successfully implemented in Jhabua district which has gone a long way in preventing land degradation and improving soil quality. Watershed Management Programmes acknowledge the linkage between land, water and vegetation and attempts to improve livelihoods of people through natural resource management and community participation. In the past five years, the programmes funded by the Ministry of Rural Development alone (implemented by Rajiv Gandhi Mission for Watershed Management) has treated 20 per cent of the total area under Jhabua district.

The Petlawad block of Jhabua is located in the northernmost part of the district and represents an interesting and successful case of Government-NGO partnership and community participation in managing watershed programmes. The Bhils in Petlawad block, for example, (Sat Rundi hamlet of Karravat village) through their own efforts, have revitalised large parts of common property resources. Each household planted and maintained one tree on the common property. They also have planted fodder grass on the pasture land and adopted social-fencing of these lands for at least two years. Even after that, they say, there would be no open grazing on these lands, but stall feeding of cattle, and they are thus confident that the pastures they have developed would sustain their cattle in future.

An interesting aspect of this experience is that before the community embarked upon the process of management of the pasture, there was encroachment on this land by a villager from an adjoining village. The villagers called the tehsildar to ascertain the rights of the common land. The ensuing conflict was tackled by the villagers by offering to make the defaulter encroaching on the CPR a member of their user group and sharing the benefits of greening the common lands/ pastures. ***(CBSE 2023)***

(i) Why did the people of Jhabua tribal community suffer from poverty?
(a) High rate of forests degradation
(b) Land degradation
(c) Illiteracy
(d) Implementation of watershed management

Ans. (a) High rate of forests degradation

(ii) How did people manage to develop pasture lands? Choose the correct option.
(a) Use of barbed wire to protect pastures.
(b) Pasture land were not under any encroachment.
(c) Pasture were common property resources hence they developed it.
(d) Government officials did not interfere in any work of the villagers.

Ans. (c) Pasture were common property resources hence they developed it.

(iii) How did the Bhils, through their own efforts revitalise the common property resources? Choose the correct option
(a) Common land was brought under cultivation
(b) They controlled open grazing on the common property resources.
(c) No tree plantation was taken up
(d) They developed water resources

Ans. (b) They controlled open grazing on the common property resources.

2. Read the case study given below and answer the questions that follow.

Based on the universal law 'Polluter pays', a silent but strong effort to restore the ecology and safeguard the human health with people's participation has taken place in Daurala near Meerut. These efforts are now bearing fruits after a span of three years when Meerut based NGO had developed a model for ecological restoration. The recent meeting of the Daurala Industries officials, NGOs, Government officials and other stakeholders at Meerut has brought out results which usually come out mainly through the court's decisions.

The powerful logics, authentic studies and the pressure of the NGO has in a way brought a new lease of life to the twelve thousand residents of this village. It was in the year 2003, that the pitiable condition of Dauralaites drew the attention of the civil society. The groundwater of this village with a population of 12,000 persons was contaminated with heavy metals. The reason was that the untreated wastewater of Daurala industries was leaching to the groundwater table and was also being used for irrigation.

The activists of the NGO conducted a door to door survey of the health status of the residents and came out with a report. The group reported that 192 deaths in the past five years have been recorded in the village due to consumption of contaminated water.

The industry came under pressure due to activism. The organisation, the village community and people's representatives sat together to find out sustainable solutions to this problem. The industrialists showed a keen interest towards checking the deteriorating ecology. The overhead water tank's capacity in the village was enhanced and a 900m extra pipeline was laid to serve potable water to the community. The silted pond of the village has been cleaned and recharged by desilting it. Large quantity of silt was removed paving way to pure water so that it percolated deep down the aquifers. Rainwater harvesting structures have been constructed at different places which has helped in diluting the contaminants of the groundwater after the monsoons. 1000 trees have also been planted which have improved the environment. ***(CBSE SQP 2023)***

(i) What type of pollution is faced by the people of Daurala?
(a) Noise pollution
(b) Air pollution
(c) Water pollution
(d) Land pollution

Ans. (c) Water pollution

(ii) Which process led to contamination of ground water?
(a) Salinisation (b) Alkalisation
(c) Leaching (d) Over irrigation

Ans. (c) Leaching

(iii) What was the most important step taken as sustainable solution to the health problem faced by the villagers?
(a) Relocation of industries
(b) Controlled irrigation
(c) Evacuation from the affected area
(d) Enhancement of water storage capacity

Ans. (d) Enhancement of water storage capacity

(iv) Which water conservation strategy help in diluting the contamination of the ground water?
(a) Rain water harvesting
(b) Universal law of 'Polluter Pays'
(c) Industrial waste treatment plant
(d) Over utilisation of ground water

Ans. (a) Rain water harvesting

3. Read the case study given below and answer the questions that follow.

Case Study : A Role Model to restore the Ecology and Safeguard Human Health in Daurala

Based on the universal law "Polluter pays", effort to restore the ecology and safeguard the human health with people's participation has taken place in Daurala near Meerut. These efforts are now bearing fruits after a span of three years when Meerut based NGO had developed a model for ecological restoration. The meeting of the Daurala Industries officials, NGOs, Government officials and other stakeholders at Meerut has brought out results. The powerful logics, authentic studies and the pressure of people have brought a new lease of life to the twelve thousand residents of this village. It was in the year 2003 that the pitiable condition of Dauralaites drew the attention of the civil society. The groundwater of this village was contaminated with heavy metals. The reason was that the untreated wastewater of Daurala industries was leaching to the groundwater table. The NGO conducted a door to door survey of the health status of the residents and came out with a report. The organisation, the village community and people's representatives sat together to find out sustainable solutions to the health problem. The industrialists showed a keen interest towards checking the deteriorating ecology. The overhead water tank's capacity in the village was enhanced and a 900m extra pipeline was laid to supply potable water to the community. The silted pond of the village was cleaned and recharged by desilting it. Large quantity of silt was removed paving way to large quantity of water so that it recharged the aquifers. Rainwater harvesting structures have been constructed at different places which has helped in diluting the contaminants of the groundwater after the monsoons. 1000 trees have also been planted which have improved the environment.

(i) What is meant by water pollution?

Ans. Water pollution is the contamination of water bodies, usually as a result of human activities, so that it negatively affects its uses. Water bodies include lakes, rivers, oceans, aquifers, reservoirs and groundwater.

(ii) Explain the role of industrialise in checking the deteriorating ecology.

Ans. The industrialists showed a keen interest towards checking the deteriorating ecology. They provided water tank capacity by laying down 900m extra pipeline to supply portable water to the Daurala community. The Silted pond of the village was cleaned and recharged by desilting it.

(iii) Analyse the contribution of the NGO in Daurala's problem.

Ans. The NGO conducted a door to door survey of health status of the residents and came out with a report that suggest that the groundwater of the village Daurala was contaminated by heavy metal. The NGO provided a model for ecological restoration such as rainwater harvesting, and plantation of thousand trees, etc.

CHAPTER TEST

01 Mark Questions

1 Which of the following is responsible for the occurrence of acid rain?
(a) Air pollution (b) Water pollution
(c) Noise pollution (d) Soil pollution

2 What causes land pollution?
(a) Fertilisers
(b) Untreated industrial waste
(c) Pesticides
(d) All of the above

3 The air pollution is a major cause of
(a) lung cancer (b) obesity
(c) Both (a) and (b) (d) heart disease

4 Which of the following is not a result of land degradation?
(a) Drought
(b) Afforestation
(c) Over irrigation
(d) Use of excessive amount of chemical fertilisers

5 Which of the following activities is the major significant contributor to water pollution?
(a) Industrial activity (b) Cultural activity
(c) Agricultural activity (d) Tertiary activities

Answers

1. (a) | 2. (d) | 3. (c) | 4. (b) | 5. (a)

03 Marks Questions

6 Describe the problems of slum in India.

7 What are the effects of water pollution on health? Suggest measures.

8 Mention the major problems associated with the urban waste disposal in India.

05 Marks Questions

9 How do slum develop in India? Explain any four miserable conditions of the residents of slum area.

10 How does industries pollute India's water bodies? Explain with examples.

11 The indiscriminate use of water by increasing population and industrial expansion has led to the degradation of quality of water. Suggest some measures to solve the issues.

CBSE

CHAPTERWISE QUESTION BANK

2024-2011

Sample Papers (1-3)

CBSE Fully Solved

SAMPLE PAPER 01

Time : 3 hrs
Marks : 70

Geography XII

1. This question paper contains 30 questions. All questions are compulsory.
2. This question paper is divided into five sections – Sections A, B, C, D and E.
3. Section A - Question number 1 to 17 are Multiple Choice type questions carrying 1 mark each.
4. Section B - Question number 18 and 19 are Source based questions carrying 3 marks each.
5. Section C - Question number 20 to 23 are Short Answer type questions carrying 3 marks each. Answer to these questions shall be written in 80 to 100 words.
6. Section D - Question number 24 to 28 are Long Answer type questions carrying 5 marks each. Answer to these questions shall be written in 120 to 150 words.
7. Section E - Question number 29 and 30 are Map based questions.

Section A

1. In which of the following types of agriculture is the farming of citrus fruit very important?

(a) Market gardening (b) Plantation agriculture
(c) Mediterranean agriculture (d) Co-operative farming

Ans. *(c)* Mediterranean agriculture

2. Arrange the following areas of commercial grain farming from East to West direction.

I. Eurasian Steppes
II. The Pampas of Argentina
III. The Velds of South Africa
IV. The Australian Downs

Codes

(a) I, II, III, IV (b) IV, I, III, II
(c) III, IV, II, I (d) I, IV, II, III

Ans. *(b)* IV, I, III, II

3. Identify the correct order of the Indian states which are arranged in the decreasing order in terms of their population density.

(a) Uttar Pradesh, West Bengal, Bihar
(b) Bihar, West Bengal, Uttar Pradesh
(c) West Bengal, Uttar Pradesh, Bihar
(d) Bihar, Uttar Pradesh, West Bengal

Ans. *(b)* Bihar, West Bengal, Uttar Pradesh

4. Which of the following is the sub-field of Economic Geography?

(a) Military Geography (b) Historical Geography
(c) Medical Geography (d) Geography of Marketing

Ans. *(d)* Geography of Marketing

5. Read the following information carefully and identify the correct option for settlement.

- These are formed due to segmentation of large village.
- These units are locally called as Panna, Palli, Nagla, etc.
- The segmentation is based on ethnicity and social factors.

Options

(a) Clustered settlement
(b) Hamleted settlement
(c) Semi-clustered settlement
(d) Dispersed settlement

Ans. *(b)* Hamleted settlement

6. Which of the following is the main characteristic of the Stage-I of Demographic Transition Theory ?
(a) High fluctuating fertility and high mortality rates
(b) Time of population explosion
(c) Decline in fertility and mortality rates
(d) All of the above

Ans. *(a)* High fluctuating fertility and high mortality rates

7. Which of the following pairs is incorrectly matched?

Location		Mineral
(a) Bella	–	Manganese
(b) Damodar Valley	–	Copper
(c) Sundergarh	–	Iron Ore
(d) Amarkantak	–	Bauxite

Ans. *(b)* Damodar Valley – Copper

8. Consider the following statements and choose the correct answer with the help of given options.
Assertion (A) Intensive irrigation has led to tremendous rise in agricultural and live stock productivity in the Indira Gandhi command area.
Reason (R) Intensive irrigation has led to excessive water logging and soil salinity.
Codes
(a) Both A and R are true and R is the correct explanation of A
(b) Both A and R are true, but R is not the correct explanation of A
(c) A is true, but R is false
(d) A is false, but R is true

Ans. (b) Both A and R are true, but R is not the correct explanation of A

9. Which of the following has a direct impact on human beings?
(a) Soils (b) Climate (c) Relief (d) Minerals

Ans. *(b)* Climate

10. Consider the following statements and choose the correct answer with the help of given options.
Assertion (A) India has adopted measures like reducing import duties, delicencing, and trade liberalisation.
Reason (R) India aims to expand its share of International Trade.
Codes
(a) Both A and R are true and R is the correct explanation of A
(b) Both A and R are true, but R is not the correct explanation of A
(c) A is true, but R is false
(d) A is false, but R is true

Ans. *(a)* Both A and R are true and R is the correct explanation of A

11. Consider the following statements and choose the correct option.
I. In mass production, each worker performs only one task repeatedly.
II. Mass production involves production of large quantities of standardised parts.
Codes
(a) Only statement I is correct
(b) Both the statements are true and statement II correctly present the reason for statement I
(c) Only statement II is correct
(d) Both the statements I and II are incorrect

Ans. *(b)* Both the statements are true and statement II correctly present the reason for statement I

12. Match the Column-I with Column-II and choose the correct option.

Column I (Copping season)	Column II (Major crop)
A. Kharif	1. Vegetables
B. Rabi	2. Rice
C. Zaid	3. Maize

Codes

	A	B	C		A	B	C
(a)	1	2	3	(b)	1	3	2
(c)	2	3	1	(d)	3	1	2

Ans. *(c)* 2 3 1

13. Which is the longest National Highway of India?
(a) NH-1 (b) NH-7 (c) NH-6 (d) NH-8

Ans. *(b)* NH-7

14. According to which approach of Human Geography does nature get humanised?
(a) Environmental Determinism (b) Possibilism
(c) Neo-determinism (d) None of these

Ans. *(b)* Possibilism

Study the following data and answer question no. 15 to 17.

Direction of India's Import trade
(In crore rupees)

Region	Imports	
	2010-11	2016-17
Europe	3323857	403972
Africa	118612	193327
North America	100602	195332
Latin America	64576	115762
Asia and ASEAN	1029881	1544520

15. Which region contributes to largest share in India's imports?
(a) Europe (b) Africa
(c) Asia and ASEAN (d) North America

Ans. (c) Asia and ASEAN

16. The largest proportion of India's exports and imports are carried out by
(a) Land routes (b) Sea routes
(c) Air routes (d) Both (b) and (c)

Ans. (d) Both (b) and (c)

17. Which among the following measures can help in increasing India's international trade?
(a) Import liberalisation (b) Licencing
(c) Increasing import duties (d) Strict patent laws

Ans. (a) Import liberalisation

Section B

18. Read the following paragraph and answer the questions that follow.

The existence of a market for manufactured goods is the most important factor in the location of industries. 'Market' means people who have a demand for these goods and also have the purchasing power (ability to purchase) to be able to purchase from the sellers at a place. Remote areas inhabited by a few people offer small markets. The developed regions of Europe, North America, Japan and Australia provide large global markets as the purchasing power of the people is very high. The densely populated regions of South and South-East Asia also provide large markets. Some industries, such as aircraft manufacturing, have a global market. The arms industry also has global markets.

Labour supply is an important factor in the location of industries. Some types of manufacturing still require skilled labour. Increasing mechanisation, automation and flexibility of industrial processes have reduced the dependence of industry upon the labours.

Speedy and efficient transport facilities to carry raw materials to the factory and to move finished goods to the market are essential for the development of industries. The cost of transport plays an important role in the location of industrial units. Western Europe and Eastern North America have a highly developed transport system which has always induced the concentration of industries in these areas.

Modern industry is inseparably tied to transportation systems. Improvements in transportation led to integrated economic development and regional specialisation of manufacturing. Communication is also an important need for industries for the exchange and management of information.

(i) Give examples of some industries which have a global market.

Ans. Industries such as aircraft manufacturing, arms industry and basic industries (e.g. iron and steel) have a global market.

(ii) What makes markets important for industries?

Ans. Markets are important for industries due to following reasons
- Industries manufacture goods and commodities and search for people who have demand for these products.
- Markets provide such locations where people who have a demand for these goods and also have the purchasing power (ability to purchase) to be able to purchase from the sellers at a place.

(iii) State two reasons which explain why the dependence of industries upon the labours has reduced.

Ans. Two reasons which explain why the dependence of industries upon the labours has reduced are given below
- Increasing mechanibation
- Automation and flexibility of industrial processes

19. Study the graph carefully and answer the questions.

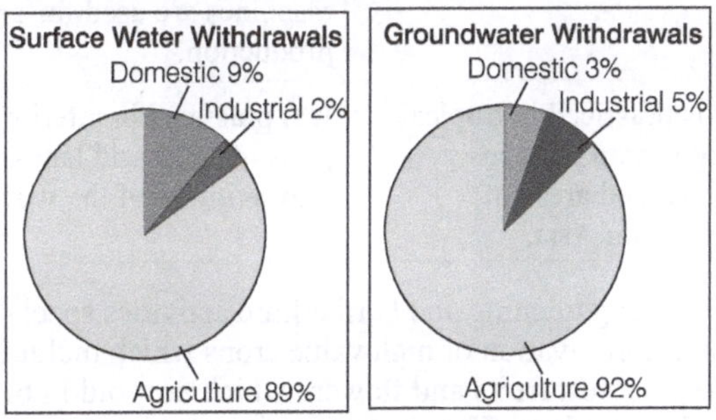

Source Earth Trend 2001, World Resource Institute, as given in Government of India.

(i) Which sector accounts for the lowest usage of surface water in India?

Ans. Industrial sector accounts for the lowest usage of surface water.

(ii) What is the reason for high usage of groundwater in agriculture?

Ans. The reason for high usage of groundwater in agriculture is it is used for irrigation.

(iii) Overuse of groundwater leads to which problems?

Ans. Overuse of groundwater leads to the following problems

- Increase in fluoride concentration
- Increase in arsenic concentration

Section C

20. Write any three differences between subsistence agriculture and commercial agriculture.

Or What do you understand by market gardening and horticulture? Analyse any three characteristics of this type of agriculture.

Ans.

Subsistence Agriculture	Commercial Agriculture
In subsistence agriculture, the local farming areas consume all or nearly all of the products locally grown.	Commercial agriculture includes growing of crops for the market which may be regional markets or international markets.
Landholdings are very small due to high density of population.	Size of landholdings is large in commercial agriculture.
It is less capital intensive and cultivation is done with primitive tools.	It is highly capital intensive and cultivation is highly mechanised as machines are used for crop production.
It is practiced in tropical regions and in densly populated areas of Monsoon Asia.	It is practiced in interior parts of semi-arid lands of mid-latitudes of the world.

Or Market gardening and horticulture activities specialise in the cultivation of high value crops which includes vegetables, fruits and flowers which are sold in the urban markets. The characteristics of this type of agriculture are

(i) This type of agriculture is both labour as well as capital intensive as it involves use of technology, building farms, transport and communication facilities, etc.

(ii) Farms are smaller in size and are located where there are good transportation links with the urban centres.

(iii) It lays emphasis on the use of irrigation, HYV seeds, fertilisers, insecticides, greenhouse gases and artificial heating infrastructure in colder regions.

(iv) It is well developed in densely populated industrial districts of North-Western Europe, North-Eastern United States and Mediterranean regions.

21. Highlight both positive and negative effects of urbanisation.

Ans. **Positive Effects**

- When people move to urban areas, the demand for goods and services, which is usually already high in more populated areas, increases even more.
- People can participate in policy making and welfare schemes.
- Rise in the standard of living.

Negative Effects

- Higher concentration of population in cities has resulted in accommodation problems, growth of slums, etc.
- In metro cities like Delhi, Mumbai, Bengaluru, etc. higher cost of living makes it difficult for lower income groups to maintain a decent standard of living.
- In cities, high rate of crimes is a result of lack of employment and education opportunities.

22. Describe the development of plantation agriculture in the world.

Or What are the specialised activities practiced in the industrial regions of Europe and America? Describe any one.

Ans. Plantation agriculture is the type of agricultural activity in which crops are grown for the purpose of profit.

Development of plantation agriculture in the world took place in the following ways

(i) The European colonialists introduced plantation agriculture in the world, mainly in their colonies situated in the tropics.

(ii) The French colonialists established cocoa and coffee plantations in West Africa.

(iii) The British established large tea gardens in India and Sri Lanka, rubber plantations in Malaysia and sugarcane, banana plantations in West Indies.

(iv) Spanish and Americans invested in the coconut and sugarcane plantations in the Philippines.

(v) The Dutch colonialists established sugarcane plantations in Indonesia.

After these colonies got independence, majority of the plantations have passed on to the governments of the independent countries.

Or Market gardening and factory and truck farming are the two specialised activities that are well developed in the industrial regions of Europe and America.

Truck Farming and Factory Farming Track farming is practiced in the peripheral areas of metropolitan cities where vegetables and milk are brought daily to the cities by trucks by travelling overnight.

This farming requires a well-developed network of roads connected with fields.

In truck farming, farmers only grow vegetables which are sold in the urban markets.

In factory farming, livestock is reared in stalls and pens. The livestocks reared include poultry and cattle, which produces products such as milk, eggs, butter, etc.

The livestock is fed by manufactured feedstuffs and it is carefully protected from diseases which is done by veterinary services.

Scientific methods of breeding are used in the selection of the best quality of breeds of livestock.

It requires heavy capital investment in terms of building, machinery and various other operations carried out in farms.

It is practiced in USA, UK and the developed countries of Western Europe.

23. "Land degradation caused by human made processes is more harmful than natural processes in India." Justify the statement with suitable examples.

Ans. Land degradation caused by human made processes is more harmful than natural processes. These are degraded lands such as degraded shifting cultivation areas, degraded land under plantation crops degraded forests due to indiscriminate cutting of trees, degraded pastures and mining and industrial wastelands. The degradation caused by human actions makes the good fertile land unsuitable for cultivation.

Fewer degraded lands such as gullied/ravinous land, desertic or coastal sands, barren and rocky areas, steep sloping lands and glacial areas are primarily caused by natural agents, but these are further aggravated human factors. This leads to permanent degradation in these lands.

The land which can be rejuvenated by using the land reclaimation techniques is mainly degraded by the man made forces. It is evident from the fact that in India man-made degraded culturable wasteland accounts for almost 6 per cent of the total geographical area of the country whereas natural degraded culturable wasteland accounts for only 2.4 per cent of the geographical area of India.

Section D

24. Explain any two methods that can be used to conserve the depleting resources of water in India.

Or What are the major problems in the development of water resources in the country? Discuss in brief.

Ans. Two methods used to conserve the depleting resources of water in the country include

Watershed Management

- Watershed management refers to the efficient management and conservation of surface and groundwater resources. It involves the prevention of runoff water and storage and recharge of groundwater by the use of percolation tanks, recharge wells, etc.
- Watershed management includes conservation, regeneration and judicious use of all resources–including land resources, plants, animals, etc.
- It involves community participation and the support of both Central and State Governments. Some of these programmes have also been implemented by NGOs.
- Programmes such as Haryali and Neeru-Meeru have been successful in conserving water for drinking, irrigation, fishing, etc.

Rainwater Harvesting

- Rainwater harvesting is a method to capture and store rainwater for various uses. It is a low cost and eco-friendly technique for preserving every drop of water. Rainwater harvesting is practiced by digging wells, recharge pits, etc.
- It increases water availability, checks the declining groundwater level and improves the quality of groundwater by dilution of contaminants like fluoride and nitrates.
- Traditional rainwater harvesting in rural areas is done by using surface storage bodies like lakes, ponds, irrigation tanks, etc. In Rajasthan, rainwater harvesting structures are known as kund or tanka.
- Rainwater can also be conserved by harvesting rainwater on rooftops and open spaces which also bridges the demand supply gap in water and conserve water for future uses.

Or The major problems in the development of water resources in the country are as follows

- **Insufficient Availability of Water** Total available water resource in India has been estimated to be around 1869 cubic km. Out of this, only 1140 cubic km water potential is available for utilisation. Availability of water in ratio of population is low and per capita availability is decreasing day by day.
- **Uneven Distribution of Water** Distribution of water resource in India is very uneven. Some areas are facing scarcity while some have surplus. Hence, it creates difficulty improperly managing the resources.
- **Over Utilisation of Water** Due to over utilisation of this valuable resource, it is difficult to provide water to all regions. Over supply of water in urban areas results in lack of water supply in other areas.
- **Deteriorating Quality of Water** Despite having access to water supply, there is a major issue of quality of water. Poor quality water and polluted water resources causes various water borne diseases such as diarrhoea.

25. Name the source of population data in India. Give a brief account on the population of India.

Or State what important steps have been taken by the Government of India to solve the problems of adolescents.

Ans. In India, population data is collected through Census which held every 10 years in our country. The recent Census was conducted in 2011. In India, spatial pattern of population distribution is very uneven. As some areas are sparsely populated, whereas other are dense. These states can be categorised into three categories

(i) **States with High Population** Uttar Pradesh (highest population), Maharashtra, Bihar, West Bengal, Andhra Pradesh, Tamil Nadu together account for 76% of population.

(ii) **States with Moderate Population** Assam, Haryana, Jharkhand, Chhattisgarh, Kerala, Punjab and Goa have moderate population.

(iii) **States with Low Population** Hilly and tribal areas like Jammu and Kashmir (now UT), Uttarakhand, All North-Eastern States (except Assam) and Union Territories excluding Delhi and Chandigarh have low population.

Population is mainly affected by climate, terrain and availability of water. For example, the North Indian Plains, deltas and coastal plains are densely populated, whereas the mountainous areas and interior areas of Central and Southern India have relatively low population. Besides these, evolution of settled agriculture and urbanisation are the socio-economic and historical factors of distribution of population.

Or The Government of India has undertaken certain policies to solve the problems of adolescents and to impart proper education to the adolescent group so that their talent are better channelised and properly utilised. These are

- The programme like SABLA for adolescent girls and SAKSHAM for adolescent boys are being executed by government to improve the nutrition level and provide skills to youth.
- Various efforts are being taken by Centre and State Governments to empower the youth and to achieve their full potential under the National Youth Policy.
- In National Youth Policy 2014, the government defined youth of age group 15-29 years and proposed to empower the youth of country to achieve their full potential.
- Kishori Shakti Yojana (KSY) is redesign version of the already existing Adolescent Girls (AG) Scheme. The objectives of this scheme are to improve the nutritional health and development status of adolescent girls, promote awareness of health and hygiene, nutrition and family care, help them gain a better understanding of their social environment and take initiatives to become productive members of the society.

26. Write with examples the three economic factors and two socio-cultural factors influencing the population distribution in the world.

Ans. The three economic factors influencing the distribution of population in the world are as follows

(i) **Minerals** Areas with mineral deposits attract industries, which generate huge employment and skilled and semi-skilled workers that settle in these areas.

(ii) **Urbanisation** Urban centres offer better employment opportunities, education and medical facilities and better means of communication which attract population.

(iii) **Industrialisation** Industrial belts provide job opportunities. These attract not only factory workers, but also transport operators, shopkeepers, bank employees, doctors, teachers and other service providers.

Two social and cultural factors influencing the distribution of population in the world are as follows

(i) **Religious and Cultural Significance** Places having religious importance and cultural significance tend to attract number of people due to which they are densely populated.

(ii) **Social and Political Unrest** Places where there is political turmoil and social unrest are not fit for living. Thus, people tend to move away from those areas. This makes them sparsely populated.

27. Explain how the size of a territory and per capita income are not directly related to human development? State with examples.

Or

How can you say that different marketing centres try to provide services by targeting different markets?

Ans. It is true that size of the territory and per capita income are not directly related to human development. It can be explained through the following points

- According to United Nations Development Programme, human development is standing on four basic pillars like equity, sustainability, productivity and empowerment. Per capita income or size of the territory is not mentioned in it.
- These pillars consider all the aspects that affect human life like health, education, access to resources of a country and other social indicators along with economic indicators. No country can achieve a desired goal of human development on the basis of per capita income alone. Human development is about all round development of people in all aspects of life.
- The economic structure of a country is the most important indicator of human development. The size of a territory does not play any role in it. The advanced countries have higher level of economic prosperity, while the less developed and backward countries are at lower level of economic growth.
- The developed country's per capita income is indirectly related to economic structure. The size of a territory and per capita income are not directly related to human development but it does play some role.

Or There are three types of trading centres or marketing centres which provide different services to target their markets. These are:

(i) **Rural Marketing Centres** These centres cater to nearby settlements. These are quasi-urban centres. Here, personal and professional services are not well-developed. These are in the form of local collecting and distribution centres. Most of these have *mandis* (wholesale markets) and also retailing areas. They are significant centres for making available goods and services which are most frequently demanded by rural people.

(ii) **Periodic Markets** These markets are found where there are no regular markets and local periodic markets are organised at different temporal intervals. These may be weekly, bi-weekly markets from where people from the surrounding areas meet their temporally accumulated demand. These markets are held on specific days and move from one place to another. The shopkeepers thus, remain busy on all the days while a large area is served by them.

(iii) **Urban Marketing Centres** These have more widely specialised urban services. They provide ordinary goods and services as well as many of the specialised goods and services required by people. Urban centres, therefore, offer manufactured goods, as well as many specialised markets develop. For example, markets for labour, housing and semi or finished products. Different services are also available in these markets like services of educational institutions such as teachers, lawyers, consultants, physicians, dentists and veterinary doctors, etc.

28. Discuss any five important characteristics of plantation agriculture in the world.

Ans. Important characteristics of plantation agriculture can be seen through the following points

- Plantation agriculture was introduced by the Europeans in their colonies situated in tropics.
- Crops which are grown in plantations are cash crops. It means that these crops are cultivated to be sold in the market for profit. These include crops like coffee, sugarcane and rubber.
- Estates or plantations are large and the capital invested in them is also huge.
- Work in these plantations is done by specialised labour and there is application of machinery and fertilisers to get high yields and a large output.
- Nearly all the production in plantation agriculture is exported to the international market. Thus, it is characterised by packaging and processing facilities.
- Managerial and technical support is provided and cultivation is done by scientific methods.

- Generally, there is single crop specialisation i.e. only one crop is cultivated at a time.
- Cheap labour and good transportation system which links the estates to the factories and markets for the export of products are essential.

Section E

29. In the given political map of the world, seven features are shown by (i), (ii), (iii), (iv), (v), (vi) and (vii). Identify the features with the help of the information given below and write their correct names on the lines marked in the map.

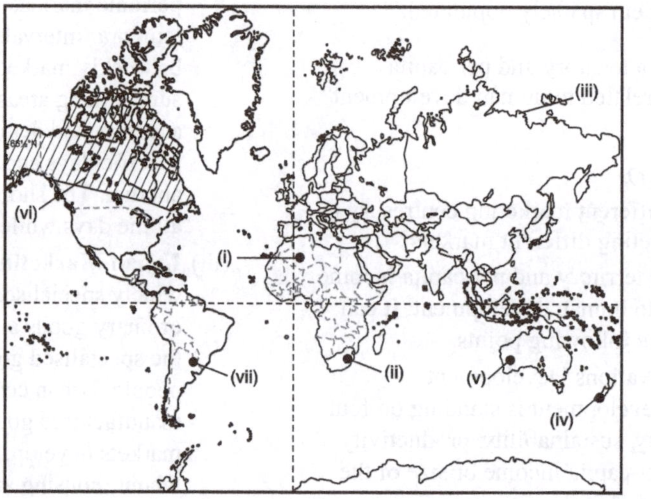

(i) The largest country in Africa in terms of area.
(ii) A major area of mixed farming.
(iii) An area of nomadic herding.
(iv) An area of extensive commercial grain farming.
(v) A major sea port in Australia.
(vi) An area where gathering is practiced.
(vii) An international airport.

Ans.

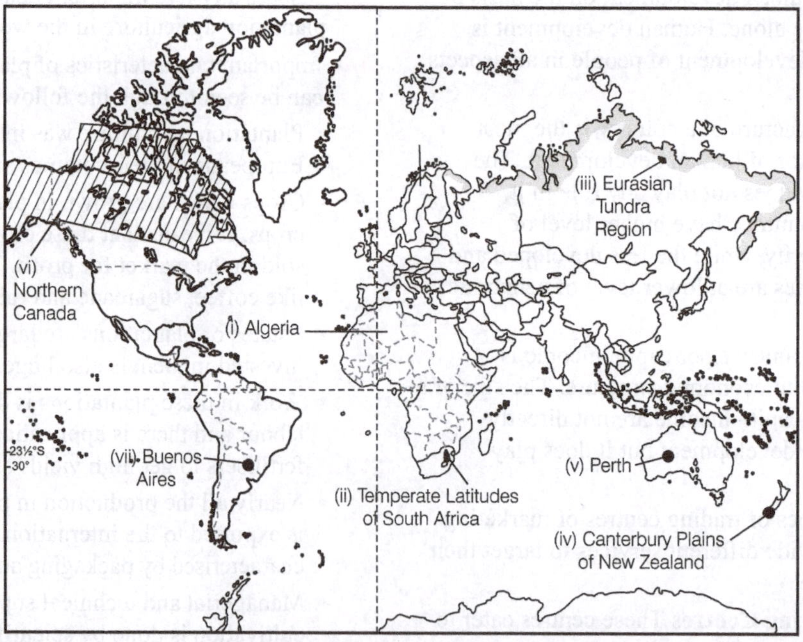

30. On the political outline map of India, mark and locate any five of the following features.

(i) State having highest population density.
(ii) Singhbhum copper mine.
(iii) Leading producer of wheat.
(iv) Mathura oil refinery.
(v) An area in Madhya Pradesh famous for the Manganese mineral.
(vi) An oil refinery in Gujarat.
(vii) An iron ore mine in Odisha.

Ans.

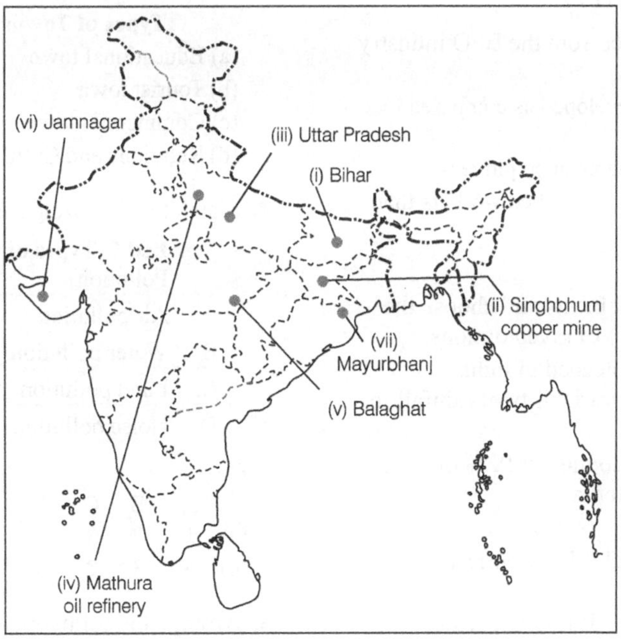

CBSE Unsolved

SAMPLE PAPER 02

Time : 3 hrs
Marks : 70

Geography XII

1. This question paper contains 30 questions. All questions are compulsory.
2. This question paper is divided into five sections – Sections A, B, C, D and E.
3. Section A - Question number 1 to 17 are Multiple Choice type questions carrying 1 mark each.
4. Section B - Question number 18 and 19 are Source based questions carrying 3 marks each.
5. Section C - Question number 20 to 23 are Short Answer type questions carrying 3 marks each. Answer to these questions shall be written in 80 to 100 words.
6. Section D - Question number 24 to 28 are Long Answer type questions carrying 5 marks each. Answer to these questions shall be written in 120 to 150 words.
7. Section E - Question number 29 and 30 are Map based questions.

Section A

1. The KPO industry is distinct from the BPO industry such that

(a) KPO industry is underdeveloped as compared to BPO industry.
(b) KPO industry has more women employees.
(c) KPO industry involves more skilled workers than BPO industry.
(d) None of the above

2. Consider the following statements and choose the correct answer with the help of given options.

Assertion (A) Irrigation is needed in India because of spatio-temporal variability of rainfall in the country.

Reason (R) Agriculture accounts for 92% of groundwater utilisation in India.

Codes

(a) Both A and R are true and R is the correct explanation of A
(b) Both A and R are true, but R is not the correct explanation of A
(c) A is true, but R is false
(d) A is false, but R is true

3. Which of the following pairs is correctly matched?

Types of Towns	Examples
(a) Educational town	– Jodhpur
(b) Tourist town	– Aligarh
(c) Commercial town	– Satna
(d) Religions and Cultural town	– Sharanpur

4. Match the following List I with List II.

	List I (Types of Pollution)		List II (Sources)
A.	Air pollution	1.	Industrial processing
B.	Water pollution	2.	Combustion of coal
C.	Land pollution	3.	Industrial waste
D.	Noise pollution	4.	Agricultural runoff

Codes

	A	B	C	D		A	B	C	D
(a)	1	2	3	4	(b)	2	4	3	1
(c)	4	3	2	1	(d)	3	4	2	1

5. Arrange the following approaches of Human Geography in chronological order.

I. Exploration and Description
II. Regional Analysis

III. Post Modernism
IV. Areal Differentiation

Codes

(a) I, II, III, IV (b) IV, III, II, I
(c) I, II, IV, III (d) II, I, III, IV

6. Consider the following statements and choose the correct option.

I. The people begin to understand their environment and the forces of nature with the passage of time.

II. With social and cultural development, humans develop better and more efficient technology.

Codes

(a) Only statement I is correct
(b) Both the statements are true and statement II correctly present the reason for statement I
(c) Only statement II is correct
(d) Both the statements I and II are incorrect

7. Which of the following States/UTs are arranged in decreasing order of their percentage of urban population correctly?

(a) Delhi, Maharashtra, Kerala, Assam
(b) Delhi, Kerala, Maharashtra, Assam
(c) Maharashtra, Delhi, Kerala, Assam
(d) Assam, Delhi, Maharashtra, Kerala

8. Consider the following statements and choose the correct answer with the help of given options.

Assertion (A) In India, the work participation rate tends to be higher in areas of lower levels of economic development.

Reason (R) A large number of manual workers are needed to perform subsistence activities.

Codes

(a) Both A and R are true and R is the correct explanation of A
(b) Both A and R are true, but R is not the correct explanation of A
(c) A is true, but R is false
(d) A is false, but R is true

9. Which of the following approaches of Human Development was developed by the International Labour Organisation (ILO)?

(a) Welfare Approach
(b) Basic/Minimum Needs Approach
(c) Income Approach
(d) Capabilities Approach

10. Which of the following is/are a basic industry?

(a) Aircraft industry (b) Iron industry
(c) Television industry (d) All of these

11. Which river supplies freshwater to the Suez Canal?

(a) Amazon (b) Nile
(c) Congo (d) Murray

12. Which one of the following types of industries produces raw materials for other industries?

(a) Cottage industries (b) Small-scale industries
(c) Basic industries (d) Footloose industries

13. Read the following information carefully and identify the correct option for the type of agriculture.

- The farms are not extensive but moderate in size.
- Important crops are wheat, barley, oats, rye and maize.
- Soil fertility maintained through crop rotation and inter cropping.

Options

(a) Commercial grain farming (b) Mixed farming
(c) Dairy farming (d) Truck farming

14. In which state is Bharmaur tribal region situated?

(a) Himachal Pradesh (b) Uttarakhand
(c) Uttar Pradesh (d) Jammu and Kashmir

Study the graph given below and answer the question no. 15 to 17.

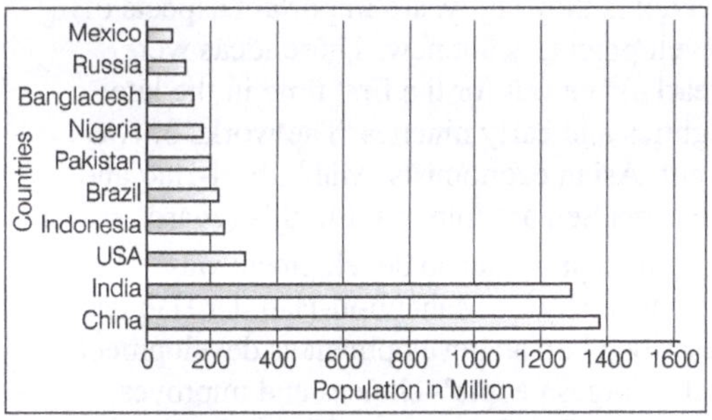

Most populous countries

15. Which among the following countries is the most populous?

(a) Mexico (b) Bangladesh
(c) Brazil (d) Nigeria

16. Which among the following continents has the largest number of most populous countries?

(a) Asia (b) North America
(c) South America (d) Africa

17. Which of the following countries is the least populous?

(a) Brazil

(b) Indonesia

(c) Russia

(d) Pakistan

Section B

18. Read the following paragraph and answer the questions that follow.

Both growth and development refer to changes over a period of time. The difference is that growth is quantitative and value neutral. It may have a positive or a negative sign. This means that the change may be either positive (showing an increase) or negative (indicating a decrease). Development means a qualitative change which is always value positive. This means that development cannot take place unless there is an increment or addition to the existing conditions. Development occurs when positive growth takes place. Yet, positive growth does not always lead to development. Development occurs when there is a positive change in quality.

The idea that the quality of life people enjoy in a country, the opportunities they have and freedoms they enjoy, are important aspects of development, is not new. These ideas were clearly spelt out for the first time in the late eighties and early nineties. The works of two South Asian economists, Mahbub-ul-Haq and Amartya Sen are important in this regard.

The concept of human development was introduced by Dr Mahbub-ul-Haq. Dr Haq has described human development as development that enlarges people's choices and improves their lives. People are central to all development under this concept. These choices are not fixed but keep on changing. The basic goal of development is to create conditions where people can live meaningful lives. A meaningful life is not just a long one. It must be a life with some purpose. This means that people must be healthy, be able to develop their talents, participate in society and be free to achieve their goals. Leading a long and healthy life, being able to gain knowledge and having enough means to be able to live a decent life are the most important aspects of human development.

(i) What is the most important feature of Human Development?

(ii) State any two reasons that can reduce the Human Development of a region.

(iii) What comes at the centre of the development in the concept of Human Development?

19. Study the map given below carefully and answer the following questions.

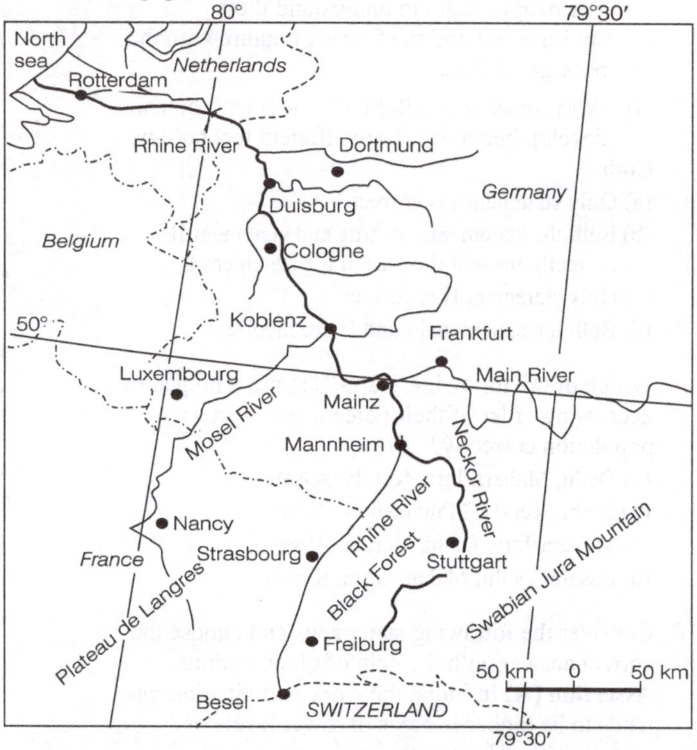

(i) Name the inland waterway shown in the map.

(ii) This waterway connects industrial areas of which countries of Europe?

(iii) State any two characteristics of this waterway.

Section C

20. "Watershed management can play an important role in sustainable development." Explain.

Or Explain any three benefits of rainwater harvesting.

21. Why is the service sector considered as an important sector in the world? How is it different from primary and secondary sectors?

Or "Though the digital means of communication have revolutionised the world but still there exists a significant digital divide." Explain.

22. Differentiate between compact settlement and nucleated settlement.

23. Explain the distribution of solar energy and wind energy in India.

Section D

24. Discuss any five factors influencing the distribution and density of population.

25. "Hill Area Development Programmes in India were drawn keeping in view their topographical, ecological, social and economic conditions." Support this statement with suitable examples.

Or

Development is a multi-dimensional concept and signifies the positive, irreversible transformation of the economy, society and environment. Support the statement with suitable arguments from India.

26. Define the main features of population growth from 1901-2011.

Or

Discuss why there is uneven distribution of population in India.

27. Explain the land use categories as maintained in the land revenue records.

28. Compare and contrast between nomadic herding and commercial livestock rearing.

Or

What is collective farming? Mention its four features.

Section E

29. In the given political map of the world, seven geographical features are shown by (i), (ii), (iii), (iv), (v), (vi) and (vii). Identify any five of the features with the help of the information given below and write their correct names on the lines marked in the map.

(i) Largest country in North America
(ii) A major airport
(iii) An area of mixed farming
(iv) An area of extensive commercial grain farming
(v) An area of commercial livestock rearing
(vi) A major airport
(vii) A major sea port

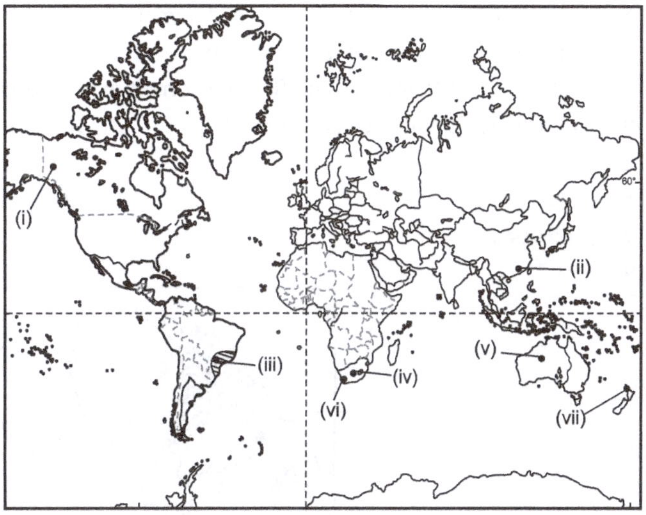

30. On the political outline map of India, mark and locate any five of the following features.

(i) The state having the highest population density
(ii) An iron-ore mine in Jharkhand
(iii) An oil refinery in Bihar
(iv) The leading cotton producing state
(v) The leading wheat producing state
(vi) A copper mine in Rajasthan
(vii) A bauxite mine in Madhya Pradesh

Answers

1. (c) KPO industry involves more skilled workers than BPO industry.
2. (b) Both A and R are true, but R is not the correct explanation of A
3. (c) Commercial town – Satna
4. (b) 2 4 3 1
5. (c) I, II, IV, III
6. (b) Both the statements are true and statement II correctly present the reason for statement I
7. (b) Delhi, Kerala, Maharashtra, Assam
8. (a) Both A and R are true and R is the correct explanation of A
9. (b) Basic/Minimum Needs Approach
10. (b) Iron industry
11. (b) Nile
12. (c) Basic industries
13. (b) Mixed farming
14. (a) Himachal Pradesh
15. (i) (c) Brazil
16. (a) Asia
17. (c) Russia
29.

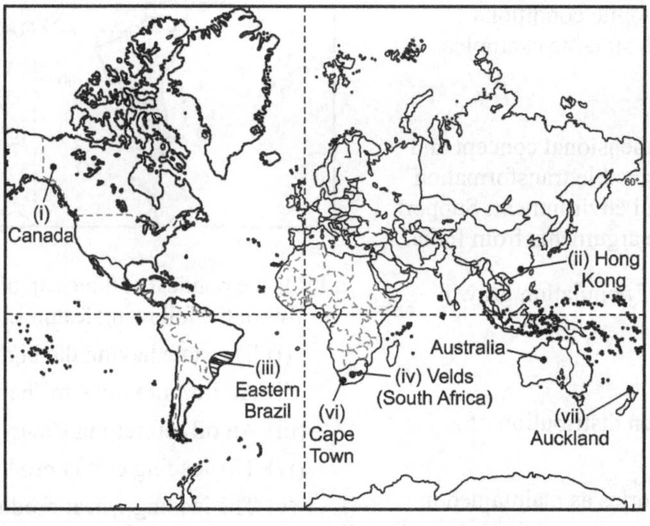

30.

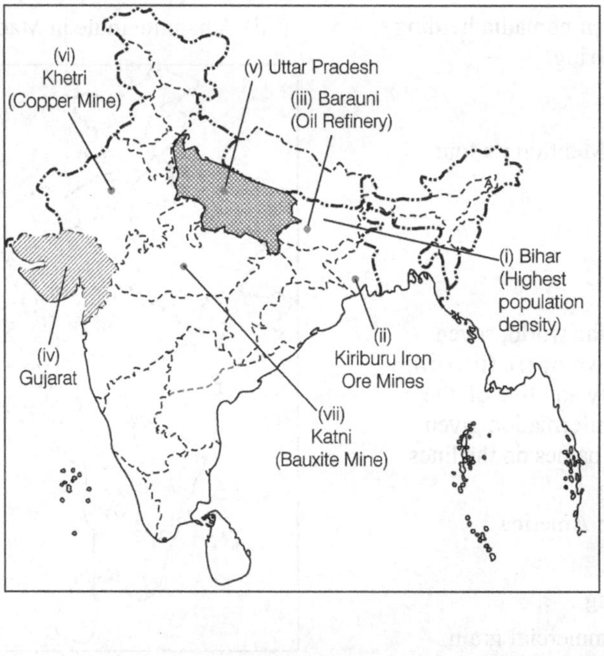

CBSE Unsolved

SAMPLE PAPER 03

Geography XII

Time : 3 hrs
Marks : 70

1. This question paper contains 30 questions. All questions are compulsory.
2. This question paper is divided into five sections – Sections A, B, C, D and E.
3. Section A - Question number 1 to 17 are Multiple Choice type questions carrying 1 mark each.
4. Section B - Question number 18 and 19 are Source based questions carrying 3 marks each.
5. Section C - Question number 20 to 23 are Short Answer type questions carrying 3 marks each. Answer to these questions shall be written in 80 to 100 words.
6. Section D - Question number 24 to 28 are Long Answer type questions carrying 5 marks each. Answer to these questions shall be written in 120 to 150 words.
7. Section E - Question number 29 and 30 are Map based questions.

Section A

1. Which of the following modes of transport can only carry freight?
(a) Airways (b) Railways (c) Pipelines (d) Roads

2. Which of the following pairs is incorrectly matched?

Railway Zone		Headquarters
(a) Central	–	Mumbai CST
(b) East Coast	–	Bhubaneswar
(c) North Central	–	Allahabad
(d) North Eastern	–	Maligaon

3. Singreni coal field is located in
(a) Telangana (b) Tamil Nadu
(c) Maharashtra (d) Punjab

4. Which of the following business is conducted in bulk?
(a) Retail trading (b) Urban marketing centres
(c) Wholesale trading (d) Periodic markets

5. Match the Column I with Column II and choose the correct option.

	Column I (Crops)		Column II (Major States of Production)
A.	Wheat	1.	Maharashtra
B.	Bajra	2.	Gujarat
C.	Groundnut	3.	West Bengal
D.	Jute	4.	Uttar Pradesh

Codes

	A	B	C	D		A	B	C	D
(a)	1	2	3	4	(b)	2	1	4	3
(c)	4	1	2	3	(d)	2	4	3	1

6. Arrange the following events in the history of international trade in a sequential order.
I. Trade on silk route.
II. Trade growth after industrial revolution.
III. Slave trade.
IV. Growth of trade between Europe and Asia.

Codes
(a) I, III, II, IV (b) II, I, III, IV
(c) I, IV, III, II (d) I, II, III, IV

7. Which one of the following sectors have been arranged in sequence according to the groundwater withdraws in India from maximum to minimum?
(a) Industrial sector, Domestic sector, Agriculture sector
(b) Agriculture sector, Industrial sector, Domestic sector
(c) Domestic sector, Industrial sector, Agriculture sector
(d) Industrial sector, Agriculture sector, Domestic sector

8. Who among the following gave the concept of 'Traffic Signal Lights' in his approach in Human Geography?
(a) Ratzel (b) Ellen C Semple
(c) Paul Vidal de la Blache (d) Griffith Taylor

9. Which of the following pairs is correctly matched?

Types of pollution		Sources
(a) Air pollution	–	Industrial processing
(b) Water pollution	–	Combustion of coal
(c) Land pollution	–	Industrial waste
(d) Noise pollution	–	Agricultural runoff

10. Which one of the following best describes the concept of development?
(a) Change in quality of the population.
(b) An increase in the population.
(c) Maintaining the consistency of income in the population.
(d) A positive change in quality of the population.

11. Consider the following statements and choose the correct answer with the help of given options.
Assertion (A) India has emerged as the leading country in medical tourism in the world.
Reason (R) There has been a positive growth in the medical facilities in India during the past 30 years.
Codes
(a) Both A and R are true and R is the correct explanation of A
(b) Both A and R are true, but R is not the correct explanation of A
(c) A is true, but R is false
(d) A is false, but R is true

12. Consider the following statements and choose the correct option.
I. Minerals are evenly distributed over space.
II. There is inverse relationship in quality and quantity of minerals i.e. good quality minerals are less in quantity
Codes
(a) Only statement I is correct
(b) Both the statements are true and statement II correctly present the reason for statement I
(c) Only statement II is correct
(d) Both the statements I and II are incorrect

13. Read the following information carefully and identify the correct option for inland national waterways.
- It stretches from Allahabad to Haldia covering around 1620 km.
- It is divided into three parts for developmental purposes.
- It is navigable by mechanical boats up to Patna.

Options
(a) NW3 (b) WW2 (c) NW1 (d) NW5

14. Consider the following statements and choose the correct answer with the help of given options.
Assertion (A) The contribution of agriculture has declined over time but the pressure on land for agriculture has not declined.
Reason (R) The number of people in India is increasing day by day.
Codes
(a) Both A and R are true and R is the correct explanation of A
(b) Both A and R are true, but R is not the correct explanation of A
(c) A is true, but R is false
(d) A is false, but R is true

Study the following graph and answer the questions no. 15 to 17.

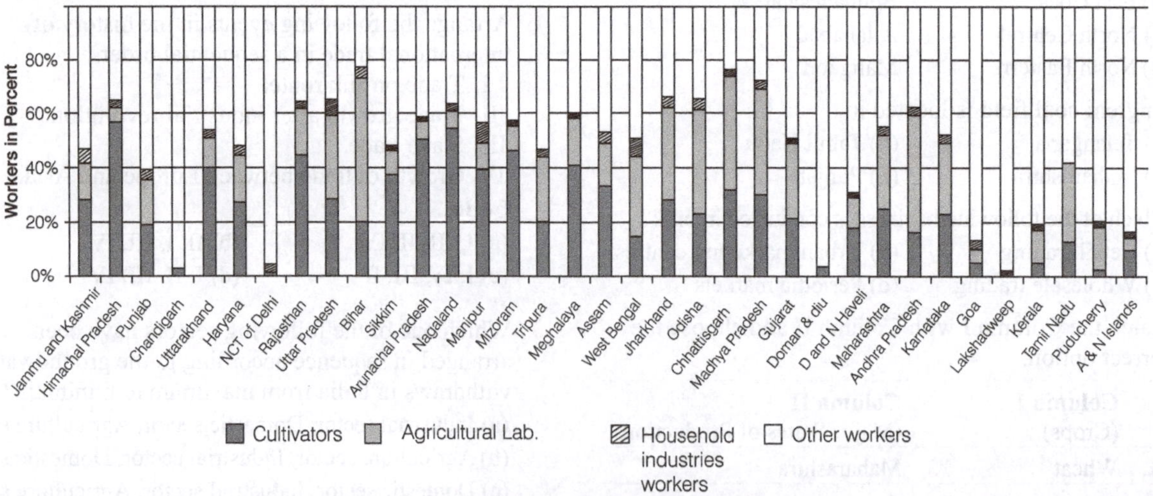

India-Occupational Structure, 2011

15. Which state has higher proportion of cultivators as compared to others?
(a) Rajasthan (b) Goa (c) Tamil Nadu (d) Puducherry

16. In which of the following state there is very high percentage of agricultural labourers?
(a) Nagaland (b) Karnataka (c) Bihar (d) Punjab

17. Majority of the workers of India are engaged in which of the following activities?
(a) Manufacturing (b) Household activities
(c) Industries (d) Agriculture

Section B

18. Read the following paragraph and answer the questions that follow.

The division of the society into male, female and transgender is believed to be natural and biological. But, in reality, there are social constructs and roles assigned to individuals which are reinforced by social institutions. Consequently, these biological differences become the basis of social differentiations, discriminations and exclusions. The exclusion of over half of the population becomes a serious handicap to any developing and civilised society. It is a global challenge, which has been acknowledged by the UNDP when it mentioned that, "If development is not engendered it is endangered" (HDR UNDP 1995). Discrimination, in general, and gender discrimination, in particular, is a crime against humanity.

All efforts need to be made to address the denial of opportunities of education, employment, political representation, low wages for similar types of work, disregard to their entitlement to live a dignified life, etc. A society, which fails to acknowledge and take effective measures to remove such discriminations, cannot be treated as a civilised one. The Government of India has duly acknowleged the adverse impacts of these discriminations and launched a nationwide campaign called 'Beti Bachao – Beti Padhao'.

(i) Which factors can create discriminations and exclusions in a society? State any two reasons.
(ii) In India, this sector of economy has the higher number of women workers.
Name it.
(iii) State the purpose of launching the Beti Bachao-Beti Padhao scheme in India.

19. Study the figure given below and answer the questions that follows.

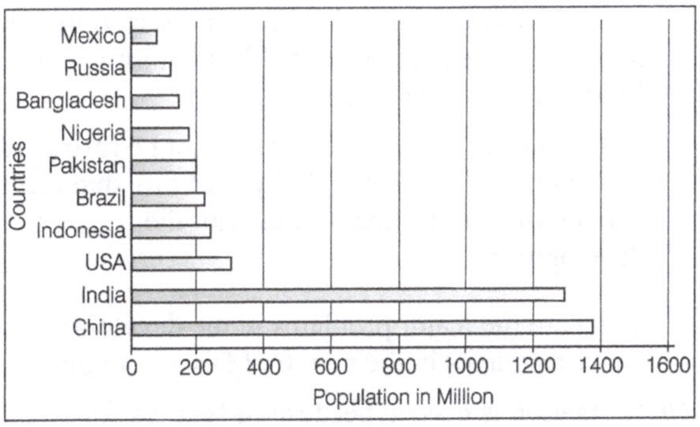

Most Populous Countries

(i) Out of the 10 most populous countries of the world, how many are located in Asia?
(ii) Which factors affect population distribution?
(iii) The fifth most populous country is located in which continent?

Section C

20. How can we define ferrous minerals? What is the importance of the category of 'other non-metallic minerals'?

Or

"Non-conventional resources are very important for producing eco-friendly energy." Explain.

21. Which states of India have high demand for irrigation? How do they benefit from irrigation water supply?

22. "Outsourcing has resulted in opening up a large number of job opportunities in several countries." Analyse the statement with three suitable examples.

Or

What do you understand by tourism? Analyse any three tourist attraction in the world?

23. State any three difference between water and air transportation.

Section D

24. Give a brief account on the scope of Human Geography.

25. "Economic development of a region is dependent upon its resources base but sometimes resource rich regions also remain backward." What measures has India taken to remove this anomaly?

Or "The concept of development cannot be restricted to economic sphere alone". In light of this statement, explain the multi-dimensionality of the concept of development.

26. What are the major problems in the development of water resources in the country? Discuss in brief.

Or "Irrigation is needed because of spatio-temporal variability in rainfall in India." Analyse the statement.

27. How air transport is advantageous for international trade? Also mention its demerits.

28. What makes high-tech industries more important in the world? State any five characteristics of this industry.

Or "The location of industries should be at a point where the production costs are minimum." Justify the statement.

Section E

29. In the given political map of the world, seven geographical features are shown by (i), (ii), (iii), (iv), (v), (vi) and (vii). Identify any five of the features with the help of the information given below and write their correct names on the lines marked in the map.

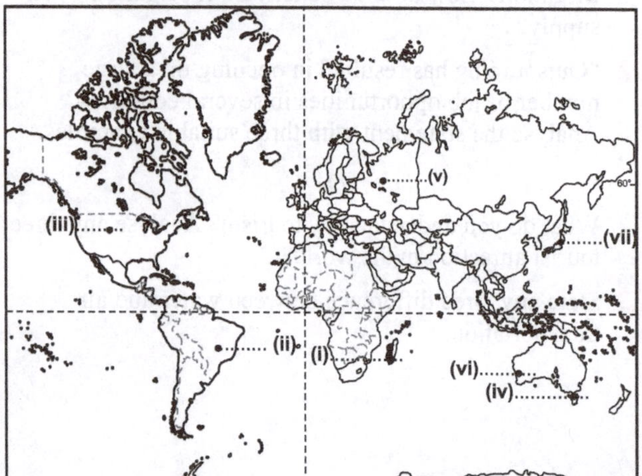

(i) An area of nomadic herding.
(ii) Largest country in South America.
(iii) An area of extensive commerical grain cultivation.
(iv) An Island where dairy farming is practiced.
(v) A major airport
(vi) A major sea port
(vii) A major airport

30. Locate and label any five of the following features on the given map of India.

(i) Shimoga manganese mine.
(ii) Major cotton producing state.
(iii) An oil refinery.
(iv) An iron ore mine Chhattisgarh
(v) A coal mine in Tamil Nadu.
(vi) Bellary iron-ore mine.

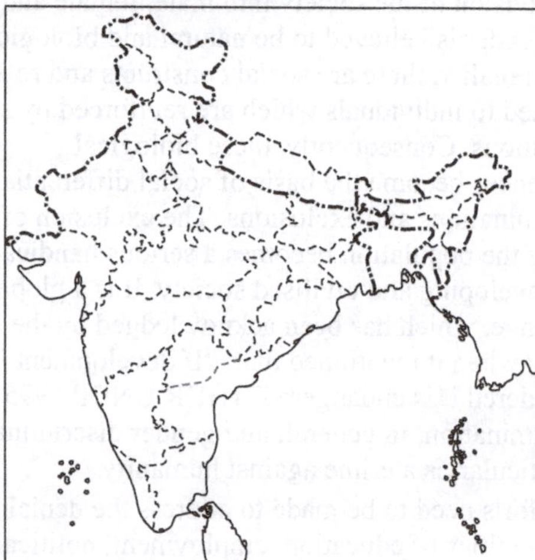

Answers

1. (c) Pipelines
2. (d) North Eastern – Maligaon
3. (a) Telangana
4. (c) Wholesale trading
5. (c) 4 1 2 3
6. (c) I, IV, III, II
7. (b) Agriculture sector, Industrial sector, Domestic sector
8. (d) Griffith Taylor
9. (c) Land pollution – Industrial waste
10. (d) A positive change in quality of the population

11. (a) Both A and R are true and R is the correct explanation of A
12. (c) Only statement II is correct
13. (c) NW1
14. (a) Both A and R are true and R is is the correct explanation of A
15. (a) Rajasthan
16. (c) Bihar
17. (d) Agriculture
29.

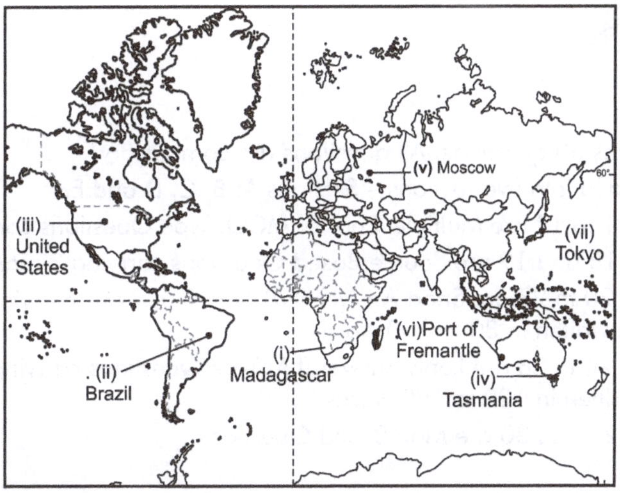

30.

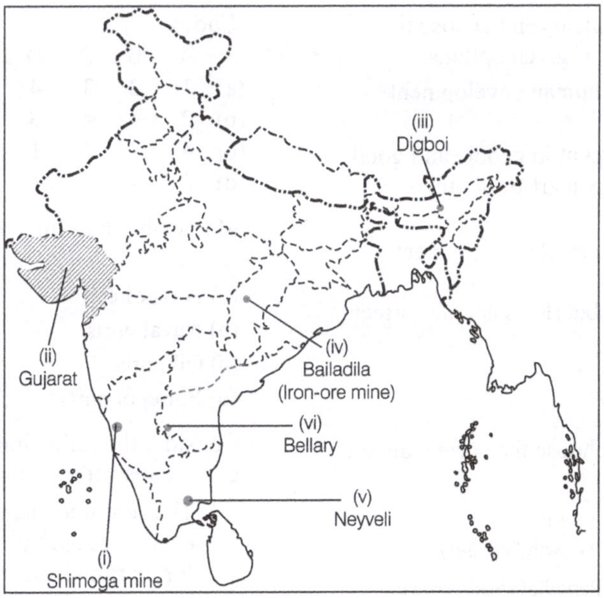

CBSE Fully Solved

LATEST SAMPLE PAPER

Time : 3 hrs
Marks : 70

Geography XII

1. This question paper contains 30 questions. All questions are compulsory.
2. This question paper is divided into five sections – Sections A, B, C, D and E.
3. Section A – Questions no. 1 to 17 are Multiple Choice (MCQ) Type Questions carrying 1 mark each.
4. Section B – Questions no. 18 and 19 are Source Based Questions carrying 3 marks each.
5. Section C – Questions no. 20 to 23 are Short Answer (SA) Type Questions carrying 3 marks each. Answer to these questions shall be written in 80 to 100 words.
6. Section D – Questions no. 24 to 28 are Long Answer (LA) Type Questions carrying 5 marks each. Answer to these questions shall be written in 120 to 150 words.
7. Section E – Questions no. 29 and 30 are Map Based Questions.

Section A

1 Consider the following statements and choose the correct answer with the help of given options.

Assertion (A) High level of human development group has 53 countries.

Reason (R) A higher investment in people and good governance has set this group apart from others.

Codes

(a) Both (A) and (R) are true and (R) is the correct explanation of A.

(b) Both (A) and (R) are true, but (R) is not the correct explanation of A.

(c) Both (A) and (R) are false.

(d) (A) is true, but (R) is false.

2 Consider the following and choose the correct answer with the help of given codes

List I (Stages of Population)	List II (Growth Features)
A. Period between 1901 to 1921	1. Period of steady growth
B. Period between 1921 to 1951	2. Phase of stagnant growth of Population
C. Period between 1951 to 1981	3. High but decreasing growth rate
D. After 1981 till present	4. Period of population explosion

Codes

	A	B	C	D
(a)	1	2	3	4
(b)	2	1	4	3
(c)	4	3	2	1
(d)	2	1	3	4

3 Maracaibo, Esskhira and Tripoli ports are classified as ………………… .

(a) Ports of call

(b) Naval ports

(c) Oil ports

(d) Entrepot ports

4 Consider the following statements and choose the correct answer with the help of given option.

I. The resource intensive approach of modern expensive agriculture has become unmanageable for marginal and small farmers due to very meager or no saving to invest in agriculture.

II. Most of such farmers have resorted to availing credit from various institutions and money lenders but crop failures and low returns from agriculture have forced them to fall in the trap of indebtedness.

Options

(a) Both the statements are true.

(b) Only statement I is true.

(c) Only statement II is true.

(d) Both the statements are false.

5 Given below is a list of pillars of human development and its indicators. Which of the following pairs is not correctly matched?

(a) Equity – Making equal access to opportunities available to everybody

(b) Sustainability – Continuity in the availability of opportunities

(c) Productivity – Resources must be used keeping in mind the future

(d) Empowerment – To have the power to make choices

6 Which one of the following is the largest linguistic group of India?

(a) Sino-Tibetan (b) Austric

(c) Indo-Aryan (d) Dravidian

7 When was the GATT transformed into World Trade Organisation (WTO)?

(a) 1st January, 1994 (b) 1st July, 1994

(c) 1st January, 1995 (d) 1st July, 1995

8 Which of the following is an example of low order service?

(a) Teacher (b) Gardener (c) Lawyer (d) Musician

9 In which of the following group of countries of the world, HYV of wheat and rice were developed?

(a) Japan and Australia

(b) Mexico and Philippines

(c) USA and Japan

(d) Mexico and Singapore

10 Consider the following statements and choose the correct answer with the help of given options.

Statement I In recent years- ropeways, cableways and pipelines were developed as a means of transport.

Statement II They were developed to cater to the demands of transporting specific goods under special circumstances.

Options

(a) Only statement I is correct.

(b) Only statement II is correct.

(c) Both the statements are correct, and statement II correctly explains statement I.

(d) Both the statements are true, but not related with each other.

11 Given below are the steps to generate geothermal energy. Arrange the following in correct sequence

I. It is so hot that when it rises to the Earth's surface, it turns into steam.

II. Groundwater in such areas (where the geothermal gradient is high) absorbs heat from the rocks and becomes hot.

III. This steam is used to drive turbines and generate electricity.

IV. Geothermal energy exists because the Earth grows progressively hotter with increasing depth.

(a) IV II I III (b) II I IV III

(c) I IV III II (d) III II IV I

12 Which of the following is not the benefit of rainwater harvesting?

(a) It increases water availability.

(b) It checks the declining groundwater table.

(c) It improves the quality of ground water through dilution of contaminants like fluoride and nitrates.

(d) Helpful in production of hydroelectricity.

13 Which of the following plans was introduced to improve the conditions of roads in India after independence?

(a) Five Year Road Plan (b) Nagpur Plan

(c) Ten Years Road Plan (d) Twenty Years Road Plan

14 If you are asked to formulate the National Water Policy, what will be the utmost important priority for you.

(a) To provide water for generation of hydroelectricity.

(b) Availability of water for industries.

(c) To provide drinking water.

(d) Availability of water for navigation.

Directions Read the following graph and answer questions no 15 to 17.

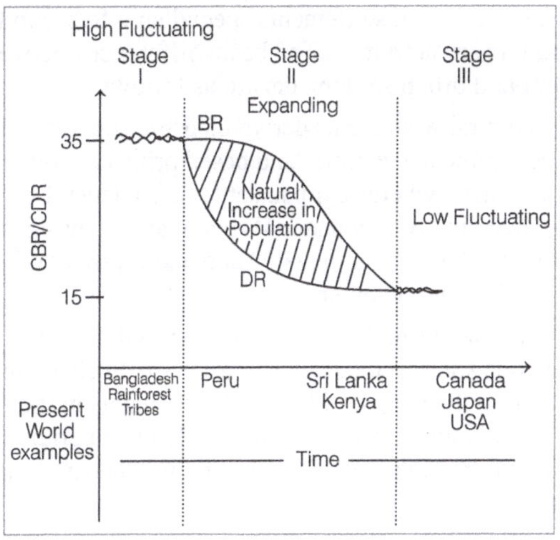

15 How does the natural increase in population occur, as per the graph?

(a) Birth Rate – Death Rate
(b) Death Rate + Birth Rate
(c) Growth Rate – Birth Rate
(d) Birth Rate + Migration

16 What does the transition from high fluctuating stage to low fluctuating stage indicate?

(a) Shift from urban industrial economy to rural agrarian economy.
(b) Shift from rural agrarian economy to urban industrial economy.
(c) Low birth and death rate to high birth and death rate.
(d) Migration from urban to rural areas.

17 From the given graph, what condition can you infer about the least developed countries?

(a) High birth rate and high death rate
(b) Low birth rate and low death rate
(c) High birth rate and low death rate
(d) Low birth rate and high death rate

Section B

18 Read the given passage carefully and answer the questions that follow.

Settlements vary in size and type. They range from a hamlet to metropolitan cities. With size, the economic character and social structure of settlements changes and so do its ecology and technology. Settlements could be small and sparsely spaced, they may also be large and closely spaced. The sparsely located small settlements are called villages, specialising in agriculture or other primary activities. On the other hand, there are fewer but larger settlements which are termed as urban settlements specialising in secondary and tertiary activities. The basic differences between rural and urban settlements are as follows:

- The rural settlements derive their life support or basic economic needs from land based primary economic activities, whereas, urban settlements depend on processing of raw materials and manufacturing of finished goods on the one hand and a variety of services on the other.
- Cities act as nodes of economic growth, provide goods and services not only to urban dwellers, but also to the people of the rural settlements in their hinterlands in return for food and raw materials. This functional relationship between the urban and rural settlements takes place through transport and communication network.
- Rural and urban settlements differ in terms of social relationship, attitude and outlook. Rural people are less mobile and therefore, social relations among them are intimate.
  In urban areas, on the other hand, way of life is complex and fast, and social relations are formal.

(a) On what basis rural and urban settlements can differ from each other.
(b) 'Towns act as nodes of economic growth.' How?
(c) Social relationships are more intimate in rural areas in comparison to urban areas. Justify.

19 Observe the given map and answer the following questions.

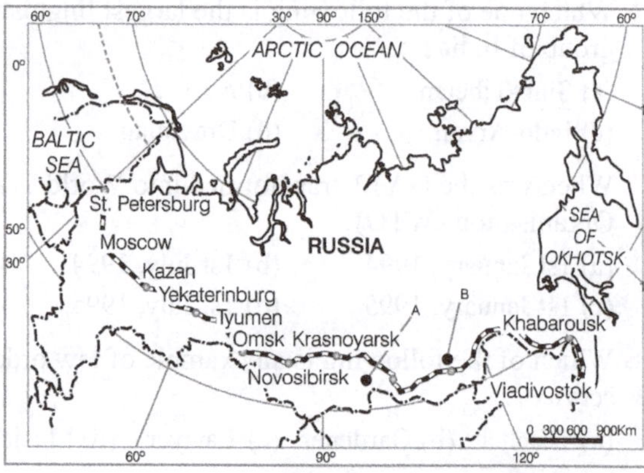

(a) Name the Railway line and the country where it lies.
(b) Name the stations marked as A and B.
(c) State two reasons why it is the most important route in Asia?

Section C

20 "The basic goal of development is to create conditions where the people can live a meaningful life". What do you mean by meaningful life?

Or

How do people's choices get affected in different aspects of life due to lack of human development?

21 What are the features of National Youth Policy?

22 How is 'Naturalisation of Humans' different from 'Humanisation of Nature'?

Or 'Geography got subjected to dualism and the wide-ranging debates started with regard to the subject matter of geography as a discipline.' Mention any three dualism that exist in Geography.

23 ''Quaternary activities centre around research and development.'' Examine the statement.

Section D

24 ''There is low yield per acre but high yield per person in the interior parts of semi-arid lands of the mid-latitudes in the world.'' Support the statement with suitable examples from different parts of the world.

25 Formulate the guidelines to promote sustainability in the Indira Gandhi Canal Command Area.

26 Land degradation in India is caused by human made processes that are more harmful than natural processes. Explain the statement with suitable examples.

Or

How has noise pollution become a serious problem in recent years in India? Explain.

27 How technological innovations are important aspect of modern manufacturing industries? Explain any five aspects.

Or

''High technology, or simply high-tech, is the latest generation of manufacturing activities.'' Justify the statement with suitable arguments.

28 What are the advantages of sea ports for India?

Or

Why is seaport termed as gateway of international trade?

Section E

29 On the given political map of the World, seven geographical features have been marked as A, B, C, D, E, F and G. Identify any five with the help of the following information and write their correct names on the lines drawn near each feature.

(i) A major seaport

(ii) An international airport

(iii) An important Seaway

(iv) An area of subsistence gathering in South America

(v) An important seaport of Asia

(vi) An area of Nomadic Herding

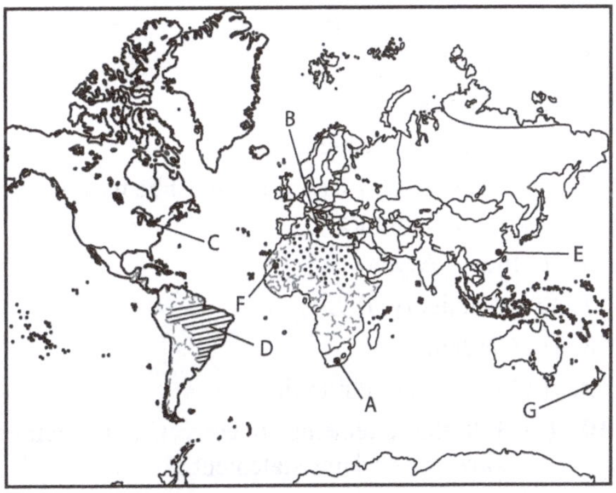

30 Locate and label any five of the following geographical features on the Political Outline map of India with appropriate symbols.

(i) An important seaport in Andhra Pradesh.

(ii) An important coal mine in Tamil Nadu.

(iii) Ratnagiri - iron ore mines.

(iv) An oil refinery in Gujarat.

(v) The state with highest population density.

(vi) The state leading in the production of jute.

(vii) An international airport in Kerala.

ANSWERS

1. (b) Both (A) and (R) are true and (R) is the correct explanation of A.

2. (b) 2 1 4 3

3. (c) Oil ports

4. (b) Both the statements are true.

5. (c) Productivity - Resources must be used keeping in mind the future

6. (c) Indo – Aryan

7. (c) 1st January, 1995

8. (b) Gardener

9. (b) Mexico and Philippines

10. (c) Both the statements are correct, and statement II correctly explains statement I

11. (a) IV, II, I, III

12. (d) Helpful in production of hydroelectricity.

13. (d) Twenty Years Road Plan

14. (c) to provide drinking water

15. (a) Birth Rate – Death Rate

16. (b) Shift from rural agrarian economy to urban industrial economy

17. (a) High birth rate and high death rate

18. (a) Rural and urban settlements are differ from each other in terms of social relationship, attitude and outlook.

(b) Towns act as nodes of economic growth because they provide goods and services not only to urban dwellers but also to the people of the rural settlements in their hinterlands in return for food and raw materials.

(c) Rural people are less mobile and therefore, social relationships are more intimate in rural areas. In urban areas, on the other hand, way of life is complex and fast, and social relations are formal.

19. (a) Trans-Siberian Railway, Russia

(b) A-Angarsk, B-Chita

(c) It is the most important route in Asia because it runs through the Chita, which is an important agro-centre and Irkutsk, a fur Centre. It also connects links to the Ukraine, Uzbekistan, Mongolia and China.

20. Meaningful life means the life which include the following

- Healthy life
- Purposeful life
- Free to achieve their goal
- Able to develop their talent

Or

The lack of human development can limit individual's choices in education, health, economic opportunities, and social and cultural factors. It can result in poor health outcomes, limited access to education and job training, discrimination and exclusion from certain groups, and reduced options for improving financial situations. To ensure individuals have the knowledge, skills, and resources to make informed decisions, it is essential to invest in human development. This will enable people to lead fulfilling lives and contribute to their communities.

21. The National Youth Policy 2014 of India launched in February 2014 proposes a holistic 'vision' for the youth of India.

Following are the feature of National Youth Policy

- It aims to provide a framework for the holistic development of young people in the country, and emphasizes the need for youth empowerment, participation, and inclusion.
- The policy focuses on five key areas that are education and skill development, health and well-being, employment and entrepreneurship, civic engagement and youth leadership, and social inclusion.
- It also recognises the importance of digital literacy and the need to address emerging challenges facing youth such as substance abuse, mental health issues, and violence.
- It seeks to promote the overall development of young people and enable them to contribute positively to society.

22. Naturalisation of Humans are different from Humanisation of Nature in the following ways

Naturalisation of Humans

- It refers to the point of view supporting environmental control on human action.

- Human listened to nature, was afraid of its fury and worshipped the natural forces.
- Many of primitive societies live in complete harmony with their natural environment.
- The physical environment for such societies becomes the Mother Nature.

Humanisation of Nature

- With social and cultural development, humans develop better and more efficient technology. They move from a state of Necessity to a state of freedom.
- People create possibilities with the resources obtained from the environment.
- Human has modified their surroundings according to their needs.
- Imprints of human may be seen everywhere on the Earth.

Or

The three dualism in geography which started wide-ranging debates in the discipline of geography are

- Whether geography as a discipline should be a law making/ the orising (nomothetic) or descriptive (idiographic).
- Whether the approach of the study should be regional or systematic.
- Whether geographical phenomena can be interpreted theoretically or through a historic-institutional approach?

23. Quaternary activities centre around research and development, due to the following reasons

- It is an advanced form of services.
- It involves specialised knowledge and technical skill.
- It involves, collection, production and dissemination of information.

24. The interior parts of semi-arid lands of the mid-latitudes in the world are the areas where extensive commercial grain cultivation takes place. Here the size of farms is very large and population is in small number. Operations of cultivation, right from ploughing to harvesting is mechanised.

Yield per person is high as the number of people working in farms is less and lot of machines is used. The size of the farms is very large due to which per acre production or yield is low even though the total production is high. This type of agriculture is practised in Eurasian Steppes, Canadian and American Prairies, Pampas of Argentina, Velds of South Africa, Australian Downs and the Canterbury Plains of New Zealand.

25. The guidelines to promote sustainability in the India Gandhi Canal Command Area are as follows

- There is an urgent need to strictly implement the water management policy.
- Water intensive crops should be avoided and instead plantation crops such as Citrus fruits should be encouraged.
- The Command Area Development programmes such as lining of water courses, land development, and levelling and warabandi system (equal distribution of canal water in the command area of outlet) shall be effectively implemented to reduce the conveyance loss of water.
- Efforts should be made to reclaim areas affected by water logging and soil salinity.
- Afforestation, shelter belt plantation and pasture development are necessary for eco- development.

26. Land degradation is generally understood either as a temporary or a permanent decline in productive capacity of the land.

The causes or factors responsible for land degradation in India are given below

(i) Soil erosion
(ii) Waterlogging
(iii) Salinisation
(iv) Alkalinisation of land

Land is constantly used without managing its fertility, it is degraded and its productivity declines. Deforestation, overgrazing, mining and quarrying too are responsible for land degradation in India. Thus, land degradation caused by human processes is more harmful than natural processes in India.

Man-made degraded wastelands such as degraded shifting cultivation areas, degraded land under plantation crops, degraded forest, mining and industrial wasteland are 5.8% of the total geographical area of the country.

In states such as Jharkhand, Chhattisgarh, Madhya Pradesh and Odisha, deforestation due to mining has caused severe land degradation.

In states such as Gujarat, Rajasthan, Madhya Pradesh and Maharashtra overgrazing is one of the main reasons for land degradation.

Or

Noise pollution has became a serious problem in recent years due to a variety of technological innovations which are as follows

- The biggest nuisance is the noise produced by traffic, because its intensity and nature depend upon factors, such as the type of aircraft, vehicle, train and the condition of road, as well as that of vehicle (in case of automobiles).
- In sea traffic, the noise pollution is confined to the harbour due to loading and unloading activities being carried.
- Industries cause noise pollution but with varying intensity depending upon the type of industry.
- Ocean noise is due to the vast increase in global shipping trade, the number of ships plying the oceans and higher speed of vessels.

27. Technological innovations through research and development strategies are an important aspect of modern manufacturing for quality control, eliminating waste and inefficiency and combating pollution.

Five aspects in this regard are as follows

- Complex machine technology is needed so that high quality goods are produced at less time.
- It requires vast capital so that machines with the latest technology can be used in manufacturing.
- Extreme specialisation and division of labour is required, that can work efficiently on the machines.
- Supply chain management technologies such as Radio-frequency Identification (RFID) and GPS tracking help manufacturers optimise their supply chain by providing real-time visibility and improving coordination.
- The manufacturers use data analytics tools to analyse large volumes of data generated by their operations, enabling them to identify patterns, optimize production processes, and make data-driven decisions.

Or

High technology or high-tech is the latest generation of industries manufacturing industries due to the following reasons

- High-Tech industries require great deal of Scientific Research and Development (R&D) and produce highly sophisticated products.
- These Industries improve their products very fast to meet the growing market demands.
- As their products are highly sophisticated therefore it requires highly skilled labour.
- Professional (White Collar) workers are main work force.
- Robotics on the assembly line, computer-aided design (CAD) and manufacturing, electronic controls of smelting and refining process are notable examples of high-tech industry.
- Neatly spaced, low, modern, dispersed, office-plant-lab buildings rather than massive assembly structures, factories and storage are mark the high-tech industrial landscape.

28. Sea ports play a vital role in the economic development of India. The advantages of sea ports for India are as follows

- **Trade Facilitation** It provide an efficient and cost-effective mode of transportation, facilitating international trade and commerce. It helps in boosting the country's economy and increasing its competitiveness in the global market.
- **Employment Generation** It provide direct and indirect employment opportunities to a large number of people, including cargo handlers, port operators, customs officials, and other support staff.
- **Regional Development** It act as a catalyst for the development of the surrounding regions, stimulating economic activity and encouraging the growth of related industries such as logistics and manufacturing.
- **Revenue Generation** It generate significant revenue for the government through customs duties, port charges, and other fees.
- **Infrastructure Development** The development of sea ports requires the creation of supporting infrastructure such as roads, railways, and warehousing facilities, which can have a positive impact on the overall development of the country.

Or

Seaports are termed as gateways of international trade due to the following reasons

- The ports act as suction points of the resources from their hinterlands. The extension of railways and roadways towards the interior facilitates the linking of the local markets to regional markets, regional markets to national markets and national markets to the international market.
- Cargoes and travellers pass from one part of the world to another through these ports.
- The ports provide facilities of docking, loading , unloading and the storage facilities for cargo.

29.

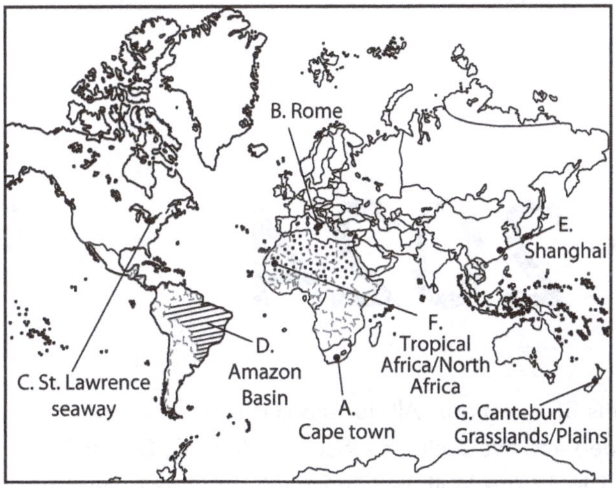
B. Rome
E.
Shanghai
F.
Tropical
Africa/North
Africa
D.
Amazon
Basin
C. St. Lawrence
seaway
A.
Cape town
G. Cantebury
Grasslands/Plains

30.

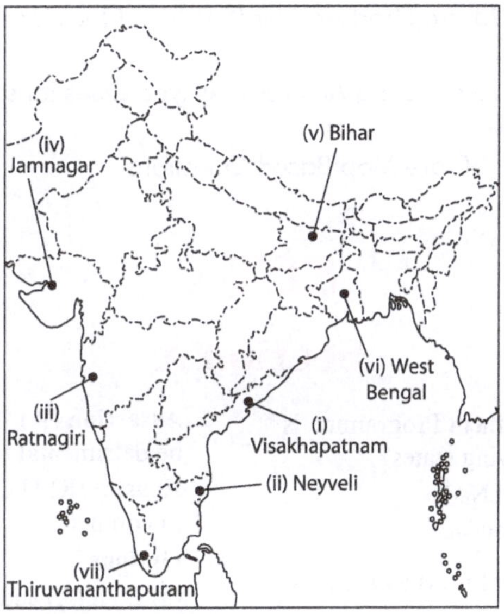
(v) Bihar
(iv)
Jamnagar
(vi) West
Bengal
(iii)
Ratnagiri
(i)
Visakhapatnam
(ii) Neyveli
(vii)
Thiruvananthapuram

CBSE Fully Solved

Solved Paper 2024

Time : 3 hrs
Marks : 70

Geography XII

1. This question paper contains 30 questions. All questions are compulsory.
2. This question paper is divided into five sections – Sections A, B, C, D and E.
3. Section A – Question nos. 1 to 17 are Multiple Choice (MCQ) Type Questions.
4. Section B – Question nos. 18 and 19 are Source Based Questions.
5. Section C – Question nos. 20 to 23 are Short Answer (SA) Type Questions. Answer to these questions shall be written in 80 to 100 words.
6. Section D – Question nos. 24 to 28 are Long Answer (LA) Type Questions. Answer to these questions shall be written in 120 to 150 words.
7. Section E – Question nos. 29 and 30 are Map Based Questions.

SET-1

Section A

1 'Neeru-Meeru' Watershed Management Programme is associated with which of the following states?

(a) Rajasthan (b) Tamil Nadu
(c) Andhra Pradesh (d) Karnataka

2 Which of the following is a means of mass awareness regarding 'water conservation'?

(a) Writing letters to the people
(b) Telephonic conversation
(c) Through TV and Print Media
(d) Personal contact with people

3 Which one of the following is the main objective of 'Jal Kranti Abhiyan'?

(a) Per capita water availability assurance
(b) Rain-water harvesting
(c) Conservation of water resources
(d) Providing sufficient water for agriculture

4 Two statements are given below. They are **Assertion** (A) and **Reason** (R). Read them carefully and choose the correct option.

Assertion (A) 'Free international trade can prove to be detrimental to the under-developed countries.'
Reason (R) Under-developed countries are not at par to compete with developed countries.

Options

(a) Both (A) and (R) are correct and (R) is correct explanation of (A)
(b) Both (A) and (R) are correct, but is not correct explanation of (A)
(c) (A) is correct, but (R) is incorrect
(d) (A) is incorrect, but (R) is correct

5 Which of the following facts, about jute cultivation in India, is true?

(a) West Bengal is the leading producer of jute.
(b) Jute is cash crop for Punjab and Haryana.
(c) Madhya Pradesh and Maharashtra are other leading jute producing states.
(d) India produces about 30% of the jute production of the world.

6 Read the following information carefully and identify the correct option for the crop.

- Grown in Kharif season.
- Mainly grown in semi-arid area in India.
- Gujarat and Maharashtra are the leading producer states.

Options

(a) Cotton (b) Tea (c) Jute (d) Sugarcane

7 Which one of the following states in India is the leading producer of manganese?

(a) Jharkhand (b) Madhya Pradesh
(c) Odisha (d) Bihar

8 Which one of the following is the largest coalfields in India?

(a) Jharia (b) Raniganj (c) Neyveli (d) Bokaro

9 Which of the following waterways and their stretches are correctly matched?

	(National Waterways)	(Stretch)
(a)	National Waterways No.1	Godavari-Krishna
(b)	National Waterways No.2	Sadiya-Dhubri
(c)	National Waterways No.3	Allahabad-Haldia
(d)	National Waterways No.4	Kottapuram-Kollam

10. Match the Column-I with Column-II and choose the correct option.

	Column-I (Railway Zone)		Column-II (Headquarters)
A.	Northern	1.	Hajipur
B.	South Central	2.	Chennai
C	Southern	3.	New Delhi
D.	East Central	4.	Secunderabad

Codes

	A	B	C	D		A	B	C	D
(a)	4	3	2	1	(b)	3	4	2	1
(c)	1	2	3	4	(d)	2	3	4	1

11 Which of the following metro-cities is not linked with the 'Golden Quadrilateral'?

(a) Mumbai (b) Chennai (c) Hyderabad (d) Delhi

12 Two statements are given below. They are **Assertion** (A) and **Reason** (R). Read them carefully and choose the correct option.

Assertion (A) "The gateways of the International trade are the ports and harbours".

Reason (R) Only heavy cargos are transported through ports and harbours in the world.

Options

(a) Both (A) and (R) are correct and (R) is correct explanation of (A)
(b) Both (A) and (R) are correct, but (R) is not correct explanation of (A)
(c) (A) is correct, but (R) is incorrect
(d) (A) is incorrect, but (R) is correct

13 Which one of the following is an example of oil port?

(a) Abadan (b) Manchester (c) Kochchi (d) Dover

14 Two statements are given below. They are **Assertion** (A) and **Reason** (R). Read them carefully and choose the correct option.

Assertion (A) "Waterway is an important mode of transport both for passengers and cargo traffic in India".

Reason (R) "It is fuel efficient and eco-friendly mode of transport".

Options

(a) Both (A) and (R) are correct and (R) is correct explanation of (A)
(b) Both (A) and (R) are correct, but (R) is not correct explanation of (A)
(c) (A) is correct, but (R) is incorrect
(d) (A) is incorrect, but (R) is correct

Direction Read the given passage and answer the question nos. 15 to 17.

Characteristics of High Human Development

High level of human development group has 53 countries providing education and healthcare is an important government priority. Countries with higher human development are those where a lot of investment in the social sector has taken place. Altogether, a higher investment in people and good governance has set this group of countries apart from the others.

Many of these countries has been the former imperial powers. The degree of social diversity in these countries is not very high. Many of the countries with a high human development score are located in Europe and represent the industrialised Western world. Yet there are striking numbers of non-European countries also who have made it to this list.

15 Which one of the following is an important priority of 'high human development index' countries?

Choose the most appropriate option.

(a) Education and healthcare
(b) Healthcare and territorial security

(c) Education and industrial development
(d) Economic development and per capita income

16 Which one of the following differentiates the higher human development countries from other?

Choose the most appropriate option.
(a) Higher gross domestic production
(b) Higher investment in social sector
(c) Higher industrialisation
(d) Higher per capita income

17 How many countries are under 'high human development index' category?

Choose the correct option.
(a) 51 (b) 52
(c) 53 (d) 54

Section B

18 Read the given passage carefully and answer the questions that follow.

Integrated Tribal Development Project in Bharmaur Region

This region lies between 32° 11 , N and 32° 41' N latitudes and 76° 22 'E and 76° 53' E longitudes.Spread over an area of about 1,818 sq km the region mostly lies between 1,500 m to 3,700 m above the mean sea level. This region popularly known as the homeland of Gaddis is surrounded by lofty mountains on all sides.
It has Pir Panjal in the North and Dhaula Dhar in the South. In the East, the extension of Dhula Dhar converges with Pir Panjal near Rohtang Pass. The river Ravi and its tributaries-the Budhil and the Tundahen, drain this territory and carve out deep gorges. These rivers divide the region into four physiographic divisions called Holi Khani, Kugti and Tundah areas. Bharmaur experiences freezing weather conditions and snowfall in winter. Its mean monthly temperature in January remains 4°C and in July 26°C.

(i) Describe the location of Bharmaur region.
(ii) Why does this region experience harsh climatic conditions? Give one reason.
(iii) Why is the region economically backward? Explain any one reason.

19 Study the given map carefully and answer the questions that follow.

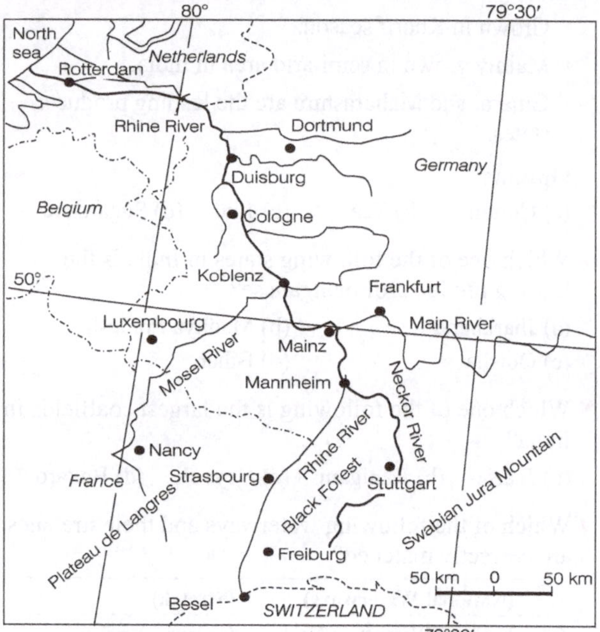

(i) Identify the given inland waterway and write its name.
(ii) Mention its two tributaries joining from East.
(iii) Write the names of terminal ports of the given waterways.

Section C

20 "Nature and human are inseparable elements in all geographical studies". Examine the statement.

Or Examine the main aspects of environmental determinism.

21 Explain the main features of periodic markets in rural areas of the world.

22 Explain the main objectives of "Smart Cities Mission" in India.

Or Explain the main features of the dispersed settlements in India.

23 "The composition of commodities in India's international trade has been undergoing a change over the years". Examine the statement with examples.

Section D

24 Analyse any five factors affecting world distribution of population.

25 Examine the main characteristics of co-operative farming in the world.

Or Examine the main characteristics of dairy farming in the world.

26 Differentiate the small and large scale manufacturing industries in the world.

27 "The distribution of urban population over India has wide variations". Examine the statement.

Or "If development is not engendered, it is endangered". Examine the statement in the context of inclusive development.

28 Describe any two sources of air pollution in India and suggest any three measures to overcome the air pollution.

Or Describe any two sources of water pollution in India. Suggest any three measures to overcome the water pollution.

Section E

29. On the given political outline map of the world, seven geographical features have been shown as A, B,C, D, E, F and G. Identify any five with the help of following information and write their correct names on the lines drawn near them.

A. A major sea-port
B. An international airport
C. An important shipping canal
D. An area of subsistence gathering
E. An area of nomadic herding
F. A terminal station of trans-continental railway
G. An area of extensive commercial grain farming

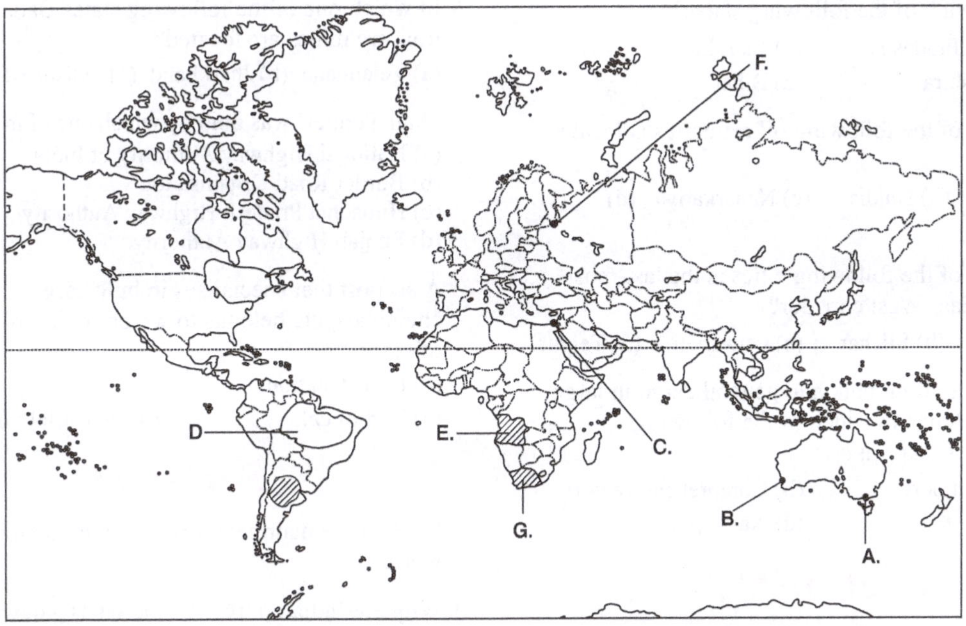

30 Locate and label any five of the following geographical features with appropriate symbols on the given political outline map of India.

A. A state leading in the production of coffee
B. An oil refinery in Uttar Pradesh
C. An important coal mining area in West Bengal
D. A major seaport along the coast of Goa
E. A state with highest population density
F. An international airport in Gujarat
G. An iron-ore mining area in Chhattisgarh

SET 2

(Uncommon Questions from Set 1)

Section A

5 Read the following statements carefully regarding rainwater harvesting and choose the correct option.

(i) Rainwater harvesting helps to capture and store rainwater.
(ii) Groundwater table is declining due to overuse.
(iii) Rainwater harvesting increases water availability for use.
(iv) Check dams help in recharging groundwater.

Options

(a) Only (i), (ii) and (iii) are correct
(b) Only (ii), (iii) and (iv) are correct
(c) Only (i), (iii) and (iv) are correct
(d) Only (i), (ii) and (iv) are correct

6 The largest concentration of sugarcane cultivation is found in which of the following states?

(a) Madhya Pradesh (b) Jharkhand
(c) Maharashtra (d) Bihar

8 Which one of the following oil refineries is located in Bihar?

(a) Bina (b) Haldia (c) Naharkatiya (d) Barauni

11 Which one of the following cities is the last-most station of East-West corridor?

(a) Imphal (b) Silchar (c) Guwahati (d) Tejpur

13 A seaport handling bulk and general cargo in large volumes belongs to which of the following categories of seaports?

(a) Industrial port (b) Comprehensive port
(c) Oil port (d) Naval port

Section C

21 Explain the main features of retail trading in the world.

23 Examine the changing pattern and composition of India's imports.

Section D

24 Examine any five factors affecting the density of population in the world.

26 Analyse the important characteristics of large scale manufacturing industries in the world.

SET 3

(Uncommon Questions from Set 1 & 2)

Section A

5 The Central Government sponsored 'Haryali' Watershed Development Project was executed by which one of the followings?

(a) District Magistrates with the help of other officers.
(b) Block Development Officers with reputed people's participation.
(c) Circle Officers with guidance of school principals.
(d) Gram Panchayats with people's participation.

7 Which one of the following is the largest producer of bauxite in India?

(a) Odisha (b) Jharkhand
(c) Chhattisgarh (d) Madhya Pradesh

8 In which one of the following states Badampahar iron-ore mines are located?

(a) Telangana (b) Jharkhand (c) Odisha (d) Chhattisgarh

10 'Atal Tunnel' was built by which one of the following?

(a) National Highway Authority of India
(b) Border Road Organisation
(c) Himachal Pradesh Highway Authority
(d) Punjab Highway Authority

13 A seaport that specialises in bulk cargo like ore,oil chemicals, etc belongs to which of the following types of seaport?

(a) Packet station (b) Inland port
(c) Port of call (d) Industrial port

Section C

21 Explain the main features of wholesale trading in the world.

23 Why are Indian ports considered as gateways of international trade? Examine.

Section D

24 Define migration.Differentiate between push and pull factors of migration.

26 Classify industries of the world on the basis of their raw materials and explain each one of them.

ANSWERS

Set 1

1. (c) Andhra Pradesh
2. (c) Through TV and Print Media
3. (c) Conservation of water resources
4. (a) Both (A) and (R) are correct and (R) is correct explanation of (A)
5. (a) West Bengal is the leading producer of jute.
6. (a) Cotton
7. (b) Madhya Pradesh
8. (a) Jharia
9. (b) National Waterways No.2–Sadiya-Dhubri
10. (b) (iii) (iv) (ii) (i)
11. (c) Hyderabad
12. (c) (A) is correct, but (R) is incorrect
13. (a) Abadan
14. (a) Both (A) and (R) are correct and (R) is correct explanation of (A)
15. (a) Education and healthcare
16. (b) Higher investment in social sector **17.** (c) 53
18. (i) The Bharmaur region lies between 32° 11' N and 32° 41' N latitudes and 76° 22' E and 76° 53' E longitudes.
    (ii) The region experiences a harsh climate because it lies between 1500 to 3700 m above sea level. Hence, it experiences freezing weather conditions and snowfall in winter.
    (iii) The region is economically backward as inhabited by the Gaddis tribal group which is mainly dependent on the rearing of sheep. The other factor due to which they lack economic development is the connectivity with the mainland.
19. (i) The Rhine Waterways
    (ii) The river Rhur and Danube joins the Rhine from the East.
    (iii) Hamburg and Dusseldorf are examples of terminal ports of the Rhine Waterways.
20. Nature and human are inseparable elements in all geographical studies because geography is an independent discipline that studies space, earth, its phenomenon, origin of human societies, their culture as well as their interaction with the surrounding environment.
    Geography is a combination of different elements which are taken from various fields and sub-fields. These elements form an effective and comprehensive system of study.
    Or The main aspects of environmental determinism are as follows
    (i) The human beings adapted to the limitations imposed by their natural environment and its various phenomena in the early stages of their interaction with their natural environment.
    (ii) The human beings direct interaction with nature and the physical environment, for human beings becomes the Mother Nature. This was because the level of technological development was very low and levels of Human Development were also primitive.
21. The main features of periodic markets in the rural areas of the world are
    - These markets operate on a specific schedule, often weekly or bi-weekly, attracting both sellers and consumers from surrounding villages and areas.
    - They primarily serve as a platform for farmers and producers to sell their agricultural products like fruits, vegetables, grains and livestock.
    - They act as a central meeting point for people beyond just trade, fostering social interaction, cultural exchange, and access to information and services.
22. The main objectives of 'Smart Cities Mission' in India are
    - To promote cities that provide core infrastructure, a clean and sustainable environment and a decent quality of life to its citizens.
    - To apply smart solutions to infrastructure and services in order to make them better.
    - To focus on sustainable and inclusive development and the idea is to look at compact areas, create a replicable model, which acts as a model for other aspiring cities.

    Or • The main features of dispersed settlements in India are
    - These settlements in India appear in the form of isolated huts or hamlets. They are found in remote jungles or on small hills with farms or pastures on the slopes.

- The dispersed settlements are formed due to extremely fragmented terrain and land resource base of the habitable areas.
- Such settlement are mainly found in Meghalaya, Uttarakhand, Himachal Pradesh, Kerala, etc.

23. The composition of commodities in India's international trade has been undergoing a change over the years. The following examples support the statement

- The share of agricultural and allied products has declined in India's exports whereas the share of crude and petroleum products have increased.
- Engineering goods have shown a significant growth in the exports. Gems and jewelleries still contribute a large share in India's exports.
- Petroleum products have shown an increase in the imports of India. This is because of its varied uses like fuel as well as an industrial raw material in industries.

24. The following factors affect the world distribution of population. These are

(i) **Availability of Water** Water is considered as life. It has many uses for human beings, such as in activities like drinking, bathing, cooking, for cattle, crops and also for industries and navigation purposes. Thus, river valleys are most densely populated areas of the world because of the availability of fresh water.

(ii) **Landforms/Relief** Plain areas and gentle slopes always remained favourable for human settlements, because plains provide such relief which is suitable for cultivation of crops, to build roadways, railways and to set-up industries.

(iii) **Climate** It has a direct impact on human beings. Humans prefer to live in normal climatic regions. Areas having harsh and extreme climates like regions with very heavy rainfall, very hot and very cold deserts are not favourable to live.

(iv) **Soils** People prefer to live in those areas which have fertile soils, as these are the base of agricultural development and allied activities.

(v) **Urbanisation** Better employment opportunities, educational and medical facilities, better means of transport and communication, better civic amenities, etc., attract people to live in the cities.

25. The main characteristics of co-operative farming in the world are as follows

- This farming is done mainly for more efficient and profitable farming.
- In this farming, a group of farmers form a co-operative society by pooling/sharing their resources voluntarily.
- Co-operative societies help farmers to buy all important inputs necessary for farming.
- Farmers also get help from these societies in processing of quality products at cheaper rates.
- It is successful in many Western European countries like Denmark, Netherlands, Belgium, Sweden, Italy, etc.

Or The main characteristics of dairy farming in the world are as follows

- This type of farming is the most modernised and efficient type of rearing of milch animals.
- It is highly capital intensive. Big investments are required in this farming for animal sheds, storage facilities for folder, feeding and milching machines, etc.
- Cattle breeding, health care and veterinery services are given more attention in this farming.
- It is mainly practiced near urban and industrial centres where demand for fresh milk and dairy products is high.

26. The small-scale and large-scale manufacturing industries can be differentiated in the following manner

Small Scale Manufacturing Industry	Large Scale Manufacturing Industry
This type of manufacturing has smaller operations such as a workshop.	In large scale manufacturing, operations are on a large scale like large factories.
It is characterised by low capital investment and simple technology.	It requires very high capital investments and advanced technology.
It uses local raw materials, simple power driven machines and semi-skilled labour.	Raw materials may be local or imported but there is large use of energy for assembly line mass production and specialised workers.
The production is consumed in local or regional markets.	The production is for export purposes in the international markets.
They are located mainly in developing countries.	They are located in both developing and developed countries.
Examples include-Disposable crockery, handbags, spices industry etc.	Examples include-Iron and steel, cement industry, automotive industry etc.

27. The distribution of the urban population in India has wide variations. These variations can be seen due to the following reasons

- The areas with established industries, particularly heavy industries, tend to attract a larger workforce, leading to the growth of cities and towns around those industrial zones. For example, Chennai, Delhi, Mumbai, Kolkata, etc.
- Government policies and initiatives aimed at promoting urbanisation in specific regions can also play a role in shaping the distribution of the urban population. The urban local bodies play a major role in the development of cities.
- The location of historical trade routes and the presence of prominent kingdoms in the past influenced the establishment and growth of urban settlements in specific regions. Major port cities of India are examples of such settlements.
- The physical factors play a significant role in any type of settlement. The urban settlements are attracted to industrial development. Hence the regions such as plains of Ganges that support the industrial development, are mostly urbanised.
- The migration pattern such as rural-to-urban migration driven by factors like job opportunities, educational facilities, or better healthcare tends to be concentrated in specific regions offering better prospects. This can lead to uneven population distribution.

Or If the development is not engendered, it is endangered. This statement approaches towards inclusive development. The statement can be substantiated with the help of the following arguments.

- When women are excluded from participating fully in the development process, their skills, talents and perspectives are not utilised. This signifies a loss of potential that could contribute significantly to economic growth, innovation, and social progress.
- The gender disparity creates an unequal playing field, limiting opportunities for women in various sectors like education, employment and decision-making. This hinders overall societal progress and hinders the effectiveness of development initiatives.
- Promoting gender equality and women's empowerment is not just about economic benefits; it's a fundamental human right. Every individual deserves equal opportunity to participate and contribute to society.
- Educated and empowered women tend to make better decisions regarding their health and the health of their families, leading to decreased child mortality and improved overall health indicators. When women have a voice in decision-making and access to resources, they contribute significantly to community development and social cohesion.

28. The sources of air pollution in India are combustion of fossil fuels, mining and industries. These processes release oxides of sulphur and nitrogen, hydrocarbons, carbon dioxide, carbon monoxide, lead and asbestos.

The three measures to overcome the air pollution are as follows

(i) Shift towards renewable energy sources like solar, wind and geothermal power to generate electricity. This reduces dependence on fossil fuels, a major source of air pollutants.

(ii) Create safe and accessible infrastructure for cycling and walking to incentivise people to adopt these active modes of transportation for short trips, reducing air pollution and promoting healthier lifestyles.

(iii) The establishment of stricter regulations and enforcing existing ones help control air pollution from industrial facilities by limiting the release of harmful pollutants into the atmosphere.

Or The two sources of water pollution in India are as follows

(i) **Natural Sources** These sources include erosion, landslides, decay and decomposition of plants and animals, etc. These sources make water polluted.

(ii) **Industrial Sources** Industries are the most significant contributor in pollution. Industries are source of a number of undesirable products including polluted waste water, poisonous gases, chemical residuals, etc.

The three measures to overcome water pollution are as follows

(i) Upgrade and expand sewage treatment plants, especially in urban areas, to effectively treat wastewater before releasing it into water bodies. This includes building new plants, improving the capacity of existing ones, and ensuring proper maintenance.

(ii) Promote the use of organic farming methods, composting, and natural pest control techniques to reduce agricultural runoff of pollutants like nitrates and pesticides that contaminate water sources.

(iii) Encourage individuals to adopt water-saving practices in daily life, such as using water-efficient appliances, fixing leaks, and minimising water usage, to collectively contribute to a significant reduction in water demand and pollution.

29.

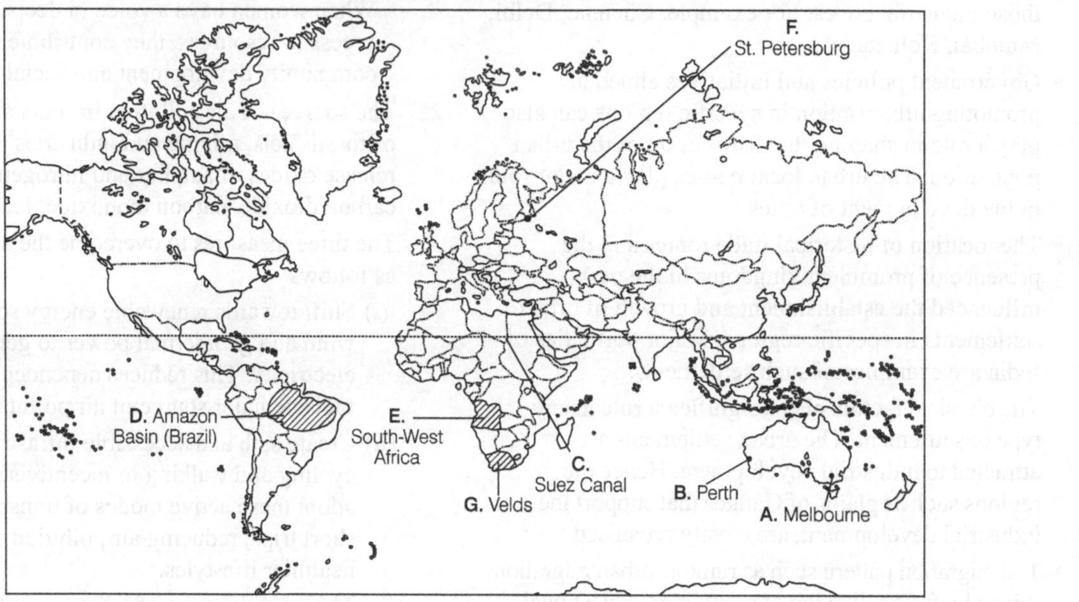

30.

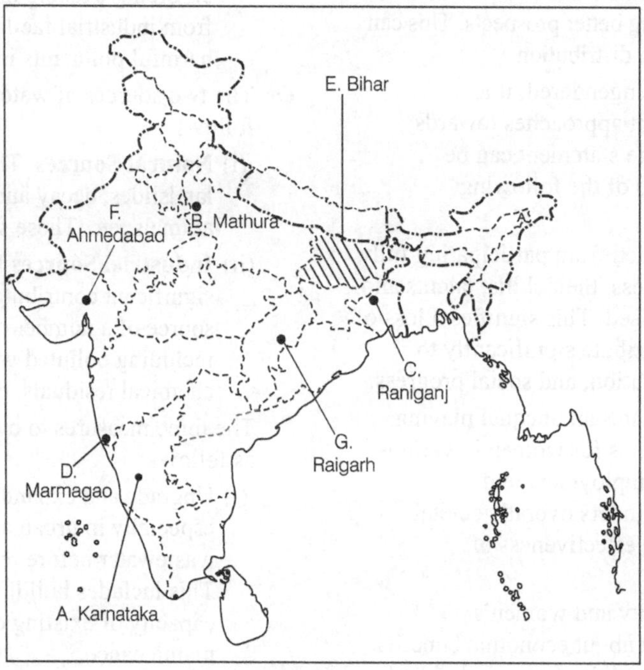

Set 2

5. (a) Only (i), (ii) and (iii) are correct

6. (c) Maharashtra **8.** (d) Barauni

11. (b) Silchar

13. (a) Industrial port

21. The main features of retail trading in the world are

- Unlike wholesale businesses that sell goods in bulk to other businesses, retail businesses sell goods directly to end consumers for their personal use.
- Retailers typically offer a wide variety of goods across different categories, allowing customers to find everything they need in one place. This can range from groceries and clothing to electronics and furniture.
- In many cases, retailers offer additional services beyond just selling products. This might include things like product demos, after-sales support, personalised recommendations, or loyalty programs.

23. The pattern of imports in India changed in pattern and composition in the following manner.

- During 1950s and 1960s, India had to import many items like foodgrains, capital goods, machinery and equipments.
- After 1970, the success of Green Revolution led to discontinuation of foodgrain import.
- In 1973, the energy crisis in India led to increase in the prices of petroleum, so, petroleum imports were increased.
- Capital goods, e.g. non-electrical machinery, transport equipment, manufactures of metals and machine tools show a steady increase in the import list of India. This is due to rising demand in the export oriented industrial and domestic sectors.

24. The factors affecting the density of the population in the world are as follows.

(i) **Availability of Water** Water is considered as life. It has many uses for human beings, such as in activities like drinking, bathing, cooking, for cattle, crops and also for industries and navigation purposes. Thus, river valleys are most densely populated areas of the world because of the availability of fresh water.

(ii) **Landforms/Relief** Plain areas and gentle slopes always remained favourable for human settlements, because plains provide such relief which is suitable for cultivation of crops, to build roadways, railways and to set-up industries. Thus, plains are densely populated in the world.

(iii) **Minerals** Industries generally are set up in those areas which have abundance of mineral deposits. Industrial set up and mining activities generate employment opportunities.

Thus, these areas are populated by semi-skilled and skilled workers. For example, Katanga Zambia copper belt in Africa.

(iv) **Urbanisation** Better employment opportunities, educational and medical facilities, better means of transport and communication, better civic amenities etc attract people to live in the cities. This leads to the process of migration from rural to urban areas. For example, mega cities like Delhi, Mumbai, Kolkata, etc are densely populated areas.

(v) **Government Incentives** Many a times government offer incentives to people to live in sparsely population areas or move away from overcrowded places.

26. The characteristics of large scale manufacturing industries are as follows.

- Large scale industrial processes consist of multiple complex activities to run the industries. The specialised and skilled labour is required in the manufacturing industries. Thus, skilled manpower is employed.
- These industries widely use huge power to run the heavy machines in the production process.
- For the quality control, special measures are taken in these type of industries.
- The main features in large scale manufacturing is the specialisation in production. Products of large-scale industries are sold in local as well as international markets.
- Iron and steel industry, ship building, textile, petro-chemical are examples of large scale manufacturing industries.

Set 3

5. (d) Gram Panchayats with people's participation.

7. (a) Odisha

8. (c) Odisha

10. (b) Border Road Organisation

13. (d) Industrial port

21. The main features of wholesale trading in the world are as follows.

- Wholesalers bridge the gap between producers and retailers, forming a crucial link in the supply chain.

- Wholesaling requires significant capital to purchase and maintain large inventories. They manage the risk of holding stock while waiting for retailers to purchase the goods.
- Wholesale markets deal only with the selling and purchasing of commodities. There is no wholesale marketing of services such as insurance, banking, transportation, etc.

23. • Cargoes and travellers pass from one part of the world to another through these ports.
- These ports provide facilities like docking, loading, unloading and storage facilities for cargo. To offer such facilities to cargo, the port authorities make some arrangements to maintain navigable channels, provide labour, arrange barges and tugs, and also provide managerial services.
- Large ports offer particularly attractive locations for lead industries and distribution-intensive enterprises.

24. Migration is one of the component of population change. It is the movement of people from one place to another.

Difference between push factors and pull factors of migration are as follows.

Push Factors	Pull Factors
The unfavourable factors which make the place of origin less attractive are known as push factors.	The favourable factors which make a place of destination more attractive are known as pull factors.
Generally, these factors result in migration from rural to urban areas.	Generally, these factors result in migration from urban to urban and rural to urban areas.
The important factors are unemployment, poverty, poor facilities of education, health sanitation, recreation, etc.	The important factors are better employment opportunities, living conditions, peace, stability, security of life, property and pleasant climate.

26. The industries of the world based on their raw materials are as follows

- **Agro-Based Industries** These industries involves the processing of raw materials obtained from the agricultural farms and fields into finished products to be sold in the rural and urban markets. Examples of these industries are food processing, sugar, pickles, fruit juices, etc.
- **Food Processing Industries** It includes canning, producing cream, fruit processing and confectionery items. Preserving techniques such as drying, fermenting and pickling.
- **Mineral-Based Industries** Minerals are the main raw materials for this industry. These are of three types
  - (i) **Ferrous Metallic Minerals based Industries** These industries use ferrous metallic minerals which contain ferrous (iron), such as iron and steel industries.
  - (ii) **Non-ferrous Metallic Minerals based Industries** These industries use raw-materials like aluminium, copper, gold. For example, jewellery, copper and aluminium industries.
  - (iii) **Non-metallic Minerals based Industries.** These industries use non-metallic minerals, such as cement and pottery industries.
- **Chemical Based Industries** A number of chemical industries use natural chemical minerals. Example of these industries are; petro-chemical industry using mineral oil (petroleum), salt, sulphur and potash industries using natural minerals, synthetic fibres. Plastic industries also use natural chemicals.
- **Forest Based Raw material using Industries** Various major and minor forests products are used as raw materials. Examples of such industries are furniture industry which uses timber, paper industry which uses wood, bamboo and grass and lac industry which uses lac obtained from forests as raw material.
- **Animal Based Industries** These industries are completely based on products obtained from animals. For example, leather for leather industry, wool for woollen textiles. Ivory is also obtained from elephant's tusks.